THE BONE BROTH SECRET

ALSO BY LOUISE HAY

BOOKS/KIT

All Is Well (with Mona Lisa Schulz, M.D., Ph.D.)
Colors & Numbers
Empowering Women
Everyday Positive Thinking
Experience Your Good Now! (book-with-audio)
A Garden of Thoughts: My Affirmation Journal
Gratitude: A Way of Life (Louise & Friends)
Heal Your Body
Heal Your Body A–Z
Heart Thoughts (also available in a gift edition)
I Can Do It® (book-with-audio)
Inner Wisdom
Letters to Louise
Life Loves You (with Robert Holden, Ph.D.)
Life! Reflections on Your Journey
Love Your Body
Love Yourself, Heal Your Life Workbook
Loving Yourself to Great Health (with Ahlea Khadro and Heather Dane)
Meditations to Heal Your Life (also available in a gift edition)
Mirror Work (book-with-audio; available March 2016)
Modern-Day Miracles (Louise & Friends)
The Power Is Within You
Power Thoughts
The Present Moment
The Times of Our Lives (Louise & Friends)
You Can Create an Exceptional Life (with Cheryl Richardson)
You Can Heal Your Heart (with David Kessler)
You Can Heal Your Life (also available in a gift edition)
You Can Heal Your Life Affirmation Kit
You Can Heal Your Life Companion Book

FOR CHILDREN

The Adventures of Lulu
I Think, I Am! (with Kristina Tracy)
Lulu and the Ant: A Message of Love
Lulu and the Dark: Conquering Fears
Lulu and Willy the Duck: Learning Mirror Work

AUDIO PROGRAMS

All Is Well (audio book)
Anger Releasing
Cancer
Change and Transition
Dissolving Barriers
Embracing Change
The Empowering Women Gift Collection
Feeling Fine Affirmations
Forgiveness/Loving the Inner Child
How to Love Yourself
Life Loves You (audio book)
Meditations for Loving Yourself to Great Health
(with Ahlea Khadro and Heather Dane)
Meditations for Personal Healing

Meditations to Heal Your Life (audio book)
Morning and Evening Meditations
101 Power Thoughts
Overcoming Fears
The Power Is Within You (audio book)
The Power of Your Spoken Word
Receiving Prosperity
Self-Esteem Affirmations (subliminal)
Self-Healing
Stress-Free (subliminal)
Totality of Possibilities
What I Believe and Deep Relaxation
You Can Heal Your Heart (audio book)
You Can Heal Your Life (audio book)
You Can Heal Your Life Study Course
Your Thoughts Create Your Life

DVDs
Dissolving Barriers
Receiving Prosperity
You Can Heal Your Life Study Course
You Can Heal Your Life, THE MOVIE (also available in an expanded edition)
You Can Trust Your Life (with Cheryl Richardson)

CARD DECKS
Healthy Body Cards
I Can Do It® Cards
I Can Do It® Cards . . . for Creativity, Forgiveness, Health, Job Success, Wealth, Romance
Life Loves You Cards (available April 2016)
Power Thought Cards
Power Thoughts for Teens
Power Thought Sticky Cards
Wisdom Cards

CALENDAR
I Can Do It® Calendar (for each individual year)

and

THE ESSENTIAL LOUISE HAY COLLECTION
(comprising You Can Heal Your Life, Heal Your Body, and
The Power Is Within You in a single volume)

All of the above are available at your local
bookstore, or may be ordered by visiting:

Hay House USA: www.hayhouse.com®
Hay House Australia: www.hayhouse.com.au
Hay House UK: www.hayhouse.co.uk
Hay House South Africa: www.hayhouse.co.za
Hay House India: www.hayhouse.co.in

Louise's Websites: www.LouiseHay.com® and www.HealYourLife.com®

THE
BONE BROTH
SECRET

A Culinary Adventure in
Health • Beauty • Longevity

LOUISE HAY AND HEATHER DANE

HAY HOUSE, INC.
Carlsbad, California • New York City
London • Sydney • Johannesburg
Vancouver • Hong Kong • New Delhi

Published and distributed in the United States by: Hay House, Inc.: www.hayhouse.com® • **Published and distributed in Australia by:** Hay House Australia Pty. Ltd.: www.hayhouse.com.au • **Published and distributed in the United Kingdom by:** Hay House UK, Ltd.: www.hayhouse.co.uk • **Published and distributed in the Republic of South Africa by:** Hay House SA (Pty), Ltd.: www.hayhouse .co.za • **Distributed in Canada by:** Raincoast Books: www.raincoast .com • **Published in India by:** Hay House Publishers India: www .hayhouse.co.in

Book design: Tricia Breidenthal
Indexer: Jay Kreider
Interior photos: Joel Dauteuil, except images on pages 20, 119, 141, 145, 147, 157, 176, 194, 215, 236, 240, 280, 352 used under license from Shutterstock
Food styling: Carolyn Himes

Library of Congress Cataloging-in-Publication Data

Hay, Louise L., author.
  The bone broth secret : a culinary adventure in health, beauty, and longevity / Louise Hay and Heather Dane. -- 1st edition.
       pages cm
  Includes index.
  ISBN 978-1-4019-5008-8 (tradepaper : alk. paper) 1. Stocks (Cooking) 2. Bones. I. Dane, Heather, author. II. Title.
  TX819.S8H39 2016
  641.81'3--dc23
                              2015033384

ISBN: 978-1-4019-5008-8

10 9 8 7 6 5 4 3 2 1
1st edition, January 2016

Printed in the United States of America

SUSTAINABLE FORESTRY INITIATIVE
Certified Chain of Custody
Promoting Sustainable Forestry
www.sfiprogram.org
SFI-01268

SFI label applies to the text stock

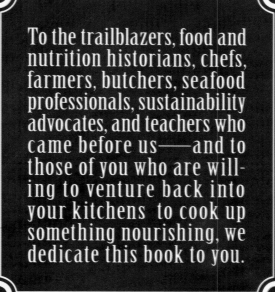

To the trailblazers, food and nutrition historians, chefs, farmers, butchers, seafood professionals, sustainability advocates, and teachers who came before us——and to those of you who are willing to venture back into your kitchens to cook up something nourishing, we dedicate this book to you.

~CONTENTS~

Preface: Let's Make Delicious Memories Together, by Louise Hay...xi
Introduction: A Little about Me, and How to Use This Book, by Heather Dane........................ xiii

PART I: THE ART AND SCIENCE OF BONE BROTH

Chapter 1: The History and Science: Is Bone Broth
Really a Health and Beauty Panacea?...3
Chapter 2: Bone Broth Orientation: Kitchen Equipment, an Overview on
Making Bone Broth, and How to Choose Quality Ingredients 21
Chapter 3: Getting Started: What Louise Eats, Guiding Principles,
Menus, and a Shopping List 45

PART II: RECIPES: DELICIOUSLY DECADENT MEALS AND HEALING ELIXIRS

Chapter 4: The Foundation: Basic Broths and Stocks..................................75
Chapter 5: The Magic: Medicinal Finishers and Healing Elixirs 105
Chapter 6: The Comfort: Soups, Stews, Sauces, Dips, and Dressings 123
Chapter 7: The Strengtheners: Meat, Poultry, Game, and Fish Dishes................159
Chapter 8: The Cleansers: Vegetable Dishes..187
Chapter 9: The Staff of Life: Grains, Breads, and Pancakes 205
Chapter 10: The Lighter Side: Salads, Pâtés, Aspics, and Smoothies 229
Chapter 11: The Celebration: Decadent Desserts 269
Chapter 12: The Sassy: Cocktails with Benefits...................................303
Chapter 13: The DIY: Beautiful Skin and Hair Masks 311
Chapter 14: To Your Health, Happiness, and Longevity.............................317

APPENDIX
Bone Broth Healing Stories 321
How to Work with Herbs and Spices 327
Recipe Contributors..335

Metric Conversion Chart 345
Resources 347
Endnotes 353
General Index 359
Index of Recipes...365
About the Authors..379

Moroccan Vanilla Spice Ice Cream.

PREFACE

Let's Make Delicious Memories Together

by Louise Hay

As I write this, I am getting close to my 90th birthday, and I am sure that it's going to be another of my best decades ever! Age means nothing when you have good health. And I've always believed that good health is a product of three things:

1. Loving yourself. Decades ago, when I wrote *You Can Heal Your Life*, this was the Dedication I wrote at the beginning of the book: "May this offering help you find the place within yourself where you know your own self-worth, the part of you that is pure love and pure self-acceptance." This book has reached well over 50 million people around the world, and it is my hope that this message continues to spread. Loving ourselves is the miracle cure. Loving ourselves works miracles in our lives. Love can go in any direction.

2. Focusing on the right thoughts. Be kind to your mind. Self-hatred is only thoughts of hate that you have about yourself. If you gently change your thinking, you will know that you are worth loving! I am so excited that science is now showing how positive affirmations change the brain and body for the better. Our words and thoughts not only change our future and our experiences, they also shape our beliefs and perceptions—which as we now know from epigenetics, have the power to change our DNA. Thinking well of yourself is an act of kindness that pays enormous dividends.

3. Focusing on the right food. In *Loving Yourself to Great Health: Thoughts and Food—The Ultimate Diet*, I joined forces with my go-to health coaches, Heather Dane and Ahlea Khadro, to share the secret to optimal health that I am less well-known for: nutrition. For all the years that I have taught, spoken, and written about positive affirmations and loving yourself, I've also been studying and applying nutritional practices that support my health, energy, and vitality. When people ask me why my skin is so vibrant or how I can still travel, teach, and enjoy life to the fullest, I tell them that it has to do with the right thoughts and the right food. In *Loving Yourself to Great Health*, we outlined how to follow a whole-foods diet as a way to dissolve dis-ease and support you in feeling your best.

> "Bones represent the structure of the Universe. When we feel we know the truth, we feel it deep in our bones."

These three simple principles are timeless. They are ancient, and yet they continue to have a starring role in the modern world. Because these three principles are the foundation of health—no matter what new trend or fad comes along—they continue to bring us "back to the basics."

To me, bone broth is like that. It's simple, it's timeless, and it's where we can go when we want to get back to the basics. Bone broth is easier to make than you might think, and it has healing properties that go deeper than we can imagine. Bones represent the structure of the Universe. When we feel we know the truth, we feel it deep in our bones. Bone broth is grounding and nourishing. And while all of this sounds wonderful, we also have science to show us the benefits that our bodies can feel with each sip.

Bone broth has been one of the secrets to my health and vitality for years, and I'd like to show you how you can make it the key to yours, if you are willing to join me in this culinary adventure. Take my hand as we walk into the kitchen and share recipes. I promise we're going to have a good time together as you read this book!

Let's all affirm: *I take in and give out nourishment in perfect balance. Nourishing myself is a joyful experience, and I am worth the time spent on my healing. It is safe to experience new ideas and new ways. I give myself permission to be all that I can be, and I deserve the very best in life. I love and appreciate myself and others. And so it is.*

Now let's go make delicious memories together!

I love you,
Louise

❧ INTRODUCTION ❧

A Little about Me, and How to Use This Book

by Heather Dane

I became known as the "21st-century medicine woman" because I'm a health detective who uses a blend of science and ancient wisdom to help people resolve chronic health conditions.

How I got here is a little unusual, but I'll sum it up as best as I can. From my father's side of the family, I get my Native American heritage. I am an Oneida Iroquois, a member of the Wolf Clan. Of the three Iroquois clans, the Wolf Clan represents the pathfinders; their responsibility is to guide people in living their lives the way the Creator intended. My great-grandmother was the clan mother, a spiritual counselor and final decision maker on important matters. Clan mothers choose and oversee the Chief, and they have the ability to make peace, ending wars.

From my father's side of the family, I learned an appreciation for the Native American practices for honoring the earth, and using plants and food as medicine. Like Chinese medicine, Native American medicine has a theme of balance—being in harmony with the rhythms of the earth. Both also have a concept of dis-ease occurring through unfulfilled desires of the soul.

From the age of ten, I experienced digestive challenges. I didn't know what was going on and neither did any medical doctors. Over the years, I was diagnosed with gastrointestinal issues ranging from gallbladder disease to candida, SIBO (small intestine bacterial overgrowth), IBS (irritable bowel syndrome), hypoglycemia (blood sugar imbalance), and malabsorption. Most of the time, I went from feeling constantly starving and wracked with cravings to feeling poisoned by the food I ate. I was a medical mystery.

By the time I got into my teens, I began to suffer from depression and eventually turned to bulimia for some relief from the worst of the digestive pain I experienced. I refused the antidepressants, pain pills, and surgery that were constantly recommended by doctors and instead began researching. In college, I majored in business and minored in nutrition and wellness. I continued to research, but it wasn't until my early 30s that I found the answer that seemed way too simple: *change your diet.*

To avoid having my gallbladder removed, I started a gut-healing diet, and it gave me miraculous relief. I recovered from bulimia, and the rest of my symptoms started falling away. About six years into my recovery, I was diagnosed with Ehlers-Danlos syndrome, an incurable collagen synthesis and processing disorder. My doctor explained that this was likely the reason for many of my symptoms because it affects the digestive organs in addition to skin, bones, joints, and ligaments. At this point, I was unfazed because my healthy diet had already healed most of my digestive issues and symptoms. But I wondered, H*mmm, how can I get collagen into my body?* This is how I stumbled upon bone broth. It took my digestion to the next level, and I've been consuming it regularly ever since.

My specialties in business were organizational development, change management, and performance improvement. I was recognized for having a gift for systems thinking, which allowed me to zero in on the root cause of "sick companies" and successfully help them get well again. While in my corporate career, I continued to study natural health because my real passion was healing the stress that created chronic illness in people's lives. More than a decade ago, I left my corporate career and started my health coaching practice. I got my professional coach certification, studied, researched, and published thousands of articles with medical and holistic doctors, and worked with some of the best minds in natural health.

Today, I practice the principles of systems thinking with my clients to uncover the root cause of health challenges. I apply nutrigenomics (how nutrition can be applied to genetic expressions), mineral balancing, and using whole foods and lifestyle changes to support my clients in achieving their best health.

HOW THIS BOOK IS LAID OUT

In Chapter 1, you will learn the history and science behind why bone broth has so many health, beauty, and vitality benefits. You'll also learn why bone broth is a panacea for some but not for others, and why you might sometimes choose meat or vegetable stock instead.

Chapter 2 gives you an overview of the kitchen equipment you'll need, the process of making bone broth, and details on choosing high-quality ingredients for your broth.

Chapter 3 helps you get started with some guiding principles and tips, along with sample menus, a shopping list, and an overview of what Louise eats for breakfast, lunch, and dinner.

Chapters 4 through 13 take you through a world of delicious recipes from a variety of cultures, showcasing the types of meals you can make with bone broth, meat stock, and vegetable broth. You will learn to make several different types of broths (meat, poultry, fish, and vegetable), soups, stews, main dishes, vegetables, grain dishes, breads, desserts, healing elixirs, beauty remedies, and even cocktails!

Chapter 14 provides encouragement for you to embrace the fact that you are worth the time it takes in the kitchen to nourish yourself. We also provide a wonderful, healing affirmation and meditation.

After reading this book, you will understand why the humble bone broth has become a widely celebrated superfood. And instead of seeing this as the latest fad, you'll learn why it is a "trend" worth sticking with for life.

AN INVITATION TO START YOUR CULINARY, HEALTH, AND BEAUTY ADVENTURE

You are about to embark on an exciting adventure into traditional foods! These are the foods that satisfy us at the deepest level of our being because they connect us back to family history, Mother Earth, and the building blocks that fuel our physical bodies and nourish our minds. I invite you to take this opportunity for self-care. The time you spend in the kitchen can nourish your mind, body, and spirit for days to come! It can bring joy to your taste buds and sustenance to your family and friends.

If you feel you don't have time to cook, Louise and I invite you to look deeper at what you don't give yourself time for. Are you doing so much that you don't have time for the things that facilitate your best health? We encourage you to take the time-saving tips in this book—and a sense of adventure—into your kitchen as a way to tell yourself what you know (deep down inside) is true: *you matter.*

I love you,
Heather

Straining broth into a mason jar.

PART I

THE ART AND SCIENCE
of Bone Broth

Bone broth ice cubes made in heart-shaped silicone molds.

CHAPTER 1

THE HISTORY *and* SCIENCE:
Is Bone Broth Really a Health and Beauty Panacea?

You know those friends who just get you? The ones you can be weird and zany with, knowing they'll love you for it? The ones who see you dancing in an elevator and join you without thinking twice? The ones who nourish you simply by their presence? We are those friends. Heather is going to share how we met:

> I met Louise at a nutrition seminar many years ago. She liked my red lipstick, and I liked her quick wit. From that point forward, we kept in touch. Even though we lived on opposite sides of the country at the time and she was 79 and I was 37, we'd get together for lunches at least once or twice per year. Most of these lunches were at Hay House conferences, where Louise was speaking. At one of them, she was up onstage and said, "Everything is thoughts and food," and I thought, *This woman gets it—no wonder she is so young and healthy*!

> Let me tell you a bit about our relationship, so that you can get a sense of why two people with so many years and miles between them became fast friends. You see, Louise is like my teenage friend. Instead of our current ages of 89 and 47, we feel transported back to age 14 when we're together. We giggle, we run around and explore things, and she makes me laugh like no one else. She's so young that I feel that young, too. We wear flapper feathers to dinner and tell people we are celebrating life. One time, we visited an adult novelty shop to see what such a place would sell. My husband, Joel, called me later that day after receiving a notification from our credit-card issuer. He asked, "Did you really spend $177 at a place called the Condom Shack?" To which I replied, "Yes, honey, Louise and I each bought a few things today." This is one of the many reasons Joel likes when I go shopping with her.

> Another time, Louise and I missed our plane sitting right there at the gate, because we were putting new apps on each other's iPads. She taught me to play solitaire and showed me how to do my hair and cut those hanger things off the inside of my shirt (what are those for anyway?), and we've experimented with new, all-natural lipsticks when we wanted

to find a nontoxic yet bold, saturated color. We've had so much fun that we decided her new name is to be Louise Play.

Over the years, we've cooked many meals together, and I've watched her natural instincts in the kitchen and seen her love of delicious, healthy food firsthand. And I've thought to myself, This woman knows how to do health right. She doesn't fret about it; she just chooses real food and trusts her body to signal what nourishes her.

The steady staple in her diet? Bone broth. Louise learned to make it from reading and watching the iconic Julia Child, many years ago and kept on consuming it because it made her feel good, energized, and strong. When people ask what Louise eats or how they can be more like her, she always talks about bone broth and affirmations. "If you get your food right and you get your thoughts right, everything just works," she tells them.

It struck me that affirmations are gentle words to change the way we think and shift us into a place of self-love, and bone broth is a gentle way to get important nutrients into the body. It's simple, and while it seems like that thing our grandmothers used to make, it's really much more than that. The whole process of making bone broth is a path back to loving and nourishing yourself. It's a way to bring pep back into your step and strength and muscle tone back into your body, and to channel your inner 14-year-old (albeit a much wiser version!).

It's based on ancient wisdom, but it's the hippest thing going in cities across America, too. It is the new green juice, done better. You are in for a big treat with this book because you will learn what makes bone broth such an enigma that it could be thousands of years old and yet the hottest thing going today. Who doesn't want more mojo? Better skin, hair, bones, and teeth? This is your elixir . . . so get ready for some delicious fun!

WHATEVER HAPPENED TO REAL, WHOLE FOOD?

Food has a magical quality of connecting human beings to memories, often those of family or special gatherings. It seems that whenever we mention bone broth, people want to talk about their grandmothers. Very quickly, we are transported into someone's kitchen in another part of the country or the world. We hear about that pot of soup that Grandma always had simmering on the stove. We smell the aromas, deep, rich, and mysterious. We feel ourselves sitting at the table and hearing old stories, feeling comforted and connected.

The soup is better than anything else we've ever tasted. We are left with a full-on sensory experience, a bit of family history, and more than anything else, the love and safety of a warm kitchen. Of people gathering together, cutting, crafting, and creating something that will nourish one another.

These days, preparing food is not the same as it was in Grandma's kitchen. We take things out of boxes and cans and bring things home in containers; often, we don't even know where our food came from. We've lost 80 percent of the sensory experience we had as kids in those warm, safe kitchens, and we've missed out on the stories shared as meals were prepared . . . our family history.

How did this happen? Since the 1950s and the invention of TV dinners, the media has ridiculed cooking. The message became: *Why do something that takes so much time and energy when you can open a box and pop it into the oven or stop at the drive-through window?*

Something interesting has happened since then, though. A few aisles down from the frozen-food section is the energy-drink section, where sales are exploding. And guess who the energy-drink companies are targeting? Millennials. If you were born between 1981 and 1997, you're a millennial, a child of baby boomers or generation Xers—the very generations who traded in their stockpots for TV dinners. In leaving real food behind, we did not gain time; we lost energy, along with nutrition.

Yet there's a quiet revolution happening now. We're putting together the puzzle pieces and seeing that what we eat absolutely matters. We're seeing a direct link between declining health and our nutrient-poor diets. These days, eight in ten parents claim to buy organic products,[1] farmers' markets are experiencing exploding growth, and Costco's organic-food sales have outpaced Whole Foods'. In 2013, sales of organic foods rose to $35.1 billion and are still growing.[2] Farmers, craftspeople, and artisans are becoming the "it" people.

Being in the kitchen is the new cool. But it might as well be rocket science if you don't know where to begin, right? Like a lab experiment, you have to put a bunch of things in a pot or bowl, mix them up, and hope it all tastes good. Our mission in writing this book is to provide you with some delicious, nourishing, home-cooked foods that are so healing to your body and soul that you'll come to enjoy your time in the kitchen!

WHAT IS BONE BROTH, EXACTLY?

Bone broth has been used as food and in healing remedies for more than a thousand years. In fact, the earliest recorded broth dates as far back as A.D. 1000.[3]

By 1765, the first restaurant in history is believed to have been opened by soup-maker A. Boulanger, who wanted to provide restorative broth to the workers of Paris who needed quick, easy, strengthening meals during the Industrial Revolution.[4] Boulanger believed so much in the powers of soup that a sign in his restaurant said: COME TO ME, ALL YOU WHO ARE WEARY AND BURDENED, AND I WILL RESTORE YOU.[5] Thus launched the use of the term *restaurant* for food establishments.

It's no wonder broths are one of the big flavor secrets used by chefs in restaurants around the world. And countless health experts talk about why this traditional broth is the best way to stay healthy in the modern world, and why it should replace coffee as our go-to pick-me-up. They use exciting terms such as *superfood, antiaging, gut healing,* and *energizing.* The most interesting thing here is that gourmet cooks and health enthusiasts meet in wholehearted agreement because homemade bone broth tastes good! Good-tasting broth makes all the difference when consumed on its own or incorporated into another recipe.

At its essence, bone broth is simply bones and water, simmered for between 1½ and 48 hours. To some, it's just "soup," but it's really so much more than that. Most broth today is being offered up by farm-to-table chefs, nose-to-tail butchers, organic farmers, and dedicated health enthusiasts—those who have rediscovered the healing benefits of this once-forgotten, humble liquid.

Bone broth is an unsurpassed source of flavor that could never be reproduced from a can. Its tastiness and health benefits can lull us back into that full-on sensory experience that we lost when processed foods and convenience gained the upper hand in our stressed-out, busy modern lives. Bone broth can satisfy our deep need for nourishment and reconnect us to those warm, safe kitchens of our memories.

We taste this broth and can feel a primal connection to our ancestors and how they prepared food. We are reminded that food is so much more than a way to satisfy hunger. Food is medicine. Food is connection. Food is love. If we're willing to pay attention, this is what we feel while savoring bone broth.

THE FOUR KEY REASONS TO CONSUME BONE BROTH

In our experience and research, we have found that there are four key reasons to consume bone broth:

1. **Bioavailable collagen.** This is the health and beauty star that makes bone broth a unique healing food.

2. **Bioavailable nutrients.** Broth contains easily digested amino acids, vitamins, minerals, and essential fatty acids.

3. **Less waste—better for your budget and the planet.** You'll find out how to use leftovers as a nutrient-dense food source.

4. **Healing flavor enhancer.** You can make delicious healing drinks, soups, and meals with this chef's secret. It's a beautiful way to let your food be your medicine.

The rest of this chapter will outline these four key components, along with the science behind the health benefits of bone broth.

#1. Bioavailable Collagen, aka the Big Deal

Collagen is one of the most studied proteins in science, and the most sought after in the beauty industry. Supplements, pharmaceuticals, nutraceuticals, processed-food additives, lotions, and potions are made to support what is projected to be a $4.4 billion industry by the year 2020.[6] What if the collagen secret was right in front of us all along? What if a simple bowl of soup were the whole-food, collagen-delivery device we've been looking for? Let's find out.

Collagen is the body's most abundant protein. While it's often referred to as "connective tissue," we like to think of collagen as "the great supporter." It supports, strengthens, cushions, provides structure, and holds the body together. Collagen makes up bones, teeth, tendons, ligaments, joints, and cartilage; and is key for beautiful hair, skin, and nails. It strengthens muscles, aids cell growth, and supports the hollow organs of your digestive system (that is, your esophagus, stomach, and small and large intestines).

The big deal in bone broth is that it's a source of bioavailable collagen. In other words, the collagen has been broken down (or denatured) into gelatin, which is easily digested and assimilated in the body. Gelatin is liquid when hot or at room temperature and becomes thick and jiggly when it's completely cooled in the refrigerator. As a kid, you may have had the boxed gelatin dessert called Jell-O, which is a highly processed, sugar-laden version of the gelatin found in bone broth.

While many specific types of collagen have been found, types I, II, and III make up 80 to 90 percent of collagen in animals.[7] Type I collagen is found in bones, tendons, ligaments, and skin; type II collagen is found in cartilage; and type III collagen is found in skin, muscle, and bone marrow.[8] Bone broth made with a variety of bones, cartilage, and skin may contain all three types of collagen.

Why is this important? Healthy human bodies produce collagen up until age 40, and then production begins to decline.[9] This brings a whole new meaning to the negative assertion that "the body falls apart after the age of 40," but you can see where that limiting belief might come from. Everything in this book will show you how to change that!

In addition to aging, stress and autoimmune conditions can adversely impact collagen production.[10] When collagen declines or is defective, some common symptoms are loose, sagging, or wrinkled skin; sagging muscles; thin or dry hair and nails; and joint issues or brittle bones.[11] Decreased or defective collagen has also been indicated in digestive issues such as GERD (gastroesophageal reflux disease) and IBS (irritable bowel syndrome).[12]

Since animal protein is the only food source of collagen (particularly the parts used to make bone broth, such as bones, tendons, ligaments, cartilage, skin, and marrow), bone broth delivers a wonderful bioavailable source for the body. Note that while plant foods do not contain collagen, they can boost it. Plant foods high in vitamins such as C, B complex, A, D, and E; minerals like silicon, sulfur, and copper; and amino acids like proline can all help build collagen in the body.

Here are some examples of foods that can support collagen production, but do not contain it:

- **Fruits:** lemons, oranges, raspberries, strawberries, and cherries
- **Vegetables:** Swiss chard, green beans, spinach, red peppers, red leaf lettuce, tomatoes,

carrots, beets, leeks, cucumbers, seaweed, and green vegetables

- **Nuts and seeds:** sunflower seeds, almonds, and walnuts

- **Essential fatty acids:** unrefined oils such as extra-virgin olive oil, coconut oil, and flaxseed oil

- **Miscellaneous:** rice wine, coffee extract (arabica), Panax ginseng root extract, cinnamon extract, and amla extract[13]

Now here's the kicker when it comes to collagen: *it also aids digestion!* Remember, bone broth denatures collagen into an easily digestible form called gelatin. Since gelatin has been popular since 1682, extensive studies have been performed on its nutritional value over hundreds of years.

Two profound digestion-boosting roles of gelatin are:

— **Protecting and sealing the intestines.** Gelatin protects the intestines by lining the mucous membrane and defending against any further issues from food or drink, which makes it a valuable option for improving digestive problems.[14]

— **Increasing total nutritional value.** Several studies found that when gelatin was combined with other foods, the total nutritional value increased considerably.[15] This may be due to gelatin's ability to aid the body's digestive process.

While studies show that consuming sources of collagen like bone broth and collagen hydrolysate (a broken-down form of unflavored beef gelatin) promote improvements in health, we also share real-life healing stories in the Appendix.

#2. Bioavailable Nutrients

Bone broth provides predigested nutrients, which makes it easier for your body to assimilate them. The actual nutritional makeup of bone broth will vary based on the types of bones, skin, cartilage, tendons, ligaments, vegetables, herbs, and spices used. In general, here are the important nutrients you may find:

— **Amino acids.** Bone broth is full of important amino acids, the building blocks of protein, which helps build and repair every tissue and organ in the body. Amino acids contribute to every function in the body, such as its growth and repair; as well as moods, energy, focus, and hormone balance. Three of the stars that are particularly abundant in collagen are: glycine, proline, and hydroxyproline. Additional amino acids you may find in bone broth are aspartic acid, glutamic acid (glutamine), serine, threonine, alanine, arginine, valine, isoleucine, leucine, tyrosine, and phenylalanine.[16] The type and amount of amino acids can vary based on type of bones and animal parts used.

— **Minerals.** With all the chronic fatigue, hormone imbalance, and adrenal fatigue we see today, mineral imbalances are likely a major contributor. Minerals are incredibly important for our health, contributing to building bones and teeth, moods and focus, and energy and hormone balance. We can all use some of that mineral mojo!

These days, we hear a lot about calcium and much less about magnesium and other minerals such as phosphorus, sulfur, potassium, iron, manganese, zinc, copper, cobalt, fluoride, and selenium. Bones and teeth are made up of more than just calcium; therefore, we need a full range of minerals for bone health and overall wellness. Bone broth contains a wide base of easily digested minerals.[17]

— **Glucosaminoglycans.** Cartilage and other connective tissue in animals contain glucosaminoglycans (GAGs), amino acid–sugar molecules that make up the network of proteoglycans, which play a supporting role in connective tissue, along with collagen.[18] GAGs essentially cushion and lubricate skin, joints, muscles, and eyes. Examples are hyaluronic acid, chondroitin sulfate, and glucosamine—you may have heard of these because they are used in supplements for joint health. Hyaluronic acid is also being used in cosmetics and eye surgery. Bone broth that gels nicely is a good source of glucosaminoglycans.

— **Vitamins and other nutrients of your choosing.** While a basic bone broth only needs a variety of bones and water, many people boost the nutrient value by adding vegetable scraps, herbs, and spices. Adding these ingredients allows you to get extra easily digested vitamins, minerals, and antioxidants into your broth. (In Part II, you'll find many options for customizing broths for your health and nutrition goals.)

— **Healthy fats.** Bone marrow, skin, meat, and the other fatty parts of beef, poultry, and fish have healthy fats that can support good moods, satiety (and therefore losing or maintaining weight), and brain health.[19] Fats also help carry important vitamins like A, D, E, and K into the body.

#3. Less Waste—Better for Your Budget and the Planet

Before supermarkets, when people lived closer to the land, human beings worked very hard to use all parts of plant and animal food, with little to no waste. We believe factory farms that cram animals into tiny spaces and force them to eat a diet that is not natural for their bodies are inhumane. Much of this industry stems from the marketing of choice cuts of meat, like steaks or chicken breast, rather than using the whole animal (also known as nose-to-tail).

For example, an entire cow could feed a family of four for a year, if they ate like their ancestors—that is, *if they ate the whole cow and not just a few choice cuts.* Choice cuts, like filet mignon and rib eye, make up only 15 percent of the cow. With growing demand for such cuts, this has meant a demand for more cows—that same family of four eating choice cuts would need many cows for a year, not just one.

And it's not just inhumane animal practices that trouble us. The same focus on a small range of foods, such as corn and wheat, has led to the overproduction of a small number of soil-depleting crops, rather than honoring the earth with a wide range of crops to support the planet's health.

If we break this down even further, we can look at the human body, which thrives on a variety of foods, including cuts of meat. Cheaper cuts of meat are actually healthier than choice cuts because they provide the most collagen, glucosaminoglycans, and essential fatty acids to aid digestion, bone, skin, and joint health.

When we plant foods that serve the ecosystem, we bring more minerals back into our soil. These minerals are devastatingly deficient in our diets today, leading to a myriad of mysterious issues that the pharmaceutical industry creates new drugs for. And since drugs don't heal deficiencies of protein, vitamins, and minerals, we continue in a vicious cycle.

The more we focus on foods that serve the health of the ecosystem, the more we find a better way for all beings—animals, plants, humans, insects . . . the entire system that must live in harmony in order to thrive.

Bone broth is also budget friendly, as it allows us to use what is considered trash in modern times. The skin and carcass of a chicken, animal bones and feet, vegetable skins and scraps, are all now used to make a nutrient-dense, healing meal. We'll even show you how to reuse bones after making broth!

#4. Healing Flavor Enhancer

For hundreds of years, chefs have been using broth as a way to add richer flavor to food. With bone broth, you will no longer have to use processed, chemical-laden bouillon cubes to flavor soups, stews, and sauces. Now you'll have a flavor enhancer that also delivers big health and beauty benefits!

THE SCIENCE: BONE BROTH AND YOUR HEALTH

While there have been some studies done on bone broth, the majority have been done on collagen, gelatin, or collagen hydrolysate (also called collagen peptides). As we've already mentioned, gelatin is the denatured form of collagen that makes your broth get more solid when refrigerated; it is also sold on the market as an unflavored powder. Collagen hydrolysate is a powdered product that is a bit more processed than powdered gelatin and has different applications (we'll explain this in more detail in Chapter 2). Please keep in mind that when we speak about gelatin, whether from bone broth or powdered, we are referring to denatured collagen.

Note: While there are many studies showing that collagen keeps the skin youthful and tight, most of the studies on antiaging skin benefits are of collagen supplements. Collagen supplements have been found to reduce wrinkles, dry skin, and scaling, and counteract natural photoaging.[20] Experts such as Kaayla T. Daniel, Ph.D., also propose that eating a collagen-rich diet may reduce cellulite.[21]

Biologist and professor Ray Peat says that the degenerative and inflammatory diseases on the rise in industrialized societies could be corrected by the use of gelatin-rich foods due to the presence of restorative amino acids such as glycine, alanine, proline, and hydroxyproline.[22]

Studies show that gelatin may also have the following benefits:

— Stronger, healthier nails[23]

— Antiaging

— Anti-tumor

— Arthritis and joint-pain relief

— Cell-protecting

— Can alleviate diabetes and lower blood sugar; supports insulin regulation

— Can improve sleep

— Helps regulate bleeding from nosebleeds, heavy menstruation, ulcers, hemorrhoids, and bladder hemorrhage

— Helps normalize stomach acid, which is useful for colitis, celiac disease, ulcers, and other inflammatory gut conditions[24]

**If you experience any challenges
with the issues above, here is
an affirmation to use:**

*In the infinity of life where I am, all is perfect, whole,
and complete. I recognize my body as a good friend.
Each cell in my body has Divine Intelligence. I listen
to what it tells me, and know that its advice is valid. I
am always safe and Divinely protected and guided. I
choose to be healthy and free. All is well in my world.*

Healing Affirmations

Since we're covering the research about health conditions that bone broth may help, we thought it would be useful to give you some affirmations for these conditions as well.

Affirmations are any statements you make. Too often, we think in negative terms, which only create more of what you don't want. A negative affirmation like *I will never get better* will get you nowhere. Stating that *I am open to feeling my best,* however, will open the channels in your consciousness to create just that.

For decades, people have reported healing benefits from using Louise's affirmations. We want to encourage you to practice thinking positively as you read this book and focus on improving your health. Continually make positive statements about how you want your life to be. However, it's important to always make your affirmations in the present tense, using phrases such as *I am* or *I have.* Your subconscious mind is such an obedient servant that if you declare in the future tense that *I want* or *I will have,* then that is where it will always stay— just out of your reach in the future!

Studies conducted on bone broth have found that it can:

— **Boost immunity.** Amino acids in bone broth, like arginine, glutamine, and cysteine, have been shown to boost immunity in humans and animals.[25]

If you are experiencing autoimmune issues or challenges with immunity, here is an affirmation to use:
I am willing to change and grow. I now create a safe future. Miracles happen every day. I go within and dissolve the pattern that created this, and I now accept a Divine healing. And so it is!

— **Alleviate the common cold and bronchitis.** In 2000, a study was published in *Chest*, the official journal of the American College of Chest Physicians, which studied chicken soup (bone broth) and found that it does indeed aid in alleviating symptoms of the common cold, such as clearing mucus, opening respiratory pathways, and providing easily digested nutrition.[26] According to medical doctor and UCLA professor Irwin Ziment, chicken soup naturally contains the amino acid cysteine, which chemically resembles the bronchitis drug acetylcysteine.[27]

If you are experiencing a cold or bronchitis, use these affirmations:
Colds: *I allow my mind to relax and be at peace. Clarity and harmony are within and around me.*
Bronchitis: *I declare peace and approve of myself. I care for me. I am totally adequate at all times.*

— **Fight inflammation.** Studies show that many of the amino acids in bone broth (such as cystine, histidine, and glycine) reduce inflammation, and L-glutamine specifically reduces gut inflammation.[28] Additionally, the same *Chest* article from October 2000 mentioned above concluded that chicken soup's anti-inflammatory benefits may be one reason it is so helpful with relieving symptoms of the common cold.[29]

If you are experiencing inflammation, here's a great affirmation to use:
My thinking is peaceful, calm, and centered. I am willing to change all patterns of criticism. I love and approve of myself.

— **Strengthen bones and teeth.** A study on the necessary nutrients for bone health found that the process of bone-formation requires "an adequate and constant supply of nutrients" as follows: calcium, protein, magnesium, phosphorus, vitamin D, potassium, zinc, manganese, copper, boron, iron, vitamin A, vitamin K, vitamin C, and the B vitamins.[30] Bone broth with vegetables and meat or fish provides a good source of all of these vitamins and minerals.

If you are experiencing issues with your bones or teeth, here are affirmations to use:
Bones: *I am well structured and balanced.*
Broken bones: *In my world, I am my own authority, for I am the only one who thinks in my mind.*
Bone deformity: *I breathe in life fully. I relax and trust the flow and the process of life.*
Teeth: *I make my decisions based on the principles of truth, and I rest securely knowing that only Divine right action is taking place in my life.*

— **Promote weight loss.** While more studies of gut bacteria and weight need to be conducted, research has shown that obese people have more of a certain type of bacteria called *Firmicutes* and less of another type called *Bacteroidetes* in their digestive tracts. The higher proportion of Firmicutes is believed to lead to a higher amount of calories extracted from food. Therefore, a higher ratio of Firmicutes to Bacteriodetes has become one of the markers of obesity.[31]

Bone broth is a good source of L-glutamine, an essential amino acid (building block of protein) necessary for the body and gut health. L-glutamine was found in studies to reduce the Firmicutes in the gut and, therefore, aid in weight loss.[32]

Many studies have also looked at whether consuming soup before a meal promoted weight loss due to a lower amount of calories eaten during the meal itself. In a study published in the November 2007 issue of *Appetite* (an international research journal specializing in behavioral nutrition and the cultural, sensory, and physiological influences on choices and intakes of foods and drinks), researchers conducted the study again and went a step further to see if eating a meal with liquid would have the same effect as soup. The finding was that ingesting soup did indeed reduce caloric intake at the next meal and that only soup—not food consumed with water—had this beneficial effect.[33]

If you are experiencing weight challenges, here is an affirmation to use:
I am at peace with my own feelings. I am safe where I am. I create my own security. I love and approve of myself.

— **Improve hydration.** Bone broth, especially when it's made from vegetables, adds electrolytes (minerals) and carbohydrates (from vegetables) to the diet. Studies have shown that drinking broth can rehydrate better than water alone due to the electrolytes.[34]

If you are experiencing any issues with hydration, use this affirmation:
I love and approve of myself. It is safe for me to care for myself. Divine right action is always taking place in my life. Only good comes from each experience. It is safe to grow up. I willingly release the past with joy. It is safe for me to let go. I am free now.

— **Restore exercise capacity with rehydration and electrolytes.** Additional studies have shown that liquids with carbohydrates and electrolytes, like a bone broth simmered with vegetables, outperform water alone when it comes to restoring exercise capacity that may be lost from dehydration and electrolyte depletion.[35]

If you are experiencing issues with fatigue or exercise capacity, here is an affirmation to use:
I *am enthusiastic about life and filled with energy and enthusiasm.*

— **Build muscle.** The amino acids in bone broth can help stimulate muscle protein synthesis. Muscle protein synthesis is essential for the ongoing growth, repair, and maintenance of skeletal muscle groups. In a study looking at healthy patients and ovarian-cancer patients, researchers found that ingesting amino acids helped stimulate muscle protein synthesis and reduced inflammation, both in healthy participants and participants undergoing cancer therapy.[36]

If you experience any challenges with muscles (overuse injuries, muscle tone, muscle wasting, cramps, inflammation, or other disorders), here is an affirmation to use:
By *choosing loving, joyous thoughts, I create a loving, joyous world. I am safe and free.*

— **Improve mood.** Your diet influences your gut bacteria, and your gut bacteria influence your brain. According to neuroscientists,

your gut bacteria are constantly speaking to your brain. The makeup of gut bacteria, called your *microbiome*, influences how the brain is wired from infancy to adulthood, along with moods, memory, the ability to learn, and how to deal with stress. When the gut microbiome is healthy, it sends happy signals to the brain; when it's unhealthy, it can send signals of anxiety. Because of this signaling, neuroscientists are starting to investigate how to manage gut bacteria to treat mood- and stress-related disorders such as depression.[37]

If you are experiencing mood issues, here is an affirmation to use:
I *love and approve of myself, and* I *trust the process of life. I am safe.*

If you are an athlete, want more energy, are looking to lose weight or feel better—or if you're a gourmet cook who enjoys the wonderful experience of delicious food—bone broth has something to offer.

For decades, food manufacturers have been trying to sell you on Gatorade, energy drinks, over-the-counter drugs, antibiotics, weight-loss potions, and energy pills. Well, there *is* something you can take for better health and better athletic performance, but it's not one of these—it's bone broth!

LEAKY GUT AND LEAKY BRAIN

Hippocrates, the father of Western medicine, said, "All disease begins in the gut." Yet it is just now beginning to be more common to look at gut health as a possible root cause or treatment option when dealing with chronic illness. It's no surprise when you learn that approximately 70 to 80 percent of the immune system is located in this area.

Unfortunately, challenges such as leaky gut are on the rise. In a healthy gut, the wall of the small intestine acts as a gatekeeper, letting through water and needed nutrients and keeping out harmful substances. However, poor diet, medications, and bacterial or fungal overgrowth can compromise the lining, causing leaky gut. Symptoms are varied but can include food sensitivities, allergies, headaches or migraines, arthritis, eczema, hives, and chronic fatigue.[38]

A leaky gut can contribute to oxidative stress or inflammation in the body, causing the blood-brain barrier to become "leaky," whereby molecules and toxins that are not supposed to enter may get into the brain.[39]

These conditions are associated with a permeable or leaky blood-brain barrier:

- ADD or ADHD
- ALS (Lou Gehrig's Disease)
- Alzheimer's disease and dementia
- Anorexia and bulimia
- Autism
- Brain fog
- Diabetes
- Epilepsy or seizures

- Infections of the nervous system such as fungal infections; viral infections; parasites; or bacterial infections that enter the nervous system, like Lyme disease, encephalitis, or meningitis
- Mood challenges such as anxiety, bipolar disorder, depression, obsessive compulsive disorder, or schizophrenia
- Multiple sclerosis
- Stroke
- Tics—brief, involuntary, repetitive, and purposeless, vocalizations or movements, like humming, yelling, shoulder shrugging, eye blinking, or grimacing[40]

Bone broth has been embraced by many who follow gut-healing diets such as the Paleo Diet, as well as gut-brain healing diets such as the Gut and Psychology Syndrome (GAPS) diet. It's also a staple of people following traditional food practices espoused by organizations like the Weston A. Price Foundation and the Price-Pottenger Nutrition Foundation.

IS BONE BROTH A PANACEA?

We don't really believe any one food is a cure-all for every health condition. However, bone broth has something very special that no other food has: a bioavailable source of collagen. When mixed in with bioavailable minerals, amino acids, glucosaminoglycans, and possibly added vitamins and antioxidants, you have a powerhouse of nutrients that can gently nourish the body.

This is not an overnight miracle, however. We've seen articles where reporters try bone broth for a week and declare it "nothing special." One week or even two weeks is typically too short a time for something as important as rebuilding the structure of your body. Most people who experience benefits with bone broth notice changes after at least a month, and more commonly after several months. Collagen is not known to be easy to rebuild, according to research, but it is possible. Perhaps this is why regular consumption is so helpful.

One Size Does Not Fit All: When Bone Broth Is Not a Panacea

Everyone is unique and at different phases in their health journey. For this reason, bone broth is not going to be a solution for everyone. If you try it and don't feel well, you may be experiencing a detoxification reaction. You could also be reacting to the glutamates, a normally healthy amino acid in bone broth that can cause problems for people with certain chronic conditions. Here's some more information about this:

— **Glutamates.** The glutamate (glutamic acid or glutamine) in bone broth is a nonessential amino acid (meaning your body can make it) with many health benefits, like aiding gut health. It's an excitatory neurochemical that stimulates the brain, which is fine if you have enough calming neurotransmitters to create balance. However, in situations where someone has a leaky gut and a leaky blood-brain barrier, consuming foods with too many glutamates is problematic, leading to unpleasant symptoms.

In cases like this, people may want to avoid bone broth and consume meat stock instead (see "For Certain Chronic Health Conditions . . ." sidebar later in the chapter). At the same time, glutamates are in many whole foods, so people may want to also avoid other foods with glutamates, such as mushrooms, broccoli, dairy (casein), tomatoes, and walnuts; along with gluten and certain condiments like soy sauce and white vinegar.[41]

— **MSG vs. glutamates.** MSG (monosodium glutamate) is a processed source of glutamate that we strongly recommend you avoid. Unfortunately, it's in just about every processed food, often disguised with the following terms: *natural flavoring, spices, vegetable protein, hydrolyzed vegetable protein, soy protein isolate, glutamic acid, enzymes, protein fortified,* and *yeast extract.*[42]

While MSG is a form of free glutamates, it's a very different form than glutamates found in real food, which could be why some people react to MSG in processed foods but not in bone broth, gelatin, or whole foods. MSG is a synthetic form of glutamic acid or D-*glutamic acid* (which may be responsible for promoting adverse health reactions) as opposed to real-food L-*glutamic acid*, which is a precursor to neurotransmitters in the body.[43]

In short, bone broth does have glutamic acid or glutamates, but most people respond well to it and experience only the healing benefits of this amino acid. Other very sensitive people with leaky guts and leaky blood-brain barriers (and often those low in magnesium and antioxidants), tend to react to glutamates in bone broth and, therefore, need to start with meat stock. We have even provided a vegetable stock recipe, just in case extremely sensitive people need to start there to build up minerals and antioxidants.

Here's what to do if you have a long-term chronic condition (including epilepsy or mood disorders), or if you don't feel well after consuming bone broth:

— **Switch to meat stock.** Meat stock is a gentler place to start because it's less concentrated and has fewer glutamates than bone broth. It's made almost exactly like bone broth, only you use a little more meat (rather than just bone), and you simmer it for 1½ to 3 hours. Consume meat stock until your symptoms resolve and then switch to bone broth, which is simmered much longer and is more concentrated.

— **Be sure to remove the fat from the broth.** If you have trouble digesting fat, it's important to either skim the fat off the broth or remove the fat that rises to the top after chilling your broth (see more in Chapter 2). It's not that the fat is bad to consume; it's just that some people with digestive challenges may have symptoms after consuming the fat.

— **Support your body.** If you are experiencing uncomfortable symptoms after drinking bone broth, drink plenty of water and consider taking a bath with your favorite essential oils or magnesium flakes (Ancient Minerals brand magnesium flakes are wonderful for calming and soothing the body, and can be purchased online from suppliers like Amazon.com). Some peppermint tea or fennel tea can be very helpful if you did consume the fat and aren't feeling well digestively. Both support the digestive system, and fennel in particular is helpful for relieving trapped gas.

— **Keep a food journal for a couple of weeks.** You can do this on your phone or carry a pad and pen with you and write down what you ate for each meal, along with this information:

- How you felt before you ate
- How you felt after you ate
- How you felt hours afterward
- How you slept that night
- How refreshed you felt when you awoke the next morning

Note that how you felt includes moods (such as anxiety, satisfaction, happiness, depression, agitation, or racing thoughts), energy (well-balanced, tired, wired, energized, and so on), physical symptoms (pain, joint issues, sleep challenges, breathing challenges, bloating, gas, digestive pain, constipation, diarrhea, or reflux), and beneficial symptoms (like feeling great, flexible, pain-free, strong, light, and so forth).

For Certain Chronic Health Conditions, You Might Want to Start with Stock

If you don't feel well after having bone broth, or you have a chronic health condition that also involves mood challenges (such as depression, anxiety, bipolar disorder, and so forth), you may want to start with meat stock first.

These guidelines are based on the teachings of Natasha Campbell-McBride, M.D., author of *Gut and Psychology Syndrome: Natural Treatment for Autism, Dyspraxia, A.D.D., Dyslexia, A.D.H.D., Depression, Schizophrenia*. Louise and Heather have both studied with Natasha to understand her principles for using meat stock and bone broth as part of the GAPS diet, which has helped thousands of people heal.

Meat stock is exactly like bone broth, with these exceptions:

- **Simmer time.** You simmer meat stock for only 1½ to 3 hours maximum (bone broth is simmered longer, often for 24 to 48 hours or more).

- **Ingredients.** You might use a little more meat and fewer bones (optional).

- **Concentration of glutamine.** Meat stock is less concentrated and has fewer amino acids than bone broth, including glutamine. This is important if you have a leaky blood-brain barrier. In situations where there is a leaky blood-brain barrier, glutamates may create a problem in the body because there isn't enough GABA, the calming neurotransmitter in the body (you can think of GABA as nature's Valium).

We recommend using meat stock until your symptoms subside, then trying bone broth and seeing how you feel. This can take a minimum of 30 to 90 days on meat stock; however, all health situations are different and you may need more time before moving to bone broth. It can be helpful to work with a health practitioner to guide you.

Vegetable stock. We have also provided a vegetable stock recipe for people who are sensitive to meat stock and want to start very simply before building up. This will not give you the collagen, amino acids, and minerals from bones, but you will get the bioavailable vitamins and minerals from vegetables to aid in your healing journey. One great option is to use the vegetables that support collagen (mentioned earlier in this chapter) in your stock. After using vegetable stock for 30 to 90 days, you may find that you can move to meat stock and benefit from the added collagen.

After two weeks, you'll begin to see the patterns that show up. You will start to see how your body is speaking to you. This is also very useful if you're working with a health practitioner because the patterns that show up can give clues about the foods that are or are not working for you, along with the possible underlying root cause.

— **Talk to a knowledgeable gut-health practitioner.** If you are working with a practitioner who understands gut health and aren't feeling well after consuming bone broth, here are some things you can ask about:

- Histamine intolerance
- Oxalates
- Glutamates

If you're working with a practitioner on your genetics as it relates to methylation or nutrigenomics (a nutritional approach that looks at how food affects gene expression), you might ask him or her to check for these gene variances (which are referred to as single nucleotide polymorphisms, or SNPs):

- MTHFR
- COMT
- GAD
- CBS

While it's beyond the scope of this book for us to cover each of these, we have seen a pattern among people who have these conditions and need to start with meat stock until their symptoms resolve. A knowledgeable practitioner may be able to help you navigate what your symptoms are related to so that you can get to the root cause. (You will find some practitioners who work by phone and specialize in nutrition and nutrigenomics listed in the Resources section at the back of the book.)

**Here are a few affirmations
to help with your digestion:**

*I digest and assimilate all new experiences
peacefully and joyously. It is safe to be me.
I am wonderful just as I am. I trust the
process of life. I am safe. There is time and
space for everything I need to do. I am at
peace. I give myself permission to be all that
I can be, and I deserve the very best in life. I
love and appreciate myself and others.*

AS YOU START YOUR JOURNEY INTO HEALING BONE BROTH . . .

Overall, whether you use bone broth or meat stock, you have a beautiful way to heal your digestion and nourish your body. Here is an affirmation to say as you begin your journey:

*In the infinity of life where I am, all is
perfect, whole, and complete. I believe in
a Power far greater than I am that flows
through every moment of every day. I open
myself to the wisdom within, knowing that
there is only One Intelligence in this Universe. Out of this One Intelligence comes all
the answers, all the solutions, all the heal-
ings, all the new creations. I trust this Power
and Intelligence, knowing that whatever
I need to know is revealed to me and that
whatever I need comes to me in the right
time, space, and sequence.
All is well in my world.*

We invite you to sip your broth mindfully, say your affirmations, and feel the connection between yourself and all things, taking your nourishment to the next level.

Imagine that there is so much love in your heart that you can heal the entire planet. Each time you make your broth, see this love filling your heart, expanding into your whole body, and radiating into the broth. Feel the broth receiving your love and healing energy. Know that when you consume this broth or cook with it, you are receiving nourishing love. As you drink your warm broth, feel a warmth beginning to glow in your heart center, a softness, a gentleness. Let this feeling begin to change the way you think and talk about yourself. Know that when you share the broth with others, you are sharing the energy of love.

Meaty oxtail bones.

⌐ CHAPTER 2 ⌐

BONE BROTH ORIENTATION:

Kitchen Equipment, an Overview on Making Bone Broth, and How to Choose Quality Ingredients

In this chapter, we outline the kitchen equipment and ingredients you'll need to start making bone broth, and we recommend that you read this information thoroughly before beginning the process. (Once you feel ready, the "Your Action Plan" section in Chapter 3 will probably be very helpful.)

The secret to a good broth is good-quality bones. At the core of them is bone marrow, which is mostly made up of healthy fat that promotes energy and a healthy brain and reproductive system.

Heather: Several years ago, Louise introduced me to bone marrow. We were at a restaurant in New York City, and it was a featured appetizer. I especially remember this night because we were wearing our feathered and bejeweled flapper headbands. People kept stopping us in the street to say how great we looked and to ask us what we were celebrating. "Life," replied Louise, with a big smile. That got them smiling even bigger and telling us how much they loved us. This happens every time I'm out with Louise. Even if people don't recognize her, they tell her that they love her, whether it's her sense of style or her mischievous grin that speaks of untold joy yet to be discovered.

The first thing Louise does in a restaurant is to check in with her "inner ding" (her intuition) about what to eat. Over the years, I began to notice that she always picks the best-tasting food on any menu. That night, her pick was the bone marrow. I wasn't sure what to expect—and, honestly, I would not have ordered it if I were on my own because it didn't sound particularly appetizing. However, after watching Louise score the best meal on the menu for so many years, it was pretty easy to just say, "I'll have what she's having." The bone-marrow appetizer was so delicious that we went back the next evening and ordered two more each, in lieu of an entrée.

This was an experience I will always remember, not just because I discovered a new food, but because it was accompanied by so much fun and laughter. That night also influenced how I make bone broth: When we returned home, Louise showed me how to roast marrowbones at 350° F and enjoy the delicious marrow once it came out of the oven. Then we put the bones into my slow cooker with some beef knuckles, oxtail, and water. To this day, it's still my favorite way to make beef bone broth.

We know that selecting bones and making broth may seem mysterious, so we'd like to invite you into the kitchen with us. The kitchen provides us with the opportunity to experiment and express our creativity; sometimes there are mistakes, and other times there are triumphs. The best times are when a mistake is actually a triumph and we craft a wonderful new recipe of our own.

The great news about bone broth is that you can't mess it up! At the heart of this process, you're simmering water with bones. Perhaps you might decide to add some apple cider vinegar, vegetables, and spices for your own health goals or signature flavors. What's most important is that you bring your sense of adventure with you!

WHAT KITCHEN EQUIPMENT DO YOU NEED?

What you need to make bone broth is really quite simple, and you may even have these items in your kitchen already. If you don't, you can often find great budget-friendly equipment at garage sales, thrift shops, and flea markets, as well as on eBay. Or family members or friends might have things in their kitchen that they never use, which they'd be happy to give to you.

The only things you really need are a stockpot or slow cooker, and a colander or fine mesh strainer; you can make do without the rest of the items in this list. (However, we also wanted to share the tools that make cooking so much easier for us.)

Essential Items

— **Stockpot.** A large, deep pot with a flat bottom and two handles on the side, this is very common for making pasta or large batches of soup on your stove top. Sizes vary based on the amount of broth you'll be making: we like using a 20-quart stockpot for our broths, but anything from 12 to 20 quarts will work.

The two types we recommend are either 18/10 stainless steel or cast-iron cookware coated with porcelain enamel (such as Le Creuset or Lodge). Note that enamel-coated cast iron is heavy and may be hard to use, while stainless steel will be lighter. We do not recommend aluminum stockpots because aluminum can leach into your broth, which can then act as a toxic heavy metal in the body. Cast iron is a good choice, but there are concerns that it can leach too much iron and have adverse effects for people who already have high iron in their bodies.

Tri-ply stainless-steel stockpots are made with stainless steel surrounding an aluminum core. These can be very good for heat conductivity without the issue of aluminum touching your food. While All-Clad is a popular choice for tri-ply stainless steel, you can often get better prices on brands like Cuisinart Multi-Clad. Shop around, and remember thrift shops and eBay!

— **Slow cooker.** A slow cooker is a countertop electric appliance used for simmering (many people use the brand name Crock-Pot generically when referring to a slow cooker). This is one of our most used and loved products because you can put your ingredients in the pot and forget about it until you're ready to strain your broth. They are most often very budget-friendly and simple to use.

The easiest type of slow cooker has the option of setting a timer for how long you want your food to cook. It could be as simple as a four-, six-, eight-, and ten-hour timed cooking option that moves to warm once it's done; a low-, medium-, high-, and warm-heating option works just as well, too.

We recommend choosing a slow cooker with a ceramic or stainless-steel interior, but there are some concerns that ceramic inserts may leach lead into food. Manufacturers like Hamilton Beach are aware of this and have models they deem lead-free, and there are other options you can look into. For example, VitaClay has a "smart organic multicooker" that uses a clay insert and does a variety of other cooking tasks, such as steaming, cooking rice, and yogurt making. These are a pricier investment than a regular slow cooker but have become very popular among health enthusiasts. You can purchase a VitaClay from Amazon.com or other online vendors.

— **Colander or fine mesh strainer.** Look for a colander with fine holes, or a fine mesh colander or strainer, as these are helpful to keep smaller pieces from escaping into your broth. (You can also line a regular colander with a few layers of cheesecloth.) We recommend choosing stainless steel because hot liquids can release toxins from plastic. You can find these at Amazon.com or your local kitchen store.

— **Long-handled spoon.** A sturdy wooden or stainless-steel spoon with a long handle can be very useful if you have to stir your broth. While stirring is not necessary, there may be times you want to use this type of spoon to work with soups, stews, and other foods you make with your broth.

— **Stainless-steel ladle.** A ladle allows you to easily scoop out broth and transfer it to bowls or storage containers.

— **Mason jars (Ball is a good brand).** These make great reusable glass storage containers for your broth, and are especially good if you want to separate out the right amount to freeze and then take out and thaw. You can often get a set of 12 pint- or quart-sized mason jars at grocery stores for a very low price, and you can reuse them over and over. You can also use any glass jars from foods you've enjoyed, like nut butters or coconut oil. However, we recommend using jars that go straight up, with no tapered curves at the top. We've found that tapered curves can be challenging when freezing broth because they tend to create a kind of trap during the freezing process and could promote breakage.

We like to put our glass jars in plastic zip freezer bags for extra protection. It also helps to label your jars with the type of stock or broth you've just made and the date you put it in your freezer.

— **Stainless-steel widemouth funnel.** This is incredibly helpful for ladling or pouring broth into your mason jars for storage, as you'll have little to no spillage when transferring your broth. You can find these online or at your local kitchen store. We like stainless steel because you'll be working with hot broth, and plastic can leach toxins when used with hot foods.

Optional Items

— **Fine mesh skimmer.** Some people like to skim the fat off the top of the broth after the first boil or during the simmering process. (We'll explain why to skim or not to skim later in the chapter.) If you do want to skim, we recommend using a fine mesh skimmer, which can be found at places like Amazon.com, your local kitchen store, or larger supermarkets. Keep in mind that when you chill the broth, the fat will rise to the top and congeal, making an easily removed "fat cap," so if you choose not to skim, you'll still be able to remove the fat after chilling the broth.

— **Silicone ice-cube trays.** Some people like to freeze their broth in small cubes and get them out to flavor soups, sauces, and other dishes. If you choose to do this, you might want to use silicone ice-cube trays because they are free of toxic BPA and phthalates found in plastic. You can purchase them in a variety of different-sized cubes based on your specific needs. The silicone is flexible, so you'll want to put the broth-filled trays in a plastic or glass container with a top, and then store it in your freezer. You can find silicone trays online or at your local kitchen store.

— **Containers to use on the go.** You can have the benefits of take-out broth from your own kitchen with two wonderful tools: (1) a Kleen Kanteen insulated widemouthed "water" bottle with café cap; and (2) a stainless-steel widemouthed thermos. If you want to drink your broth on your way to work or once you get there—or maybe you just want to wander around town contemplating life while consuming broth—a Kleen Kanteen will keep your broth warm, and the café cap will allow you to sip to your heart's content. A widemouthed thermos is also fantastic for taking soups, stews, and broth with you (Thermos is a popular stainless-steel brand). Heather used to take two thermoses to work and have plenty of broth and soup for meals and snacks during long days at the office. Both of these items can be purchased at your local kitchen store or from sites like Amazon.com.

— **Immersion blender.** This is a hand-held blender that you can put right into a pot or bowl to blend up ingredients. While it's not needed for bone broth, it can be useful when making blended soups or adding "finishers" (spices, flavorings, and other healthy ingredients) to your broth. The trick to using an immersion blender is to protect yourself from splattering by starting it on low, wrapping a tea towel around the pot or bowl, and using a very deep pot or bowl with a lot of liquid. We recommend 400 watts or greater if you plan to use it often because the motor tends to last longer. Cuisinart and Braun make nice immersion blenders, and you can buy them at some kitchen stores or online.

— **Regular or high-speed blender.** This is not necessary for bone broth making, but can be very useful for recipes in this book. While fancy high-speed blenders like Vitamix or Blendtec are highly prized in health communities, you can use a regular blender for most recipes. Remember to check Costco, eBay, and thrift shops for bargains on any blender, including Vitamix and Blendtec.

— **Food processor.** This is another appliance that can be useful for many kitchen tasks, including mixing, pureeing, slicing, dicing, and julienning; many of our recipes use the "S-blade," which is the attachment that mixes and purees ingredients. (Along with her slow cooker, Heather values her food processor the most.) Kitchen Aid and Cuisinart are the brands we've both loved over the years, but there are many good brands out there. You can find these in many kitchen and department stores, along with online and in some thrift shops.

— **Electric mixer or stand mixer.** We don't use these often, but do find them very handy for saving time when mixing ingredients. They are great for whipping egg whites and desserts and mixing liquid batters, for example.

HOW TO MAKE BONE BROTH OR STOCK

Now that you know what you'll need, it's time to familiarize yourself with the process of making broth.

1. Decide on the Flavor You'd Like to Make—Neutral, Flavored, or Finished

As we created the recipes for The Bone Broth Secret, we realized that there are different options when it comes to flavoring a broth. We're going to describe the uses of three types here so that you can get an idea of how we used them in the book. Then in each recipe in Part II, we will suggest the type of broth you might want to use.

— **Neutral broths** are almost flavorless (or perhaps have a very mild flavor) and can be used in a variety of recipes without imposing a meat flavor on the dish. These broths are typically made with bones only and no meat (or very little meat, like oxtail), since the meat is where the flavor is. Neutral broths are exceptionally good for sneaking into desserts and cocktails. As you'll see in Chapters 11 and 12, with neutral broths you get the health benefits without actually tasting the broth in the recipe.

— **Flavored broths** are typically the result of those made with bones, meat scraps, vegetables, herbs, and spices; they'll have some flavor from the meat, vegetables (such as onions and garlic), and spices. They can make really nice sipping broths or the basis of savory dishes, but would not be appropriate for making desserts.

— **Finished broths** are flavored with add-ins that we're calling "finishers," which can range from spices to bitters to fish sauce (a condiment popular in Thailand and Vietnam, made of fermented anchovies). In restaurants selling bone broth, we've seen finishers like sea salt, herbs, spices, fish sauce, and even options like bone marrow. At home, you can add any spices or flavors—the key is to use the ones you love. Remember, quality is key: organic spices, fresh herbs, and sea or Himalayan salt (as opposed to table salt) are high-quality options with healing benefits.

2. Choose Your Bones and Ingredients

To make a basic meat stock or bone broth, all you really need are bones and water. Everything else is optional!

— **Bones.** While there are lots of guidelines on how many bones to use, we suggest using enough bones to fill ⅔ of your pot, leaving room at the top to just cover them with water. (Keep in mind that you will adjust this if you're using vegetables because they take up room in the pot as well.) Look for the following:

- *Collagen- and cartilage-rich animal parts, which are key for rich gelatin*— skin (like chicken skin for chicken broth, pig skin for a meat broth, or fish heads and skin for fish broth), knuckles, feet, joints (chicken feet for chicken broth, and beef or pig's feet for meat broths), necks, heads, or tails (like oxtail).

REMINDER: BONE BROTH VS. STOCK

Remember, for health purposes, we are following the Gut and Psychology Syndrome (GAPS) definition of stock (bones and possibly more meat, simmered from 1½ to 3 hours) and broth (mainly bones, simmered over 3 hours) outlined at the end of Chapter 1.

- *Meaty bones*—these may be clean of meat or still have some on them (rib bones, marrowbones, thighbones, and so on).

- *Mixing bones*—some purists like to make a broth using only bones from one animal because they want to match it to the recipe they'll be using it for, such as beef bones for a beef stew. You'll likely want to separate fish bones from poultry and meat bones because fish bones require less simmering time, but mixing poultry and meat bones in the same broth is just fine. We have many recipes that will provide a springboard for you to experiment with different types of bones and see what you like best.

— **Water.** We recommend using filtered or springwater instead of tap water for the most pure, healing bone broth.

— **Optional ingredients:**

- *Apple cider vinegar*—adding an acid like apple cider vinegar, lemons, or white vinegar is popularly believed to help pull minerals from bones. This was debunked in a study done in 1934, which we'll explain later in the chapter. We still like to use apple cider vinegar, but it is technically optional when it comes to making a gelatin- and nutrient-rich broth. If using apple cider vinegar, the general guideline is to use approximately 2 tsp. per quart of water. Some people like to use more, so it's often based on preference. If you use it, here's what you'll do: Add the water, bones, and apple cider vinegar to your pot. Allow to sit for one hour at room temperature. Then begin cooking according to your recipe.

- *Vegetables*—these add flavor and nutrients to your bone broth.

- *Herbs and spices*—another flavor- and nutrient-enhancing choice.

3. Prepare Your Bones for Broth Making

Here are some options:

— **Raw bones.** You can keep it simple and use raw bones. You may also have bones that were cooked as part of a meal, like a chicken carcass and bones.

— **Browned bones.** Many people like to brown bones first for added flavor and a nice, clear broth. You'll find that some recipes in this book call for browned bones and others for raw bones; this is to give you variety so that you can see what you prefer. Once you decide what you like best, you can either brown or not brown the bones for any of our recipes. If you do want to brown them, you can set your oven to 350° F and roast the bones for about 45 minutes to an hour, turning them at the 30-minute mark.

— **Parboiled bones.** This refers to putting the bones in a stockpot, covering them with water and bringing to a boil, then reducing the heat to medium high and boiling for 5 minutes. You then drain and discard the water and start the process of making broth. Parboiling is used to remove blood and impurities from the bones, yet most people only use it for pig's or beef feet and skip it for other bones and parts. Try it if you want, though, and see what you think!

4. Fill Your Stockpot or Slow Cooker with Bones, Water, and Other Ingredients, and Simmer

Per our earlier guidelines, fill your pot. Set your slow cooker to low; if using a stockpot, set your burner to high, bring the water to a boil, and then reduce the temperature to low so that you have no more than a simmer. Your meat stock will simmer for 3 hours max; your bone broth will simmer much longer, depending on the recipe you're following.

A WORD ABOUT KITCHEN SAFETY

Most people are comfortable with a slow cooker that's on for 24 hours or more; fewer are comfortable keeping their stove burners on for hours while they are away or asleep. Modern kitchen safety would suggest that you always attend your stockpot while the stove is on, yet our ancestors didn't do that and kept the back burner going for days with pots of soup. Louise never worries about leaving her stockpot on the back burner while doing other things around the house, but she makes sure to turn off the burner when she goes out. Heather uses a slow cooker and is comfortable with going to bed or leaving home for an hour or two while it's on. It's up to you to decide what feels comfortable for you, and to always consider the safety of your home, pets, and family when you engage in slow cooking.

5. Skim the Fat While Simmering the Broth . . . or Not

When you bring bone broth to a boil, foam rises to the top, which is referred to as "scum." The scum has some amino acids and impurities that could include toxins. Chefs and traditional cooks often teach to skim the scum off with a fine mesh strainer so that the impurities are removed. This can be a bit of a challenge because the fat globules are floating in liquid and can be hard to strain out. We do find this to be difficult and like to take the easier way out, which is to strain the broth through a fine mesh strainer into jars and chill in the refrigerator. The fat will rise to the top of the chilled broth, and can be taken off very easily with a spoon.

To find out whether it's a good practice to skim, we went to one of Dr. Natasha Campbell-McBride's GAPS team members, nutrition expert Caroline Barringer. She said, "Dr. Natasha doesn't speak much about skimming, but here's my take: if the scum is from quality bones, I think it's fine to leave it in (if it doesn't bother you). If it does bother you, skim away!

"If using commercial factory–farmed animal bones, keep in mind that some of the scum will be from bone marrow, and toxins are held in fatty tissues (adipose and fatty organs like bone marrow). *If you cook a stock or broth with bones and meat from commercial animals, definitely skim off the scum and avoid eating the marrow and fat.* Although Dr. Natasha says she has people who choose to eat commercial meat (for financial reasons or due to lack of access to other options) and do not skim or remove anything, and they still heal quite well. So in the end, I like to leave it up to each individual to do what they feel is right for them. I think there's some bioindividuality that will be a factor in deciding to skim or not to skim."

We agree with Caroline and highly recommend skimming or removing the fat cap from your broth if you're using conventional factory–farmed animals so that you can reduce the toxins you consume.

Cooking Tip: Getting a Clear Broth

Cloudy broths are perfectly fine! But if you want a clear broth for aspics or consommé, or because you prefer them, you can do the following:

1. **Brown the bones.** Make sure to wipe off the browned bones and dry them before making your broth.

2. **Slow simmer** your broth without letting it come to a boil.

3. **Skim the fat** as you're cooking.

4. **Strain your broth several times.** You can do an extra good job with a cheesecloth-lined fine mesh strainer, straining your broth through it a few times.

5. **Refrigerate.** You can also refrigerate your broth and remove the fat cap, plus any brown sediment that falls to the bottom of your broth. These are easily removed once your broth has chilled into a gel.

6. **Make a raft out of egg whites.** Aspics are the foods that often require clear broth, and in Chapter 10, several of the recipes provide instructions to make a "raft" with egg whites to soak up the cloudiness. This simple step results in a very clear broth! We tend to do this if we want clear broth, skipping the skimming and multiple straining steps.

6. Strain Your Broth
Once It's Fully Simmered

Once you've finished simmering your stock or broth for the amount of time you desire, you're ready to strain out the liquid. Take a fine mesh strainer or colander with fine holes (you can add a layer or two of cheese-cloth if you like, to catch any of the fine debris) and place it over a very large glass or stainless-steel bowl.

It's usually most prudent to put your colander or fine mesh strainer over a bowl in the sink and slowly ladle the broth into it, allowing the liquid to be collected in the bowl. Another option is to use a Pyrex measuring cup to scoop out the broth and pour it through the fine mesh strainer into the bowl, which will allow it to go faster. Some people prefer to place a widemouth funnel and small fine mesh strainer over a jar and ladle the broth straight into it.

Having someone help with this step can make it easier, but it's not necessary if you're cooking on your own. Take your time—your goal is to get nice, strained liquid into your bowl or jars. Some people strain it more than once, although this isn't necessary. As we've mentioned, once you put your broth into the refrigerator and it cools sufficiently, the fat will rise to the top where it can be easily removed.

Once your broth is cooled, you'll have a thick, jiggly gelatin instead of a liquid . . . at least this is the goal. If you didn't get a thick gel, that's okay; it will still be good and nutrient-rich.

7. Store Your Broth

How you store your broth depends on what will be most convenient for how you want to use it. We like to store ours in quart-sized mason jars, but some people like to put theirs in pint-sized jars or even various sizes of silicone ice-cube trays to be used as needed.

Your stock or broth should last up to seven days in the refrigerator and up to six months in the freezer. Many experienced broth makers say that theirs lasts longer in the refrigerator if they leave the fat cap on the broth until they're ready to start using it—once the fat cap is removed, they find they have to use it up within five to seven days.

Keep in mind, though, that how long your broth lasts in the refrigerator can vary based on a lot of factors. This is why we recommend using your senses; for example, smelling it can give you your biggest clue. Our ancestors used their senses in cooking much more than we do today: They'd know by smell, taste, and even by touching the food and getting an intuitive signal whether or not it was right for them. We invite you to learn to use your senses and trust your intuition.

Two people consuming broth daily can likely use two or three quart-sized jars in a week. If you're committed to making bone broth a part of your regular diet, you might consider taking a new jar out of your freezer as soon as the one in the refrigerator is almost empty. This way, you'll always have thawed bone broth when you need it. (However, if you use it less regularly or you want more convenience, you may want to freeze in smaller containers and thaw as needed.)

Here are some tips to reduce the chance of breakage if freezing broth in glass jars:

- Fill the jar ⅔ of the way with broth, leaving ⅓ of it empty. This leaves room for the expansion that happens when liquids freeze. Leave the jars on your countertop with the caps off while the liquid cools to room temperature before refrigerating. We recommend putting the jars in the refrigerator for 24 hours before freezing them so that there will be less temperature shock when you put them into the freezer.

- Put your jars into plastic freezer bags as one more layer of protection. (It can also help you remember what you made if you label the jars or bags with the type of broth and date you made it.)

8. Get Ready to Use Your Broth (a Word about Gelatin and Fat Caps)

When we first started making bone broth, we found that most of our broths still came out nice and thick with gelatin even though we weren't always doing everything "right." We've since learned that the process is often much easier than it seems.

After you simmer your broth, it will be hot, so you won't be able to tell how much gelatin it has. Once you strain and refrigerate it for 24 hours, you'll get to see the end result:

— **The fat cap.** The first thing you'll see when you take your broth out of the refrigerator to use it is that the fat has risen to the top. This is the fat cap, and depending on the type of bones you used and whether you skimmed or not, its thickness and hardness will vary. This fat cap is a preservative for your bone broth, so we recommend leaving it on until you're ready to consume your broth. If you used commercial factory–farmed animal bones and parts or farmed fish, we recommend discarding the fat cap (see the skimming information earlier for more on why), rather than consuming it or using it for other cooking.

If you used organic and grass- or pasture-fed animals, or wild fish, you have the option of removing and reusing the fat in your recipes. Many cooks use it for sautés, soups, and stir-fry dishes. Home cooks most commonly use beef tallow, pig lard, or chicken fat (called "schmaltz") for cooking; Louise's favorite is duck fat.

— **Rendering your saved fat.** When you scrape the fat off the top of your broth, store it in a jar or covered bowl in the refrigerator until you're ready to render it. While it's perfectly fine to use as is, without rendering you'll have bits of broth and proteins on your fat, which can affect the taste and ease of use in cooking, and it can go bad faster. When you render the fat, you're cleaning it so that it lasts longer and is easier to use. Here's how:

- Place the fat in a saucepan on low heat.

- Once it melts, allow it to cool and put it in a glass bowl or leave it in the pan and place it in the fridge. Chill it for several hours or until the fat is solid again.

- Take the solidified fat out of the refrigerator, and place the bottom of your pan or bowl into some hot water (you can fill your sink or use a larger bowl of hot water). This will loosen the fat from the container.

- Carefully turn your pan or bowl upside down, and using a spoon, butter knife, or spatula, gently remove the fat from the container onto a plate. You will now see that the impurities have all solidified in a layer at the bottom (now facing you on top) and are a darker color.

- With a chef's knife or butter knife, scrape the darker layer of debris from the fat, making sure to scrape it all off so that only the clean, white fat remains.

- Break off the amount you think you'll use over the next two weeks and store that in your refrigerator; store the rest in small batches in your freezer. We keep ours in little glass jars, labeled with the type of fat and date of rendering; then we place the jars in plastic freezer bags for added protection from breakage. Some people use silicone

containers or ice-cube trays to store cubes of fat in the freezer.

— **Using your broth.** Underneath the fat cap is your broth, and you can use it as you please—in a recipe, or heated up to consume alone or turn into a soup.

What you're aiming for is a thick gel that barely moves when you shake the jar after it's been refrigerated. If it's too thick to pour and has to be scooped out with a spoon (with a consistency like the Jell-O desserts some of us had as kids), you know you got a really rich source of gelatin (that's your denatured collagen!). Perhaps it's gloppy and gelled but not too thick—that's fine, too!

If your bone broth didn't gel, it's still good and full of minerals and amino acids, and you'll still be able to use it for most of the recipes in this book. For those that require more gel, we'll give you tips for using a high-quality powdered gelatin that you can add to your broth. This will allow it to thicken up nicely.

Here's what might have happened if your broth didn't gel:

- You had too few bones or used too much water.

- You didn't have enough collagen-rich bones or skin— feet, necks, backs, and knuckles are wonderful for this.

- You boiled your broth, which broke down the collagen too much. You'll get a better result if you stay at a slow simmer, rather than boiling. A slow cooker makes this really easy. On the stove top, once the water starts to boil, reduce the temperature to the lowest setting to simmer your broth.

- You made meat stock, which won't gel as much as longer-simmered broth.

— **As we said, you can use unflavored powdered gelatin to create a gelatin-rich broth if your recipe calls for it.** You can do this with your bone broth, meat stock, or vegetable stock to bump up the collagen or if you need to use a gelled broth for one of the recipes in this book. Here's how:

- Warm your broth or stock, and add 1 Tbsp. of unflavored powdered beef gelatin per 1 quart of broth or stock. Once this mixture cools, you will have a gelled broth or stock. (See more about recommended brands of gelatin later in this chapter.)

9. Reuse the Bones: Budget and Planet Friendly

This practice of reusing bones varies across the board depending on the home cooks, chefs, and butchers you talk to. For example, Aaron Rocchino, owner of the Local Butcher Shop in Berkeley, California, makes a gelatin-rich stock by long-simmering the bones, straining out the liquid and setting it aside, and then taking the same bones and doing another long simmer. This second simmer is a process known as *remouillage* (remoistening), and it extracts more flavor and minerals from the bones. Both of these liquids can then be simmered together, reducing into rich, concentrated stock.

Many farmers and home cooks do a different type of remouillage, where instead of putting the two broths together in a pot, they save their bones from their first batch of broth and use them again to make a stand-alone second batch—and sometimes they even make a third batch from the same bones as the first and second batches.

What happens if you use the same bones to make new batches of bone broth? You do get fewer minerals and amino acids and less gelatin when you reuse the bones, but there is still some value to them. If you're making meat stock, you'll likely be able to use the bones several more times because they've only been simmered a maximum of 3 hours. Yet how many times you reuse them is up to you and will depend upon personal preference: If you're doing longer-simmered bone broths, you can use them again once or twice, as long as they're not disintegrated. Fish bones disintegrate faster, so you'll likely only use them once.

If you want more gelatin when reusing bones, consider adding a split pig's foot, a beef knuckle, beef feet, or some chicken feet to bump up the collagen a bit more.

HOW TO CHOOSE BONES, MEAT, AND OTHER BASIC INGREDIENTS

When it comes to great stock and broth, the quality of ingredients is everything. When you eat animal protein, you're consuming everything that animal has consumed. In other words, its diet is pretty important. And if you're like us, you care about the humane treatment of animals—we believe in letting them roam free and eat their natural diets, and treating them well from the beginning to the end of their lives. More farmers are doing this now. We call them "ethical farmers" because they truly care about their animals and the people who purchase meat from them.

In this section, we'll give you guidelines on how to choose ethically raised meats, poultry, and game, along with sustainable fish (which are not endangered and have a strong, thriving population).

First Things First: Using Leftovers

The best thing about making a stock or bone broth is that you're most often using scraps from previous meals, which makes it an economical way to use food as your medicine, as well as to stock your larder.

We think of bone broth as the meal that keeps on giving. Let's say you start with a whole chicken or even just some legs and

Vegetables for broth or stock.

thighs. You cook these, and when the meal is done you save the bones, which you can use immediately or freeze. After you make broth with those bones, you then use it for other soups, sauces, stews, grain dishes, desserts, and so much more! During the course of a week, you can take leftovers from one meal and use them to make soup the next day. In this way, every meal is a marriage of the wonderful dishes that came before it. And the flavor just keeps getting better.

If you don't have any bones or vegetable scraps in your home, you can start by taking a trip to your local health-food store, farmers' market, or grocery store.

Choosing Meat and Poultry

The gold standard in making bone broth is organic grass- or pasture-fed and grass- or pasture-finished meat and poultry. This means that there were no antibiotics or hormones used, and the animal was able to roam freely, eating its natural diet. While these are also the most expensive options, keep in mind that when you make bone broth, you get many meals from one purchase of animal protein by using leftovers.

Another option is to purchase just the bones, bone marrow, and parts like the neck, back, and joints. You can typically find these items for a lower price from your farmer or butcher, or in the meat or freezer section at your health-food store.

Here are some important concepts to understand when shopping for animal protein:

— **Organic.** According to the United States Department of Agriculture (USDA), organic meat, poultry, and eggs are "given no antibiotics or growth hormones. Organic food is produced without using most conventional pesticides; fertilizers made with synthetic ingredients or sewage sludge; bioengineering; or ionizing radiation."[1]

While organic meat and poultry is an excellent choice, these animals may be fed a non-natural diet, unless they're grass- or pasture-fed.

— **Grass- or pasture-fed**. Grass- and pasture-fed animals are allowed to roam free, eating their natural diets. It is best for animals' health and welfare if they're able to roam free outside, eating what their bodies truly need.

There are some differences between grass- and pasture-fed animals and animals fed with grains. First of all, the meat of grass- and pasture-fed animals is leaner. If you're used to eating grain-fed animal protein, you're probably used to that particular taste and the appropriate cooking methods, so switching to grass- and pasture-fed animals may be an adjustment at first. However, over time you may begin to notice what Stanley A. Fishman did when making the transition. In his book *Tender Grassfed Meat: Traditional Ways to Cook Healthy Meat*, Fishman says, "Good grassfed beef, when properly cooked, has a depth of flavor, a dense, meaty texture, a good clean mouthfeel that no grain fed beef can ever come close to. It just tastes better. Much, much better."[2] This type of animal protein typically needs less seasoning because the natural diets provide a rich flavor all on their own.

If you've tried cooking grass- or pasture-fed animal protein in the past and it didn't turn out well, we have many suggestions in the recipes section of this book for preparing such meat and poultry so that it's flavorful and tender. As you return to slow-cooking techniques, you'll find out the secrets of our ancestors for delicious meals with much greater nutrition. These animals have the healthiest bones, cartilage, joints, meat, and skin, making them the best choice for bone broth.

Now, one thing to keep in mind is that some animals, like poultry and pigs, do have additional feed to support their natural diets, even if they roam free. In this case, make sure to look for organic pasture-fed animals so that you get the healthiest animal protein. And note the following:

- *Grass-fed and grass-finished*—when meat is grass-finished, this means that the animal was allowed to eat its natural diet of grass throughout its life. In addition to this being the most humane life for animals, it also makes for the best-tasting meat. Proper cooking techniques help to bring out the natural goodness.

- *Grass-fed and grain-finished*—when meat is grain-finished, this means that the animal ate its natural diet for most of its life and was then sent to a feedlot where it ate non-native feed, including hay, grains, corn, soy meal, potatoes, and silage.[3] If the animal was organically raised, this feed will be organic. If the animal was conventionally raised, the feed will be conventional and include genetically modified foods.

— **Hormone and antibiotic free.** You typically find hormones and antibiotic use in nonorganic animals. In 2012, the U.S. Food and Drug Administration (FDA) created guidelines for the judicious use of antibiotics in animals because their use was creating bacterial resistance, which "poses a serious public health threat."[4] Since then, there have been more guidelines on the use of antibiotics in animals, but the medications are still being administered today. Animals are also routinely given growth hormones to fatten them up.

Many health advocates feel that consuming the meat of animals raised with hormones and antibiotics is the reason why people have so many health issues today. We recommend looking for better sources of animal protein that are hormone and antibiotic free.

— **Conventional or factory farmed.** These terms may apply to any meat or poultry not labeled *organic*, *grass-fed*, or *pasture-fed* and could refer to cage-free and free-range poultry and eggs as well. Very often, these animals are penned into small spaces and fed a diet that is not natural for their digestive systems, which can lead to poor health or illness. We feel that these animals are inhumanely treated. They often get sick and require antibiotics, growth hormones tend to be used to get them fattened up, and they're typically fed GMO (genetically modified organism) feed. All of this results in more toxins and lower-quality meat and poultry.

— **Wild game.** Examples of wild game are antelope, bison, wild boar, elk, venison (from deer), guinea fowl, pheasant, quail, rabbit, wild geese, and ducks. With the increasing popularity of these lean meats, many are now being raised on farms. We recommend looking for farmers you trust when choosing game, or asking your butcher or health-food store for information on how the game was raised, fed, and treated.

— **Eggshells.** If you choose to use eggshells in your broth or stock, make sure you know how they were processed before packaging. Many commercial eggs (even organic ones) have to undergo a cleaning with chlorine; in some cases, mineral oil (a petroleum product) is also used after the chlorine. Since an eggshell is porous, like our skin, this can get into the egg itself and residue may stay on the eggshell. Many farmers' markets sell organic pasture-fed eggs, and you can talk to the farmer about how they're processed.

A Word about GMOs— Genetically Modified Organisms

When choosing animal protein, it's important to know how the animals were raised and what their diet consisted of. As we stated previously, when you consume animal protein, you're also consuming what those animals consumed during their lifetime. If they received antibiotics, hormones, and GMO foods, you are consuming these things as well. Many people have heard about GMOs by now, but to recap, these are plants or animals that have been genetically altered with DNA from other plants, animals, bacteria, or viruses.[5]

Unless the feed of grain-fed or grain-finished animals is organic, you can be sure that the corn, soy, and other feed crops are GMO. One of the big concerns these days is that Roundup Ready seeds by Monsanto have been genetically modified to resist the toxic herbicide glyphosate; when farmers use these seeds, they must use glyphosate as an herbicide on their crops to compensate. Scientists were on the fence about how harmful glyphosate was to human health; then in March 2015, the International Agency on Research for Cancer (IARC), a specialized cancer agency of the World Health Organization (WHO), assessed glyphosate and found that is "probably carcinogenic to humans."[6]

While the findings infuriated Monsanto and their supporters, it confirmed the concerns of food activists, politicians, scientists, and many countries that have banned GMO foods. The controversy still lives on today, and there is a growing number of activists calling for proper labeling and the elimination of GMO foods.

Selecting Fish: Wild vs. Farmed

For fish broth, you want to use non-oily wild fish, like Alaska or walleye pollock, sea bass, cod, and halibut. Oily fish (such as salmon and anchovies) have fats that can become rancid while cooking the broth.

Wild fish are the best option because they swim in open waters, eating their native diets, such as other fish, algae, and seaweed. They tend to be higher in protein and omega-3 fatty acids and have less disease. In contrast, farmed fish are penned in; eat a non-native diet such as GMO corn, soy, and canola; and are exposed to antibiotics, hormones, neurotoxins, pesticides, artificial dyes, and other toxins.[7]

Mercury can be an issue in both wild and farmed fish. If you look for cold-water fish and smaller species, you're likely to find less mercury contamination. Other concerns include sustainability; for example, overfishing is a concern for certain species. This can change from year to year, so talk to the experts at the seafood counter in your local store or check fishwatch.gov. Many stores are starting to put notices at the fish counter about sustainable choices.

Fish is a great source of iodine, which is a wonderful mineral for thyroid health, energy, and metabolism.[8] If you live in a coastal area, you may be able to access people in the fishing industry, like fishmongers, who can save wild carcasses for you. Fish broth in general can be a very affordable and easy way to make bone broth at home.

What about radiation in fish? We talked this over with Robert Ruiz, chef and owner of the Land & Water Company restaurant in Carlsbad, California, and noted fish expert. Robert has worked closely with the National Oceanic and Atmospheric Administration (NOAA) scientists about fish health and sustainability. In his work with the scientists, he's gotten access to research showing that by the time fish was taken out of the water and processed for selling (even the fish that swam off the shores of Fukishima), it was considered safe to eat. Larger carnivorous fish may have more radiation than smaller fish feeding on algae and plankton; however, even larger fish have been measured at what experts consider a "low five Banana Equivalent Dose (BED)" of radiation. *Banana Equivalent Dose* is a term scientists use to simplify comparisons about radiation emissions. A fatal dose is 80 million BED.[9]

Sourcing Sustainable, Humanely Raised Animal Protein

You may be able to source your animal protein from farms, butchers, fishmongers, or other providers who are meticulous about pure, humanely raised animals. In the Resources section, we provide some ideas for how to find high-quality sources of meat, poultry, game, and fish in your area.

CHOOSING AND USING OPTIONAL INGREDIENTS

If you want to add ingredients to your broth beyond bones and water, the items in this section are good choices.

Organic Vegetables

Organic vegetables are non-GMO and free of toxic pesticides, and we recommend using them whenever possible, whether you're making a vegetable stock or adding scraps to your meat stock or bone broth. Vegetable stock is very easy to make and consists of simmering vegetables in water for an hour and then straining the broth to drink or use in recipes. (We have a wonderful basic vegetable stock recipe for you in Chapter 4.)

For bone broths or stocks, you don't have to add vegetables, and in some cases, you won't want to (such as with bone broth you'll use for making desserts). Having said that, they do make a wonderful addition for flavored broths created for drinking alone or using in many recipes; adding vegetables also ups the ante on vitamins and minerals.

If you can't find organic vegetables, we recommend looking up the list of the "dirty dozen" each year that outlines which vegetables are the most affected by pesticides. You can find these lists on the Environmental Working Group's website (ewg.org).

Keep in mind that you can offset the higher price of organic vegetables when making broth and stock because you get to use the waste that you'd normally throw away or compost. Tough ends of asparagus, onion skins, kale and collard stalks, the ends of bok choy—all of these things are perfect for bone broth because while they're not what you'd typically eat, you can still get all their great benefits when you simmer them.

When we asked our broth-making friends about adding vegetables to bone broth, many of them said they added the vegetables during the last hour of simmering, others added them just after soaking the bones in apple cider vinegar and water, and still others put them in right at the beginning with the bones.

One reason to put the vegetables in during the last hour of simmering a broth for 3 hours or more is that all the nutrients will be extracted from the vegetables within that hour, and there is no need to cook them any longer. Some people feel that if you do cook them longer, it will change the taste of the broth, and not for the better; others like putting the vegetables in right from the beginning. There are no hard-and-fast rules here, so follow your own intuition and experiment!

Apple Cider Vinegar

If choosing to use vinegar, you can use any type. However, many people feel that white vinegar does not result in the best taste; additionally, rice or white vinegar can be a challenge for very sensitive people who have digestive challenges and a leaky blood-brain barrier. We recommend using apple cider vinegar because it won't influence the taste of your broth. Look for the organic, unpasteurized, unfiltered kind—this type contains beneficial live enzymes and, therefore, appears to have debris floating in it. You can find brands like Bragg in your health-food store or online.

Vinegar is included as a necessity in most cookbooks about bone broth because it is believed to help extract important minerals from the bones. The guideline used most often by traditional-foods experts is to soak the bones in water and apple cider vinegar for an hour before you begin cooking your bone broth. We do this, and leaders in the industry like Sally Fallon Morell, Kaayla T. Daniel, and Dr. Natasha Campbell-McBride all teach this. It's a standard process that's been passed down for years, but one that we started asking questions about in our research for this book.

In 1934, a study on bone and vegetable broth was published in the *Archives of Disease in Childhood*, an international peer-reviewed medical journal. In this study, researchers at the King's College Hospital in London noticed that a bone and vegetable broth was widely used to feed infants in England, and they wanted to understand the nutritional properties. After analyzing the broth, they found the following:

- Apple cider vinegar is not needed to pull minerals or amino acids from the bones.[10]

- The vegetables only needed to be simmered for 30 minutes to 1 hour to fully extract their minerals.[11]

This surprised us, so we called Kaayla T. Daniel, co-author with Sally Fallon Morell of *Nourishing Broth: An Old-Fashioned Remedy for the Modern World*. Kaayla, a long-time researcher of bone broth, had reviewed the study and felt that it was very sound. We then asked if she thought that the vinegar was added for other reasons, like to remove impurities from the bones—perhaps akin to parboiling, a purification technique used in Chinese bone soups. She said that this could be a possibility.

We concluded along with Kaayla that what happens in the kitchen is part science and part alchemy. It's possible that the apple cider vinegar is not needed at all, and this is great news for the people who forget to put it in! In other words, there is no such thing as needing to be perfect when it comes to making broth. A lot of traditions are passed down from generation to generation for reasons we may never know, and it's up to us to decide what feels right to us. Your kitchen is the perfect place to learn to trust your intuition! As Kaayla likes to say, "Relax and enjoy your broth!"

Herbs and Spices

Herbs (green, leafy parts of plants used for seasoning) and spices (dried, concentrated, and aromatic parts of plants) are wonderful additions to your bone broth. They're concentrated sources of phytonutrients, which means that they're chock-full of life-giving antioxidants. In this book, our recipes include herbs and spices added during simmering to bring flavor to the broth, or they're added as medicinal "finishers" to enhance flavor for sipping broths.

Our recipes use herbs and spices liberally for their health properties and for their ability to balance the six tastes in Ayurvedic medicine (sweet, salty, sour, bitter, pungent, and astringent). When you balance the six tastes, your body feels more satisfied, calm, and grounded. This also reduces cravings! Check out "How to Work with Herbs and Spices" in the Appendix to learn even more about specific herbs and spices and their medicinal properties, and for more information about using them to balance the six tastes.

WHEN TO USE POWDERED GELATIN AND COLLAGEN HYDROLYSATE (COLLAGEN PEPTIDES)

If you're out of bone broth and still want the benefits of denatured collagen, you can use unflavored powdered gelatin or collagen hydrolysate (also called collagen peptides).

Unflavored powdered gelatin is available on the market with varying levels of quality. While you may be familiar with products like Jell-O desserts or Knox powdered gelatin, we're not recommending these sources because they're derived from factory-farmed cows. The powdered gelatin we recommend is high quality, from hormone- and antibiotic-free grass- or pasture-fed animals. Brands like Great Lakes and Vital Proteins beef gelatin are some good options, as both of them derive their gelatin from grass-fed cowhides.

Many health enthusiasts are adding unflavored powdered gelatin to foods for its digestive health benefits and because it's an easily absorbed form of protein; it is finding its way into beauty remedies for hair, skin, and nails as well. While powdered gelatin has many of the same health benefits as the gelatin found in bone broth, we feel that bone broth is superior for a couple of important reasons: (1) powdered gelatin has fewer types of collagen than bone broth because the powdered kind is made only with skin;[12] and (2) powdered gelatin requires more processing. From a metaphysical perspective, the more processed something is, the more distant its connection to the earth, to your kitchen, and to the interaction you have with the experience of nourishing yourself.

At the same time, we know that people get busy and may want to use powdered gelatin here and there as part of their health and beauty regimen. It's a wonderful, convenient way to get the benefits when you are short on time or have run out of bone broth. And it has some applications that make it a better option in certain desserts and beauty remedies. (We will share some fun recipes using unflavored powdered gelatin with you in Part II.) Just keep the following in mind:

— **Gelatin vs. collagen hydrolysate.** Gelatin is best used in foods that you want a gelling or binding agent for (like the Marshmallow recipe in this book). It needs to be dissolved in warm water before using.

Collagen hydrolysate or collagen peptides are more processed than gelatin, and some people find them easier to digest. You don't have to put collagen hydrolysate in warm water to dissolve, so it's easy to use in smoothies, mix into water, or add to just about any food for an extra collagen bump without waiting for it to dissolve. Great Lakes brand makes a product called Collagen Hydrolysate and Vital Proteins brand makes a product called Collagen Peptides, both of which are available for purchase online.

— **Gelatin, collagen hydrolysate, and MSG.** One concern about gelatin powder is whether it is a source of MSG (monosodium glutamate). In Chapter 1, we talked about glutamates found in bone broth and meat stock versus in processed foods. One thing to keep in mind is that powdered gelatin is more processed than bone broth and meat stock, so some people may be more sensitive to powdered gelatin and collagen peptides than broth or stock.

While many people following a healing protocol report that they do well with gelatin, it's important to listen to your body. If you have any uncomfortable symptoms after consuming foods with powdered gelatin, you may want to go back to Chapter 1 and take a look at the information on glutamates.

Buying Ready-Made Bone Broth

More and more farmers, butchers, health-food stores, and restaurants are selling bone broth these days. On top of this, you may find Asian restaurants that don't specifically mention bone broth, but still use authentic slow-cooked broth as the basis for their bone soups, pho, seolleongtang, sup tulang, tonkotsu soup, or bah kut teh. Since bone broths have long been made in cultures all over the world, always ask how a restaurant makes their dishes. You may discover some great soups, stews, and meals infused with real bone broth.

The main thing to look for is the quality of the bones used. Going back to the section in this chapter about choosing good animal protein and bones, remember to ask for organic and/or grass- or pasture-fed meat and poultry, and ask whether the feed that was supplemented for poultry and pigs was either organic or non-GMO. Ultimately, choose what you feel most comfortable with. Remember what Dr. Natasha Campbell-McBride said—she has seen people heal with all varieties of bone broth, so if you can't get your hands on the quality you like, start where you can and build from there.

When it comes to store-bought bone broth, check the freezer section. You may find a good one that's made locally; call the individual or company who made the broth and ask them if it's a thick, rich gelatin and how they made it. Or ask at your local Weston A. Price Foundation chapter, which often has recommendations for where to get good bone broth. You can also purchase broth online and have it delivered to your door. We have provided a starter list of companies making bone broth in the Resources section of the Appendix, including those who sell online.

You can now find bone broth in health-food stores in Tetra Paks or aseptic packaging. In their book *Nourishing Broth*, Sally Fallon Morell and Kaayla T. Daniel say that these soups are rarely nutrient- or gelatin-rich (you can see for yourself if they gel when you chill them in the refrigerator), and the flash-heating required for aseptic packaging can damage the amino acids in the bone broth.[13]

CHANNELING YOUR WHAT-THE-HELL ATTITUDE

If you haven't been in the kitchen for a while, you may feel like making bone broth is pretty daunting. However, when you really get into it, you'll see how easy it can be to put bones and water in a pot and simmer it up. Sometimes all it takes to truly enjoy time making home-cooked foods is changing the way you think.

Since Louise has always been the master at changing the way people think, let's hear from her about creating the right mind-set for making broth:

> One of my favorite Julia Child quotes is: "The only real stumbling block is fear of failure. In cooking you've got to have a what-the-hell attitude." So I encourage you to have a what-the-hell attitude when it comes to your soups and broths!
>
> Making broth is a great place to try things in the kitchen. You don't have to be an experienced cook to do this! I'm always trying new things. I have some bone broth simmering almost every day, and depending on the mood I'm in, I'll add whatever catches my fancy. It could be fish sauce, some green vegetables, or my favorite spice mix of the moment (right now it's fennel, fenugreek, sea salt, and black pepper, a mixture that Heather and I created for its anti-inflammatory, metabolism-boosting, feel-good dose of TLC). One day, Heather visited my kitchen

and we got to talking about bitters and how they help with digestion. Without further ado, into the broth went a few drops of cardamom bitters! We had great fun taste-testing the bitters-enhanced broth. It added a festive, almost cocktail-like taste.

> Broths and soups can be your art. If you mess up, you can always fix it with a little more water or a dash of this or that. With soup, you can learn to listen to your intuition and just go with it. Every day can bring a new taste discovery. It doesn't have to take long either. We have plenty of five-minute soups to share with you. What the hell—why not start today?

In the next chapter, we'll give you some guiding principles for getting started in the kitchen, along with menus and shopping lists. You'll also get a peek at what Louise eats for breakfast, lunch, and dinner. Our adventure continues!

Roasted marrowbones, Heather's Easy Oxtail Broth, and the Healing Elixir Vegetable Stock.

～CHAPTER 3～

GETTING STARTED:

What Louise Eats, Guiding Principles, Menus, and a Shopping List

O nce you've made bone broth, incorporating it into your daily meals is pretty easy. In fact, you now have the basis for a kind of at-home fast food!

Most experts recommend consuming two 6- to 8-ounce cups of bone broth per day for healing benefits. How much you consume is up to you, and we recommend that you let your body lead you. Listen to your body as you consume broth; pay attention to how you're feeling. In order to get in touch with how food affects your energy, health, and moods, you can use the food-journal approach that we outlined in Chapter 1.

Here are some ideas for including bone broth in your routine (note that we have provided recipes for each of these options in Part II of this book):

1. Drink the broth instead of coffee. Broth can be consumed on its own (plain), or with finishers like spices, raw butter, sea salt, pepper, fish sauce, or fresh herbs. This makes an energizing hot beverage that many people use as a coffee replacement.

2. Make a fast soup. You can heat up your bone broth along with some other meats, vegetables, and eggs to make wonderful, quick soups. These can become a true fast food in your own kitchen. Once you start making these soups, you'll realize that you can make them just as fast as opening a can or box and microwaving.

To make things go even faster, try this: Wash and chop some vegetables and store them in a glass jar or container in your refrigerator. When you wake up in the morning or get ready for work, open your jar of bone broth and scoop out a cup or two (you might decide to dilute it with water; we'll show you how to do all of this in the recipes section). Heat it up in a saucepan and then add some seasonings (maybe sea salt and pepper with some herbs) and some of your chopped vegetables, allowing it to simmer for 3 to 5 minutes. If you want, you could throw in some leftover meat slices, a couple of eggs, or whatever animal protein you have on hand. Now you have a delicious soup!

There are many soup recipes to get you started in Chapter 6, but you'll likely come up with your own creative favorites!

3. Use it as a quickie meal when on the road or off to work. Put your hot broth, some spices, and some vegetables and leftover cooked meats (or an egg or two) into a wide-mouthed thermos, and take it to work. The broth will cook the rest of the ingredients so that you have a nice soup for lunch! This is one thing that Heather did consistently when she was working 12-hour days at her corporate job. She'd take five minutes to get the soup prepped into two large thermoses and have it for lunch, dinner, and snacks. It was easy to make, pack, and consume on workdays, and it was delicious! This is also a great idea for traveling, as it will help you avoid the fast food or convenience stores found along the way.

4. Use it to start other recipes. Bone broth can be used in place of water to make scrumptious sauces; simmer grains; poach eggs, fish, chicken, and meat; and even to make dessert! Your broth can become a key collagen-rich ingredient for many delicious recipes, kicking the health benefits up a few notches. Who wouldn't want better skin, hair, nails, digestive health, and joint health, just from eating a wonderful meal?

5. Make healing elixirs and beauty remedies. You may also want to make some medicinal healing remedies or beauty treatments with your bone broth, which can be a really wonderful way to make food your medicine. We have recipes to get you started on making broth a delivery device of sorts for all kinds of healing herbs and spices. Over time, you may want to experiment with some of your own, tapping into the wisdom of herbology, Chinese medicine, Ayurvedic medicine, and other health approaches.

If you're working on a health condition, you may want to consume 2 cups or so of broth per day. If you're using broth as part of a wellness-focused routine, then do what feels right for your body. Overall, enjoy the process!

Perhaps you want to channel your inner teenager. Or go back in time and revel in how wise our ancestors were when they realized that water, bones, and vegetables could create a healing elixir. Maybe you'll channel your spiritual side and drink your broth to feel your connection to the earth. Or to simply experience how making the broth is actually an act of self-love and nourishment. The more you do this, the healthier you'll feel—because ultimately, you will have declared that you're worth the time it takes to deeply nourish yourself. And you are!

LOUISE SHARES HER DAILY MEAL ROUTINE: "I'M A BONE BROTH GIRL, THAT'S FOR SURE!"

Someone at Hay House once told me that the most popular search phrase on HealYour Life.com is "What does Louise Hay eat?" After a good laugh, I thought, *What a great question*!

First and foremost, I consider myself a bone broth girl. It's a staple in my diet because it makes me feel so good. I've learned in all my years that listening to my intuition, what I call my inner ding, is the best guidance I can follow.

Heather and I talked a lot in Chapter 1 about the health benefits of bone broth, and we also gave you affirmations to use while you drink it. I truly believe in affirmations and food as two of your best healing tools. The thoughts you think and the food you eat can make all the difference in your health. They did in mine.

You see, I grew up very poor. We didn't have much money, so my mother did the best she could with our meals. We had whatever vegetables we could gather from our garden, and wheat berries and oatmeal for grains. We had goats that I milked, and about twice per year, we'd have goat meat and rabbit to eat. Once a month, my father would get a Milky Way candy bar and he would have half, then my mother, my sister, and I would split the other half in three. This was our only big treat. We didn't have much love at our meals. In fact, there was more anger than love. So when I left home, I decided that every meal was going to be a celebration!

Guess how I started to celebrate? I went to a diner and had Cherry Coke and Boston cream pie for *breakfast* every day for about two weeks! I still laugh when I think back to those days. After two weeks of that I said, "Okay, Louise, that's enough."

While I was married, I began following Julia Child. There are two things I remember most about her, besides her being an incredible icon in the cooking world: one is that she taught me how to make bone broth; the other is that I heard her husband say how much he loved her bottom! From this point on, I developed a love of cooking.

Later, when I was diagnosed with cancer, affirmations and food were my chosen protocols, instead of allopathic medicine. Every day, I ate the 2-oz. servings of pureed asparagus that had been recommended to me by a natural-health professional. I recommitted to working with my thoughts because I knew Life was asking me to walk my talk with courage. And it worked.

Decades later, at 89 years old, I believe that I'm about to enter the greatest years of my life. Every day is a celebration. Every meal is a celebration. I focus on bringing love, joy, and laughter into my life as often as I can. I play more. I am cooking more and having parties with my friends. I feel good. I listen to my body. I don't follow a "diet." I just listen and follow my inner ding.

What I truly believe is that if it doesn't grow, don't eat it. And whatever you eat, do it with love.

Here is what my day's meals look like:

— **Before breakfast.** The first thing I do is drink 32 ounces of water. Doing this feels so good as I wake up to start my day. It took me a while to work up to drinking this amount, so I started by drinking whatever I could and progressed from there. Now when I finish, I tell myself what a great job I did!

I have my bedroom set up so that I can heat a mug of bone broth right there in the morning. After I've had my water, I get a hot-water bottle and my mug of bone broth, and I settle into my bed all nice and comfy with the hot-water bottle on my tummy. I sip my bone broth and do my meditation and affirmations. I thank Life for all the goodness it has given me. Then guess what happens? It's bowel time! The bone broth really gets things going in the morning. If I have time, I'll get back into bed and read for a bit before starting my day.

The rest of my meals are based on two things: (1) What my inner ding feels is right for my body that day, and (2) what's in the kitchen. I tend to eat what is in season, except for asparagus, which continues to be a staple vegetable in my life. If it's not in season, I will buy frozen asparagus.

— **Breakfast** may be one of the following:

- *Fruit*—could be berries, cooked apples, mango, bananas, or soaked dried apricots.

- *Smoothies*—I love ones with kale, asparagus, romaine lettuce, green powder, broccoli, zucchini, and maybe some vegetable broth. I might add some combination of the following: colostrum, probiotics, coconut water, hemp seeds, coconut powder, bone broth or collagen peptides, and a spice mix made of ground cinnamon, fennel, fenugreek, dulse seaweed, and cardamom.

- *Eggs*—I like 3 egg yolks and 1 egg white. It's so good that way! The yolks are a perfect food, full of healthy fat.

- *Quinoa flakes*—I like these because they cook really fast. Sometimes I even take them on trips for an easy breakfast when I want a break from restaurant food. I like cooking my quinoa flakes in bone broth, then adding one of my favorite nut or seed butters, cinnamon, and spices.

— **Lunch and dinner** are often similar in nature. I keep it simple because I like simple meals. You can take something simple and put it on a nice plate and it looks incredible. I like to use what's in my fridge, and my main focus is to always have vegetables, protein, and bone broth.

Here are some examples of what I enjoy:

- Salad with some kind of animal protein and aioli or a great dressing or rémoulade.

- Butter-lettuce wraps with egg salad or tuna salad.

- Pâtés, like liver pâté or duck mousse.

- Ground meat or poultry burgers, which are so fast to make. I actually make single patties out of the ground meat I buy and put them into the freezer, wrapped separately. This allows me to take them out one at a time and cook them when I'm ready. You don't even have to thaw the meat to start cooking it, but I like to take it out before lunch and let it thaw a little first.

- Fish.

- Chicken thighs or turkey wings.

- A sliced avocado with the juice of a lemon squeezed over it and some sea salt.

— **Desserts and snacks.** I don't eat many desserts, except for the ones that Heather and I make, because I know those are full of good ingredients. (See Chapter 11 for ideas.)

For snacks, I might have hummus, a scoop of a nut or seed butter, or whatever leftovers I have in the refrigerator. I also love having a slice of the yummy Herb Bread made with bone broth, which is in Chapter 9.

Heather and I compiled the recipes in this book based on the kinds of things I love to eat. Most of them are very simple, like our five-minute soups. These are meals that we love to have and make for dinners and parties together with our friends. We hope you will love them, too. They'll show you how to make bone broth a part of your life.

I think you'll see how, once you have your bone broth, you can use it to make meals quickly with whatever is in your refrigerator. If you sip your broth while saying your affirmations and bring love into every meal, you will get all the benefits of the nutrients in your delicious food!

See if you can bring a sense of play into your day. Celebrate every meal because it's an important way to love yourself, nurture yourself, and prepare yourself for all the good that Life has in store for you.

GUIDING PRINCIPLES FOR MAKING BROTH AND USING OUR RECIPES

Before we get down to brass tacks with our shopping list and menus, we'd like to offer you the following words of wisdom.

Guiding Principle #1:
The Kitchen Is Where We Play

We do not work in the kitchen; we play. We put on music or a great show. We dance. We invite our friends in and we laugh. This is where we have adventures and experiments, where we bring on our "what the hell" attitudes and just go for it. And let's just really lay out what's happening here . . . this is where we fuel our bodies for all the good things we want to do and be in life. There is nothing more important than this, but we won't get there unless we enjoy the process!

We also like to add dance breaks to our cooking routine, as Heather explains:

The dance break began one day in Pasadena, California, at a Hay House event. I was traveling with Louise, and it was my first time spending quality time with Maya Labos (Wayne Dyer's assistant and right hand for over 30 years). Someday over a bone broth cocktail, Maya and Louise will have to tell you the story of how they first met!

On this night, we had just returned from Louise's talk onstage with Cheryl Richardson and were on our way to dinner. The hotel elevator had some jazzy music playing, and I'm not sure which one of us started it, but suddenly the

three of us had our arms in the air and were dancing away. That's when I realized that these women were good dancers . . . and the dance break was born. From this point on, Louise and I started doing dance breaks in the kitchen. We'd dance while things were simmering or before getting started on our culinary adventure.

Dancing actually improves memory and boosts mood, but all that aside, it just feels good! At any time—whether reading this book or making food in the kitchen—if you're feeling overwhelmed, call a dance break!

Guiding Principle #2:
You Are Worth Healing

In Part II of this book, we provide you with recipes that range from basic broths all the way through main courses, desserts, cocktails, and beauty remedies—our goal is to give you many ways to incorporate bone broth into your daily life and routine.

Some of the recipes call for seemingly odd or new ingredients that may have you wondering why you have to go out of your way to get them. Why are they not right there at your corner market? We know; we have the same frustration.

The thing is, most people who are healing from something are finding themselves having to give up certain foods, with gluten, sugar, and dairy being the usual suspects. These days, it's getting even more complicated thanks to food allergies and sensitivities to compounds found in many foods we consider healthy. Some compounds you may have heard of are histamine (a messaging molecule found in plant and animal foods), oxalates (a naturally occurring substance in many plant and animal foods), thiols (a compound in some sulfur-rich foods), and FODMAPS (fermentable oligosaccharides, disaccharides, monosaccharides, and polyols found in some grains, beans, vegetables, and fruits). People with leaky gut and related digestive issues are reacting to so many foods these days that some end up with only a few things that they can eat without reacting.

Because of all of this, if you do Internet searches you can find something "bad" about any food, even the ones you think are "good." However, in this book, we'd like you to keep the following in mind:

— **We use alternative flours and specialty ingredients because we care about your gut health!** The bottom line is, the usual ingredients at the local grocery store are not working for a growing population of people. For these folks, finding cookbooks with ingredients they can actually eat is nearly impossible. In addition, more parents are trying desperately to find ways to heal their kids, who seem to be even more sensitive than generations before us.

— **We love and care about you, so we're offering recipes that contain ingredients known to be easier to digest and, therefore, gentler on your gut.**
For example:

- We provide refined sugar–free, dairy-free, gluten-free, and grain-free options for people experiencing autoimmune conditions and small intestine challenges.

- We use many herbs and spices to boost antioxidants that go after damaging free radicals, fight inflammation, balance the body, and reduce cravings.

Because mainstream grocery stores have not yet caught up with how to meet these healing needs (not to mention the fact that they make a great profit with processed foods), many alternative ingredients like these are harder to find in your local market or health-food store. Later in this chapter, we provide a shopping list with how to find these ingredients online so that they can be sent right to your door, often with free shipping.

— **Such ingredients are cheaper in the long run.** While these ingredients may seem more expensive, they're higher quality, and you may find that because they're so nutrient dense (and balanced), you feel satisfied and nourished with much less than with typical processed foods. We've also noticed something interesting, both in our own lives and in those of our clients and friends: When gut-healing, nourishing foods are eaten, less is spent on trips to the doctor and beauty remedies. Hair, skin, and nails tend to glow with good health as the body is fed with love. Moods start to improve. Sleep gets deeper and better. These are the priceless benefits of eating well.

Keep in mind that you are also welcome to substitute ingredients. Don't let a weird ingredient or a budget concern stop you from loving your body with good food! Let's all enjoy this process together. We're discovering the lost art of making delicious food in our own kitchens—making things that are customized to our own taste buds, our own desires for that day or week. This is one of the ways we satisfy, nurture, and love ourselves. It's how we can express our creativity. It's how we slow down and say, "Yes, I matter. I'm good enough. I deserve the time it takes."

Guiding Principle #3: Learn to Work with Herbs and Spices

Herbs and spices are the most impressive yet most forgotten casualties of the processed-food industry. They have been deliberately pushed aside so that food manufacturers can focus on your cravings with just the right mix of sweet, salt, and fat tastes, which they want you to eat more of.

Herbs and spices are the righteous and unsung heroes of the food world: They conquer your cravings. They balance your taste buds, which creates satisfaction in your body. They deliver more phytonutrients and antioxidants than most other foods; for example, it takes ½ cup of blueberries to deliver the same antioxidants found in a tiny ½ teaspoon of ground cloves.[1] (If you want to learn more about the health benefits of herbs and spices, go to the "How to Work with Herbs and Spices" section in the Appendix.)

Guiding Principle #4: Remember That Mistakes Can Be Delicious

Heather has a recipe on her website for "oddball cookies," which was a giant mistake that actually turned out well because she stayed with the recipe. It all started to go wrong when she tried putting garlic and other savory spices together into a sweet cookie recipe. It got to the point where it tasted pretty bad and she could have abandoned it altogether, but she had used so many good ingredients that she didn't want to just give up. So she added in more coconut butter and the great mistake hider: a bunch of raw cacao. Things got a little better. Then she added more sweet spices like cinnamon, then some vanilla for a richer taste. It all came together, and people loved the result!

Another time, Heather made a raw cookie recipe and nothing she did could make it work. She hoped that dehydrating the cookies would make a difference; when it didn't, she put the big batch in the freezer and told her husband to use them in his smoothies, as they were full of great ingredients like nut butter and great spices. He was already putting nut butter in his smoothies, so he'd throw in a couple cookies and get the protein and good fats without having to add any nut butter. He loved it, and they got to make use of the cookies.

We find that most mistakes either have happy results or can be used in creative ways. Crumbly bread becomes stuffing or soup thickener—just check out our Messed-up but So Delicious Pan Bread, which was fantastic tasting, but fell apart. We were going to throw away the recipe until we tried the bread pieces in a salad, cooked up with turkey burgers. We both swooned at how delicious it was. It tasted a bit like hush puppies, and we decided that the recipe was too good not to share. So you'll get to see for yourself how delicious mistakes can be used in unexpected ways!

Guiding Principle #5:
Channel Your Inner Child
—Eat What Makes You Happy

We have so many options in the recipes section that we invite you to channel your inner child and pick some that make you feel happy, excited, and maybe just a bit mischievous. Pick some that make you want to dance around the room and shout, "Life loves me!" After all, where do you think Louise got the idea for that affirmation? It came from pure joy.

All of life is a joy, especially when you celebrate all of it, including your meals. With the recipes we've provided, you can even celebrate dessert knowing that you are doing good things for your beautiful body.

Let's all affirm: I *bring joy to all things in my life. I now celebrate my meals with all of my senses, engaging in the full experience that my body is receiving. This is love, I am love, and so it is!*

MASTER SHOPPING LIST

The shopping list that follows focuses on whole foods and gives you guidelines for what to look for. It is not specific to the menus, but we have listed the ingredients that are called for in our recipes and included notes on where you can find specialty items that might not be in your grocery or health-food store.

Many people who develop a love for whole foods find themselves enjoying farmers' markets, where they can save money and interact with the people growing their food. Many farmers you meet at these markets have CSA (community-supported agriculture) programs for budget-friendly boxes of vegetables, fruit, meats, game, poultry, raw milk, eggs, fresh-cut flowers, and more. It's a great, affordable way to support your local farmer.

Note that if you cannot find these foods at your local grocery, health-food store, or farmers' market, you can typically get them online at sites like Amazon.com, Vitacost.com and iHerb.com. The Resources section has more details on where to find ingredients.

Whole Foods, Organic Preferred

Typically found on the perimeter of the grocery store, these include produce, the fish and meat counters, and some refrigerated areas. Bones and meat can be found in the freezer section as well, and health-food stores that carry bone broth often stock it in the freezer section.

Fruits and Vegetables: A Rainbow of Colored Vegetables

- *Red*—beets, red leaf lettuce, radishes, red Swiss chard, red onions, tomatoes, and red bell peppers. (Note that tomatoes and red bell peppers are in the nightshade family, which is not well tolerated by everyone. If you experience digestive pain, reflux, tremors, or joint pain, you may want to avoid or eliminate these and reintroduce them after two weeks to see if you're sensitive to them.)

- *Orange*—carrots, pumpkin, sweet potatoes, and butternut squash.

- *Yellow*—summer squash, yellow onions, and corn. (Many people have corn allergies or sensitivities, so make sure you can tolerate corn and that you choose organic to avoid GMO corn.)

- *Green*—artichokes, arugula, bok choy, broccoli, brussels sprouts, cabbage, chayote, collards, cucumbers, dandelion greens, endive, escarole, frisée, green beans, green leaf lettuce, kale, microgreens, romaine lettuce, snap peas, snow peas, spinach, sprouts, Swiss chard, watercress, and zucchini; as well as fresh herbs such as basil, cilantro, dill, fennel, mint, parsley, rosemary, sage, and thyme.

- *Blue/purple*—radicchio, shallots, turnips, and eggplant. (Eggplant is a nightshade, so please see the above note about tomatoes and red bell peppers.)

- *White*—cauliflower, garlic, white onions, white asparagus, mushrooms, and ginger.

Animal Protein, Bones, and Gelatin

The ideal is organic and grass- or pasture-fed meat and poultry and wild-caught fish. You want to make sure that the animals you consume are free of hormones and antibiotics.

- Grass-fed and finished meats and bones, such as oxtails, marrowbones, knuckles, beef feet (feet are the hooves), thighbones, and the like.

- Game meats and bones, such as bison, Cornish game hen, duck, goose, lamb, pheasant, quail, rabbit, venison, and so on.

- Organic pasture-fed poultry, eggs, and chicken feet, wings, necks, and backs.

- Organic pasture-fed pork and split pig's feet (whole feet often come split in half).

- Wild-caught fish and bones (for broth making, choose non-oily wild cold-water fish, such as Alaska or walleye pollock, sea bass, cod, and halibut); check fishwatch.gov and seafoodwatch .org for sustainability information. Note that wild-caught shrimp from North America are most likely to be sustainably caught.

- Unflavored powdered beef gelatin—use this for recipes that need gelling; must be dissolved in warm water. Great Lakes Beef Gelatin or Vital Proteins Beef Gelatin are great options.

- Hydrolyzed collagen or collagen peptides—this is the unflavored powdered gelatin that does not gel and is great for smoothies or other liquids that do not require gelling. Great Lakes brand collagen hydrolysate or Vital Proteins brand collagen peptides are great options.

Healthy Fats and Oils (Choose Organic, Unrefined Oils)

- Borage oil
- Coconut oil (extra virgin)
- Cod-liver oil
- Flaxseed oil (in the refrigerated section)
- Grass- or pasture-fed animal fats, such as raw butter (this may be hard to find, so organic or cultured butter are good alternatives); ghee; lard from pork; tallow and suet from lamb or beef; goose, chicken, or duck fat (you may have plenty of this type of fat from the top of your bone broth; see Chapter 2)

- Hemp-seed oil
- Macadamia-nut oil
- Olive oil (extra virgin)
- Pumpkin-seed oil (you may have to purchase this online if it's not available in-store)

Whole-food Sweeteners

- Blackstrap molasses
- Fruit (like fresh apples)
- Lo han guo (we do not use this in any of our recipes, but it's a good natural sweetener)
- Maple syrup (*Note*: Names of grades have changed, but as long as you buy one of the organic Grade A types, the only difference is the color and taste. If you used to enjoy Grade B maple syrup, the new name is "Grade A dark with robust taste.")
- Medjool dates
- Raw honey
- Stevia

Gluten-Free Grains and Beans

- Amaranth

- Buckwheat

- Lentils

- Millet

- Quinoa

- Rice—consider Lundberg brand Organic California White Basmati because it has been found to be lower in arsenic than other brands

Sea Salt, Spices, and Herbs

Look for organic herbs and spices and real sea salt or Himalayan salt, and choose Ceylon cinnamon instead of cassia cinnamon. If you want the best bargains for your budget, go to MountainRoseHerbs.com and purchase bulk spices online. Mountain Rose Herbs focuses on organic, pesticide-free, wild-crafted herbs and spices. You can learn more about the medicinal properties and how to work with herbs and spices in the Appendix.

These are the herbs and spices used most often in our recipes:

- Allspice

- Basil

- Bay leaf

- Black pepper

- Cardamom

- Cinnamon (We recommend seeking out Ceylon, the "true cinnamon," instead of cassia cinnamon because cassia could have health risks if consumed in large quantities. You can find organic Ceylon cinnamon at MountainRoseHerbs.com.)

- Cloves

- Coriander

- Cumin

- Fennel

- Fenugreek

- Ginger

- Hing (asafoetida)

- Nutmeg

- Oregano

- Rosemary

- Sea salt and Himalayan salt

- Thyme

- Turmeric

Wine, Vinegar, Fish Sauce, and Lemons

If you're sensitive to glutamates, your best bet is to make broths and stocks with either apple cider vinegar or lemon juice. Many of our experts prefer the taste and ease of use of apple cider vinegar for broths and use lemons for flavoring. The rest of the items on this list are great to have on hand for flavoring and show up in some of the recipes in this book:

- Apple cider vinegar
- Fish sauce—this is a condiment popular in Thailand and Vietnam, made of fermented anchovies and sea salt. Look for a brand with no sugar, like Red Boat (this is made only with wild-caught anchovy and sea salt and can be purchased at Amazon.com).
- Rice vinegar (check the label and make sure there is no sugar)
- Mirin—a sweet rice wine often used in Japanese cooking
- Madeira (or cooking sherry)— Madeira is a Portuguese fortified wine that can add an exquisite taste to many recipes. It's one of Louise's favorite flavor secrets.
- Lemons
- White wine

Specialty Flours

- Almond flour (also called almond meal), made from ground almonds. NOW Foods Real Food Raw Almond Flour has the non-GMO verified label, but it can be a challenge to find organic almond flour. If this is important

to you, you can make your own with our recipe in Chapter 9.

- Organic coconut flour is made from ground, defatted coconut meat. Two good options are NOW Foods Organic Coconut Flour and Let's Do Organic Coconut Flour.
- Organic rye flour is lower in gluten than wheat and is used in our sourdough bread recipe in Chapter 9. Sprouted rye flour is the easiest for the body to digest and may be found in your health-food store or online.

Miscellaneous Specialty Ingredients

- Bitters are helpful for balancing recipes and aiding digestion. Urban Moonshine Citrus Digestive Bitters contain a concentrated extract of dandelion root and leaf, burdock root, orange peel, fennel seed, yellow dock root, angelica root, gentian root, and ginger root.
- Bonito flakes are fine, sashimi-quality, steamed, air-dried, and aged skipjack tuna flakes that come in a bag. They're typically found in the ethnic foods section of the grocery store.
- Bragg Liquid Aminos is a flavoring agent made from

non-fermented, non-GMO soybeans. (Note that some people with gut or mood issues are too sensitive to use this product.)

- Coconut aminos is a liquid soy-free flavoring alternative to soy sauce, tamari, and Bragg Liquid Aminos, containing coconut sap and sea salt. Some people with gut issues may be sensitive to this, but perhaps less so than the aforementioned products. Coconut Secret brand uses organic coconuts and does not add MSG.

- Coconut butter is coconut meat mixed with coconut oil and has a very rich, almost frosting-like taste, although it is unsweetened. Also called coconut cream or coconut manna, you can find organic coconut butter in your health-food store. Some popular brands are Artisana, Nutiva, Kevala, and Let's Do Organic. You can also order it from TropicalTraditions.com, Amazon.com, and other sites.

- Cultured vegetables, like sauerkraut or kimchi, make a great side dish for many of our recipes. Look for the kinds with no vinegar or sugar, like Gold Mine Brand or Rejuvenative Foods brand.

- Katsuobushi or bonito flakes (you can get these at Asian markets or many grocery stores, or from Amazon.com).

- Kombu seaweed (you can get this at most grocery stores or health-food stores, or from theseaweedman.com).

- Mustard—several of our recipes call for this. Our favorite mustards have apple cider vinegar instead of white distilled vinegar, such as Whole Foods' 365 Everyday Value brand German mustard and Dijon mustard; the German mustard is a blend of stone-ground mustard and horseradish. Eden Organic Brown Mustard is also made with apple cider vinegar.

- Organic flaxseeds or flax meal (seeds last longer and can be easily ground into flax meal, but flax meal saves you the step of grinding). These are usually found in the bulk section of your health-food store, where you can often save money. You can also buy them packaged, such as in Bob's Red Mill Organic Golden Flaxseed Meal and NOW Foods Certified Organic Flax Seed Meal. Flaxseeds can be found in packages by Arrowhead Mills and NOW Foods as well.

- Pomegranate molasses is a concentrated form of pomegranate juice used for flavoring, most often in Middle Eastern dishes (not the same as pomegranate paste). Some people use it in place of an acid, like vinegar or lemon juice, and it's a nice way to flavor or finish broth. Look for brands with no added sugar (read labels), like Alwadi 100% Natural Pomegranate Molasses or Sadaf. You can also make your own (see instructions in Chapter 5 in the medicinal finishers section).

- Raw cacao is a less processed version of cocoa powder or chocolate, and Essential Living Foods Cacao Nibs and Earth Circe Organics Balinese Cacao Nibs are two popular brands. Cacao nibs are usually used to add flavor and texture to desserts, but raw cacao powder is the easiest to work with. However, some testing has shown that the processing of cacao into powder can increase the cadmium levels. If this concerns you, cacao beans or nibs can be ground up in a coffee grinder or high-speed blender to make a fresh, fragrant powder that we think is even better

tasting. All raw cacao used in our recipes is unsweetened.

- Raw cacao butter is the white chunks of cacao butter that have the smell and slight flavor of cacao, but is just the fat without the dark color or theobromine found in cacao. Raw cacao butter is a nice base for white chocolate desserts as an alternative for people who have sensitivities to chocolate. Sunfood is a popular brand for raw organic cacao butter.

- Smoothie ingredients you might like (many of these are available online if you cannot find them in your health-food store):

  - Camu camu powder (powder made from the camu berry, considered a superfood and a good source of wholefood vitamin C)

  - Chia seed powder (you can also grind up whole chia seeds in a coffee grinder)

  - Colostrum (the first milk of cows, full of concentrated nutrients to support immunity; Surthrival.com has a quality product)

  - Green powders, such as Ormus Greens by Sunwarrior, Premier Greens by Premier Research Labs,

Perfect 3 Grass Blend (perfectsupplements.com), and Wheat Grass Powder by NOW Foods

- Hemp-seed powder (you can also grind up whole hemp seeds in a coffee grinder)

- Pomegranate juice

- Tart cherry juice concentrate by Dynamic Health

- Young coconut water

- Tamari—a version of soy sauce made with no wheat. Make sure to read the label to be sure you're getting a wheat-free tamari. San-J Organic Wheat Free Tamari does not add MSG and can be purchased online.

- Tamarind paste—a concentrated paste of the fruit of tamarind—is a good source of antioxidants and has a sweet and sour taste.

SAMPLE MENUS

Adding bone broth to your diet doesn't have to mean a full-scale change in what you choose for breakfast, lunch, or dinner. If you want to dip your toe in the water, you can simply fill your mug or to-go cup with broth once or twice per day and feel your body glowing from the inside out. This stuff isn't called liquid gold for nothing!

If you want to go whole hog or just submerge yourself into the bone broth world a bit more, you can begin to add a little here and there to your daily meals.

When we asked our friend and bone broth expert Caroline Barringer how she incorporated it into her diet, she paused and said, "What? What do you mean?" We all laughed. You see, as a 14-year veteran of bone broth making, Caroline doesn't even think about it anymore. She's constantly adding broth to soups, stews, pâtés—she even freezes the broth into cubes and sucks on them while on long phone calls. This is our kind of woman!

Whatever conventional or oddball way you want to add bone broth to your life, get it into your belly and your body will love you for it! Here are some ideas:

Breakfast

- Drink a cup of your favorite broth, stock, or soup (you may want to add one of the finishers in Chapter 5 to your broth or stock)

- Quinoa, Broccoli, and Leek Pilaf

- Sassy Green Smoothie

- Collagen-Rich Fruit Smoothie

- Lulu's Salad in a Glass

- Breakfast Lamb Stew

- Pancakes or Waffles (Grain Free)

- Maya's Finnish Sourdough Rye Bread with butter and sea salt (or coconut oil and sea salt)

- Herb Bread with Aioli, butter, nut or seed butter, or coconut oil
- Messed-up but So Delicious Pan Bread sautéed in beef tallow or bone broth
- Eggs Your Way Soup or Pureed Green Bean Soup

Lunch and Dinner

- Chicken Burger Salad with Aioli and Messed-up but So Delicious Pan Bread
- Farm-to-Table Aspic and Maya's Finnish Sourdough Rye Bread
- Pâté Plus with soup or a salad
- Oeufs en Gelée with Herb Bread
- Oxtail Pâté rolled in butter lettuce and dipped in Aioli
- Everyone's Favorite Egg Salad over a bed of romaine lettuce
- Lobster Salad Extravaganza with Simple Asparagus
- Tempting Tuna Salad rolled in butter lettuce or over a bed of mixed greens
- Cornish Game Hen with White Wine Mustard Sauce, Caramelized Onions, and Cardamom Carrots
- Honey Mustard Chicken

- Easy Turkey Meatloaf Cupcakes with Kabocha Squash Topping and Simple Asparagus
- Cleansing Cilantro Soup with Pâté Plus in romaine lettuce wraps
- Hearty Hamburger Soup with Herb Bread
- Cactus and Seafood Soup with Magic Zucchini and Carrots
- Goat and Vegetable Stew
- Easy Eye of Round Roast with Mashed Celery Root
- Maori Puha Boil Up with Best Brussels Sprouts

Snacks

- Carry bone broth, soups, or stews in an insulated Kleen Kanteen or a widemouthed thermos for snacks on the go
- Maya's Finnish Sourdough Rye Bread
- Herb Bread
- Simply Delicious Salmon Salad, Lobster Salad Extravaganza, or Tempting Tuna Salad rolled in butter lettuce
- Turkey or Bison Meatloaf Cupcakes

- Any of the pâtés on Herb Bread or in butter lettuce or romaine lettuce

Desserts (Note That These All Freeze Well)

- Consider doubling the ice-cream recipes if you want to make the dessert one time and have plenty of leftovers for your freezer.

- Apple Tarte Tatin and Cinnamon New Year Cake both go well with Moroccan Vanilla Spice Ice Cream.

- Try the Chocolate Drop Cookies, and do the Great Chocolate Experiment included in the recipe.

SAMPLE DINNER PARTY MENUS

Here's another way to celebrate! In order to write this book "Louise Play" style, we decided to have dinner parties every weekend so that we could test out our recipes with our group of friends. You would have loved to see their faces when we told them they were having bone broth cake and ice cream for dessert! But they came anyway. And they loved it. They especially loved when we told them they would be coming for a meal and leaving with better skin.

Meatloaf Cupcakes
Casual Dinner Party Menu

These wonderful "cupcakes" are made of bison meatloaf and have celery root mash on top as the "frosting." They look delightful and bring joy to children or the child inside of us.

Don't let the menu fool you, though, as this is just the kind of casual meal that has an understated elegance and is as at home in the backyard as it is in the formal dining room. What makes it so appealing is the ease of preparation, sense of playfulness, and the surprisingly sophisticated tastes in the menu.

Serves 8 people

Appetizers

- Herb Bread or Maya's Finnish Sourdough Rye Bread (from Chapter 9), with butter or hummus (Majestic brand is a nice raw organic hummus, or choose your favorite brand)

- Vegetable Crudités (endive, cut zucchini, carrots, celery, cucumber, yellow squash, and so on)

Main meal

- Bison Meatloaf Cupcakes with Mashed Celery Root Topping (Chapter 7)

- Simple Asparagus (Chapter 8)

Dessert

* Vanilla Cake with Berry White Chocolate Frosting (Chapter 11)

Cornish Game Hen Easy-Yet-Elegant Dinner Party Menu

If you want to serve an elegant meal that's reminiscent of the French countryside, this is the one. The good news is, it's so easy that you can serve it at the end of a long workday and still remain unhurried as your guests arrive.

The Cornish game hen can be prepped in less than 10 minutes and slowly cooks for 6 hours in the slow cooker. So you can put it in around lunchtime and forget about it until it's ready when your guests arrive for dinner—without worrying about burnt or dry poultry.

The appetizers and desserts can be made a couple of days in advance, then prepped for the evening meal the night before or the morning of.

Serves 8 people

Appetizers

* The Best Liver Pâté Ever! (this recipe from Chapter 10 can be made the day before or the day of the party; it also freezes very

Preparing for Parties "Louise Play" Style

Louise: When I was married, I did a lot of gourmet cooking. My husband loved my cooking. Every year for my birthday, he'd take me to whatever restaurant I chose. When it was his birthday, he always wanted me to cook a delicious meal. Kitchens were small in New York City, where we lived, but I still loved to cook. In this tiny kitchen, I'd make all sorts of delicious things. I had my favorite cookbooks, and I loved trying new things.

My routine when getting ready for parties went like this: I'd put on my makeup, do my hair, and choose the perfect hat—we all wore hats in those days. Next, I would take a bath! I must have made quite a sight, taking a bath all made up with my hat already on. Well, I've always been practical. I figured that if I ran short on time, I'd have the important things done first!

There was one time when I grabbed a honey jar too fast and it shattered on the floor. There I was, broken glass and honey everywhere, but that night, my system of getting ready served me well. I had the whole mess cleaned up—and my hair, makeup, and hat were perfection!

These days, everyone is more casual, which means we get to share the food preparation! Whether you gather together with friends to make a meal for your dinner party or have everyone bring part of the meal, the theme these days is to keep it simple. I hope you enjoy the simple party menus we've provided here. And if you like, you can try doing your hair and makeup (and maybe a hat) before bathing, too!

well and can be thawed out the night before)

- Aioli (this recipe from Chapter 6 can be made up to 5 days before your party)

- Herb Bread (this recipe from Chapter 9 freezes well and can be made well in advance of your party or made up to two days in advance if you don't want to freeze it)

Main meal

- Cornish Game Hen in White Wine Mustard Sauce (this recipe from Chapter 7 is best made the day of the party, but could be made the day before and reheated, if you are short on time)

- Caramelized Onions (this recipe from Chapter 8 can be made up to two days before your dinner party)

- Best Brussels Sprouts (this recipe from Chapter 8 can be made the day of or the day before your party)

Dessert

- Apple Tarte Tatin (for this recipe from Chapter 11, you can prep the crust and freeze it well in advance of your dinner, or make the whole dessert a couple of days before the dinner; check the recipe instructions for ideas on how to do this)

- Moroccan Vanilla Spice Ice Cream (make this recipe from Chapter 11 weeks before the event if you like!)

Chinese Hot Pot Menu

This is by far the easiest party menu ever! There is very little preparation, and the beauty of this meal is that everyone cooks together.

Hot pot meals are considered the ultimate in communal cooking—they're meant to be shared with friends and loved ones who want to gather together in the most social of meal experiences. You take a single burner or two, plug them in on a center island or table, and place pots of hot broth on the burners. The group gathers around, customizing their meal fondue-style. Thinly sliced meats, shrimp, and chicken; vegetables; and rice noodles all cook within 3 minutes in these communal pots.

With fine mesh strainers, slotted spoons, or hot pot strainer scoops (all of which can be purchased at Amazon.com or your local kitchen store), you can put the foods you want for your meal into the hot broth and allow them to cook. Your guests who are new to hot pot meals will be surprised by how fast everything cooks.

Serves 10–12 people

Broth

- 10 cups of bone broth (make this well in advance to freeze and take out to thaw a day or two before the party, or make fresh one to two days before the party). The best options from our recipes are Louise's Favorite Bone Broth, Kitchen Sink Bone Broth, Heather's Easy Oxtail Broth, The Local Butcher Shop Bone Broth, and Balanced and Bright Bone Broth. A lightly flavored chicken broth is also a great option. (All recipes are in Chapter 4.)

Vegetables

- 2 cups spiral-cut, julienned, or thinly sliced half-moons of yellow summer squash and zucchini

- 6 baby bok choy or 1 head large bok choy, thinly sliced lengthwise

- 1 head of broccoli, chopped up (use florets and save stems for future bone or vegetable broth)

- Pickled Ginger (this is exceptionally good if you use the optional carrots in the recipe in Chapter 8)

Noodles

- Organic rice noodles (you can often get these gluten free, fast-cooking noodles in your grocery or health-food store, and of course they're available online; King Soba Organic Thai Rice Noodles is a good brand)

Meat, poultry, and fish

- 1 lb. chicken thighs

- 1 lb. beef eye of round

- 1 lb. jumbo shrimp

Dipping sauces (Typically, there are 3 to 4 dipping sauces. Our group of 12 did not eat much of the dips and enjoyed the food on its own.)

- Make your own sauce: The recipes in Chapter 6 for Artichoke Tahini Sauce and Aioli are great options (or if you want a shortcut you could purchase one, like Majestic Garlic's basil dip, from your health-food store)

- Coconut Secret Coconut Aminos or wheat-free tamari (you can typically get these at your health-food store or from sites like Amazon.com)

- Organic German mustard (this is mustard and horseradish—you can also mix Dijon mustard with prepared horseradish)

Dessert

- Cinnamon New Year Cake (this recipe from Chapter 11 freezes well and can be made well in advance and frozen or made the day of the party)

- Moroccan Vanilla Spice Ice Cream (this can be made weeks

Louise's Chinese New Year Hot Pot Party, and the Bone Broth Tribe

Heather: Recently, we had a group over to Louise's house for a Chinese New Year Hot Pot party. It was the first one we had ever hosted, and it was a chance to have bone broth take center stage in a communal meal. We had two single burners placed on Louise's kitchen island with saucepans of hot broth. All 12 people gathered around the pots and helped each other with the cooking. We'd put in some eye of round meat and bok choy, then pass it around to those who wanted it. In another pot, someone would be making rice noodles, broccoli and shrimp. The meat, chicken, and shrimp cooked quickly and perfectly, and we laughed and expressed surprise at how fun and easy it was.

Louise had set her table so beautifully, and we all took our seats, enjoying the dips and the side dish of marinated ginger. We passed a book of Chinese New Year proverbs around, opening to any page and reading out loud to the group. Something magical happened that night: It was a blending of old friends and new. We got to know each other better as we cooked together, simmering and spooning up food for one another, and going back for seconds. This group became the "Bone Broth Tribe," gathering on a weekly basis thereafter for adventures in community, nourishment, and joyful laughter. These were our taste testers for this book. Something about the hot pot experience allowed us to blend together in supportive community.

Never underestimate the power of food when it comes to creating a loving connection. If you want a truly unique community experience, this is it!

in advance or up to 2 days before your party)

- Optional: fortune cookies (even though we don't eat the cookies, we like to get them just for the fortunes!)

Tools

- One or two single burners. You can use your stove if you like; it's up to you! If you want to use burners, you can get them at your local kitchen store or department store, or from Amazon.com. They start at around $13 and go up from there. Heather takes a single burner on trips to heat bone broth and other healthy foods while traveling and staying in hotel rooms—it has come in handy many times!

- A deep saucepan for each burner (about 8- to 10-cup capacity)

- One or two stainless steel fine mesh strainers (OXO fine mesh strainers have a silicone handle and all stainless strainer, and these were our favorite hot pot tools)
- Optional: tongs, slotted spoons, or hot pot strainer scoops to scoop smaller things out of the broth; chopsticks for the meal

YOUR ACTION PLAN FOR ENJOYING BONE BROTH

Now that you've learned about bone broth, meat stocks, and vegetable broths, it's time to get them into your belly! Remember, Chapters 1 through 3 give you all the basics for getting started, but here are some additional steps to support you:

1. Decide How You Want to Start

— If needed, tailor to your health goals: If you have a health condition you're working on, Chapter 1 will guide you on whether to start with vegetable broth, meat stock, or bone broth.

— Choose your favorite recipes: Look at the recipes in this book and decide which ones appeal to you most. Once you've chosen the ones you want to make, identify which broth is required and make a list of ingredients you need. For the most part, you'll be able to use a meat or chicken broth for just about any recipe. Fish broths are less versatile, but don't let that stop you—they are a gentle source of iodine and full of flavor for many delicious recipes. Remember, you can freeze your broth in jars or as ice cubes and use it as needed.

— It may be easier if you make one type of broth first and choose recipes based on it. The only time you'll need a neutral (relatively flavorless) broth is for desserts or cocktails. You can always use unflavored powdered gelatin to make desserts until you start making neutral broth.

— If you do start with a neutral broth, you'll be able to make any of the recipes in the book. This may seem like the best place to start, but you might have an easier time at first making flavored broths because you may want to use bones and meat scraps from previous meals, without having to trim off all the meat. It can be much faster to have a chicken for dinner, for example, then throw what's left over (wings, neck, carcass with meat and skin, and so forth) into your pot and start simmering.

— No matter where you start, we have plenty of recipes and suggestions for how you can use powdered gelatin as a substitute in desserts and neutral broth recipes!

— Start collecting bones and vegetable scraps. The beauty of bone broth is that you can eliminate a lot of food waste in your kitchen, which is great for your budget! Gather odds and ends of vegetables, peels, bones, and meat scraps, and store them in your freezer until you're ready to make your next batch. If you're ready to start now and don't have everything you need, you can purchase bones from your farmer or fishmonger, or at the seafood or meat counter in your local store. Some people like to get bone-in meat, like a chicken or beef shank, cook a meal, and then use the leftover bones. The easiest way to do this is with a chicken—a whole bird makes a wonderful broth, both while cooking (if you slow cook it using some water, like our Cornish Game Hen recipe) and by using the carcass afterward.

2. Assess Your Kitchen and Storage Tools

— Do you have the tools you need for broth or stock? Take a look around your kitchen: Chances are, you have a large stockpot or slow cooker; if not, put that on your list to purchase. A stockpot, large mixing spoon, and good fine mesh strainer are all you really need to get started with making stock and broth.

— Decide whether you have the storage tools you require. Take a look at the other kitchen tools in Chapter 2—such as storage containers, a funnel to pour broth into jars, a ladle, and ice-cube trays—and decide what you feel will work best for you. We find that having a funnel and ladle to pour broth from the stockpot into jars makes the whole process so much easier. However, you can always use a small cup to transfer soup into a jar, no funnel or ladle needed!

— For storage, we love using glass mason jars because they are easy to find at the grocery store, take up less room in the refrigerator, make it easy to remove the fat cap when ready to use the broth, and are easy to freeze. You may also want to use recycled jars from coconut oil, nut butters, or anything else that comes in a glass jar.

3. Make a Plan

Now that you have a sense of what you have and what you might need in terms of ingredients and kitchen tools, write down your plan:

— First, give yourself plenty of time, especially if you're starting something new. If you rarely cook and are getting ready to jump into this culinary adventure, go slowly and be kind to yourself. Give yourself a week or two to gather everything you need on your list if that feels good. In some cases, you may be ordering ingredients online, and you'll be waiting for them to arrive. Some of you may be more comfortable in the kitchen and can easily gather everything you need. If you're ready to dive right in, that's great, too!

— What foods or ingredients do you need to shop for? Make a list that you can take with you when shopping. Keep in mind that every locale is different and you may not have all of the ingredients in a recipe that you'd like to make. While we strive to offer substitutions, in some cases the ingredients you need may only be available online. Remember, it's okay if you cannot access organic or grass- and pasture-fed ingredients. The key here is to do your best with what you have and trust that the more you consume real, whole food, the more your body will respond with good health.

— Set aside some time! This one is really important, as most of us are already so busy as it is. If you look carefully at your calendar, what can you remove so that you have time to shop for ingredients and make your broths and meals? Is there something you have on your calendar that is not enriching your life or supporting your goals? That's the perfect thing to remove from your schedule. If you're a busy parent, perhaps this is a good time to engage the kids in some chores around the house, so you can take them off your plate.

Maybe you can get the family together and have a wonderful Sunday in the kitchen, playing music and preparing food for the week. Freeze what you don't need now and take it out to thaw for a fast meal later in the week. Put food in individual containers that you can take to work or the kids can take to school. Invite friends over and cook together. Turn on your favorite music, podcast, or radio show and listen to something uplifting while you cook. You can turn time in your kitchen into time for yourself, or time with family and friends, to create a more joyful experience.

4. Shop for Your Ingredients

Earlier in the chapter, we provided a master shopping list for you. This is a good tool to have alongside your normal grocery list, to remind you of ingredients you'd like to have on hand.

You may have a variety of options for sourcing ingredients. Some people love to support their local farmers and fishmongers; others don't have access to these and look to their local grocery or health-food store. Use what you have access to nearby. The last thing you want is to become overwhelmed by having to seek out ingredients, so do the best with what you have near you and make substitutions if necessary. If you're on a healing diet, you are likely more familiar with seeking out specialty ingredients and perhaps you already have a process for finding what you need.

Here are some options to consider:

- Farmers' markets.
- Health-food or grocery store (your health-food store is more likely to have specialty ingredients that many people on healing diets seek out, like coconut flour, raw cacao, and almond flour).
- Farm CSA (community-supported agriculture) program—some farms have these programs, and you can either pick up your box of food at the farm or the farm may deliver to a spot in your area. You can often find out about these online at LocalHarvest.org.
- Local fish merchant—ask around or check with your local Weston

A. Price Foundation chapter for ideas (www.westonaprice.org/get-involved/find-local-chapter).

- Online providers—Amazon.com, iHerb.com, Vitacost.com, MountainRoseHerbs.com, and other online providers often sell specialty ingredients that may be hard to find in your health-food store.

- Check the shopping list in this chapter and the Resources section at the end of this book for more options.

5. Go Slowly, and Be Gentle with Yourself

Like the tortoise and the hare, most things follow the old adage, "Slow and steady wins the race." The goal with making broth and getting back into your kitchen to make real food is to take your time and develop this new habit slowly. You are building a new habit for a lifetime, so there is no rush to get it all done right away. Take one step at a time. Perhaps what you feel you can do right now is buy a vegetarian soup and add gelatin, or purchase bone broth from a local supplier. That's great! Any step, however small it feels, is a worthy place to start. Over time, these small steps build and turn into big rewards.

As you start clearing your calendar to make way for time in the kitchen to nourish yourself, you may be able to add more steps. We've heard many reports from our clients that once they made time for cooking, they started to feel better and more energized, which inspired a passion for being in their kitchens to keep the cycle going. Cooking is a beautiful way to show yourself through your actions that you love taking care of yourself, and that you're worth it!

6. Make Your Broth

Channel Julia Child and take a "what the hell" mind-set when you start making your broth. You have your ingredients and kitchen tools—you're ready! This process may seem foreign, but you can do it. You'll see that it's so much easier than you think, and you can work with whatever end result you get. The broth will be rich with healing nutrients, and once you have it, you can make many wonderful meals quickly and easily.

If this is your first time, congratulate yourself for making it to this point, and be sure to celebrate your broth when it's done!

7. Store Your Broth and the Fat

Think about how much broth you'll need for the coming week for the recipes you've chosen, as well as for sipping. Keep the amount you'll need in your refrigerator, and if you have some left over, put it in the freezer. If you run out sooner than you think that week, you can always take a jar out and thaw it for the next day.

Leave the fat cap on top of your broth until you're ready to use it so that it stays fresh longer. Remember to use your senses—smell, sight, taste, and your intuition are all excellent guides for whether your broth and fat are still good or not!

8. Use the Broth and Fat

Now that your broth is done, you can start using it in the recipes you've chosen. Keep in mind that some of the recipes take a few minutes, while others take a bit longer. Set aside the time you need for each recipe and remember that you are investing this time in your own self-care and nourishment. Also, some of the recipes are healing elixirs for medicinal and beauty goals—give yourself some meditative spa time for these because they can be an important part of your relaxation and self-care for the week.

9. Listen to Your Body

Chapter 1 contains tips for listening to your body and deciding if a stock would be better for you than a broth. If you make a bone broth and find that it's too much, you can always freeze it for later or dilute it with a lot of water. It's never wasted! Diluting with water can be a great strategy because you'll still get the flavor and nutrients, but in a less concentrated way. If you are so sensitive that even diluted bone broth is too strong, store it in the freezer until your gut has healed with meat stock and you're ready to move into bone broth. It will be there, ready and waiting for you!

10. Repeat the Process

As you prepare and consume meals, continue to save bones and vegetable scraps in your kitchen, storing them in your freezer until you're ready to make your next batch. Perhaps you're ready to try new recipes or move to another level in your kitchen adventures.

Making broth can become a rewarding part of your regular routine, allowing you to support your health and reduce waste. It allows you to reconnect with the earth and connect to the feeling of home and hearth once present in our ancestors' kitchens. Most of all, you will delight in the incredible-tasting recipes you can make with this flavorful "chef's secret." Perhaps you will venture into making your own creative recipes, learning what tastes work best for your unique palate. This is the cycle of nourishment . . . the cycle of life.

LET'S GET COOKING!

Now that you've learned the basics of making bone broth, you're ready to start your first batch. The next chapter includes recipes for making basic broths and stocks that can be sipped on their own or used as the beginning of many delicious recipes. Join us as we venture into making broths!

Maya's Finnish Sourdough Rye Bread.

PART II

· RECIPES ·

DELICIOUSLY DECADENT MEALS

and Healing Elixirs

Vegetable scraps for Louise's Favorite Bone Broth or Vegetable Broth recipe.

~CHAPTER 4~

THE FOUNDATION:
Basic Broths and Stocks

W e'd like to take a moment to remind you of what we talked about in Chapter 2, that there is a difference when it comes to the flavor of bone broth or stock. For the purposes of this book, we are going to describe the uses of three types of broths—*neutral*, *flavored*, and *finished*—so you can get an idea of how we used the broths in recipes. In each recipe, we will suggest the type of broth you might want to use.

Here's a brief refresher:

1. **Neutral broths** are almost flavorless (or have only a very mild meat flavor) and can be used in a variety of recipes without imposing a meat flavor on them.

2. **Flavored broths** will have some flavor from the meat, vegetables (such as onions and garlic), and spices. These can make a really nice sipping broth or the basis of savory dishes, but would not be appropriate for making a dessert.

3. **Finished broths** are flavored with add-ins that we call "finishers." Finishers can be any flavorings, ranging from herbs and spices to bitters or fish sauce, and are described in detail in Chapter 5.

cu

One other note before we get started with the recipes: You'll notice that some of them come from chefs, butchers, farmers, or healers who happen to be located in California (specifically Southern California). The reason for this is that we both live and have many friends here, with whom we swap recipes and talk broth. However, this is by no means meant to convey that we don't recognize the contributions of talented individuals worldwide.

We know there are many lovers of animals and food out there, so get to know those in your area by visiting farmers' markets, striking up a conversation with your local butcher or favorite chef, or simply doing an Internet search for like-minded people. We're sure you'll find your own tribe of bone broth enthusiasts in no time!

LOUISE'S FAVORITE BONE BROTH
OR VEGETABLE BROTH
(Neutral or Flavored)

This recipe and process can be used for making any meat, poultry, or fish broth, or you can collect vegetables and just make veggie stock. If you make the meat and poultry broths with vegetables, you'll get a flavored broth. If you leave the vegetables out and focus only on bones, you'll have a neutral broth.

Heather: Louise is brilliant in the kitchen. She has a gift, both in the kitchen and in life, for making things simple and streamlined. We wanted to start this chapter with Louise's bone broth recipe and process because it makes broth and stock making easy. Even the experts have told us that once they learned Louise's process, they started doing it, too!

This recipe sets the tone for making bone broth or stock because it gives you an easy way to gather ingredients from kitchen scraps at your own pace; then when you're ready, making the broth is easy. It helps you practice zero waste beautifully, while saving scraps to make a nutrient-rich broth.

This broth can be sipped or used in recipes for more flavorful grains, soups, and more!

Gathering Ingredients (Go at Your Own Pace)

Open a large paper shopping bag and place it in one of your freezer drawers or shelves. If your freezer has limited space and is just one big bin, you may want to use zip-top plastic bags and label them with the contents (such as "broth veggies," "broth bones: unused," "broth bones: used 1 time," and so on).

Over the course of the week (or several weeks), throw all bones and meat scraps into the bag in your freezer. If you want to make neutral broths, you can start a separate bag for vegetable scraps, peelings, and the odds and ends that you chop off. Some examples are onion or garlic skins, carrot peelings, salad scraps, artichoke tips, the tough ends of asparagus, kale stems, and pea pods. You can also throw all the vegetable scraps and bones in one bag if you're planning to make a flavored broth.

Keep adding vegetable scraps, meat scraps, and bones to your bag in the freezer until it's full and you're ready to make your broth.

If you are ready to make broth and don't have enough meat and bones to get started, you can go to the health-food store or farmers' market and purchase the necks, feet, backs, and wings of a chicken. Other options for a gelatin-rich broth are lamb necks, pig's feet, beef feet, marrowbones, or beef bones. Add these to your bag until you're ready to make the broth.

Add 1 or 2 (3") pieces of seaweed, like wakame or digitata, for extra minerals.

Vegetable broth option: To make a veggie broth, eliminate the meat and bones and use only vegetable scraps.

Making the Broth or Stock

Put all of the contents from the bag in your freezer into a stainless-steel stockpot. Alternatively, you can use your slow cooker to make this even easier!

Pour enough water so that it just covers the top of your bones, meat, and vegetables. Add ¼ cup apple cider vinegar. Let this sit for 60 minutes, to allow the apple cider vinegar to set in.

Add 2 tsp. sea salt and 10 black peppercorns. Add more if needed when the broth is finished and you taste it.

Turn your burner to high heat, put a lid on the pot, and bring the water to a boil (or set your slow cooker to high). As soon as it's boiling, turn the heat down to very low and allow the pot to simmer as follows (use the low setting on your slow cooker):

1 hour for vegetables only (veggie stock)

3 hours for meat stock

Up to 24 hours for bone broth

You may find that your water reduces a bit after many hours of simmering and bones are peeking out over the water. If this happens, you can add more water to cover the bones.

If you're using a slow cooker, always use the lid; if you're using a stockpot, use the lid once the water comes to a boil, but be sure to leave the lid slightly open so that air can escape. Some people like to leave the stockpot uncovered for the last hour of simmering.

When your broth has finished simmering, strain the liquid out of the pot with a fine mesh strainer, making sure to ladle the broth in jars or a large bowl.

You may now compost your vegetable scraps and save your bones for another use, if desired (see Chapter 2 for more on reusing bones). If you have any meaty bones and want to make pâté or add the meat to stews and soups, set them aside for future use.

Put the broth into the refrigerator. When it chills and you're ready to use it, remove the fat layer that will accumulate on the top (you can save this to use for cooking fat).

Start a new bag of bones and vegetable scraps in your freezer for your next batch of bone broth and repeat the steps. Your body will love you for continuing to nourish it in this manner!

Roasted marrowbones.

HEATHER'S EASY OXTAIL MEAT
STOCK *and* BONE BROTH
(Neutral)

This makes a neutral, gelatin-rich bone broth that is ideal for desserts or just about any recipe. It's very easy and uses bones that tend to be more available in grocery or health-food stores. Bone marrow and oxtail meat are two of our favorite treats that you can consume as a side benefit of making this broth.

☞ **Hands-on prep time:** 15 minutes ☜
Total prep time: 4–25 hours
Yield: 3–4 quarts

1 (7") marrowbone (split down the middle, if possible)—use several marrowbones totaling up to 7" if you have smaller pieces

3–4 lbs. oxtail bones—this is usually somewhere around 4–6 bones

1 split pig's foot (half a pig's foot)—you can use a whole one if the foot doesn't come split

¼ cup apple cider vinegar

Preheat oven to 350° F.

Put the marrowbones with the split middles facing up (if you have split marrowbones; otherwise, just put the smaller pieces or whole marrowbone in flat), oxtails, and pig's foot into a deep baking dish (to catch the melted fat).

Roast the marrowbones, oxtails, and pig's foot in the oven for about 30–40 minutes or until the oxtail meat is darker brown. If you like, turn the oxtail bones and pig's foot over at the 15-minute mark (*optional*).

Once the bones are roasted, remove the marrow from the marrowbones. It's a delicious delicacy with a sweet, light taste, full of rich, good fat; a little goes a long way. You can serve the marrow warm and sprinkled with sea salt for a meal or an appetizer, or save it by scooping it out and putting it into a jar or storage container. You can use this in our Chocolate Drop Cookie recipe, or just warm it up and enjoy (spread on the Herb Bread or Maya's Finnish Sourdough Rye Bread, yum!). We recommend you save it and find your favorite ways to enjoy this healthy fat.

Once the bones are roasted, add them to your chosen pot and add enough water to just cover the bones and meat. Then add the apple cider vinegar. You can use a slow cooker, a stockpot on your stove top, or a Dutch oven in your oven:

— **Slow cooker:** Set your slow cooker to low and simmer for 1½–3 hours if you're making meat stock, or for 24 hours if making bone broth. You don't have to let the bones sit in apple cider vinegar and water for an hour first because it will take time for the slow cooker to warm up.

— **Stove top:** Let the bones, water, and apple cider vinegar sit for an hour before turning on the burner. After an hour, put the burner on medium high, bring to a boil, and then reduce the heat to the lowest temperature to simmer. Simmer for as long as you like (up to 3 hours for stock, and up to 24 hours for richer broth).

— **Oven:** Add the apple cider vinegar and put the covered Dutch oven in your oven. Set the oven at the lowest temperature you have to choose from (or about 150°–200° F). Allow to simmer up to 3 hours for meat stock, and up to 24 hours for richer bone broth. Because it will take time for the oven to preheat, you don't have to wait an hour with the apple cider vinegar soaking into the bones before cooking.

You may find that your water reduces a bit after many hours of simmering and bones are peeking out over the water. If this happens, you can add more water to cover the bones.

If you're using a slow cooker, always use the lid; if you're using a stockpot, use the lid as well, but you may want to leave the lid slightly open so that air can escape. Some people like to leave the stockpot uncovered for the last hour of simmering.

No matter which cooking option you choose, if you're simmering your broth for 24 hours, you can still remove the oxtails and meat at the 1½-hour mark, or you can let them stay in the broth and simmer the whole 24 hours. This is up to you and based on whether you want the meat earlier for meals or pâté.

Once the stock or broth is finished simmering, allow it to cool down. Then get a large bowl and a fine mesh strainer to strain the broth. With a cup, jar, or ladle, pour broth through the strainer, saving the liquid in your large bowl and straining out the bones. Set the strainer with bones aside for a moment.

You can now ladle the liquid into your favorite-sized jars or ice-cube trays and store them in the refrigerator or freezer. Make sure your broth is cooled down to room temperature before putting it into the freezer, especially if it's in glass jars. You don't want them to break because of extreme temperature changes.

Now remove the bones, saving any you intend to use again for another stock or broth. Remove the meat from the oxtail bones and set it aside in a storage container to use as a meal or to make pâté (see Oxtail Pâté recipe in Chapter 10). You can also freeze the meat for later use in soups and stews.

Once your bones are at room temperature, put them in a bag or storage container and store them in your freezer if you're using them again. We like to label them with the type of bones and as "used," as well as how many times they've been used, so we can plan for future broths.

Heather Shares Three Ways to Enjoy Oxtail Meat

You have three options with the oxtail meat:

1. First is the way Louise and I did it in her kitchen, which was probably the tastiest. After roasting the oxtails and marrowbones, remove the fatty center of the marrowbone and enjoy it right then (it's optional to remove the marrow, but we think you'll find this delicacy delicious and full of brain-healthy fat) or put it in a separate container to save it for another recipe. Put the cleaned marrowbones and oxtail into your pot and simmer them for 1½ hours and take out the oxtail, removing the meat and saving the bones. You can stop simmering right there and use the broth as meat stock. The meat stock will be relatively clear and neutral in flavor. Alternatively, you can return the cleaned bones back into the broth and keep simmering for a total of 24 to 48 hours, for a rich bone broth with a darker, slightly golden brown color and neutral flavor.

2. Option two is the lazy option I use in my own kitchen. After roasting the bones and removing the cooked marrow from the marrowbone, I throw one large split marrowbone (about 7" long), one half of a split pig's foot, and about 6–7 oxtails into my slow cooker and simmer for 24 hours. The next day, I strain out the bones and oxtails, remove the oxtail meat after it cools and either enjoy the meat as meals over the next few days (sprinkled with a little sea salt) or I turn it into pâté, which is easy to digest and makes a great, easy appetizer for guests (see the Oxtail Pâté recipe to make this delicious dish).

3. As a third option, you can simply freeze the oxtail meat and use it as needed for future soups, stews, and snacks.

THE
LOCAL BUTCHER SHOP
BONE BROTH
(Neutral)

This recipe by **Aaron Rocchino,** owner of the Local Butcher Shop in Berkeley, California, makes a neutral, gelatin-rich bone broth that is ideal for desserts or just about any recipe.

☞ **Hands-on prep time:** 10 minutes ☜
Total prep time: Up to 48 hours
Yield: Approximately 4 quarts broth

4 lbs. raw beef bones

3 lbs. raw pork bones and skin (pork skin is incredibly rich in collagen and can be purchased from your local butcher; alternatively, you can use one split pig's foot)

½ cup apple cider vinegar

Add beef bones, pork bones, and skin into a large stockpot (or slow cooker).

Add water to cover the bones by about an inch or two.

Add apple cider vinegar.

Let the pot sit for about an hour or two so that the vinegar can start to extract minerals and nutrients from the bones.

Next bring the bones, water, and vinegar to a boil (your burner and slow cooker would be set to high). After it boils, reduce the heat to a very low simmer, and let it cook for 2 days straight (48 hours).

You may find that your water reduces a bit after many hours of simmering and bones are peeking out over the water. If this happens, you can add more water to cover the bones.

If you're using a slow cooker, always use the lid; if you're using a stockpot, use the lid as well, but you may want to leave the lid slightly open so that air can escape. Some people like to leave the stockpot uncovered for the last hour of simmering.

Once done, strain the liquid through a fine mesh strainer, catching the broth in a large bowl or your storage jars. Cool down the liquid (some butcher shops and chefs do an ice bath, while the home cook will often leave the broth to cool on the countertop).

Put the broth in your refrigerator to chill. Once completely cold, peel off the fat cap and discard (or you can use it to cook with later). If you leave the fat cap on, your broth will last about twice as long in the fridge. Without the fat cap seal, it will generally last about 3–4 days.

You could also freeze the broth, and it will last you a good 6 months.

KITCHEN SINK
BONE BROTH
(Neutral)

This recipe by **Brian Merkel,** head butcher at Belcampo Meat Co. in San Francisco, makes a neutral, gelatin-rich broth that is ideal for desserts and just about any recipe.

This is the broth made 24 hours a day at Belcampo Meat Co., a full-service, nose-to-tail butchery and restaurant featuring local, sustainable, organic, grass- and pasture-fed meats and poultry. Sometimes it's heavier on one type of bone than another, or sometimes they have a lot of meat trim with tendons that gets thrown in, creating a darker, more deeply flavored broth. Feel free to experiment with types of bones as well as degrees of roasting.

Hands-on prep time: 30 minutes
Total prep time: 25½–49½ hours
Yield: Approximately 4 quarts broth

- 1 whole pig's foot split in half (a pig's foot is typically sold split in two)

- 3 lbs. meaty beef bones cut into 1"–2" chunks (ask for tendon knucklebones and/or kneecaps)

- 2 lbs. meaty pork bones cut into 1"–2" chunks (neck bones work well, but any pork bones will do)

- 1 lb. meaty chicken bones (backs, wing tips, whole carcasses)

- 8 chicken feet (replace with chicken bones if you can't find them)

- *Optional:* Pork skin, if you can get some (it's best if you trim off the fat)

Preheat oven to 400° F.

Parboil: Put pig's foot in your stockpot covered with boiling water for 20 minutes to purify. Once boiled, drain and discard the water.

Place bones and pig's foot in a thin layer on a roasting tray. Roast in your oven for 45–60 minutes, until well browned but not burned.

Remove bones from the oven and place them in a slow cooker or large stockpot and just cover the bones with water. Set to a very gentle simmer—never boil! Simmer for at least 24 hours or as long as 48 hours; skim off the top occasionally.

You may find that your water reduces a bit after many hours of simmering and bones are peeking out over the water. If this happens, you can add more water to cover the bones.

If you're using a slow cooker, always use the lid; if you're using a stockpot, use the lid as well, but you may want to leave the lid slightly open so that air can escape. Some people like to leave the stockpot uncovered for the last hour of simmering.

Strain through a fine mesh strainer 1–3 times, until you have a nice amber liquid and there are no meaty bits floating around.

Chill overnight, then remove the fatty layer on top when you're ready to use the broth (you can save the fat for cooking later, if you like).

From left to right: chicken feet, chicken neck, marrowbones, oxtail, beef feet, and pig's foot.

BALANCED & BRIGHT
BEEF BONE BROTH
(Neutral)

This signature bone broth by **Quinn Wilson,** owner of Balanced & Bright Bone Broth, has taken the greater San Diego area by storm! Customers routinely line up to get cups, quarts, and even gallons of her healing broth.

☞ **Hands-on prep time:** 20 minutes ☜
Total prep time: 37½–48½ hours
Yield: 4–5 quarts

3 lbs. beef femur (thigh) and knucklebones (You can ask for cut thighbones so that they're smaller in size. Make sure they're small enough to fit in your slow cooker.)

1 (2"–3") piece of fresh ginger

2 star anise pods

1 Tbsp. apple cider vinegar

1 tsp. cardamom

Preheat oven to 425° F.

Place your bones on a greased baking sheet and put them into the oven, allowing them to bake until the bones become dark brown in color. Time will depend on your oven, since temperatures can vary, but this usually takes 35–40 minutes.

While the bones are baking, slice the ginger into thin strips or disks and place in your slow cooker. Next, add in the star anise.

When the bones are done browning, let them cool for 10–15 minutes. Once cooled, add them to your slow cooker, and add just enough water to cover them.

Add the apple cider vinegar and allow to sit for 15–20 minutes.

Add more water until the slow cooker is full; set it to low heat and allow to cook for 36–48 hours.

You may find that your water reduces a bit after many hours of simmering and bones are peeking out over the water. If this happens, you can add more water to cover the bones.

If you're using a slow cooker, always use the lid; if you're using a stockpot, use the lid as well, but you may want to leave the lid slightly open so that air can escape. Some people like to leave the stockpot uncovered for the last hour of simmering.

Add the cardamom during the last hour of cooking.

Turn off heat and allow the slow cooker to cool for 1 hour.

Remove the bones; carefully strain the broth into your storage containers. Allow to cool in the refrigerator overnight.

A thick to thin layer of fat will solidify on the top of the broth; this fat will act as a preservative for your broth in the refrigerator. When you're ready to use the broth, remove the fat from your container— using a butter knife, gently loosen the fat from the container's sides and pop out. (You can save this fat in a separate container and use as cooking fat in other recipes per instructions in Chapter 2.)

When you're ready to use your broth, place it in a pot on the stove and gently simmer until heated throughout.

Pour into your favorite mug and season in your favorite style.

FARMER LESLIE'S
BONE BROTH RECIPE
(Neutral or Flavored)

This recipe by **Leslie Pesic and Dave Heafner** of Da-Le Ranch Farm in Lake Elsinore, California, has two steps. Step 1 will give you neutral broth, and continuing to step 2 will give you flavored broth. And note that while this is a beef bone broth recipe, it also works for lamb, pork, and chicken as well.

☞ **Hands-on prep time:** 30–40 minutes ☜
Total prep time: 37–49 hours.
Yield: 4–5 quarts (8–10 pints) of very condensed broth

About 1 lb. of each of the following:

Marrowbone

Knucklebone

Neck bone

Thighbone (these are easier to work with if you request cut thighbones)

Feet bones (1 beef's foot)

Uncooked meat for additional flavoring, such as:

- meaty shank
- flanken ribs
- short ribs

1 cup Bragg apple cider vinegar

Optional ingredients (these come in during step 2): If you use the bones only, you will get a neutral broth. If you add the items below, you will have a very rich, flavored broth that is ideal for making fast, delicious soups and stews:

1 large onion, unpeeled (do not use sweet Vidalia-type onions)

2 large heads of garlic, unpeeled

5 stalks of celery

4 medium carrots

2 Tbsp. garlic powder

½ tsp. ground celery salt

2 dried bay leaves

Cooking tips from the farm:

Vegetable amounts are by preference. Adjust to fit your palate, and enjoy experimenting! If you have sensitivity to any of the ingredients, leave them out.

Since you're straining the vegetables out, you don't have to dice them; however, you can if you like.

Instructions for Step 1—Meaty Bone Broth Only:

Place bones and apple cider vinegar in stockpot. Add water until bones are just covered.

Set the burner to high until liquid boils. Watch it so that the liquid doesn't start to boil over (which happens in our kitchen sometimes!).

Reduce heat to lowest setting and simmer with the lid on. Allow to simmer, covered, for about 36 hours.

You may find that your water reduces a bit after many hours of simmering and bones are peeking out over the water. If this happens, you can add more water to cover the bones.

If you're using a slow cooker, always use the lid; if you're using a stockpot, use the lid as well, but you may want to leave the lid slightly open so that air can escape. Some people like to leave the stockpot uncovered for the last hour of simmering.

Stir occasionally, if desired. Skim the "bone scum" from the top of the water each time you stir.

After meat has completely pulled away from the meaty shank (about 6–8 hours), and bones have fallen out of the ribs, use a slotted spoon and remove meat. Nibble on the meat if you choose, or set aside for another purpose. You could use it in another dish, use it to garnish salads, feed it to the dogs . . . use your imagination.

After 36 hours, remove bones, and strain broth into a large stainless bowl or another stockpot. You should have about 4–5 quarts.

Allow to cool on counter. Then put in the refrigerator to gel overnight.

Optional: If you want to do a second session with the bones, you don't need to wash out your stockpot—just put the same bones back in, add water and apple cider vinegar, and it's ready to start over. You should add another beef foot to try to develop more gelatin in this batch.

Stop here if you want a less flavored broth that can be used in a wide variety of recipes.

Instructions for Step 2—Richly Flavorful Vegetable Bone Broth:

Go to this step for a nutrient-dense and flavor-concentrated broth that can make flavoring soups and stews really easy.

Remove broth from fridge, and remove the layer of fat. Reserve it for other uses of your choosing or discard (see Chapter 2 for more on using the fat).

Add broth to your stockpot and set the burner on high. Add unpeeled onions, garlic, celery, carrots, garlic powder, bay leaves, and celery salt.

Bring to a boil, and reduce heat. Cook covered overnight, or until vegetables are very mushy.

Remove from heat, allow to cool, and strain the liquid into mason jars. Store in the refrigerator or freezer. Discard the vegetables, unless you want to use them for another recipe—most of the flavor and nutritional value will be gone, but they're still a source of fiber.

SAVORY BEEF BROTH
WITH AROMATIC SPICES
(Flavored)

This recipe is by **Nick Brune,** executive chef at Local Habit in San Diego and owner of Eco Caters, a catering company dedicated to handcrafted, organic, sustainable foods made 100 percent from scratch. This is a flavored bone broth with aromatic spices that taste delicious and are great for heart health, digestion, skin health, and sleep!

Nick has traveled the world learning how different countries and cultures infuse their foods with delicious taste. Originally from Louisiana, when he came to California, he was inspired by the commitment to organic, fresh foods and a focus on improving agriculture. Nick came up with a new style of food to honor his love of Louisiana's mix of cultures and California's fresh focus—he calls it California Creole, and it's delicious! In his broths, like this one, you can taste the alchemy of culture, memory, and love of the land.

When you make and consume this broth, you may be reminded of the power food has to reunite and reconnect us. It can allow us to honor the blending of cultures, tastes, and ideals; it can bring our senses and our passions together. Broths made with love absolutely have the ability to uplift and inspire.

☞ **Hands-on prep time:** 30 minutes ☜
Total prep time: Up to 8 hours
Yield: 3–4 quarts bone broth

5 lbs. beef bones with meat (such as knuckle and oxtail)

¾ lb. whole shallots

1 whole garlic clove

8 allspice berries

2 whole cardamom pods

¼ cup whole coriander seeds

½ cup fish sauce

½ cup wheat-free tamari or coconut aminos (if you're sensitive to either of these, you can use ½ cup apple cider vinegar and 1 Tbsp. blackstrap molasses)

Preheat oven to 375° F and roast bones until nice and brown, about 45 minutes.

Place whole shallots and garlic with skin onto baking sheet and bake for 15 minutes at 375° F. Remove the garlic after 15 minute and set aside. Return the baking pan with shallots back into the oven and continue baking for another 10–15 minutes. Remove when shallots are soft.

Remove the skin from the garlic and shallots and discard or save for future broths. Place garlic and shallots in a large stockpot or slow cooker.

Toast allspice, cardamom, and coriander in a sauté pan on low—you'll begin to smell the aromas when they're done. Once lightly toasted, add them to the stockpot or slow cooker.

Add roasted bones and cover them with about 2" of water. Add fish sauce and either tamari, coconut aminos, or your apple cider vinegar/molasses mixture.

Bring to a low simmer on the stove top or set your slow cooker to low. Simmer for 4–6 hours while skimming every 20–30 minutes (you can also wait to skim until the end).

You may find that your water reduces a bit after many hours of simmering and bones are peeking out over the water. If this happens, you can add more water to cover the bones.

If you're using a slow cooker, always use the lid; if you're using a stockpot, use the lid as well, but you may want to leave the lid slightly open so that air can escape. Some people like to leave the stockpot uncovered for the last hour of simmering.

Remove from heat and let rest at room temp for 1 hour.

Strain through a fine mesh strainer lined with cheesecloth and refrigerate for up to 3 days. If you did not skim, you can remove the fat cap after your broth is chilled (you may still find a small fat cap even if you did skim). Freeze any excess broth for up to 2 months.

CHICKEN AND PORK
BONE BROTH
(Flavored)

This recipe by **Nick Brune,** executive chef at Local Habit in San Diego, is a savory flavored bone broth that makes an incredible base for soups, stews, and other meals. With a broth like this, you'll likely enjoy sipping it on its own with no adornments, or making an easy egg drop soup. Let your creativity take you where it may!

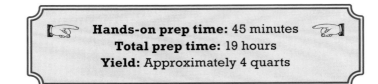

Hands-on prep time: 45 minutes
Total prep time: 19 hours
Yield: Approximately 4 quarts

5 lbs. pork bones

1–2 chicken backs (depending on the size of your pot)

1 large yellow onion

1 head garlic

6 allspice berries

1½ Tbsp. whole coriander seeds

2 bay leaves

¼ cup Bragg Liquid Aminos (or use apple cider vinegar for people sensitive to Liquid Aminos)

½ cup bonito flakes

Sea salt, to taste

Preheat oven to 400° F.

Put all pork bones and chicken backs in separate pans (with rims to contain melted fat) and roast until nice and caramelized (browned), about 30 minutes. The pork bones should take a little longer.

Remove bones from oven. Empty all fat that has built up in the pans and set aside for use for other cooking needs. Put the bones in a large stockpot (with lid) and add cold water until the bones are just covered. (You can make this recipe in your slow cooker on a low setting, if you like.)

Set your stove-top burner to medium high and heat until the broth comes to a low simmer. Turn heat down to low and cover the pot, leaving at least a 1" gap open for heat to escape, and simmer overnight for about 12 hours.

You may find that your water reduces a bit after many hours of simmering and bones are peeking out over the water. If this happens, you can add more water to cover the bones.

If you're using a slow cooker, always use the lid; if you're using a stockpot, use the lid as well, but you may want to leave the lid slightly open so that air can escape. Some people like to leave the stockpot uncovered for the last hour of simmering.

After 12 hours, you'll prepare the onions: Preheat oven to 350° F. Cut the onions in half and leave the skins on, then place them directly in a deep baking sheet. Cook for 30 minutes; remove onions from the oven, allow them to cool, and remove the skins.

While the onions are baking, you can put the coriander seeds into a skillet on low heat and toast them—when you begin to smell the aroma, they're done (about 2–3 minutes).

Peel the garlic and cut the cloves in half. Add the onions to your pot along with garlic, allspice, coriander, bay leaves, Bragg Liquid Aminos (or apple cider vinegar), and bonito flakes. Add more water, if needed, to just cover the bones.

Simmer for another 6 hours with all ingredients—remove the lid for this. After the 6 hours of simmering, taste the broth and season with sea salt.

Remove pot from the stove and let the broth cool for 1 hour.

Next strain the broth through a fine mesh strainer lined with cheesecloth, catching the broth in a large bowl. Cool to room temperature and refrigerate for up to 3 days, or freeze up to 2 months.

HEALING ELIXIR
VEGETABLE STOCK
(Vegan; Lightly Flavored)

This recipe by medical intuitive **Rhonda Lenair** does not contain gelatin because it's a vegetable broth. It can be used for sipping or any recipe that calls for stock.

We wanted to share this recipe with you because it's a beautiful option if you're not ready for bone broth or meat stock, or if you want to do a periodic health cleanse or gentle detox. This broth is extra gentle, and it also makes a nice "green drink" if you're not inclined to have powdered green drinks.

☞ **Hands-on prep time:** 20 minutes ☜
Total prep time: 1 hour and 20 minutes
Yield: 3–4 quarts

Use whatever combination of these vegetables you have on hand; you do not have to use all of them. You're aiming to fill ⅓–½ of the stockpot with vegetables.

Kale

Cauliflower

Something from the onion family: leek, shallots, or onion

Carrots

1–2 heads garlic (you can just rough-cut in half and even leave the skins on)

A beet or two (you don't even have to cut it, but if you want, cut in half once)

¼ cup fresh ginger (can be in large pieces)

Half a head of purple cabbage

Chopped red or Vidalia onion

3–6 cups finely chopped parsley and/or cilantro or fresh basil

Watercress (use this every third time you make the broth, because it's a diuretic and you may not want to put it in every time)

Dandelion greens

Shredded Swiss chard (this can restore electrolytes)

Optional: Chopped eggplant (this is a nightshade, so avoid using if it bothers you; it does have anticarcinogenic benefits, though, so can be helpful)

Optional: Kombu seaweed (about a 2" piece)

Use whatever amount of each vegetable you feel drawn to adding—there is no need to be exact! It doesn't matter how you cut the vegetables because this recipe is all about broth, and you'll be discarding the vegetables after simmering them.

In a 12-quart stockpot, add whatever vegetables you want to use and add enough water to cover them.

Bring water to a boil over high heat. Once it's boiling, lower the temperature to low or medium low, put the lid on the pot, and simmer for 1 hour.

After an hour, ladle the broth through a fine mesh strainer into a glass bowl or jars.

Discard the vegetables into your compost bin and save the broth. After an hour of simmering, all of the nutrients are in the broth, and what you have left is the fiber in the vegetables. Regardless, some people don't like to waste any ingredients and ask if they can consume the vegetables. You can certainly do this if you like, although they may not taste very good.

Serving suggestions:

Sip the broth as is for a morning or afternoon energizer.

Make a soup with the broth. To do this, just heat up the broth and add:

- Leafy greens (kale, collards, bok choy, Swiss chard, dandelion greens, a couple basil leaves, and so on)

- Your favorite spices (such as sea salt, pepper, thyme, rosemary, or turmeric). You can start with ⅛–¼ tsp. of the spices you like and then taste, checking to see if you want to add more.

- Ladle the soup into bowls, and put a little toasted sesame oil on top of each serving.

This Healing Elixir Vegetable Stock gets its nice color from purple cabbage.

LAMB
BROTH[1]
(Lightly Flavored)

This recipe by the **Price-Pottenger Nutrition Foundation** is a mild, lightly flavored broth, ideal for sipping or soups, sauces, and stews.

When it comes to nature's best sources of zinc and iron, nothing beats red meat. And when it comes to red meat, nothing beats lamb for both flavor and nutritional value. Lamb is rich in easily absorbed minerals and B vitamins, particularly B_6 and B_{12}. It's also nature's best source of carnitine, an amino acid that the body uses to transfer fatty acids across the membranes of the mitochondria where they can be used as a source of fuel to generate energy, and an especially important nutrient for the heart. Always eat lamb as a whole food—that is, with the fat that accompanies it. Lamb fat is stable and nutritious; it is a good source of palmitoleic acid, a 16-carbon monounsaturated fatty acid that has strong antimicrobial properties.

Look for lamb labeled organic, or that comes from New Zealand (where it grazes on rich, green pasturage) or Iceland (where the animals eat mineral-rich mosses and lichens). Tender cuts should be eaten raw, rare, or medium-rare; tougher cuts can be braised in broth to make stews. Lamb riblets are a lesser-known cut of meat worth seeking out for their rich flavor.

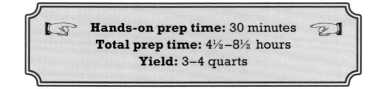

☞ **Hands-on prep time:** 30 minutes ☜
Total prep time: 4½–8½ hours
Yield: 3–4 quarts

About 2 lbs. of lamb riblets

2 Tbsp. vinegar or lemon juice

1 onion, chopped coarsely

Several sprigs fresh thyme, tied together

1 tsp. dried green peppercorns

Preheat oven to 350° F.

Place lamb riblets in a stainless-steel baking pan and bake until they are nicely browned, between 20–30 minutes.

Transfer to a pot and cover with water, so it is just covering the meat. Add some hot water to the baking pan and stir to deglaze the drippings. This is a great source of flavor.

Add the drippings to the pot and bring to a rolling boil. Skim any scum (fat) that rises to the surface.

Add remaining ingredients and reduce heat to a simmer; cover and cook gently for 4–8 hours.

You may find that your water reduces a bit after many hours of simmering and bones are peeking out over the water. If this happens, you can add more water to cover the bones.

If you're using a slow cooker, always use the lid; if you're using a stockpot, use the lid as well, but you may want to leave the lid slightly open so that air can escape. Some people like to leave the stockpot uncovered for the last hour of simmering.

Strain broth through a strainer, catching the broth in a bowl or ladling it into jars, and allow to cool. Some people love to save the meat for salads or stews, while the broth can be used in soups, sauces, and stews.

cu

BEEF OR LAMB
STOCK ᴼᴿ BROTH
(Lightly Flavored)

This recipe by **Kim Schuette,** CN, Certified GAPS Practitioner, makes a lovely broth with some added flavor and nutrients from the herbs, spices, and vegetables. If you want to make a broth that's ideal for adding nutrition and flavor to soups, stews, and other recipes, a flavored one like this would make an excellent choice!

> ☞ **Hands-on prep time:** 45 minutes ☜
> **Total prep time:** 3½–48½ hours
> **Yield:** Approximately 3–4 quarts

4–5 lbs. of marrowbones and knucklebones

3 lbs. of meaty ribs or neck bones

1 calf's foot or beef foot, if available, cut into pieces (*optional*)

2 tsp. Celtic sea salt

½ cup raw apple cider vinegar

Assortment of vegetables, as desired (avoid adding starchy vegetables, like parsnips, winter squash, potatoes, sweet potatoes, and yams):

- 1–2 medium yellow onions

- 2–4 carrots

1 tsp. black pepper

Bouquet garni (this is a bundle of fresh herbs tied together using cooking twine):

- 2 fresh bay leaves

- 3 sprigs each of fresh thyme, rosemary, and sage

- If you don't have fresh herbs, you can alternatively use dried herbs tied up in cheesecloth, making a kind of "tea bag" of herbs. To do this, use 1 bay leaf and 1–2 tsp. of each dried herb.

3 sprigs of fresh parsley (or 1 Tbsp. dried)

Optional ingredients for variety:

Garlic

Ginger

Lemon rind

2–3 sliced celery stalks (for those not following the Gut and Psychology Syndrome introduction diet)

Instructions for stock:

Optional step for more flavor: If you want more flavor in your broth, you may roast the meaty bones in a roasting pan. Set your oven to 350° F and bake until the meat is well browned.

Place the bones, meat, and joints into a large stock-pot or slow cooker.

Add remaining ingredients. Fill pot with water until it just covers the bones and vegetables.

Allow pot and its contents to stand for 60 minutes, giving the raw apple cider vinegar time to draw minerals out of the bones. After 60 minutes, bring the water to a boil (you can do this in your slow cooker by setting it to high at first).

Once the water starts to boil, reduce the heat to a simmer and cook for 3–4 hours (if you're making broth instead of stock, skip the next 3 steps and go to the instructions for making broth).

Add parsley during the last 10 minutes of cooking.

Using a fine mesh strainer, strain the stock into jars for storage.

Debone and reserve the meat for eating. It will be delicious and tender.

Instructions for broth:

After simmering the stock for 3–4 hours, remove the meaty bones with a large fork or tongs and debone the meat, reserving it for another meal. Return the bones to the pot, add additional water to cover the bones (if needed), and continue to simmer for 36–48 hours.

You may find that your water reduces a bit after many hours of simmering and bones are peeking out over the water. If this happens, you can add more water to cover the bones.

If you're using a slow cooker, always use the lid; if you're using a stockpot, use the lid as well, but you may want to leave the lid slightly open so that air can escape. Some people like to leave the stockpot uncovered for the last hour of simmering.

Add the parsley during the last 10 minutes of simmering.

CHICKEN, PHEASANT, OR TURKEY
STOCK ᴏʀ BROTH
(Flavored)

This recipe by **Kim Schuette,** CN, Certified GAPS Practitioner, is delicious and provides some added flavor and nutrients from the herbs, spices, and vegetables. If you want to make a broth that's ideal for adding nutrition and flavor to your poultry soups, stews, and other recipes, a flavored broth like this would be an excellent choice!

☞ **Hands-on prep time:** 30 minutes ☜
Total prep time: 3½–25½ hours
Yield: 3–4 quarts

1 whole chicken, pheasant, or turkey

2–4 chicken, pheasant, or turkey feet
(*optional*)

1–2 chicken, pheasant, or turkey heads
(*optional*)

2 Tbsp. raw apple cider vinegar

Assortment of vegetables, as desired (avoid adding starchy vegetables, like parsnips, winter squash, potatoes, sweet potatoes, and yams):

- 1–2 medium yellow onions

- 2–4 carrots

Bouquet garni (this is a bundle of fresh herbs tied together using cooking twine):

- 2 fresh bay leaves

- 3 sprigs each of fresh thyme, rosemary, and sage

- If you don't have fresh herbs, you can alternatively use dried herbs tied up in cheesecloth, making a kind of "tea bag" of herbs. To do this, use 1 bay leaf and 1–2 tsp. of each dried herb.

3 sprigs fresh parsley (or 1 Tbsp. dried)

2–3 celery stalks, sliced (if you are not following the Gut and Psychology Syndrome introduction diet)

1–2 tsp. sea salt

Instructions for stock:

Rinse poultry, feet, and heads in water. Cut whole bird in half down the middle lengthwise. Place the parts in the pot.

Add remaining ingredients, except the parsley and sea salt. Fill pot with water (you can use a stockpot or slow cooker).

Allow the pot and its contents to stand for 60 minutes, giving the raw apple cider vinegar time to draw minerals out of the bones. After 60 minutes, bring the water to a boil, then reduce the heat to a simmer and cook for 1½–2 hours (if using a slow cooker, set your slow cooker to high to bring to a boil and then reduce heat to low for simmering).

Add parsley and sea salt during the last 10 minutes of cooking.

Remove the chicken and other large parts. Debone and reserve the meat for eating—it will be delicious and tender.

Strain the stock through a small-holed colander or fine mesh strainer. Catch the broth in a large bowl or ladle it into jars.

Instructions for bone broth:

After simmering the stock for 3–4 hours, remove the meaty bones with a large fork or tongs and debone the meat, reserving it for another meal. Return the bones to the pot, add additional water to cover the bones (if needed), and continue to simmer for 36–48 hours.

You may find that your water reduces a bit after many hours of simmering and bones are peeking out over the water. If this happens, you can add more water to cover the bones.

If you're using a slow cooker, always use the lid; if you're using a stockpot, use the lid as well, but you may want to leave the lid slightly open so that air can escape. Some people like to leave the stockpot uncovered for the last hour of simmering.

Add the parsley and sea salt during the last 10 minutes of simmering.

FISH STOCK
or BROTH
(Flavored)

This recipe from **Kim Schuette,** CN, Certified GAPS Practitioner, may seem unusual. However, Kim is a wonderful cook and nutrition expert, and this broth is absolutely delicious!

Louise: The first time I made fish bone broth, I must admit that it seemed daunting. The first thing I did was go to the fish market and ask for bones. I had no idea what to expect, but I certainly didn't expect to be greeted with a three-foot-long fish skeleton! I thought to myself, *Louise, what have you done?* then grabbed the package and ran off, without giving myself a chance to change my mind.

When I got home, I opened the wrapping and stood looking at this long fish bone. It would never fit into my stockpot. *So now what?* I wondered. I went to my closet, found a hammer, and put the fish in the sink. A couple good whacks and the bone had broken down enough to fit in the pot. *Now that wasn't too bad!* I thought.

Four hours later, I had the best thick, gelatinous fish broth one could imagine! I was so proud of myself for doing something new, especially something that scared me at first. If you've never made fish broth or stock, join me in this affirmation: *Life loves me, and I am always willing to learn new things.* It works for me, and I know it will work for you, too!

> **Hands-on prep time:** 30 minutes
> **Total prep time:** 2–4½ hours
> **Yield:** 3–4 quarts of stock or broth

2 medium, whole, non-oily fish, such as sole or snapper (alternatively, you can use just the fish bones or a cleaned fish carcass, or for added nutrition, include some fish heads)

2 Tbsp. raw apple cider vinegar

Assortment of vegetables, as desired (avoid adding starchy vegetables, like parsnips, winter squash, potatoes, sweet potatoes, and yams):

- 1–2 medium yellow onions
- 2–4 carrots

Bouquet garni (this is a bundle of fresh herbs tied together using cooking twine):

- 2 fresh bay leaves
- 3 sprigs each of fresh thyme, rosemary, and sage

- If you don't have fresh herbs, you can alternatively use dried herbs tied up in cheesecloth, making a kind of "tea bag" of herbs. To do this, use 1 bay leaf and 1–2 tsp. of each dried herb.

3 sprigs of fresh parsley or 1 Tbsp. dried

1–2 tsp. Celtic sea salt

Optional ingredients for variety:

Garlic

Ginger

Lemon rind

2–3 sliced celery stalks (for those not following the Gut and Psychology Syndrome introduction diet)

Instructions for fish stock:

Rinse the fish in water. If using a whole fish, remove meat from the bones and reserve for making a separate meal (such as the Pan-Seared Snapper or Halibut recipe in Chapter 7).

Place bones—and, if you're using them, the fins, tails, skin, and heads—in the pot.

Add remaining ingredients. Fill pot with water (up to 4 quarts) so that it just covers the fish.

Allow the pot and its contents to stand for 60 minutes, giving the raw apple cider vinegar time to draw minerals out of the bones.

Turn your burner to high and bring the water to a boil. Once the water boils, reduce the heat to a simmer and cook for 1–1½ hours.

Add parsley and salt during the last 10 minutes of cooking.

When the stock is cooked, remove the fish bones and other large parts.

Strain the stock through a colander, capturing the stock in a large bowl.

Instructions for fish broth:

To make fish bone broth, follow the above recipe, but simmer the broth for 4 hours.

You may find that your water reduces a bit after many hours of simmering and bones are peeking out over the water. If this happens, you can add more water to cover the bones.

If you're using a slow cooker, always use the lid; if you're using a stockpot, use the lid as well, but you may want to leave the lid slightly open so that air can escape. Some people like to leave the stockpot uncovered for the last hour of simmering.

DASHI FISH
STOCK
(Flavored)

Robert Ruiz, chef and owner of the Land & Water Co. restaurant in Carlsbad, California, contributed this recipe because, while it's not technically a bone broth, it is a fish stock that's super easy to make. He learned to make dashi broth in Hawaii and said that the Hawaiians believed it could cure cancer. The fish is a skipjack tuna that has been dried, fermented, and smoked. And kombu seaweed is full of flavor and iodine, for thyroid health.

> **Hands-on prep time:** 15 minutes
> **Total prep time:** 2 hours
> **Yield:** 3–4 quarts of stock or broth

1 sheet of kombu seaweed

2 cups katsuobushi or bonito flakes

Fill your stockpot with 6 cups water and add the sheet of kombu. Let it sit for 30 minutes.

After 30 minutes, set your burner to medium and bring the water to a simmer. Just before the water starts to boil, remove the kombu and turn the heat to high until the water boils. *Note:* If you leave the kombu in the broth, it could get slimy or create a bitter taste, which is why it's removed after the nutrients have soaked into the water. You can discard the kombu in your compost bin. Some people like to save and eat this tough sea vegetable by cutting it up thin or pureeing it, then adding to thick soups or stews.

Let the water boil for about 5 minutes. Add the katsuobushi or bonito flakes and immediately turn off the heat, allowing the pot to sit for 30 minutes.

After 30 minutes, strain the stock through a colander, capturing the stock in a large bowl or ladling into jars.

Use as the basis of soups, sauces, and stir-fry dishes.

⌐ CHAPTER 5 ⌐

THE MAGIC:
Medicinal Finishers and Healing Elixirs

In this chapter, we offer a variety of delicious remedies for your health goals. We'll start with a wide range of medicinal finishers, and then move on to some wonderful healing elixir recipes.

MEDICINAL FINISHERS—FLAVOR BOMBS FOR YOUR BONE BROTH!

As mentioned earlier in the book, *finishers* or *add-ins* are terms that some chefs and butcher shops use to describe the ingredients added to plain bone broth to give it flavor and pizzazz. This is not about making soup by adding vegetables or meats; it's just about flavoring the broth with herbs, spices, or natural condiments.

If you think of a coffee shop, once you get your cup of Joe, you walk over to the milk, cream, and sugar station. They may also have cinnamon or other fun additives so that you can customize your coffee flavor even more. Similarly, at establishments serving bone broth to go, you might have the option of adding finishers to flavor your broth. Typical offerings are sea salt, herbs, spices, and fish sauce (a condiment made of fermented anchovies and sea salt, which is often used in Thai and Vietnamese cooking).

We'd like to elevate the whole idea of finishers by giving you options that are both delicious and have great health benefits. We invite you to come up with finishers of your own as well—you can refer to the "How to Work with Herbs and Spices" section in the Appendix to tailor your finishers for your taste buds and your health goals. Have fun with them!

Tips

— Neutral broths make the best blank canvas for finishers. If your broth has flavor, taste it first, before adding any extras. You may not need anything at all, or perhaps only some sea salt and black pepper.

— Grinding dried herbs and spices before using them boosts the flavor and aroma.

— We offer mostly dried herb and spice options here for convenience because they keep for long periods of time and require fewer trips to the grocery store. You may want to experiment with fresh herbs and spices as well.

— If you have limited time to get out the door each morning, premix your favorite spice combination for fast and easy shaking into your broth. You could also consider bringing a small shaker of your favorite spice mix with you so that you can add it on the fly at work.

— An insulated Kleen Kanteen makes sipping on the go really easy.

— When experimenting with new finishers of your own, add ⅛ tsp. of each herb or spice one at a time and taste. From there, you can decide if you want more of the spices, adding just a bit more at a time until you have the blend you like. Smell the spices to see what you think will go together.

Chai Drink and
Energizing Chai Hot Chocolate.

FINISHER
RECIPES

You can use any bone broth or meat stock, or our Healing Elixir Vegetable Stock, for these recipes. Remember that the neutral broths will be most flexible, while flavored broths may need some adjustments.

The spices in these recipes were carefully selected with the guidance of Eyton Shalom, M.S., L.Ac., who collaborated with us on the Chinese-medicine and Ayurvedic aspects of each finisher. We also consulted our favorite spice resource book, *Healing Spices: How to Use 50 Everyday and Exotic Spices to Boost Health and Beat Disease*, by Bharat B. Aggarwal, Ph.D., with Debora Yost.

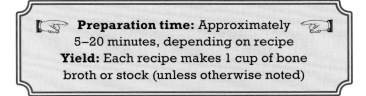

Preparation time: Approximately 5–20 minutes, depending on recipe
Yield: Each recipe makes 1 cup of bone broth or stock (unless otherwise noted)

Heat up 1 cup of bone broth (unless otherwise noted) in a saucepan on low heat. If you want to make more than 1 cup at a time, adjust the spice amounts accordingly.

Add your herbs and spices or other ingredients, and simmer for 3–5 minutes.

Sip or pour into a thermos to take on the go.

You can shake spices in after simmering as well.

Some of the recipes that follow have custom instructions, which will be noted.

For All-Day Energy

— **Option #1, Energizing Chai Hot Chocolate or Latte:** 2 cups bone broth, 2–3 Tbsp. raw cacao, 1 Tbsp. maca powder, 2 Tbsp. butter, 2–3 tsp. honey, 1½ tsp. ground cinnamon, ¼ tsp. ground cardamom. *Optional:* ½ tsp. vanilla extract (for a richer taste).

Mix the ingredients as they're being warmed in a saucepan on the stove top, then blend up well in your blender. (Using a blender is optional, but better. *Safety tip:* Remove the center cap and cover the opening with a folded tea towel before turning on your blender. This will allow air to escape so that the hot liquid doesn't cause the top to blow off your blender.) Add some almond milk or rice milk if you like a chai-latte taste.

— **Option #2:** 1 tsp. pomegranate molasses and ¼ tsp. ginger.

Amazon.com carries a 100 percent natural pomegranate molasses by Al Wadi. You can also make your own with 4 cups pomegranate juice, ½ cup honey, and 1 Tbsp. lemon juice, cooking on low until it reduces to a syrupy consistency. This may take up to an hour with some occasional mixing while cooking.

— **Option #3, Saffron Tea:** Heat your bone broth on medium heat, bringing it to a simmer. Add 5 strands saffron and reduce the heat to low, heating for 15 minutes with the lid on. Remove the lid after 15 minutes and allow tea to cool down for a few minutes before straining and drinking.

— **Option #4, Rocket Stock:** see recipe in this chapter.

To Ease Acid Reflux

— **Option #1:** 20 caraway seeds steeped in bone broth for 3–5 minutes (you can chew the seeds or strain them out and just drink the broth).

— **Option #2:** See the Fermented Turmeric Finisher in this chapter.

To Combat Allergies or High Histamine (Including Nighttime Itching or Skin Issues)

— Add ½ tsp. ground cardamom and ½ tsp. ground fenugreek to meat stock or the Healing Elixir Vegetable Stock.

For Anti-Stress, Anti-Anxiety, Cholesterol Regulation, and Heart Health

— **Option #1:** ½ tsp. oregano, ½ tsp. basil, ¼ tsp. sea salt, and ¼ tsp. black pepper.

— **Option #2:** ¼ tsp. lemongrass, ½ tsp. cardamom, ¼ tsp. ginger, and ⅛ tsp. fenugreek.

— **Option #3, Bone Broth Hot Chocolate:** 1½ cups neutral bone broth, 2–3 Tbsp. raw cacao, 1½ Tbsp. coconut oil, 2–3 tsp. honey, 1 tsp. cinnamon, and ¼ tsp. cardamom.

This is even better if you put everything in a blender and blend up for a few minutes. (*Safety tip:* Remove the center cap and cover the opening with a folded tea towel before turning on your blender. This will allow air to escape so that the hot liquid doesn't cause the top to blow off your blender.) Add some almond milk or rice milk if you want a creamier flavor.

— Option #4, Saffron Tea: Heat your bone broth on medium heat, bringing it to a simmer. Add 5 strands saffron and reduce the heat to low, heating for 15 minutes with the lid on. Remove the lid after 15 minutes and allow tea to cool down for a few minutes before drinking.

To Enhance Digestion, Balance Blood Sugar, and Promote Weight Loss

— Option #1: ½ tsp. cinnamon, ⅛ tsp. ground dulse (seaweed), ⅛ tsp. ground fennel, ⅛ tsp. ground fenugreek, ⅛ tsp. ground cardamom.

— Option #2: 4 drops Scrappy's Cardamom Bitters (available at Amazon.com) or ¼ tsp. ground cardamom.

— Option #3: 1 Tbsp. coconut oil, 1 tsp. raw honey, 1 tsp. ground cinnamon, ¼ tsp. allspice, ⅛ tsp. ground juniper berry, ⅛ tsp. cloves, dash sea salt.
Blend everything in a blender, if possible. (*Safety tip*: Remove the center cap and cover the opening with a folded tea towel before turning on your blender. This will allow air to escape so that the hot liquid doesn't cause the top to blow off your blender.)

— Option #4: ⅛ tsp. fennel, ⅛ tsp. fenugreek, ¼ tsp. allspice, ⅛ tsp. black pepper, pinch sea salt.

— Option #5: 1 ginger tea bag steeped in bone broth.

— Option #6: 4 drops Swedish bitters or Urban Moonshine Citrus Bitters.

— Option #7: 1 tsp. ground goji berry, ⅛ tsp. fennel, ⅛ tsp. ground five spice, dash ground white pepper, dash black pepper, 1–2 drops fish sauce, ⅛ tsp. ground ginger.

— Option #8, Chai Drink: 1 cup coconut milk, 1 tsp. ground cinnamon, ½ tsp. ground cardamom, ¼ tsp. ground ginger, ⅛ tsp. ground clove. *Optional*: ¼ tsp. dried orange peel or 1 drop Urban Moonshine Citrus Bitters.
Blend up in your blender, then simmer in a saucepan on low heat for a few minutes. Pour into a thermos and allow to steep until you are ready to drink.

For Cleansing, Anti-Inflammatory, and Detoxifying

— Option #1: 1 tsp. sea salt, 1 tsp. black or white pepper, and 1 tsp. turmeric.

— Option #2: ¼ tsp. garlic powder, 1 tsp. sea salt, 1 tsp. black pepper, and ½ tsp. paprika.

— Option #3: See Fermented Turmeric Finisher in this chapter.

Medicinal finishers.

To Alleviate Gas and Bloating or Irritable Bowel Syndrome

Note that these can be good for trapped gas in conditions like small intestine bacterial overgrowth or candida:

— **Option #1:** 1 tsp. coriander seeds (dry roast by heating on low in saucepan until you can smell it, then add the bone broth and the rest of the ingredients), a dash of hing (asafoetida), ⅛ tsp. tamarind paste, ⅛ tsp. turmeric, and ⅛ tsp. ground ginger.

— **Option #2:** 20 fennel seeds, crushed just a bit with mortar and pestle or spice grinder (or you can use the back of a spoon on a cutting board to break the seeds a bit), steeped in bone broth for 10 minutes (can strain out seeds or just chew them while sipping broth). You can heat your bone broth on low, adding these seeds in; cover the pan for 5 minutes, then remove from the heat and leave covered for another 5 minutes (or you could put it in your thermos and let it steep there).

To Boost Mood and Memory

— **Option #1:** 2 tsp. thyme, 1 tsp. rosemary, 1 tsp. sea salt, and 1 tsp. black pepper.

— **Option #2:** 8 strands saffron, ⅛ tsp. cinnamon, ⅛ tsp. ground ginger (or 2 thick slices fresh ginger), ⅛ tsp. nutmeg, ⅛ tsp. black pepper, and ½ tsp. honey. Combine bone broth and all ingredients and heat on low for 15 minutes, covered. Uncover and allow to cool for a few minutes.

Invent Your Own

Here are some options that Brian Merkel offers at Belcampo Meat Co. in San Francisco:

— Basic seasonings such as sea salt or fish sauce.

— Premixed finishers:

- Calabrian chili peppers (these come packed in oil, so remove the stems and strain the oil, then blend the chili peppers into a paste with fresh rosemary and lemon juice). Brian tells us that this gives the bone broth a hot kick with a depth of flavor that is very popular with Belcampo customers.

- Cilantro, garlic, ginger, and lemon juice.

Finishers are fun and delicious! They're a great way to get creative and follow your intuition. The following pages introduce more medicinal finishers and healing elixirs and offer some guidelines to start making your own!

FERMENTED
TURMERIC
Finisher

This recipe by **Brian Merkel,** head butcher at Belcampo Meat Co. in San Francisco, is an excellent medicinal finisher for bone broth. It's also a great addition for soups, stews, sauces, and aspic recipes. It blends well with coconut milk and makes a great marinade for pork or chicken.

Turmeric is a root that has so many healing benefits it's almost considered a panacea. In his book, *Healing Spices*, biochemist and author Bharat B. Aggarwal calls turmeric the "leading crusader against disease" because it has been found to protect and improve every organ in the body.[1] If you want an anti-inflammatory, cancer-preventive spice that can also aid digestion, regulate cholesterol, boost moods, support skin health, and soothe the liver and gallbladder, turmeric may be your best bet.[2]

☞ **Hands-on prep time:** 25 minutes ☜
Total prep time: 2 weeks to ferment
Yield: 2 cups of turmeric paste

2 quarts water

6 Tbsp. sea salt

2 cups fresh organic turmeric, peeled and sliced into ½" pieces

1 cup fresh organic ginger, peeled and sliced into ½" pieces

¼ cup raw honey

2 tsp. black pepper

2 Tbsp. fresh lemon juice

Make the brine: combine water and salt into a saucepan. With your burner on low, warm the brine just enough to easily dissolve salt.

Divide the roots evenly into 2 quart-sized mason jars (each will have 1 cup turmeric and ½ cup ginger). Fill each jar with brine, leaving a couple inches free at the top.

Cover each container with cheesecloth or a clean towel and fasten with a rubber band or string. Place in cool, dark place (60°–70° F is ideal) for 2 weeks.

After 2 weeks, remove the roots, saving the brine. Blend the ginger and turmeric in a food processor or blender until you have a paste. Add a small amount of brine, enough to maintain a liquid consistency. You can save the remaining brine for future fermentation.

Now add the honey, pepper, and lemon juice; blend until smooth.

Serving suggestions:

Add turmeric sauce to your favorite broth as a finisher. Try 1–2 tsp. mixed into your cup of bone broth.

Add to soups, stews, or aspics for extra flavor and nutrition.

Medicinal finishers.

ROCKET
STOCK

This is the bone broth version of "Bulletproof Coffee," a product created by Dave Asprey that has taken the Paleo and health world by storm. Bulletproof coffee starts with a mold-free, high-quality coffee bean; once the coffee is brewed, it's blended up with butter and MCT (medium chain triglyceride) oil, sort of like a hacked café au lait.

Dave Asprey based his tweaked coffee recipe on a tea with yak butter that he tasted in Nepal, and we've heard that loggers in Vermont have been drinking coffee with butter for decades. So while it's not a new idea, Asprey has breathed new life into a forgotten tradition that is now fueling people's enthusiasm for caffeine tempered with healthy fats.

Our friend and nutrition expert **Caroline Barringer,** NTP, CHFS, created what we think is an improved version of Bulletproof Coffee with this recipe. After watching people drink takeaway coffee cups of bone broth from kiosks in New York City, Caroline thought, *Why not add some healthy fats and bump up the energy even more?*

Incidentally, the MCT oil you hear a lot about from Bulletproof Coffee enthusiasts is a refined derivative of coconut oil. This means it's been processed and thus removed from its whole-food form. Since refined fats can lose beneficial properties and cause challenges for the liver, we recommend using coconut oil instead, which is what Caroline has called for here.

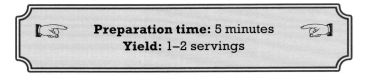

☞ **Preparation time:** 5 minutes ☜
Yield: 1–2 servings

1–2 cups bone broth of choice

Sea salt, to taste

1 Tbsp. butter or ghee

1 Tbsp. coconut oil

Combine warmed broth, sea salt, butter, and coconut oil in a blender. (Remove the center piece in the top of the blender and cover the hole with a folded tea towel—this will allow air to escape, so the hot broth doesn't blow the lid off your blender.)

Blend on high for 1–2 minutes. The mixture should be slightly frothy and emulsified.

Pour into your favorite mug and enjoy!

Variation: For added nourishment, you can also whisk in a tablespoon or two of gelatin or collagen peptides (Vital Proteins has both products) after blending your Rocket Stock.

HEALING ELIXIRS

Eyton Shalom, M.S., L.Ac., says that in Chinese medicine, broth has a warm and light quality and is easy to digest. That's because in making it, you take the essence of hard-to-digest ingredients like bones and meat, and turn them into liquid form, where they can be easily digested and assimilated. Broth is very healing.

Bones also contain *jing*, which in Chinese medicine is the deepest level of energy in the body. Chinese medicine focuses on "nourishing life," which is essentially about preserving jing rather than wasting it. In the world of food, the way you can promote life is by respecting the general laws of digestion. It's a warm process of transforming material into energy. With bone broth, cooking has already done this work for you.

When customizing your elixirs, here are some guidelines for choosing broth for the time of year or health condition you may be experiencing:

— **Chicken broth:** Chicken is easy to digest and supports energy. The energy you get from it is a lifting energy (think chickens jumping on the roof of a henhouse). It's great for any time of year, including summer. Chicken broth is an ideal healing remedy for colds, but not such a good option if you have eczema because it can bring things to the surface.

— **Beef, pork, lamb, and goat broth:** In Chinese medicine, these are thought to nourish life. They are ideal in late autumn or early winter. We often eat heavier foods in the winter to store up energy, as our digestive fire is stronger to support this process. Think about nourishing your body and the adrenals, or building and storing up energy (jing) during the winter season so that you're ready for spring.

Beef can make an ideal remedy any time of year because it's considered neutral. Beef broth, in particular, can be great for congenital weakness, infertility, low libido, menopause and andropause (male menopause), and pregnancy.

HEALING
CHICKEN
Soup

This recipe from **Eyton Shalom,** M.S., L.Ac., is a medicinal, healing elixir that makes its own chicken bone broth. We know from experience and scientific studies that chicken soup is very healing. When Eyton was recovering from walking pneumonia and swollen lymph nodes while in acupuncture school, for instance, this is the recipe that helped him heal.

From a Chinese-medicine perspective, Eyton says that any condition with swelling, mucus, and phlegm may find this soup extra healing. It's also helpful for people with a "heat illness," which in Chinese medicine could include symptoms like fever, chronic infective sinusitis, headaches, chronic skin outbreaks, sweating, or anxiety.

The seaweeds kombu and wakame are great because they're decongesting, but they're best left out of the recipe if you find that you're cold all the time or experiencing weak digestion, diarrhea, or chronic fatigue.

The healing herbs are wonderful; in fact, if you already have chicken bone broth and just want to have some healing broth, you can simmer the herbs and spices in your broth for 10–20 minutes, then sip. (You can learn more about the healing benefits of Chinese herbs in the "How to Work with Herbs and Spices" section of the Appendix. We also show you where to get them in the Resources section.)

☞ **Hands-on prep time:** 30 minutes ☜
Total prep time: 6½ hours
Yield: 8–10 servings

Whole chicken or chicken parts (bone-in legs, thighs, breast with skin on)

6 slices fresh astragalus root (or 1 Tbsp. dried ground astragalus)

7 codonopsis roots (about 1 Tbsp. ground coconopsis)

1 Tbsp. dried, ground dioscorea

¼ tsp. ground schizandra berries

2 Tbsp. whole goji berries, ground in a spice grinder

2 tsp. dried ground ophiopogon

1 (2") piece of kombu (see earlier note about when not to use this seaweed)

¼ cup dried wakame (see earlier note about when not to use this seaweed)

1 Tbsp. dried lily bulbs (or 2 fresh lily bulbs, rinsed, cleaned, and petals removed); avoid this ingredient if you have diarrhea

10 whole coriander seeds or 2 tsp. ground coriander

1 fresh pear, chopped into small pieces (this helps nourish the lungs)

2 tsp. sea salt

Black pepper, to taste

Optional: rice or quinoa

If using a whole chicken, cut it into parts. Rinse the chicken and pat it dry.

Put chicken parts in a large stockpot or slow cooker. Add enough water to just cover the chicken.

Setting your burner to high, bring the liquid to a boil, then reduce to a slow simmer. Simmer for 4–6 hours. If you're using a slow cooker, set it to high to bring to a boil, and then reduce the heat to low for 4–6 hours. Your chicken will be moist and tender.

Add all other ingredients, except the coriander and fresh pear. If you're using dried lily bulbs, wait until the last 45 minutes of cooking to add them in.

Add coriander and fresh pear in the last 45 minutes of cooking (this is when you'd also add dried lily bulbs, if using them instead of fresh).

Optional: If you want, you can add a cup of uncooked rice or quinoa (we recommend soaking it first; see instructions at the beginning of Chapter 9) in the last hour of cooking and just keep adding water, if needed. The grains will soak up the liquid and make a porridge-like consistency.

Add sea salt and pepper.

Serving suggestions:

Enjoy as is. Or drink the liquid only and save the chicken for another meal, if you just want the healing broth.

DONG QUAI
CHICKEN
Soup

This recipe from **Eyton Shalom,** M.S., L.Ac., is a medicinal, healing elixir that makes its own chicken bone broth. Dong quai and astragalus are adaptogenic herbs that protect the body from stress. This combination is especially good for someone experiencing anemia, chronic fatigue, hormone imbalance, or any conditions of weakness.

The healing herbs are wonderful; in fact, if you already have chicken bone broth and just want to have some healing broth, you can simmer the herbs and spices in your broth for 10–20 minutes, then sip. (You can learn more about the healing benefits of Chinese herbs in the "How to Work with Herbs and Spices" section of the Appendix. We also show you where to get them in the Resources section.)

> ☞ **Hands-on prep time:** 30 minutes ☜
> **Total prep time:** 6½ hours
> **Yield:** 8–10 servings

Whole chicken or chicken parts (bone-in legs, thighs, breast with skin on)

1 Tbsp. dried dong quai root (2–4 knobs, if using fresh dong quai root); avoid using this herb if you are pregnant, have diarrhea, or have digestive pain.

1 Tbsp. dried astragalus (or 6 slices fresh astragalus)

1 cup fresh or 2 Tbsp. dried shiitake mushrooms

Sea salt and black pepper, to taste

Optional: Honey, to taste

Toasted sesame oil, to taste

Green onion, sliced thin, to taste

Dong quai root.

If using a whole chicken, cut it into parts. Rinse the chicken and pat it dry.

Put chicken parts in a large stockpot or slow cooker. Add enough water to just cover the chicken. Add the dong quai, astragalus, and shiitake mushrooms.

Setting your burner to high, bring the liquid to a boil, then reduce to a slow simmer. Simmer for 4–6 hours. If you are using a slow cooker, set it to high to

bring to a boil, and then reduce the heat to medium for 4–6 hours. Your chicken will be moist and tender.

Add sea salt and pepper. You can also sweeten this soup with a bit of honey, if desired, to balance the taste of the medicinal herbs.

Serving suggestion:

After ladling soup into each bowl, add toasted sesame oil and green onion.

INDIGESTION
AND JOINT HEALTH
Remedy

Bone broth and bay leaves are both wonderful natural joint health and digestive health remedies. This recipe, which uses any bone broth or stock, shows you how to make a "tea" specifically to treat joint pain, such as arthritis, bunions, gout, or related issues. You may also want to try this if you're experiencing indigestion.

Keep in mind that this remedy serves as a cleanse or light detox, so your body will be releasing things it no longer needs. Whenever you cleanse, you'll probably have symptoms, so plan ahead, perhaps by taking the weekend to get started. Note that the recipe is designed to help dissolve the salts that have accumulated in the joints, so as they dissolve, they may prompt frequent urination as a way to release from your body. This is a very gentle cleanse, though.

☞ **Hands-on prep time:** 5 minutes ☜
Total prep time: 8–12 hours
Yield: 1 serving

1⅓ cup chicken bone broth or stock
(you can also use the Healing Elixir
Vegetable Stock)

1 Tbsp. crushed dried bay leaves

Optional: ⅛ tsp. ground juniper berry

Pour chicken bone broth into a saucepan (you can also use meat stock or vegetable stock). Add crushed dried bay leaves (and optional ground juniper berry, if desired). Simmer for 5 minutes.

Put in a thermos overnight to steep. In the morning, strain out and discard the bay leaves, catching the liquid in a cup. Sip this in small amounts throughout the day (not all at once).

Repeat this procedure for 3 days, making a fresh 1⅓ cup batch each day. You will then take 7 days off and repeat the procedure for another 3 days. At this point, you can either stop here or wait another 7 days and repeat the procedure from the beginning.

The process will look like this:

- **The night before Day 1:** Make the bay leaf bone broth tea and steep overnight.

- **Day 1:** Sip the broth slowly throughout the day and prepare another batch to steep that night.

- **Day 2:** Sip the broth slowly throughout the day and prepare another batch to steep that night.

- **Day 3:** Sip the broth slowly throughout the day. (You don't make any more tonight.)

- **Days 4–10:** Take these days off.

- **The night of Day 10:** Prepare a 1⅓ cup batch of bay leaf bone broth tea and steep overnight.

- **Days 11–13:** Repeat the steps from days 1–3. After day 13, you may either stop here or wait 7 days and repeat the procedure from the beginning.

PROBIOTIC
TONIC RECIPE[3]

This recipe by **Ariane Resnick,** author of *The Bone Broth Miracle: How an Ancient Remedy Can Improve Health, Fight Aging, and Boost Beauty,* calls for either flavored or neutral broth.

When Ariane's family took probiotics in the 1980s, friends and neighbors thought they were insane. It was not yet the time to discuss the "healthy bugs" living in everyone's intestines. Thankfully, that time for talking is now upon us, and probiotics are becoming well known as a necessary part of life. Whether you have intestinal issues, autoimmune illness, or just want to ensure your lasting health, your belly needs lots of healthy bacteria in order for you to thrive. Combine probiotics with the gut-healing properties of bone broth, and you have a recipe for happiness inside.

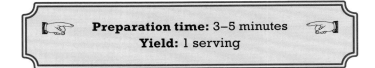

Preparation time: 3–5 minutes
Yield: 1 serving

½ cup bone broth

½ cup liquid probiotics: unflavored kefir, unflavored kombucha, or fermented vegetable juice

1 tsp. miso paste

Heat broth until just warm.

Remove from heat and whisk in miso paste.

Add liquid probiotic and stir briefly. Be sure not to add probiotics to hot liquid, as that will kill the beneficial bacteria.

⌒ CHAPTER 6 ⌒

THE COMFORT:
Soups, Stews, Sauces, Dips, and Dressings

///

CACTUS AND SEAFOOD
SOUP

This recipe by **Caroline Barringer,** NTP, CHFS, calls for fish broth. You can also use fish stock or dashi stock.

Nopales (also referred to as prickly pear or nopal cactus leaves) are a powerhouse of healing properties. In addition to being a delicious part of traditional Mexican cuisine, they also have brain- and immune-boosting benefits. Studies have shown that these vitamin- and amino acid–rich cacti have antimicrobial, antioxidant, anti-inflammatory, hypoglycemic, and neuroprotective properties.[1] Now that makes it worth seeking them out for this delicious soup!

To find nopales, go to the produce section and look for flat, green, prickly paddles the shape of an oval; they're also sometimes sold in cut strips. While nopales are available year-round, they may not be available in your supermarket or health-food store. If you have a Mexican market nearby, this will be a great place to find nopales; you can also order them online at establishments like Melissas.com. These are typically very affordable and can be a great addition to your meals!

We are grateful to Caroline for contributing this recipe so that more people can learn how to cook with this fun, nutritious Mexican staple. This soup is a bit spicy; however, we offer some suggestions for those averse to spicy foods so that you can enjoy a milder version.

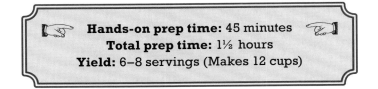

Hands-on prep time: 45 minutes
Total prep time: 1½ hours
Yield: 6–8 servings (Makes 12 cups)

1 quart fish broth (any fish broth of choice)

4 medium nopales

1 chayote (this is a small green squash; substitute ½ cup peeled and chopped celery root or turnip if none are available)

2 medium yellow onions

2 tsp. sea salt

4 dried guajillo peppers. (Pronounced *gwah-HEE-yoh*, these peppers are mild and somewhat sweet in flavor with only a little heat. You can reduce this to 1 dried guajillo pepper or leave them out if you're concerned about them being too spicy. You can find these online if they're not available at your local market or Mexican market.)

2 cloves of fresh organic garlic, whole

1 Tbsp. lard (substitute butter, if needed)

2 Tbsp. organic olive oil

1 bunch organic cilantro, without stems

1½ cups of unfarmed bay scallops, fresh or frozen

12 medium shrimp, cut in half

If your quart of fish broth is frozen, either place the container in hot water to allow it to thaw while you're prepping other parts of this recipe, or place it in a saucepan over medium low heat to thaw more quickly.

With a sharp paring knife, *carefully* scrape away the prickly points from each of the nopales paddles. Please use caution—the points are *very* sharp! Be sure to completely trim around the edges and cut away any brown parts that may be at the very base of the stem. Rinse each paddle well to ensure that all of the prickly parts have been removed. The final step here is to cut the nopales into thin strips. Once sliced, rinse a final time and set aside. (If your supermarket sells nopales precut, this can save you time.)

Peel the chayote squash and then dice into 1" cubes; rinse the cubes in cool water. (Substitute ½ cup peeled and cut celery root or turnip if you cannot find chayote.) Place the nopales and chayote in a medium-sized pot and cover with water.

Cut one of the onions in half crossways. Peel away the outer skin and place only one half (as a whole piece) into the pot with the chayote and nopales. Sprinkle in 1 tsp. of sea salt.

Bring to a boil and then reduce heat to low. You'll see that the simmering water becomes slightly thick and gooey—this is completely normal and a common occurrence when cooking with cactus. Once the nopales, chayote, and onion are soft (about 20 minutes or more), strain them and set aside.

While you're waiting for the chayote, nopales, and onion to soften, tear the stems off the dried guajillo peppers. Place peppers in a small pot; completely cover them with water and bring to a boil. Reduce heat to medium low and simmer until the peppers are tender, about 10–15 minutes.

Strain the guajillo peppers completely (discard and do not reuse the simmering water) and place them into a blender (a NutriBullet or Magic Bullet works really well), along with 2 cloves of garlic and 1½ cups of cool water. Blend until no large pieces of the pepper can be seen. The blended guajillo peppers will have a beautiful and bright red-orange color!

Next, cut up the remaining half of the first onion, as well as the whole second onion (1½ onions total). Cut the onions crossways so that you create rings (as if you were going to dip them in batter and make onion rings).

In a stockpot, melt 1 Tbsp. lard (or butter) and 1 Tbsp. olive oil over medium heat. Add the onion rings and sauté until they begin to sweat and soften.

Add the cilantro to the stockpot (leave cilantro sprigs whole; do not dice or chop) and allow it to cook along with the onion until it is fully wilted.

Add the softened chayote, nopales, and onion to the stockpot. Add the second Tbsp. of olive oil and mix well.

Cover the entire mixture in the stockpot with 1 quart of warmed fish broth. Sprinkle in 1 tsp. of sea salt and stir well.

Now it's time to add the rich red-orange guajillo peppers! Place a fine mesh strainer over the stockpot, and pour the blended peppers into the pot through the strainer. Discard the seeds.

Allow the soup to simmer for an additional 10–15 minutes undisturbed.

Add the fresh bay scallops and whole shrimp and cook for 7–10 minutes, or until the shrimp are pink and tender (but not rubbery).

Serve immediately.

Serving suggestions:

For an authentic Mexican meal, top the soup with cubed ripe avocado and homemade masa-flour tortilla chips. For quick and delicious chips, buy the non-GMO, organic, sprouted corn or rice tortillas by Food for Life; or the non-GMO, organic, whole-grain tortillas by Ezekiel 4:9. Cut tortillas into triangles and fry in very hot pastured-lard bath until crispy (pieces of corn tortilla should sizzle and bubble immediately when you place them into the lard bath; if they don't, the lard is not hot enough).

Lay fried triangles out on a paper towel to absorb excess lard, and sprinkle with sea salt while still warm. Allow the chips to cool, then add them to the soup to soak up the broth and for an extra-special treat. Some chopped fresh jalapeño (for those who like it extra hot) or salsa verde will also complement this delicious and mildly spiced soup.

CLEANSING
CILANTRO SOUP
(Easy On-the-Go Soup)

This recipe can use any bone broth or stock, including the Healing Elixir Vegetable Stock. It's a wonderful soup to use when you are doing a cleanse or have overindulged for a period of time and want to get back on track. It tastes wonderful and is very easy on the digestive system.

☞ **Preparation time:** 20 minutes ☜
Yield: 2–4 servings

1 Tbsp. coconut oil, ghee, or butter

1 Tbsp. herbes de Provence spice blend; or if you don't have this on hand, use:

- 2 tsp. thyme
- 1 tsp. marjoram
- ½ tsp. rosemary
- ½ tsp. fennel

2 cups sliced leeks

3 cups fresh cilantro, chopped

2 cups bone broth, meat stock, or vegetable stock—the more flavorful your bone broth, the fewer spices you need in this soup

1 carrot, sliced

2 zucchini, sliced

1 tsp. sea salt

Black pepper, to taske

Put the coconut oil, spices, and leeks into a saucepan and sauté on low heat for 2–3 minutes.

Add cilantro and sauté on low for 2 more minutes; remove from the heat and set aside.

In a separate saucepan, add the bone broth and carrots and simmer for 5 minutes or until the carrots are soft. Add the zucchini slices and simmer for 1 minute.

Add the broth, zucchini, and carrots to the saucepan with the coconut oil, leeks, spices, and cilantro. With your immersion blender (or in your food processor with the S-blade), blend the vegetables up until smooth. The soup is now ready to serve. Season with sea salt and pepper.

Thermos soup instructions: To make this as a thermos soup, sauté the coconut oil and spices in one saucepan; add the bone broth and sliced vegetables into your blender or food processor with the S-blade and blend into a smooth puree. Add the vegetable puree to the saucepan with the coconut oil and spices; bring to a boil, mixing well. Remove from heat and pour into your thermos. Your vegetables will be cooked in the broth in your thermos and ready to eat at your next meal. Season with sea salt and pepper.

Serving suggestions:

Eat this soup on its own if you're doing a cleanse.

If you want a heartier soup, add your choice of ground meat, leftover chunks of meat or chicken, eggs, or cooked grains.

Serve with Maya's Finnish Sourdough Rye Bread or the Herb Bread.

Cleansing Cilantro Soup with Maya's Finnish Sourdough Rye Bread.

EASY
HOMEMADE
Tomato Sauce

This recipe is flexible and can use any red meat or poultry bone broth or stock (flavored or neutral), or the Healing Elixir Vegetable Stock. It makes a sauce that is fast, easy, and delicious!

There is almost no substitute for tomato sauce, especially if you love cacciatore, meatloaf, or pizza. The sauce in this recipe is a healthy alternative to the canned and jarred varieties that line supermarket shelves.

Keep in mind that tomatoes are nightshades. Therefore, if you're experiencing arthritis symptoms or otherwise just avoiding nightshades, this recipe would not be for you until your symptoms subside.

> ☞ **Hands-on prep time:** 20 minutes ☜
> **Total prep time:** 50 minutes
> **Yield:** 4 cups

4 large hothouse tomatoes (approximately 4 cups tomatoes, pureed)

1 Tbsp. butter, ghee, or coconut oil

½ cup bone broth (flavored or neutral, or stock)

2 cloves garlic, minced or pressed

1 Tbsp. dried oregano

2 tsp. dried thyme

2 tsp. dried basil

1 tsp. black pepper

1 tsp. sea salt

1 bay leaf

Put 4 cups of water into a saucepan and bring to a boil.

Put another 4 cups of cold water into a large bowl.

Make an X cut in the bottom of each tomato (this makes it easier for the skin to come off); put the tomatoes into the boiling water and boil until the skin starts to come off (about 1 minute).

Once skin starts to come off, remove tomatoes from boiling water with a slotted spoon and put them into the cold water. (The cold water will make it easier for you to handle them.) Once the tomatoes are cool enough to handle, peel them.

Some people recommend that you squeeze the tomatoes to remove the seeds as well. If you like a really smooth sauce or if you have diverticulitis or a related large intestine challenge, this is a good idea for you. Otherwise, you can skip that step.

Put the tomatoes into a food processor with the S-blade or a high-speed blender and puree. Alternatively, you can mash them up with a large fork or potato masher.

Add the butter (or ghee or coconut oil) into a medium-sized deep skillet or braising pan (with lid) with the burner on low. With the lid off, heat the butter and add the minced or pressed garlic, oregano, thyme, basil, and black pepper. Allow to heat on low for 2 minutes, until the aromas are released. This releases the medicinal properties of the herbs and spices.

Add the pureed tomatoes into the skillet. Now add the sea salt and bay leaf.

Put the lid on the skillet and simmer on low for at least 30 minutes. When finished, remove the bay leaf and serve warm.

Serving suggestions:

Use as a tasty sauce for anything you like.

Mix with a poultry dish to make a cacciatore.

Serve with meatloaf or meatballs.

If you need a gluten-free pasta option, consider 100 percent buckwheat soba noodles topped with this sauce. You can typically find these noodles in your health-food store or online. Make sure you check the ingredients because some brands add other things in with the buckwheat and others are 100 percent buckwheat.

EGGS
YOUR WAY
Soup

Eggs have been put into soups in all sorts of ways in all cultures. Whether poached, scrambled, or hard-boiled, people seem to love eggs in soup. We do, too! Adding an egg to broth is a simple way to create a satisfyingly light, yet hearty meal.

Feel free to make this egg soup any way you like, as this recipe can use any type of broth.

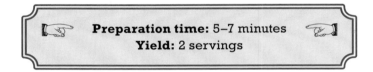

Preparation time: 5–7 minutes
Yield: 2 servings

1½ cups bone broth or meat stock (flavored or neutral)

Optional spices: All of these go together, so use them all if you like, or any combination.
If you're using a flavored broth, make sure you taste it to see what is needed. Sometimes you won't need to add anything, or perhaps just some sea salt and ground pepper. These spices work very well for a neutral or lightly flavored broth, like chicken bone broth:

- 1 tsp. thyme
- ½ tsp. paprika
- ½ tsp. black pepper
- 1 tsp. sea salt

4–6 eggs

Combine broth (or stock) and your spices of choice in a medium-sized saucepan.

Set your burner to medium high and simmer for a few minutes.

Turn your burner down to low and add the eggs. This recipe serves 2, so add the number of eggs you want for 2 people.

How you do the eggs is your choice. You can poach them or mix them right in like egg drop soup. Some people like to scramble the eggs first and then add them to the broth. Others like to take already pre-pared hard-boiled eggs from the refrigerator, slice them in half, and add them to the broth. This is totally up to you and whatever you have on hand!

- If you would like to poach the eggs, simmer the broth on low and carefully crack the eggs into the broth so that the yolk stays whole. Simmer until the egg whites are cooked and the yolks are the way you like them (we enjoy them slightly soft). You can cook them longer to get fully cooked yolks if you prefer.

- If you like egg drop soup, mix the egg into the broth for a few minutes and the soup will be ready as you see the egg white turn opaque.

Serving suggestions:

Pour into bowls and enjoy!

Add a side dish of cultured vegetables, like sauerkraut or kimchi.

Serve with a side dish of your favorite vegetables, the Celery Root Mash, or the Mashed Kabocha Squash.

Eggs Your Way Soup.

HEARTY
HAMBURGER
Soup

This recipe makes a hearty, tasty meal that cooks up in minutes for a fast breakfast, lunch, or dinner. It has a nice, deep spicy-savory flavor from the turmeric (not hot spicy, just flavorful). This makes a wonderful fall, winter, or early spring meal.

If you're feeling depleted or your blood sugar has become low, this is a nice meal that can help to perk you up and restore your energy. Serve it anytime you want to feel a sense of grounded satisfaction, or when you feel like you need a little extra strength or rejuvenation.

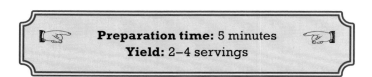

Preparation time: 5 minutes
Yield: 2–4 servings

2 Tbsp. coconut oil, ghee, or butter

2 tsp. turmeric

2 tsp. black pepper

3 cups bone broth, meat stock, or the Healing Elixir Vegetable stock (you could also use 2 cups broth or stock and 1 cup water)

½ lb. ground beef (this also works with ground bison, lamb, turkey, or chicken)

2 tsp. sea salt

Optional: 1 cup thinly shredded bok choy or thinly sliced yellow summer squash and zucchini

Add coconut oil, ghee, or butter to a saucepan and set your burner to low.

Add the rest of the spices, except for the sea salt. Warm the spices in the coconut oil for 2 minutes or until you can smell their aromas.

Add the bone broth or stock and sea salt. Simmer for 1 minute.

Add the ground beef in small chunks. Decide if you want any sliced vegetables, like bok choy and yellow summer squash. Add them if you want them. Simmer the broth with meat (and vegetables, if using) for 3 minutes or until the meat has changed color and looks done. Ground meat, bok choy, and yellow squash cook very fast in broth.

Taste the broth and, if you want, you can dilute it with more water. If you really want to strengthen your body, mind, and spirit after feeling depleted, the rich broth is wonderful as is. However, if you want to feel lighter, dilute it a bit. Start by adding ¼ cup water and taste. Notice how that feels in your body—does it need to be lighter? Add another ¼ cup water and taste again. Continue to add water until the broth feels right to your taste buds and body.

Add more sea salt and pepper, if needed.

Thermos soup instructions: If you're making a thermos broth for work or a road trip, you can bring the broth to a boil, turn off the heat, and add the ground meat (making sure it's broken up into small chunks first) and, if desired, the thinly sliced vegetables. Then pour the soup into your thermos and put on the cap. The meat and vegetables will continue to cook in the broth and be ready by the time you want to eat your meal.

Serving suggestions:

Serve as a soup or ladle some hamburger with a little broth over a plate of finely shredded lettuce and cultured vegetables.

This soup goes well with the Herb Bread.

LOUISE'S
HEALING
Asparagus Soup

This recipe can use any meat or poultry bone broth or the Healing Elixir Vegetable Stock. Not only is it delicious; it's very healing, too! This soup has anti-inflammatory, cancer-preventive, metabolism-boosting, and digestion-supporting properties.

This is the recipe Louise used as part of her nutritional healing regimen when she was diagnosed with cancer, and with great results—her healthy thoughts and food resulted in dissolving the cancer naturally!

Louise: After receiving a cancer diagnosis many years ago, my natural-health practitioner suggested that I eat 2 ounces of pureed asparagus three times per day. I carried asparagus puree around in little film containers because that's all there was in that size back then. I still love asparagus to this day and often have it several times per week. This soup is a wonderful way to get the healing properties of asparagus into your diet, along with some medicinal spices.

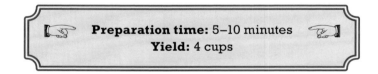

Preparation time: 5–10 minutes
Yield: 4 cups

2 Tbsp. butter, ghee, or coconut oil

1 tsp. black pepper

2 tsp. turmeric

½ tsp. ground cumin seed

1 clove garlic, minced

3 cups broth or stock

2 cups asparagus, chopped

1 tsp. sea salt

Add the butter to a 3-quart saucepan and set the burner to low. Melt the butter and add the black pepper, turmeric, and ground cumin. Heat for 2 minutes on low, to release the aromas and medicinal properties of the spices. Add the minced garlic and heat for 2 more minutes.

Add the broth and raise the heat to high, bringing the broth to a boil. Once the broth is boiling, add the asparagus and reduce the heat, bringing the water to a simmer. Simmer for 5 minutes or until the asparagus is soft.

Now add the sea salt and puree the soup. You can do this with a handheld immersion blender or your food processor or blender. You can also use a potato masher to mash up the asparagus, blending it with the broth. Blend until smooth.

Pour into bowls and serve. Add sea salt, pepper, butter, sesame oil, or bite-size pieces of avocado to each bowl, to taste.

Serving suggestions:

Serve with your favorite meat, poultry, or fish dish.

Serve with the Herb Bread or Maya's Finnish Sourdough Bread.

Louise's Healing Asparagus Soup.

MAORI PUHA
BOIL UP[2]

This recipe by **Nick Polizzi,** author of *The Sacred Cookbook: Forgotten Healing Recipes of the Ancients,* does not need bone broth because it creates its own chicken stock while you are simmering the soup!

Centuries ago, the Maori traveled to New Zealand from Polynesia. Isolated there, they developed their own unique culture, including language, mythology, customs, and art. In their early history, the Maori were quite dynamic in that they not only hunted and gathered, but also maintained large community gardens full of vegetables like sweet potato and taro root. There was no such thing as private property in Maori culture until European settlers enforced it. Rather, their spiritual philosophy was based on a responsibility to protect the earth for the benefit of all. Pretty beautiful, right?

Although the arrival of foreigners and decades of conflict put their population into decline in the 19th century, in recent years traditional Maori culture has enjoyed a revival along with a renewed interest in their culture and cuisine.

The boil up is a Maori method cooking that has changed little through the years. Root vegetables such as sweet potatoes, spinach, and watercress are cooked in a meat or vegetable stock.

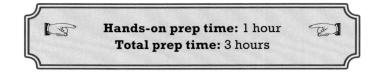

Hands-on prep time: 1 hour
Total prep time: 3 hours

1 whole free-range chicken

2 quarts of water

1 bunch of puha (watercress is a great substitute)

1 bunch leeks, sliced into ½" pieces

1 sweet potato, peeled and diced

½ white onion, chopped

6 tomatoes, chopped

1 small pumpkin, seeded, peeled, and diced

3 green onions, thinly sliced

2 Tbsp. sea salt

Rinse the chicken and place into a stockpot with the water and sea salt. Bring to a boil; lower heat and simmer for about 1 hour or until the meat is falling from the bones.

Meanwhile, soak the puha or watercress in cold water for 5 minutes, then pull it out and spin or towel dry. Set aside. Repeat this process with the leeks.

Remove the chicken from the pot and set aside to cool. Add the sweet potato, white onion, tomatoes, pumpkin, and leeks to the pot of stock; simmer for 15 minutes.

Separate the chicken meat from the bones and skin (save the bones for a future bone broth). Break meat into large pieces and add back to stock along with the green onions. Simmer for an additional 15 minutes.

Add puha or watercress and serve in bowls.

Serving suggestion:

Goes very well with a scoop of quinoa or wild rice mixed into each bowl.

TOM YUM
SOUP[3]

This recipe by **Nick Polizzi,** author of *The Sacred Cookbook: Forgotten Healing Recipes of the Ancients,* calls for chicken or vegetable stock, although you can also use chicken bone broth or any neutral bone broth.

Aside from being among the most popular dishes in Thailand, Tom Yum Soup's powerful combination of herbs and spices make it a "super soup." Recent scientific studies of this signature dish have many experts dumbfounded: Apparently, it is a hundred times more powerful than any other food for inhibiting tumor growth. It also appears to have significant immune-boosting power, and is an effective natural remedy for combating cold and flu viruses.

But most importantly, it is delicious and perfect for a cold autumn or winter day!

Preparation time:
Approximately 50 minutes
Yield: 2 servings

3–4 cups chicken or vegetable stock

1 stalk lemongrass, minced, using the lower ⅓ only (discard the remainder)

3 cloves garlic, minced

½ tsp. red chili paste (adjust to taste)

Juice from ½ fresh lime

½ cup fresh shiitake mushrooms, sliced thinly

12–15 jumbo shrimp, shelled and deveined (It's important to only use jumbo shrimp for this recipe because of their immense flavor, but make sure not to overcook them. Save the shells in your freezer for the next time you make fish stock.)

1 green bell pepper, sliced

1 red bell pepper, sliced

½ cup cherry tomatoes, halved

½ can coconut milk (or make your own with ½ cup water and 1½ Tbsp. coconut butter, blended thoroughly in your blender)

2 Tbsp. fish sauce

1 Tbsp. sea salt

1 tsp. honey

⅓ cup fresh cilantro, roughly chopped (or 2 Tbsp. dried ground coriander)

Pour stock into a deep pot and turn heat to medium high; add prepared lemongrass. Boil 5–6 minutes, or until fragrant.

Reduce heat to simmer. Add garlic, chili paste, lime juice, and mushrooms to broth; continue simmering for another 5 minutes.

Add shrimp, red and green peppers, and cherry tomatoes. Simmer 2–3 minutes, or until shrimp are pink and plump.

Lower the heat and add ½ can coconut milk, fish sauce, sea salt, and honey. Simmer a few more minutes.

Serve in bowls with fresh cilantro sprinkled over (or shake in some ground dried coriander). Enjoy!

Serving suggestions:

Serve with the Herb Bread or Maya's Finnish Sourdough Rye Bread with Aioli.

CHARD
SOUP[4]

This recipe by the **Price-Pottenger Nutrition Foundation** is great with any type of bone broth or stock, including the Healing Elixir Vegetable Stock. This soup helps restore the body's alkaline reserve.

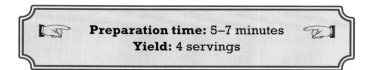

Preparation time: 5–7 minutes
Yield: 4 servings

1 cup cooked chard, preferably steamed

3 cups stock or broth

1 Tbsp. arrowroot powder

1 Tbsp. butter

¼ tsp. nutmeg

Blend the first three ingredients and heat until soup thickens.

Add butter and nutmeg; mix together, allowing the butter to melt, and then serve in mugs.

Serving suggestions:

Enjoy with the Herb Bread or Maya's Finnish Sourdough Rye Bread.

Swiss chard.

PUREED
GREEN BEAN
Soup

This soup is so delicious that it makes us bounce in our seats when eating it! It's fast, easy, full of vitamins and minerals, and flexible enough to allow you to add a variety of things for a different soup each time you make it.

☞ **Preparation time:** 7–10 minutes ☜
Yield: 4 servings

1 Tbsp. butter

2 tsp. turmeric

1 tsp. black or white pepper

1 tsp. sea salt

2 cups flavored beef bone broth (or any other stock or broth)

3 cups green beans

Add butter to a saucepan and set the burner to low, allowing butter to melt.

Add turmeric and pepper and heat on low for 2 minutes, allowing the spices to release their aromas and medicinal properties.

Add bone broth and raise heat to high, bringing broth to a boil. Add sea salt.

Trim ends off green beans (save for future broths or stocks). When broth boils, reduce to simmer and add beans. Heat for 3–5 minutes.

When beans are soft, puree the soup. You can do this with a handheld immersion blender, a food processor, or a blender. Blend until completely pureed.

Optional: Choose one or more of the following to add to your soup:

- A few chunks of Messed-up but So Delicious Pan Bread to thicken and flavor
- 2–4 eggs
- Some oxtail meat from Heather's Easy Oxtail Meat Stock and Bone Broth
- Some ground meat or poultry (this cooks fast)

Serving suggestions:

Serve warm in bowls and add a little extra butter or coconut oil, sea salt, or ground pepper, to taste.

GOAT AND VEGETABLE
STEW

This recipe from **Eyton Shalom,** M.S., L.Ac., calls for lamb broth or stock. You can also use any neutral bone broth or the Healing Elixir Vegetable Stock.

> ☞ **Hands-on prep time:** 20 minutes ☜
> **Total prep time:** 2–4 hours
> **Yield:** 4–6 servings

1 lb. goat stew meat (substitute lamb or beef brisket if you can't find a good source of goat meat)

1 large or 2 small yellow onions, diced (about 1½ cups)

3 garlic cloves

2 Tbsp. ghee, butter, or coconut oil

2½ tsp. cumin seeds

12 cardamom pods (or 2 tsp. ground cardamom)

1½ tsp. black peppercorns

½ tsp. turmeric

2 cups bone broth or stock

2 tsp. sea salt

2 large carrots, cut in big chunks (so they don't get overcooked)

2 cups green cabbage, shredded

Rinse the goat meat and pat dry with a paper towel; set aside.

Dice the onions and mince the garlic; set aside.

Put ghee in a large braising pan (that has a lid) or Dutch oven; set your burner to low. Once the ghee has melted, add the cumin, cardamom, black peppercorns, and turmeric; heat for 1 minute.

Add the goat meat and turn the heat up to medium, browning the meat for 5 minutes. Add the diced onions and minced garlic and sauté for another 2–3 minutes.

Add bone broth, sea salt, and carrots. Add additional water so that there is 4" of liquid over the meat.

Turn up the heat and bring the liquid to a boil. Then lower the heat and bring the liquid to a rolling simmer for 2–4 hours (maximum).

Finally, 45 minutes before the meat finishes cooking, add green cabbage.

Serving suggestions:

Serve in bowls over the Mashed Celery Root or cooked quinoa or rice.

Enjoy with the Herb Bread or Maya's Finnish Sourdough Rye Bread.

Goat and Vegetable Stew.

BALANCED & BRIGHT
QUICK PHO & LUNCHES
to Go

This recipe by **Quinn Wilson,** owner of Balanced & Bright Bone Broth, can use any bone broth or stock, or the Healing Elixir Vegetable Stock.

This is a fantastic, easy lunch idea that is perfect for days at work or on the road. You simply put whatever ingredients you choose into a mason jar (1 pint or 1 quart—your choice) and let the broth heat all the ingredients into a lovely, portable soup.

If you're going to be out for several hours, you can make this soup in a widemouthed thermos the morning before you leave and have a nice lunch, dinner, or snack when you need it!

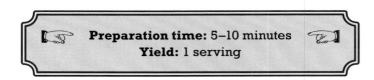

Preparation time: 5–10 minutes
Yield: 1 serving

You can choose ingredients with a theme in mind or just add your favorites; this is best made with your imagination. Here are some suggestions:

Any thinly sliced vegetables of your choice (zucchini, carrots, radishes, tomatoes, onions, cabbage, broccoli or cauliflower florets, and so on)

Any thinly sliced cooked meats such as chicken, meat, or shrimp

Fermented vegetables and hot sauces (such as kimchi, sauerkraut, beets, or sambal)

Any aromatic herbs (such as basil, chives, parsley, or cilantro); a good guideline is ¼ tsp. of each herb per jar

Sea salt and pepper, to taste

Rice noodles

Enough bone broth to fill a pint- or quart-sized mason jar (your choice), with room for add-ins

The night before, prepare your sliced vegetables, meats, and any other accoutrements (spices, fats, and the like) you desire. Place in a mason jar, making sure you leave room for the bone broth and rice noodles.

When you're ready to eat, simply heat your bone broth on the stove. When heated, carefully pour the bone broth into the jar. Add the rice noodles; once they have softened into the jar, place the top back on the mason jar. Let sit for 5–7 minutes.

Season to taste.

Balanced & Bright Quick Pho and Lunches to Go.

AIOLI:
GARLIC MAYONNAISE
with a Healthier Twist

This recipe uses neutral or lightly flavored bone broth. (If you didn't get a good gel in the bone broth you have on hand, add 1 Tbsp. unflavored powdered gelatin per quart of broth, which should give you enough gel.)

Many commercial brands of mayonnaise use unhealthy refined oils, which are heated and treated, removing antioxidants and creating dangerous free radicals. Making your own aioli—a garlic-flavored version of mayo—is really easy and worth the time because you can use a healthy, unrefined oil; in this case, extra-virgin olive oil. While some homemade aioli recipes call for canola oil, we recommend you avoid this oil because it's highly processed. Extra-virgin olive oil makes a tasty aioli on its own and does not need to be mixed with other oils.

You'll have aioli in your refrigerator for a couple of weeks, and you'll know it's full of good fats for your brain and body.

☞ **Preparation time:**
Approximately 10 minuntes
Yield: 3 cups ☞

1 whole egg

1 Tbsp. apple cider vinegar

2 egg yolks

1 Tbsp. Dijon mustard (choose one that uses apple cider vinegar, like 365 Everyday Value brand)

3 Tbsp. bone broth (neutral or lightly flavored)

1 tsp. sea salt or Himalayan salt

2 cups extra-virgin olive oil

Optional spices for flavor and balance of tastes:

1 tsp. thyme

1 tsp. basil

1 tsp. black pepper

2 large cloves garlic

Aioli with Maya's Finnish
Sourdough Rye Bread.

Peel the garlic cloves and cut them in half length-wise. Put garlic in a small saucepan, cover with cold water, and bring to a boil. Then discard the water and return garlic to the pan.

Add about ½ cup of water to the saucepan with the parboiled garlic. Add the apple cider vinegar and a pinch of sea salt. Bring the water to a boil and add the whole egg. Allow the egg white to fully cook and the yolk to stay runny. This will take about a minute or two.

Remove from heat and remove the egg and garlic with a slotted spoon, discarding the water.

Put the cooked egg and garlic into your food processor with the S-blade or blender. Add the 2 egg yolks (discard the whites or save them for another recipe), the mustard, bone broth, and sea salt. Turn on the food processor or blender (low or medium speed for the blender).

Take the olive oil and very slowly pour it in, so it's dribbling slowly into the food processor or blender. This is key because if you pour too fast, the aioli will not thicken properly (emulsify). In order for emul-sification to happen, time your pouring so that it takes 2 minutes to pour the olive oil slowly into the running food processor or blender. This is a good time to meditate, do your breathing exercises, or say your affirmations! The slow pouring is worth it. You should start to see the aioli thicken like mayon-naise or pudding.

Once all the oil is slowly poured in and the aioli has thickened, turn off your food processor or blender and taste. If you've used a flavored broth, see if you like the flavor as is. If it needs a little more, con-sider adding some black pepper, dried basil, and/or dried thyme per the ingredients listed earlier under optional spices. You may also decide that you want a little more sea salt. Add the spices you want and blend thoroughly. Do not over-blend; just blend until all ingredients are mixed in.

Note: Sometimes when you first blend up aioli, you may detect a bitter taste from the garlic; this goes away after you refrigerate it for 24 hours. Some peo-ple like to remove the germ (center) of the garlic cloves to reduce the potential for bitterness. We haven't seen this make a huge difference after the garlic has been boiled, so do what you feel is best based on your own tastes. (If, however, your garlic contains a green germ, you may want to remove it.)

You're ready to serve!

Serving suggestions:

Use in place of mayo.

Use as a dipping sauce for vegetables, fish, meat, or poultry. It makes a wonderful dip for shrimp cocktail.

Dip the Herb Bread in it.

Use in the Everyone's Favorite Egg Salad, Tempting Tuna Salad, Simply Delicious Salmon Salad, and Lobster Salad Extravaganza recipes.

LOUISE'S
FRENCH RÉMOULADE
with Aioli

Rémoulade is a mayonnaise-based dip or sauce. It's equally wonderful with meat, vegetable, or seafood dishes. For this recipe, you will make our Aioli recipe from earlier in the chapter and add some spices.

Louise: I love rémoulade! One time, I saw some at the health-food store and got so excited that I brought it home without even reading the ingredients. It wasn't until I tasted it that I realized it was full of hot spices and was Cajun-style! I love spices, but hot spices are not my favorite. I began to think about making my own French rémoulade, and the result is this recipe. If you love the Cajun version, you can leave out the pickles and capers and add some of your favorite Cajun mustard and hot spices.

Preparation time:
Approximately 10 minutes
Yield: 1¼ cup

1¼ cups Aioli

1 tsp. fresh tarragon (or ¼ tsp. dried tarragon)

1 Tbsp. capers (drained and rinsed)

1 Tbsp. chopped dill pickle

1 Tbsp. chopped anchovy or anchovy paste

1 tsp. turmeric

1 tsp. paprika

2 tsp. horseradish (fresh grated or prepared)

Put all ingredients in your food processor or blender. You can leave anything out that you don't like, such as anchovies, capers, or pickles. Blend everything up. It will be a bit thinner than the Aioli, with the addition of capers, pickles, and horseradish.

Taste and see what you think. Add a little more sea salt and black pepper if you like.

You're ready to serve!

Serving suggestions:

Use in place of mayonnaise in recipes.

Use as a sauce for vegetables, fish, meat, or poultry. It makes a wonderful dip for shrimp cocktail.

Dip the Herb Bread in it.

Use as a salad dressing.

ARTICHOKE
TAHINI
Sauce

This recipe makes a delicious sauce for green beans and other steamed vegetables, or can be used as a dip.

> **Preparation time:** 25 minutes
> (add 1 hour if soaking artichokes)
> **Yield:** Approximately 1½ cups

2 Tbsp. ghee or butter

¼ cup bone broth (neutral meat or poultry broth, or vegetable stock)

½ cup red onion, diced

2 tsp. dried dill

2 tsp. dried oregano

2 tsp. ground rosemary

1 tsp. Herbamare (organic sea salt and herbs) or regular sea salt

1 tsp. black pepper

12-oz. jar of artichoke hearts in water (*Optional:* drain the water from the jar, put the artichoke hearts in a bowl, and soak in just enough water to cover the artichokes. This removes citric acid. After an hour, drain the artichokes.)

2 Tbsp. tahini (or almond butter or sunflower butter)

¼ cup oil from the top of a tahini jar (or sesame oil)

Put the ghee or butter in a small skillet and set the burner to low, allowing the butter to melt. Add the bone broth, onion, dill, oregano, rosemary, Herbamare (or sea salt), and black pepper, and sauté on low until the onions are translucent.

Remove from heat and let cool; then pour into your food processor with the S-blade and add the artichokes, tahini, and tahini oil (or sesame oil).

Process until fully blended. Add more Herbamare or sea salt to taste.

Serving suggestions:

This recipe works well warm or cold. Use as a salad dressing, dip, or sauce for vegetables, poultry, and white fish.

Pour on top of cooked vegetables or chicken, or chill in the refrigerator for at least 1 hour and serve as a dip for the Herb Bread or raw vegetables.

Artichoke Tahini Sauce.

DO IT YOUR WAY
SALAD
Dressing

This recipe uses collagen hydrolysate (or collagen peptides; see the shopping list in Chapter 3 for more information). You can leave this out if you don't have any on hand. You can also use neutral or flavored bone broth or stock instead.

Too many salad dressings on the market are full of refined fats and trans fats, which are not great for building a healthy brain. The good news is that you can make your own salad dressing in just minutes! In this recipe, we give you options for changing things up when you want new flavor sensations.

☞ **Preparation time:** 5 minutes ☜
Yield: Just over 1⅓ cup dressing

1 cup extra-virgin olive oil

⅓ cup raw apple cider vinegar

1 Tbsp. collagen hydrolysate (collagen peptides) or bone broth (If you use a flavored bone broth, meat stock, or vegetable stock, make sure to taste it first to get a sense of the flavor you're working with. Since this is such a small amount, it should only add subtle flavor to the dressing.)

1 tsp. sea salt

1 tsp. black pepper

Whisk all ingredients together, or place in a blender and blend up well, and you have an easy, delicious vinaigrette!

Variations:

- Honey Dijon: 1 Tbsp. Dijon mustard and 2 tsp. honey (taste and add another tsp. honey if you want a sweeter dressing)

- Herby Vinaigrette: Add ½ tsp. dried thyme and ½ tsp. dried basil
- Lemon Vinaigrette: Add 1 Tbsp. lemon juice
- Balsamic Vinaigrette: Replace the apple cider vinegar with ⅓ cup balsamic vinegar

WHITE WINE
MUSTARD
Sauce

This recipe works best with poultry bone broth or stock, although any broth or stock with a mild flavor will do.

This is a lovely, quick gourmet sauce that goes beautifully with poultry, rabbit, fish, lamb, and vegetable dishes. (Please see p. 180 for a photo of the sauce on a Cornish game hen.) You can even make a batch and use it as a salad dressing or sauce to add to soups, broths, and stews. It freezes well, so you can make extra and have it on hand for that last-minute meal or dinner party.

☞ **Hands-on prep time:** 10 minutes ☜
Total prep time: 20 minutes
Yield: 3 cups

2 Tbsp. crushed fresh garlic (or 2 diced shallots or ½ cup diced red onion)

1 cup white wine

1 cup water

½ cup Dijon mustard

½ cup coconut butter

1 cup bone broth (any broth or stock will do, although a neutral broth or mildly flavored poultry broth or stock would be preferred)

2 Tbsp. ground rosemary

2 tsp. dried thyme

1 tsp. dried basil

1 tsp. black pepper

1 tsp. sea salt

Add all ingredients except sea salt to a sauté pan or saucepan on low heat. Mix this thoroughly and add sea salt, simmering on low for 10 minutes.

Taste the sauce and see if you'd like to add a little more sea salt or pepper.

Remove from the heat and set aside until your main meal is ready to serve.

Serving suggestions:

Serve over vegetables, lamb, poultry, burgers, or salads, or in soups or stews.

Drizzle over poached or scrambled eggs.

Use as an alternative to mayonnaise in egg salad.

Roasted marrowbones.

CHAPTER 7

THE STRENGTHENERS:

Meat, Poultry, Game, and Fish Dishes

///

BISON MEATLOAF CUPCAKES
WITH MASHED CELERY ROOT
Topping

This recipe calls for red meat bone broth, but poultry broth or stock or the Healing Elixir Vegetable Stock will also work.

While the meatloaf cakes are great all by themselves, they're even more fun with the Mashed Celery Root recipe as a topping, so they look like frosted cupcakes. (The Mashed Celery Root recipe is in Chapter 8.)

These meatloaf cupcakes are so fun that children—or the little child inside each of us—will be thrilled when eating them. They're wonderful both as a celebratory casual meal or a dressed-up gourmet experience. What's even better is that they're so fast to make that you'll have more time to enjoy with family and friends. That makes this dish the perfect dinner-party treat!

1 large yellow onion, diced (about 1½ cups)

1 cup fresh fennel (stalks or bulb), diced small

½ cup coconut oil or butter

1 Tbsp. rosemary

2 tsp. turmeric

2 tsp. fenugreek

2 tsp. allspice

2 tsp. black pepper

2 tsp. garlic powder

2 tsp. sea salt

1 cup Madeira

2 cups bone broth (red meat bone broth preferred; poultry broth or stock or the Healing Elixir Vegetable Stock will also work)

2 lbs. ground bison meat

Bison Meatloaf Cupcakes with Mashed Celery Root Topping.

Preheat oven to 350° F.

Sauté onions and fennel and all spices (except for sea salt) in 1 Tbsp. coconut oil for 5 minutes in a 3-quart saucepan on low heat. Add bone broth, sea salt, and Madeira; simmer for 10 minutes on the lowest temperature.

Remove pan from the heat; mix in the bison meat and sea salt. Add the rest of the coconut oil and mix thoroughly.

Grease cupcake pans for a total of 24 cupcakes. (The recipe will make 24 large cupcakes, and most people will want 2 of them.) If you only have one cupcake pan, use a loaf pan for extra meatloaf. Scoop the meatloaf into your cupcake pan, just enough to fill each hole. You don't need to fill them too full.

If you're using silicone cupcake pans, put them on a baking sheet so that it's easier to put them into and take out of the oven. Put the baking sheet into the oven and cook for 7–12 minutes, or until the meat is cooked to your liking. One guideline is that bison is done when a meat thermometer reads 160° F.

While the meatloaf cakes are cooking, make the Mashed Celery Root.

Once the meatloaf cakes are cooked and your Mashed Celery Root is prepared, you're ready to assemble the "cupcakes"! Scoop some mashed celery root on top of your meatloaf cakes (the amount is up to you). Some people like to put the mashed celery root through a frosting piping kit to make beautiful frosted-looking cupcakes.

Serving suggestions:

Serve these meatloaf cakes alone or with the celery root on top, like a frosted cupcake.

Serve with the Simple Asparagus, the Best Brussels Sprouts, or your favorite soup.

CRISPY SHORT RIBS
WITH LIME, CILANTRO,
and Mint

This recipe by **Nick Brune,** executive chef at Local Habit in San Diego, uses beef broth or stock of your choice, flavored or neutral.

This is a very ambitious recipe, but it's worth the time for an out-of-this-world chef-inspired meal! If you want to cut corners, you can stop after simmering the ribs in the broth. However, if you want a true taste and kitchen adventure, keep going until the end and experience the rewards of the amazing flavor in this dish!

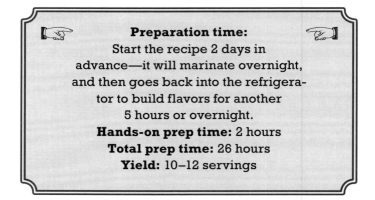

Preparation time:
Start the recipe 2 days in advance—it will marinate overnight, and then goes back into the refrigerator to build flavors for another 5 hours or overnight.
Hands-on prep time: 2 hours
Total prep time: 26 hours
Yield: 10–12 servings

6 lbs. boneless short ribs

⅔ cup fish sauce

1 cup minced shallots

¼ cup minced garlic

¼ cup extra-virgin olive oil

1 Tbsp. black pepper

¼ cup chili flakes

1 whole split pig's foot

2½ quarts beef broth

Butter or beef tallow

5 limes

Garnish: green onions, bean sprouts, mint sprigs, fresh cilantro

Optional: hot Thai chilies

Put short ribs into a deep glass baking dish or casserole dish.

Put fish sauce, shallots, garlic, olive oil, black pepper, and chili flakes into a bowl; mix well with a whisk. Pour mixture over short ribs.

With your hands, mix the short ribs in the oil-and-spice mixture until ingredients are evenly distributed. Cover with plastic wrap and allow to marinate overnight in the refrigerator.

The next day, remove ribs from the refrigerator, and let them sit on the countertop for about 30 minutes to come to room temperature. (If using a slow cooker, skip this step.)

— In using a slow cooker: Put the ribs, pig's foot, and broth into your slow cooker and set to low for 8 hours. It's done when the ribs are tender.

— If cooking in the oven: Preheat oven to 300° F. Put the ribs, pig's foot, and broth into a large Dutch oven with a lid. (A great trick is to cut some parchment paper about the size of your pot and put it over the pot, then add aluminum foil and your lid. This will seal in the steam and protect your meat from the foil.) Simmer in the oven for 2½–3 hours or until the meat is completely tender. Then remove from the oven and cool with the lid still on.

Once the meat is done, remove the meat and pig's foot from the slow cooker or Dutch oven. Strain the broth through a fine mesh strainer, collecting the broth in a large bowl.

Once the meat has cooled a bit, pull the beef until it's completely shredded. You can do this by putting it into a shallow casserole dish and using two large forks to pull the meat apart and shred it.

Return the broth and pig's foot to the pot and simmer for another 30 minutes on a slightly higher heat. (You can either use the slow cooker or cook at medium high on the stove top.) Strain the broth again.

Now it's time to build. Place your pulled beef in a large bowl and slowly add enough broth to moisten everything—should be about 1½–2 cups (save excess broth for sipping or future recipes). Finally, place your beef in an even layer on a large baking sheet, cover with parchment, and then place another large baking sheet over the top.

Place in fridge with about 5 lbs. of weight evenly distributed on the baking sheets for about 4 hours (best if overnight).

To serve, remove meat from baking sheet and cut into squares or use kitchen shears to make patties. Heat a large cast iron or stainless-steel skillet on high heat for 1 minute. Add some butter or beef tallow to coat the bottom of the pan lightly.

Pan sear your patties on both sides for 1½ minutes or until golden brown.

Place the beef patties on your plate and garnish with green onions, bean sprouts, mint, cilantro, hot Thai chilies, and more broth if you like.

Cut limes into quarters and squeeze over the meat for added flavor.

Serving suggestions:

Enjoy with your favorite green salad.

Serve with the Mashed Celery Root or Best Brussels Sprouts.

EASY
EYE OF ROUND
Roast

If you haven't tried eye of round roast, it may be because you've heard that while it's budget-friendly, it can be tough. Well, we debunk this by slow cooking this roast for a tender result!

We love using a slow cooker or slow-cooking method for a couple of reasons. One is because it's so darn easy! The other is because grass-fed meat is less fatty and, therefore, can sometimes be trickier to get that just-right tenderness. So if you want easy, sure-thing results (and we do!), the slow cooker is a stellar way to get it. However, we also give you some cooking alternatives if you don't have a slow cooker.

This eye of round roast is just as good for a casual family dinner as it is for a formal affair with guests—you can dress it up any way you like.

☞ **Hands-on prep time:** 20 minutes ☜
Total prep time: 8½–16 hours
Yield: 4–6 servings

Easy Eye of Round Roast.

1–2 lbs. eye of round roast

1 cup Madeira (you can use ¼ cup apple cider vinegar if you don't want to use wine)

5 cloves garlic

1 cup red onion, sliced thin or diced

2 Tbsp. coconut oil, butter, ghee, or beef tallow

2 cups bone broth or meat stock (lamb, oxtail, or any meat broth you like)

2 bay leaves

1 Tbsp. thyme

1 Tbsp. rosemary powder or leaves

1 Tbsp. black pepper

1 Tbsp. sea salt

½ tsp. cloves

Optional—marinate the meat for extra flavor:

Add the Madeira (if substituting with apple cider vinegar, also add ¾ cup olive oil), garlic, and onions to a blender and blend together. If you don't have a blender, mince the garlic and whisk everything well.

Pierce the roast all over with a sharp knife (about 1"-deep cuts); pour the Madeira mixture over the meat and store in your refrigerator overnight. If you didn't plan that far ahead, no worries! Just let the meat sit for at least 30 minutes on your counter-top. If you like, you can stuff additional garlic cloves (peeled and cut in half or quarters) in the holes you pierced into the roast. This will add rich flavor to the meat.

Optional—browning the meat for extra flavor:

Some people love to brown meat. It's not necessary, although it can provide extra delicious flavor. If you're in the mood to try it, put the butter, ghee, beef tallow, or coconut oil in the bottom of a braising pan, deep skillet, or Dutch oven, and set your burner on low.

If you marinated the meat, add the meat and extra marinade to the pan.

If you didn't marinate the meat, add the Madeira, fat (coconut oil, butter, ghee, or beef tallow), garlic, and onions to the pan. If you're opting not to use the wine, set the apple cider vinegar and olive oil aside until you're ready to cook the roast in the broth.

Heat on low for a few minutes. While it's heating, pierce the roast all over with a sharp knife (about 1"-deep cuts). If you like, add some garlic cloves (peeled and cut in half or quarters) into the holes you just pierced.

Add the roast to the pan. Set your burner to medium high, and sear the meat on all sides for a few minutes each.

No-fuss method—skip the browning and marinating:

Sauté the Madeira, fat (coconut oil, butter, beef tallow, or ghee), garlic, and onions in a skillet; cook down to reduce the Madeira by ½ or ¾. You're creating a nice, concentrated flavor. If you're opting not to use the wine, set the apple cider vinegar and olive oil aside until you're ready to cook the roast. You can add the vinegar to the water and broth in the next step. Just sauté until the garlic and onions are soft and fragrant.

While the Madeira mixture is reducing, pierce the roast all over with a sharp knife (about 1"-deep cuts). If you like, add some garlic cloves (peeled and cut in half or quarters) into the holes you just pierced. This will add rich flavor to the meat.

Instructions for cooking the roast:

Place the roast in your slow cooker, Dutch oven, or stockpot. (If you skipped browning and marinating, pour the reduced Madeira mixture over the roast now.) Add just enough water to cover the roast; add the bone broth and bay leaves.

Cook the roast using the following methods. You'll know it's ready when you insert a sharp knife and it cuts the meat effortlessly. You can use a meat thermometer to make sure it's done, if you like. Press the meat thermometer into the thickest part of the roast—when the internal temperature reads 125°–130°, it's medium-rare.

— In *the oven*: Preheat oven to 250° F and cook in a Dutch oven (with lid on) for about 6 hours.

— In *a slow cooker*: Set on low (or for 8 hours if you have a timed slow cooker). After 8 hours, you should have very tender meat.

— On *the stove top*: If you don't have a Dutch oven, you could use a stockpot on your stove top. Bring to a boil and then set to the lowest temperature on your burner, simmering for 4–8 hours with the lid on. Check at 4 and then 6 hours.

After 4–5 hours of cooking, add your spices. You could add them right at the beginning, but you'll get better flavor if you add in the last hours of cooking.

Serving suggestions:

Slice the roast very thin and serve with the Celery Root Mash (for a meat and potatoes–type meal without the starch) or your favorite steamed vegetables, like the Simple Asparagus. It goes well with the Cardamom Carrots and Caramelized Onions, too.

At the end of cooking, you'll have bone broth infused with the flavor of the eye of round and spices in your slow cooker. You can use this as a thin gravy to put over your roast or on mashed celery root or whatever vegetable you're serving. You can also thicken it up by adding some celery root mash to the liquid and using a whisk or immersion blender, or putting the whole thing in a blender.

A side of cultured vegetables, like sauerkraut or kimchi adds a well-rounded, palate-pleasing sour taste and provides a nice dose of digestion-enhancing probiotics.

Thinly slice any leftover meat and store in the refrigerator or freezer for easy snacks or meals later in the week.

HONEY MUSTARD
CHICKEN

This recipe is geared toward healing the intestines. And good news, it's also delicious and easy to make! The bonus of this recipe is that you'll have some nice meat stock at the end to save for future recipes.

We served this for dinner at Louise's home one night, and Maya Labos (from the "dance break" section in Chapter 2, and of Maya's Finnish Sourdough Rye Bread fame in Chapter 9) absolutely loved it. We think you will, too!

> ☞ **Hands-on prep time:** 30 minutes ☜
> **Total prep time:** 1½–4½ hours
> **Yield:** 8 servings

8 chicken thighs, bone-in

1 cup bone broth (chicken bone broth or stock, or almost any vegetable, meat, or poultry broth or stock)

1 cup white cooking wine (whatever you have on hand)

¼ cup apple cider vinegar

4 cups broccoli, about 2 large heads, chopped into florets

½–⅔ cup raw honey (If you like things less sweet, start with ½ cup honey and adjust to your preference once the dish has been fully assembled.)

2 Tbsp. Dijon honey mustard

2 tsp. sea salt

1 tsp. turmeric

1 tsp. black pepper

½ tsp. cumin

¼ tsp. allspice

Optional spices for flavor and balance:

¼ tsp. lemongrass

3 cloves garlic

Put chicken thighs into a slow cooker. Add bone broth, white wine, apple cider vinegar, and just enough water to cover the chicken. Put the slow cooker on high for 4 hours.

— *Stove-top option*: If you don't have a slow cooker, add the chicken, wine, and vinegar to a stockpot or Dutch oven, then add just enough water to cover the chicken. Bring the mixture to a boil; reduce to low heat and simmer for 3 hours. When the chicken is done, it will nearly fall right off the bone because it's so tender.

— *Oven option*: Preheat oven to 350° F. Place the chicken, bone broth, wine, and vinegar into a Dutch oven, then add just enough water to cover the chicken. Cook for approximately 25 minutes or until the meat has reached an internal temperature of 165° F. You can also use a Pyrex casserole or deep baking dish, adjusting the amount of water to accommodate the size of your baking dish. The chicken will still come out wonderfully.

While the chicken is cooking, make the honey mustard glaze. (Consider using a 6-quart saucepan or large braising pan to make the glaze so that you can easily add the chicken and broccoli into the sauce at the end.) Add the honey, mustard, and all spices into the saucepan; set your stove to the lowest heat setting. If you're using garlic, mince it up and add it to the glaze as well. Heat on low for 5–7 minutes, then remove from heat and set aside.

Once you've made the glaze, steam the broccoli. In a saucepan or skillet on medium low, add a couple cups of water and place the florets in a steamer basket. Steam for 5–10 minutes, occasionally checking for the texture you like. Drain the liquid and discard, or save it for a future soup.

Once the chicken is cooked, drain the liquid into a glass storage container, saving the broth for future recipes. (Tip: You can make a soup with the leftovers from this dish. Take this bone broth, add some leftover chicken and a little sea salt and ground pepper, and you have a whole new meal!)

Allowing the chicken to cool a bit, or using tongs, take the meat off the bone (it should come off really easily and you can use a knife or fork, if needed).

If the honey-glaze mixture is in a big enough saucepan, it's great to add the chicken and broccoli into it and heat it all up for a few minutes on a low setting, mixing thoroughly in the honey glaze. If the saucepan is too small, place the chicken on a serving platter, then pour the honey glaze over it and mix well.

Taste the final result and see if you want to add a touch more honey, sea salt, or pepper, or leave it as is.

Serving suggestions:

Serve warm as is, or over a bed of rice or quinoa.

Serve with a side salad, or over a bed of romaine lettuce or arugula.

BAKED
LEMON TURKEY
Breast[1]

This recipe by the **Price-Pottenger Nutrition Foundation** uses chicken bone broth or any poultry stock or neutral broth or stock.

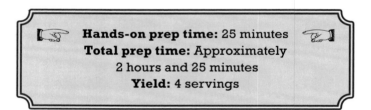

> **Hands-on prep time:** 25 minutes
> **Total prep time:** Approximately
> 2 hours and 25 minutes
> **Yield:** 4 servings

½ turkey breast with skin on (3–4 lbs.)

1 cup chicken broth (or any poultry or vegetable broth)

1 large clove garlic, peeled and minced

1 medium lemon, sliced into rounds

1 medium onion, peeled and sliced

1 Tbsp. fresh sage, chopped (or 1 tsp. dried)

1 Tbsp. fresh basil, chopped (or 1 tsp. dried)

1 tsp. sea salt

Preheat oven to 325° F.

Place turkey in a large baking dish. Cut several slits in top of breast skin, and plug with garlic. Place lemon slices on top of turkey, and surround bottom of breast with onion.

Pour in the broth and, if needed, add a bit more water so that the turkey breasts are sitting in about 2" of liquid. Mix seasonings in a bowl and spinkle evenly over the breasts.

Bake for 20 minutes per pound, basting as needed.

When the turkey is browned, cover the pan with foil or a silicone baking mat, and continue baking for another 30–50 minutes. (You can also check for doneness by putting a meat thermometer into the center of the breast to see when it reaches 165°).

Remove turkey to a cutting board, then let sit a few minutes before slicing.

Serving suggestions:

This dish would go well with a salad or any of your favorite cooked greens.

Serve with the Mashed Celery Root and Best Brussels Sprouts.

Serve with the Cardamom Carrots and Caramelized Onions.

The Pickled Ginger (with the optional carrots suggested in the recipe) would also go well with this dish, along with some raw, cultured vegetables, like sauerkraut.

EASY TURKEY
MEATLOAF CUPCAKES
with Kabocha Squash Topping

Your inner child is in for a treat! These wonderful meatloaf cupcakes look like a dessert, with kabocha squash as the frosting. They are a savory treat with just the right amount of naturally sweet tastes for a perfect balance that satisfies your taste buds and your body. This recipe calls for flavored or neutral poultry stock, although you can also use vegetable stock or neutral meat broth or stock; and it uses the Mashed Kabocha Squash recipe in Chapter 8.

If you've had a busy day and just want to get dinner on the table, this is a fast, delicious way to do it. You can skip the kabocha squash topping, but if you've baked it ahead of time, the whole recipe will go very fast.

These cupcakes are equally delightful as a casual meal or a gourmet lunch or dinner. Most of all, they're just plain fun! The first time we served this to our recipe testers, the Bone Broth Tribe, they oohed and ahhed through the whole meal, saying that the kabocha squash topping took everything over the top, worthy of a gourmet restaurant.

☞ **Hands-on prep time:**
15 minutes–1 hour
Total prep time: 20 minutes–1 hour
Yield: 10–12 cupcakes ☜

1 cup coconut oil (can substitute butter, ghee, or our favorite blend: ½ cup coconut oil and ½ cup ghee)

2 cups diced red onion (about 1 large or 2 medium onions)

5 stalks celery, sliced thin

1 Tbsp. thyme

1 Tbsp. basil

2 tsp. ground rosemary

2 tsp. black pepper

1 tsp. fennel

1 tsp. fenugreek

1 cup bone broth (ideally, use flavored or neutral poultry broth or vegetable stock)

2 tsp. sea salt

1 cup Madeira (You can substitute cooking sherry or a sweet red wine. You can leave this out entirely, but note that it does add a nice, gourmet taste.)

6 strips bacon (cut into small pieces)

1½ lbs. ground turkey (or ground chicken)

Easy Turkey Meatloaf Cupcakes
with Kabocha Squash Topping.

We recommend you make the Mashed Kabocha Squash recipe first, if you haven't baked the squash ahead of time, so you can make the turkey meatloaf while the squash is cooking. You can even cook the squash in your slow cooker the night or morning before you serve this meal, so it's all ready when you get home from work.

For a super-fast option, you can use sweet potatoes for this recipe: cut them into small pieces and boil for 10–15 minutes while the meatloaf is cooking. This will cut the time quite a bit if you weren't able to plan ahead but still want to experience this delicious meal. Once tender, drain the water, then mash the veggies with a potato masher or put in your food processor.

Preheat oven to 325°.

Put coconut oil, onion, celery, and all spices (except sea salt) into a large sauté pan, and set your burner to medium low. Allow the spices to warm up and release their aroma. Sauté until the onion is translucent, then add the bone broth and sea salt. Simmer for 5 minutes.

Add Madeira and keep simmering for another 5 minutes.

Now add the cut bacon and ground turkey to the pan and continue to simmer on the lowest temperature setting as you mix everything up well. We like to then transfer the mixture into a food processor with S-blade and pulse it a few times to really blend everything together well. Alternatively, you could pour the meatloaf mixture into a mixing bowl and stir with a wooden spoon.

Grease a 12-cupcake pan with coconut oil, butter, or ghee. You may want to use a silicone cupcake pan on top of a cookie sheet (which would allow you to get the cupcake pan into and out of the oven more easily). Now you're ready to fill the cupcake pan: Scoop in just enough to fill the cupcake hole. You don't need to fill it too full.

Put your meatloaf cupcakes into the oven and cook for about 10 minutes. You'll know they're done because they'll shrink in size and get juicy. You can touch a cake in the middle to see if it feels a bit bouncy like a sponge. Or use a meat thermometer—it's done when the meat thermometer reads 155°–160°.

Remove from the oven to cool a bit, then place on plates or a serving platter and put the kabocha squash on top like frosting. You can be as sloppy or as artful as you like! Some people like to use a cake-decorating set and pipe the squash onto the meatloaf for a beautiful presentation. Or you could just put the squash next to the meatloaf cupcakes for a no-fuss way of serving. We tend to be more rustic and do whatever is easy!

Serving suggestions:

Serve with the Simple Asparagus, Best Brussels Sprouts, a side salad, or your favorite soup or broth.

BREAKFAST
LAMB STEW²

This recipe by the **Price-Pottenger Nutrition Foundation** calls for lamb broth, although you can use any red meat broth or stock.

If you're new to lamb, you are in for a treat! It's packed with nutrition, and many people find it to be an easier-to-digest red meat. Tender cuts can be eaten raw, rare, or medium-rare; tougher cuts can be braised in broth to make stews. Always eat lamb as a whole food—that is, with the fat that accompanies it.

☞ **Hands-on prep time:** 30 minutes ☜
Total prep time: 12–16½ hours
Yield: 6 servings

---

2 lbs. lamb stew meat, with fat

1 cup red wine

3–4 cups lamb broth

1 Tbsp. butter

1 Tbsp. olive oil

1 (6-oz.) can tomato paste

Several sprigs fresh rosemary and thyme, tied together

2 cloves garlic, peeled and mashed

2–3 whole cloves (or ¼ tsp. ground)

1 tsp. dried green peppercorns, crushed (or substitute capers or ½ tsp. crushed black peppercorns)

2–3 small pieces fresh orange peel

5–6 red-skinned potatoes (or substitute 3 cups chopped celery root if you want a non-starchy alternative)

6–8 medium-sized carrots, peeled and cut into strips (about 3 cups)

2 Tbsp. arrowroot powder dissolved in 2 Tbsp. water

Salt and pepper, to taste

Breakfast Lamb Stew.

Marinate lamb in wine in the refrigerator for several hours or overnight. Remove from wine and dry pieces very well with paper towels; save the marinade.

Add butter and olive oil to a deep braising pan or Dutch oven with lid; set the heat to low, allowing the butter to melt. Once melted, add the stew meat and turn the heat up to medium high. You want all of the meat in a single layer in the pan for browning, so cook the meat in batches if your pan is not big enough.

Brown the meat on all sides, removing to a plate for subsequent pieces of meat if they don't all fit in the pan at once.

When the meat is browned, pour the fat off into a bowl, then add the leftover marinade and the broth to the pan. (You can save the fat for other cooking purposes.) Bring to a rolling boil, and skim off any scum that rises to the surface.

Reduce heat and add browned meat, tomato paste, herbs, garlic, cloves, peppercorns, and orange peel to the pan.

Place in a 300° F oven and cook for 3–4 hours with the lid on (check tenderness at the 3-hour mark).

Add potatoes or celery root 1 hour before the stew finishes cooking.

Add the carrots 30 minutes before the stew finishes cooking; remove the lid for the final 30 minutes. You can add some water or broth if the stew looks too dry.

Just before serving, transfer pan to the stove, and over medium heat stir in the arrowroot mixture to thicken the sauce.

Add salt and pepper to taste.

Serving suggestions:

Serve with your favorite green vegetables.

Enjoy with the Herb Bread or Maya's Finnish Sourdough Rye Bread.

RABBIT
IN WHITE WINE
Mustard Sauce

If you want to serve a really special meal that is pretty easy to make, this is the one that will delight your guests. It can either be rustic, farm-to-table style, or high end and sophisticated, depending on the side dishes you choose. It works best with poultry bone broth or stock, although any broth or stock with a mild flavor will do, and uses the White Wine Mustard Sauce from Chapter 6.

You will need a slow cooker for this recipe. If you don't have one, you can use a braising pan. Just make sure you meet these requirements if you do: (1) the braising pan must be big enough so that all of the rabbit meat fits into the pan (at least 12" in size); (2) you must have a lid and use it while you cook the rabbit (it will take 1–3 hours on low heat); and (3) you will want the liquid to almost fully cover the rabbit for the best cooking results. The rest of the steps are exactly the same.

Louise: I founded Hay House, Inc., in 1984; in 1988, Reid Tracy, Hay House's current President and CEO, joined the company. Over the years, we've traveled quite a bit together for speaking events, and have many wonderful memories. Once we were at an event in rural Italy, and I'll always remember the restaurant we found there. Reid was excited because they had rabbit, his favorite, on the menu. The first day we arrived for lunch, Reid ordered the rabbit. The waiter, who did not speak English, told us through hand gestures and playacting that the rabbit was too fast to catch! We laughed and ate something else on the menu. Every day for a whole week, we'd walk through the olive trees to get to the same restaurant so that Reid could have his rabbit. And every day, the rabbit was too fast to catch. Today, I dedicate this recipe to Reid, who I know will love it dearly. I think you will, too!

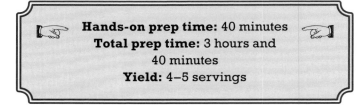

☞ **Hands-on prep time:** 40 minutes ☜
Total prep time: 3 hours and
40 minutes
Yield: 4–5 servings

1 rabbit (approximately one 6-lb. rabbit or two 3-lb. rabbits)

Coarse sea salt (approximately ¼ cup)

3 Tbsp. coconut butter (or butter)

White Wine Mustard Sauce

Please read all of these instructions first, before preparing the rabbit:

If the rabbit still has organs, carefully cut them out of the interior and put them aside. You can save the organs and make delicious pâté with them another time.

Rinse the rabbit well with water and pat it dry. Cut it into serving pieces. (There are several excellent "how-tos" for cutting up a rabbit on YouTube, and we recommend you watch them because it makes the process so much easier. Or you may be able to get your butcher to cut it up for you.)

Salt the rabbit pieces well by rubbing coarse sea salt all over each of them. Then set the pieces aside at room temperature for 30 minutes to an hour.

Add 3 Tbsp. coconut butter to the sauté pan and put the heat on medium high; brown the rabbit pieces. It will take 8–10 minutes to do both sides of the meat. You want a nice, brown color so that the flavor is locked into the meat. This is especially important for game, which is low in fat.

Keep in mind that your pan may be too small to brown all the rabbit pieces at once. This is okay—just cook the meat in batches in the pan, being sure that the pieces are in a single layer and the sides of the meat don't touch each other. When each batch is done, put in your slow cooker or braising pan.

Continue browning at a moderate pace, until all pieces of rabbit are done. Remember, if the meat is sticking while you're browning, it just needs more time to brown on that side. Do not turn the meat too often; 4–5 minutes on each side will likely be enough.

Once the rabbit is browned, set aside and make the White Wine Mustard Sauce. Pour the sauce over the rabbit in your slow cooker or braising pan. The sauce should be mostly covering the rabbit meat, but it's okay if some of the meat is not fully submerged. Add water if you need more liquid to cover the pieces. Cook the rabbit:

— *On the stove top*: In large braising pan, set your burner to medium high, and bring the rabbit and sauce to a simmer, then reduce the heat to low and simmer for 1½–2 hours. Make sure that the sauce is not coming to a boil or bubbling too much. If it is, use a burner diffuser or move to a back burner. Check at the 1½-hour mark, and every 15 minutes thereafter, to see when the meat is fork tender—this means that the meat is easily pierced and removed from the bone with a fork or just shy of falling-off-the-bone tender. Some describe the texture as "velvety chicken." This is much easier to achieve in a slow cooker, but if you don't have one, just make sure not to let the heat get too high.

— *In the slow cooker*: It's up to you how long you want your meat to cook; you can do it on a low heat setting for 6–8 hours. We have found that it's nice and tender at the 6-hour mark.

When the rabbit is finished cooking, remove it to a serving platter and put the sauce into a gravy boat. Pour some sauce over the rabbit on the serving platter, and reserve the rest to add to each individual dish when ready to eat.

If you're a wine lover, this dish goes well with a Bordeaux Blanc, pino grigio, or French chardonnay; or a Belgian-style beer.

Serving suggestions:

Serve with one or two of the following: the Cardamom Carrots, Caramelized Onions, Simple Asparagus, Mashed Kabocha Squash, or Herb Bread.

cu

Cornish Game Hen with White Wine Mustard Sauce, Cardamom Carrots, and Carmelized Onions.

CORNISH GAME HEN
WITH WHITE WINE
Mustard Sauce

Cornish game hens are much smaller than chickens, and make an elegant change to the usual chicken dinner. They are especially lovely for an elegant meal, when you want to keep things simple but are going for a special presentation.

This is the kind of meal you can make for a dinner party after a long day of work because there isn't much preparation; you can use any broth or stock, although poultry broth or the Healing Elixir Vegetable Stock would be best. You can make the birds a day in advance, or put them in a slow cooker the morning or afternoon before your dinner party, giving yourself at least 6 hours to slow cook them. They will go much faster in your oven, if you're short on time.

We recommend the White Wine Mustard Sauce from Chapter 6 to accompany this meal. While the game hens are wonderful without the sauce and can certainly be served on their own, the sauce ups the ante for flavor and presentation. If you have extra sauce, it can serve as gravy or vegetable or salad dressing, or be used the rest of the week for leftovers and soups. Some people like to double the sauce recipe for this reason. You can freeze the extra if you like.

While many recipes will say that a whole Cornish game hen serves 1 person, we've found that half of a bird served with vegetable side dishes is generally a good portion size. Some variation will depend on whether you get a smaller game hen or a larger one (birds typically range from 1¼–2 lbs. each).

> **Preparation time:** The sauce can be made up to 3 days before serving, if you want to plan ahead and save time.
> **Hands-on prep time:** 35 minutes
> **Total prep time:** 1 hour and 25 minutes (oven cooking); 6 hours and 35 minutes (slow cooker)
> **Yield:** Approximately 6 servings

6 cloves garlic

½ onion

2 Tbsp. butter

1 Tbsp. ground rosemary

1 tsp. tarragon

½ tsp. ground ginger

1 tsp. black pepper

1 tsp. basil

2¼ cups bone broth (while poultry bone broth would be best, any broth or stock will do)

1 tsp. sea salt

3 Cornish game hens 5 cloves garlic

6 sprigs fresh thyme (or 2 tsp. dried)

White Wine Mustard Sauce

If using your oven, preheat to 450° F; skip this step if using your slow cooker.

Make the butter mixture:

Mince 1 clove of garlic and dice the onion. You can do this very quickly if you have a food processor: Put the garlic clove and onion in your food processor with the S-blade and pulse a few times until you have tiny chunks. You don't have to be perfect with this because it's going in the butter mixture to be spread under the skin of the game hen; just go for small pieces.

Put the butter in a saucepan; set your stove burner to the lowest temperature. Add the garlic and onion, and cook on low for 2 minutes.

Add the rosemary, tarragon, ginger, black pepper, and basil. Heat on low for 1 minute until the aromas are released.

Add 1/4 cup bone broth and sea salt. Raise the heat to medium high and bring to a simmer, then turn off the heat and allow to cool for a few minutes. Pour the mixture into a small bowl.

Season the Cornish game hens:

If your hens came with giblets, remove them and set aside for use in another meal. Rinse the hens and pat them dry.

If cooking in the oven, put your hens into a deep casserole dish or Dutch oven. Put them right in the slow cooker if you're slow cooking them.

With the cavity of the hen facing you, slide your fingertips under the breast skin, gently lifting the skin off the breast to make a pocket of space. This should happen very easily.

Now that you've made a space under the skin, dip your hands into the bowl of butter mixture and spread it on the breast meat, just under the skin. You can use a silicone brush or a baster, if you like. Pour any excess butter mixture into the cavity of the hens and over the top of the skin.

Place the sprigs of thyme under the skin on each side of the breast, 1 sprig per side of each hen. If using dried thyme, evenly spread some under the skin of each breast.

Put 1 clove of garlic in the cavity of each hen, and 2 cloves in the pan or slow cooker you're cooking them in.

Add 2 cups bone broth or stock in the pan you're cooking the hens in.

Cook the Cornish game hens:

— In *the oven*: Reduce the oven temperature to 350° F. Place the game hens in the oven and cook for 45 minutes–1 hour. A lidded Dutch oven will result in moister hens; if you don't have a lid, you could baste the hens every 10–15 minutes with the bone broth and juice at the bottom of the pan. You can check to make sure your game hens are ready by using a meat thermometer in the breast of the chicken—the internal temperature will read 165° F when they're done cooking.

— In *the slow cooker*: Slow cooking the hens will guarantee you a very moist end result. Set your slow cooker to 6 hours, or put it on high for 1 hour, then reduce to low for the last 5 hours. The meat will be fall-off-the-bone tender.

Prepare the White Wine Mustard Sauce while the hens are cooking.

Serve the hens by cutting them in half and laying the cut half down on the plate. Drizzle the sauce over them; put the excess sauce in a gravy boat to have at the table.

Serving suggestions:

This dish is wonderful when served with one or two of these vegetable side dishes: the Caramelized Onions, Simple Asparagus, Best Brussels Sprouts, or Magic Zucchini and Carrots.

If you're running short on time, a simple spring mix salad would go well with this dish, too.

PAN-SEARED
SNAPPER OR HALIBUT

Since fish broth calls for non-oily fish, we created this recipe to make a tasty meal with the fish you remove from the bones. This recipe is flexible and can be used with almost any non-oily fish; it calls for fish stock or broth (or dashi stock), but you can use any neutral broth and stock or the Healing Elixir Vegetable Stock.

We've served this recipe at dinner parties, and it's always a treat because it tastes great and cooks really fast. This is especially good if you want to spend more time with your guests or if you want a fast meal after a long day at work.

Hands-on prep time: 10 minutes
Total prep time: 30 minutes–2 hours and 20 minutes (depending on marinating time)
Yield: 4–6 servings

3 cloves garlic

6 Tbsp. olive oil

3 Tbsp. lemon juice

1 tsp. ground ginger (or 1" fresh ginger, peeled and sliced thin)

1 tsp. turmeric

2 tsp. thyme

1 tsp. sea salt

1 tsp. black pepper

2 lbs. halibut or red snapper

2 Tbsp. fish broth or stock

Mince the garlic.

Add the olive oil, lemong juice, garlic, and all spices into a deep, rectangular, glass baking dish or container, and mix together well. Add the fish and turn it around in the oil-and-spice mixture, coating it well.

Allow the fish to sit and marinate in the oil and spices for 10 minutes–2 hours (store in your refrigerator if marinating for more than 10 minutes).

Add fish and oil-and-spice mixture to a skillet; add the broth. Cook on medium heat on your stove top for 2–4 minutes on each side (halibut may cook faster than snapper). You'll know it's done when the fish flakes easily with a fork. You can always cut the fish in half and take a look at the middle, too—if it looks wet and solid in the center, it still needs to cook a bit.

Add sea salt and pepper to taste.

Serving suggestions:

Serve with the Best Brussels Sprouts or Simple Asparagus.

Serve with the Healing Elixir Vegetable Stock.

Enjoy with the Herb Bread.

Pan-Seared Halibut.

Best Brussels Sprouts.

∾ CHAPTER 8 ∾

THE CLEANSERS:
Vegetable Dishes

BEST
BRUSSELS
Sprouts

This is one of our favorite go-to recipes. It's easy and fast, and it goes with just about anything. Plus, everyone always loves it! Brussels sprouts cook a lot faster when they're shredded, and they always look good on the plate as a salad topper or side dish.

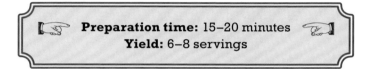

☞ **Preparation time:** 15–20 minutes ☜
Yield: 6–8 servings

1 lb. brussels sprouts (about 4 cups shredded)

3 cloves garlic, minced

½ cup diced onions

1 Tbsp. duck fat, butter, or ghee

1 tsp. thyme

1 tsp. basil

1 tsp. ground rosemary

1 tsp. black pepper

½ cup Madeira

½ cup bone broth or stock (any meat, poultry, or vegetable broth or stock)

1½ tsp. sea salt

Clean brussels sprouts, cut off the ends (save for future bone broth or vegetable stock), and remove any blemished outer leaves. Shred them in your food processor with the slicer attachment or cut up into thin shreds. Set aside.

Put the duck fat, butter, or ghee in a skillet, braising pan, or wok (with lid); set the heat to low, allowing the fat to melt.

Add the thyme, basil, rosemary, black pepper, garlic, and onions; sauté on low until the onions are translucent.

Add the Madeira, bone broth, and sea salt; simmer on medium low for 3–5 minutes.

Add the brussels sprouts and set the heat to low. Put on the lid and allow to simmer on low for 5–10 minutes, or until the shreds are as soft as you like them. Once the brussels sprouts are cooked to your liking, remove them from the heat.

Season to taste with more fat, sea salt, or pepper.

Serving suggestions:

Serve on its own, over a salad, or with your favorite main dish.

This recipe is so flexible that it goes with just about anything. Try it with the Bison Meatloaf Cupcakes with Mashed Celery Root or the Pan Seared Snapper or Halibut.

CARDAMOM
CARROTS

These are a nice, naturally sweet change from typical cooked carrots, as the cardamom gives them a rich taste. They wonderfully accompany burgers, meat, game, and just about any entreé that you want to serve with a special side (see photo on p. 180)—but they're so good on their own that you could make a meal or snack out of them as well.

☞ **Hands-on prep time:** 15 minutes ☜
Total prep time: Approximately 1 hour
Yield: 8 servings as a side dish

10–12 carrots (about 3–4 cups, julienned)

2 Tbsp. butter, ghee, or coconut oil

2 tsp. cardamom

1 tsp. cinnamon

1 tsp. black pepper

2 tsp. thyme

1 tsp. basil

⅛ tsp. ground celery powder

1 cup bone broth (can also use meat stock or the Healing Elixir Vegetable Stock)

1½ tsp. sea salt

Peel carrots, then julienne them. If you have a food processor, you can use the julienning attachment to make this really fast and easy. A mandoline is also an option to make julienning easier.

Add coconut oil, butter, or ghee to a skillet with lid (at least 3½ quarts); set your burner to low, allowing the fat to melt. Add cardamom, cinnamon, black pepper, thyme, basil, and celery powder, and heat on low for 3 minutes, to allow the spices to release their aromas and medicinal properties.

Add bone broth and sea salt. Turn the heat up to medium and simmer for 10 minutes, then add carrots. Reduce the heat to low and put the lid on the pan; cook 30–45 minutes, or until carrots are soft. Add more salt and pepper to taste.

Serving suggestions:

Serve on their own or as a topping for burgers or salad. They're also delicious on romaine lettuce with steamed slices of zucchini and yellow squash, drizzled with a little coconut oil.

CARAMELIZED
ONIONS

Caramelized onions make a great flavor enhancer for meat, poultry, and vegetable dishes. A couple tablespoons in soup or broth, and you have a wonderful new flavor. They add gourmet flair to just about any meal (see photo on p. 180), and many people find them easier to digest than raw or lightly cooked onions.

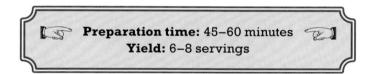

Preparation time: 45–60 minutes
Yield: 6–8 servings

3 medium-sized onions; red, yellow, or white all work

2 Tbsp. coconut oil, butter, or beef tallow

¼ cup bone broth (if you use flavored, choose something that will harmonize with the meal you intend to serve the caramelized onions with, like chicken bone broth for poultry, or beef or pork bone broth for red meat dishes)

Cut the onions about ⅛" thick. If you have a food processor, you can use your slicing attachment to make this go really fast.

Put the coconut oil in a large braising pan or deep skillet (that has a lid) and heat on the lowest temperature, spreading the coconut oil on the bottom of the pan.

Add the bone broth and simmer on low for 2–3 minutes Add the onions, spreading them evenly along the bottom of the pan.

With the burner on the lowest temperature, put the lid on your pan and simmer for 45 minutes to an hour, or until all of the onions are very soft and translucent. You can either remove them from the heat when they're soft but not too mushy, if you like them more stewed, or you can caramelize them. If you do caramelize them, you'll cook them until they are a deep, rich brown.

Toward the end, as the onions are getting brown, you'll want to scrape the bottom of the pan with a spatula—you may have to add a little more bone broth, coconut oil, or butter to keep them from sticking to the pan and burning.

If you like, you can add a little balsamic vinegar into the pan to deglaze it. This also adds a little flavor.

Serving suggestions:

Season with sea salt and black pepper.

Caramelized onions make a great side dish for meat or poultry dishes; try serving with the Cornish Game Hen or Rabbit in White Wine Mustard Sauce.

The Magic Zucchini and Carrots or Simple Asparagus go very well with this dish. Adding cultured vegetables, like sauerkraut or kimchi, as a side dish along with caramelized onions is really tasty as well.

Add to a plain broth or soup to bump up the flavor.

MAGIC
ZUCCHINI
and Carrots

If you want to wow your guests (or indulge yourself!) for lunch or dinner, this side dish is the one to serve. It's a real crowd-pleaser for its light taste—you'll surely get recipe requests from even the picky eaters!

☞ **Hands-on prep time:** 15–20 minutes ☜
Total prep time: 1 hour
Yield: 6–8 servings

---

4 medium carrots

1 zucchini

1 yellow summer squash

1 cup mirin

¼ cup extra-virgin olive oil

¼ cup bone broth or stock

1 tsp. sea salt

2 tsp. dill weed (or 1½ Tbsp. fresh)

1 tsp. oregano

Preheat oven to 350° F.

You can cut these vegetables however you want:

— If you're in a hurry and not concerned about presentation, you can rough cut them into chunks.

— You can avoid chopping altogether by using one of the slicing attachments on your food processor and slice them into half-moons or rounds (a fast and easy kitchen trick).

— You can amp up the presentation for a fancy dinner by julienning them (again, your food processor may have an attachment for this—bonus!).

— Make flat strips (that is, long, thin slices) in your food processor or with a mandoline.

— As one more creative alternative, you could make thin spaghetti-like spirals with a spiralizer. (This can be really fun for kids or the kid in you!)

Put all ingredients into an uncovered casserole dish and mix well. Bake for 20 minutes (if you're doing long, thin slices or spirals, cook for 10–15 minutes). The vegetables are done when they're slightly soft when pierced with a fork. Save the excess liquid for another recipe.

Serving suggestions:

Serve as a side dish, snack, or salad topper. The excess liquid makes a great salad dressing if using this dish as a salad topper.

It's delicious as a topping for the Mashed Celery Root, with the excess liquid drizzled on as "gravy."

Top with the Aioli or Lulu's French Rémoulade.

Zucchini, yellow summer squash, and carrots for Magic Zucchini and Carrots.

MASHED
CELERY ROOT

This recipe makes a fast comfort food that tastes as good as mashed potatoes without all the starch. (You can also make it with turnips, if celery root is not available.)

A member of the carrot family, celery root or celeriac is found in the produce aisle during the fall and winter seasons. Many health-food stores carry organic celery root, and you'll often find celeriac in bins near the turnips at the grocery store. In fact, it's kind of like a knobby turnip, and not considered a pretty vegetable—but, as with all things, don't let looks deceive you!

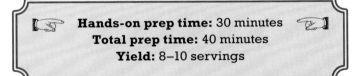

Hands-on prep time: 30 minutes
Total prep time: 40 minutes
Yield: 8–10 servings

3 celery roots (about 1–2 lbs. each)

½ cup butter or coconut oil

1 Tbsp. rosemary

1 Tbsp. basil

2 tsp. pepper

2 tsp. garlic powder

½ cup Madeira

1 cup bone broth (any red meat or poultry bone broth or stock, or vegetable stock)

2 tsp. sea salt

Peel the celery root. You can use a peeler or just cut the skin off with a good knife.

Add about 3 cups water to a saucepan and turn the heat to high, bringing the water to a boil while you chop the celery root into chunks. They can be large chunks—keep it simple.

Add the celery root to the water and boil until the pieces are soft, about 10 minutes. When they're cooked, you should be able to insert a fork or knife very easily into the chunks.

While the celery root is boiling, in another saucepan on low heat, add 1 Tbsp. butter or coconut oil and all of the spices, except the sea salt. Allow the spices to warm in the oil for 2–5 minutes to release their aromas and bring out their medicinal qualities. Add the Madeira and cook for 3 more minutes; remove from the heat, and add the bone broth.

Once the celery root is soft, remove from the heat and strain out the water (save it for a future broth or recipe). Now add the celery root to the saucepan with the spices and bone broth. Add the rest of the butter or coconut oil and sea salt, and heat on the lowest temperature to mix everything in.

If you have an immersion blender, you can use that to puree the celery root right in the saucepan. If you don't have a handheld blender, you can either use a potato masher or a fork, or put the mixture into your food processor or blender and blend it all up.

Now it's ready to eat! Season to taste with extra sea salt or pepper.

Serving suggestions:

Serve this as a side dish for anything you'd want to pair with mashed potatoes.

This makes a great breakfast mash with eggs and bacon.

Serve with the Simple Asparagus or Best Brussels Sprouts or your favorite soup.

A little red leaf lettuce, a drizzle of olive oil, and some of this Mashed Celery Root on top is a really great vegan/vegetarian meal! The celery root warms the lettuce, and it makes a lovely comfort food.

This is an excellent choice when traveling because it tastes great cold, too!

Mashed Celery Root.

MASHED
KABOCHA
Squash

This recipe is best made with a neutral meat bone broth or stock, or the Healing Elixir Vegetable Stock. You can use a flavored broth or stock as well, just make sure you take into account the flavor of the broth (vegetables, seasonings used, and so on) because it will influence the flavor of the mashed squash. You may be able to leave out several of the spices if your broth has a lot of flavor.

A winter squash, kabocha squash is the ultimate comfort food. It looks like a flatter, green pumpkin, and has a sweeter, almost meatier taste and drier texture as compared to a butternut squash. Some say it tastes a bit like sweet potatoes. You can use butternut squash, sweet potatoes, or buttercup squash as a substitute if you can't find kabocha squash at your grocery store, health-food store, or farmers' market.

☞ **Hands-on prep time:** 20 minutes ☜
Total prep time: 1 hour
and 20 minutes
Yield: 6–8 servings

1 large kabocha squash	2 tsp. thyme
1 onion, diced	2 tsp. black pepper
1 cup coconut oil	1 cup bone broth or stock
2 tsp. cinnamon	1 tsp. manuka honey (or 1 tsp. molasses)
1 tsp. allspice	2 tsp. sea salt

Cook the squash:

— *Oven method*: Preheat oven to 350° F. Rinse the squash, pat dry, and pierce the skin with a sharp knife several times (this lets hot air out while cooking). Place in a glass dish and bake for about 45 minutes to an hour. You'll know it's done when you can easily insert a knife in the center. It should be soft to the touch.

— *Slow-cooker method*: Rinse off the squash, pierce it several times with a sharp knife, and put it into your slow cooker on low for 8 hours. You'll know it's done when you can easily pierce it with a sharp knife and it's soft when you touch it.

Add the onion, 2 Tbsp. of the coconut oil, and all the spices (except for the sea salt) to a sauté pan; sauté on low until the onions are translucent. Add the bone broth, honey, and sea salt to this mixture; continue to sauté for 2 more minutes. Turn off the burner and reserve this mixture until the squash is finished cooking.

Once the squash is fully cooked, remove it, allow it to cool a bit, and cut down the center with a sharp knife. Remove the seeds (some people like to save these, wash them off, and then soak and roast them for a treat).

Scoop out the squash into a mixing bowl and add the onion mixture and the rest of the coconut oil; mix thoroughly. If you want a really creamy texture, use a potato masher or your food processor with the S-blade.

Serving suggestions:

This is the perfect topping for the Turkey Meatloaf Cupcakes. It goes equally well with your favorite grain dishes and meat, poultry, or fish dishes.

Serve with the Simple Asparagus, the Best Brussels Sprouts, a side salad, or your favorite soup or broth.

Mashed Kabocha Squash.

SIMPLE
ASPARAGUS

This recipe is so fast, simple, and delicious that it's sure to be a hit no matter when you serve it! Asparagus is full of glutathione, a detoxifying antioxidant, and rich in important vitamins, minerals, and anti-inflammatory properties. It's the perfect fast food for when you get home from work and want a quick, comforting meal that is easy on your digestive system. This recipe is flexible because it goes with just about any dish you're making, and adds a touch of class to any plate.

☞ **Preparation time:** 5–10 minutes ☜
Yield: 6–8 servings

---

2 bunches asparagus

2 cups bone broth (any meat or poultry broth or stock, or veggie stock)

2 Tbsp. butter or duck fat

1 Tbsp. ground rosemary

1 Tbsp. basil

1 tsp. black pepper

1 tsp. sea salt

Remove tough woody ends of the asparagus (save them for your bone broth or veggie stock!).

Fill a 6-quart stockpot or 3½-quart braising pan with the broth or stock. If you want to steam the asparagus instead of boiling it, put a steamer basket in the pot. Add water, as needed, so that there's enough to cover the asparagus (if boiling) or the water level is just below the steamer basket.

Set the burner to high and bring to a boil. Add the asparagus, and reduce the heat to a low simmer for 4–7 minutes, or until the asparagus is how you like it. Everyone is different—some like it al dente and others like it soft.

Once the asparagus is cooked to your liking, strain out the water (save it for your next batch of broth or stock, or for other cooking uses). Set the asparagus aside in a bowl for a moment.

Add the butter or duck fat back to your empty pan. Set the burner to low and melt the fat; add in all of the spices and heat on low for 2 minutes. Add the asparagus back in and toss in the fat and spices for 2–3 minutes.

Season to taste with more fat, sea salt, or pepper.

Serving suggestions:

Serve on its own, over a salad, or with your favorite main dish.

This recipe is so flexible that it goes with just about anything. Try it with the Bison Meatloaf Cupcakes with Mashed Celery Root Topping for a casual yet gourmet dinner treat.

BALANCED & BRIGHT
SEARED VEGGIE
Sauté

This recipe by **Quinn Wilson,** owner of Balanced & Bright Bone Broth, calls for beef bone broth and also uses beef tallow. However, you can use any type of bone broth, stock, or the Healing Elixir Vegetable Stock.

    This easy, tasty veggie dish is perfect when you want a nutritious meal in minutes.

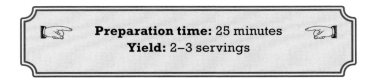

Preparation time: 25 minutes
Yield: 2–3 servings

1 Tbsp. beef tallow (See Chapter 2 for more on rendering fat from the fat cap on top of your beef bone broth. You can use butter or ghee if you don't have any tallow on hand.)

1 head broccoli (stem removed, peeled, and sliced lengthwise; cut broccoli florets lengthwise, in quarters or half depending on size)

2 medium carrots, sliced on an angle (1 cup)

1 Tbsp. ginger

6 cloves garlic

¼ cup beef bone broth

Sea salt, to taste

Olive or sesame oil for drizzling

In a large sauté pan, heat the tallow on medium high heat (just before it begins to smoke). If the fat begins to smoke, turn down the heat.

Once the tallow is hot and melted, add the broccoli and carrots. Allow the vegetables to sear on one side in the pan. When they begin to brown, toss them gently in the pan, about 3–5 minutes total. Finely mince the garlic and ginger, then add to the bone broth; allow to steam until liquid evaporates.

Turn off heat. Gently toss the vegetables to distribute the garlic and ginger; generously toss with sea salt (start with 2 tsp. and taste).

Transfer to your serving dish. Drizzle with olive oil or sesame oil, depending on taste.

Serve immediately. (It's also excellent served cold.)

Serving suggestions:

Serve with your favorite grain, meat, poultry, or fish dish.

Serve over a bed of lettuce for a fabulous warm salad.

Enjoy with the Herb Bread or Maya's Finnish Sourdough Rye Bread and Aioli.

PICKLED
GINGER

This side dish is perfect when you want a sweet-and-sour taste as a side dish. It's particularly good for Asian food or if you're doing a Chinese hot pot party. It's also a great substitute for fermented foods, soy sauce, wheat-free tamari, and Bragg Liquid Aminos, if these foods trigger reactions in you.

This recipe calls for any lightly flavored or neutral bone broth or stock (but not fish stock). You can puree it to make it into more of a thick sauce—or just leave it as is and have it as a side dish for burgers, salad, or anything you can dream up!

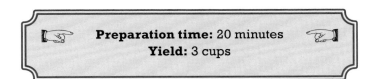

Preparation time: 20 minutes
Yield: 3 cups

3 cups fresh ginger, peeled (or 2 cups ginger and 1 cup carrots, if you want to have a ginger-carrot dish, which makes a nice alternative)

½ cup bone broth (lightly flavored or neutral broth or stock)

1½ tsp. sea salt

1 cup raw apple cider vinegar or sugar-free rice wine vinegar

⅓ cup raw honey

Peel ginger, and either julienne or slice in very thin rounds. You can julienne with your food processor or a mandoline to make it easier (if you decide to use carrots, too, cut them the same way).

In a saucepan, heat ginger (and carrots, if using) and bone broth on medium until roots are soft (5–7 minutes). Add sea salt, vinegar, and honey; mix thoroughly.

Allow to cool, then store in a glass jar. Can be served warm or cold.

Serving suggestions:

Serve with a Chinese hot pot party meal.

Use as a side dish for burgers, or serve with fish, meat, or poultry dishes.

Use in place of fermented vegetables for any dish.

Top a salad, or puree to add to soups or salad dressing.

⊸ CHAPTER 9 ∾

THE STAFF OF LIFE:
Grains, Breads, and Pancakes

Before we get to the recipes in this chapter, we'd like to take a moment to talk about the importance of soaking nuts, seeds, and grains. Soaking removes the anti-nutrient phytic acid, which binds up the minerals and essentially steals them from the body. We need minerals for all enzymatic functions in the body—they're our energy spark plugs and give us our mojo! So for optimal digestion, be sure to take the time for this step.

How to Soak Nuts and Seeds

- Put the nuts or seeds in a glass or stainless-steel bowl. (Note that 2–3 cups of nuts or seeds at a time is useful for recipes, while 1–2 cups at a time is useful for snacks. If you want to make more and freeze them, consider up to 6 cups at a time when soaking.)

- Add enough filtered water to cover them.

- Add about 1 tsp. sea salt per cup of nuts, and mix well.

- Cover the bowl with a lid or plate and leave it on the counter for 8–12 hours. You can do this before going to bed.

- After 8–12 hours, drain the water, rinse the nuts or seeds, and either put them in the refrigerator (lasts 3 days to 1 week) or the freezer (lasts about 2 months).

- *Optional*: You can also dry your nuts or seeds. Put them in a single layer on a baking sheet and put in the oven on the lowest temperature. Heat until dry (10–20 minutes). If you have a food dehydrator, set it to 115° F and dehydrate for 2–5 hours or until dry. They will last a couple of weeks in your refrigerator or several months in your freezer.

How to Soak Grains

- Put grains in a glass or stainless-steel bowl (follow the same quantity guidelines as previously mentioned for nuts and seeds).

- Add enough filtered water to cover them.

- Add 1 Tbsp. of apple cider vinegar for every cup of grains, and mix well.

- Cover with a lid or plate and let sit on your countertop for 8–12 hours.

- After soaking, drain and rinse the grains in a fine mesh strainer. Fine mesh is especially important for small grains, like millet.

- You can cook with them immediately; or store the soaked grains in your refrigerator for a few days, or in your freezer for about a month.

cu

HOW TO
MAKE YOUR OWN
Almond Flour

In this chapter and in some of the dessert recipes in Chapter 11, almond flour is one of the ingredients used. Almond flour, coconut flour, and other grain-free flours have been helpful for people with gut issues, allowing them to enjoy breads and desserts that are easier on their small intestine.

Organic almond flour (also called almond meal) can be very pricey. For this reason, you might want to make it yourself. Note that you can save time if you find organic almonds that have already had their skins removed, but we still recommend that you soak them overnight to make them easier to digest (unless they've been soaked or sprouted already).

> **Hands-on prep time:** 15–30 minutes
> **Total prep time:** 9–13 hours
> **Yield:** 4 cups

4 cups organic almonds

1 Tbsp. sea salt

Soak your almonds according to the instructions at the beginning of this chapter. Once they've been soaked, drain them, blot dry with paper towels, and remove their skins. Simply squeeze the almonds, and their skins should come right off. Be careful, though, as the almonds shoot out of the skin! (You can also peel the skins off.)

Now you're ready to dehydrate the almonds in your food dehydrator at 115° F, for about 2–4 hours until they're completely dry. If you don't have a food dehydrator, put them in the oven on the lowest temperature until they're dry (10–20 minutes).

Once dehydrated, pulse the almonds in your food processor with the S-blade, or in a high-speed blender—don't leave it unattended because the almonds can turn to butter if overprocessed. Pulse them until you get a grainy mixture that looks like almond meal, and you're good to go!

Use almond flour in your favorite recipes; it can often substitute well for coconut flour. However, if the recipe calls for regular flour, you may have to make some creative adjustments; for example, you may need to add more liquid or adjust spices for the flavor.

Keep in mind that almond flour does not act like gluten flours, so it won't have the same flexibility or create the same air pockets that regular breads have. It will tend to make better quick bread-style breads than fluffy breads that rise.

Storage: Store in your refrigerator for a few weeks or in your freezer up to 6 months.

cee

HERB BREAD

(Grain Free)

This recipe can use any type of bone broth (flavored or neutral). The broth should be fairly solid when chilled; if it's not, add 1–1½ Tbsp. unflavored powdered beef gelatin when you are heating up the broth.

This is a moist and flavorful bread that will keep you grounded and satisfied. It contains medicinal, antioxidant, and anti-inflammatory spices; it's also received rave reviews from our recipe testers, the Bone Broth Tribe. It is protein rich and has healthy fats, which makes it a very satisfying snack, appetizer, or accompaniment to a main meal.

Most grain-free breads don't do well as sandwich breads, and this one is no exception. It's easy to digest, though, which makes it worth the change of habit. So cut this bread into thick pieces and use as a side with a salad; dip it in soups; spread it with aioli, butter, or pâté; or use it for whatever suits your fancy!

> ☞ **Hands-on prep time:** 10 minutes ☜
> **Total prep time:** 1 hour
> **Yield:** 1 loaf, with approximately 10 thick slices

½ cup bone broth (chicken broth is exceptionally good, but any gelled broth works)

2 eggs

3 Tbsp. flax meal

1½ tsp. ground rosemary

1½ tsp. basil

1 tsp. sea salt

1 tsp. black pepper

1 cup coconut butter

2 Tbsp. coconut oil

2 Tbsp. butter

¼ cup almond flour

1 tsp. baking soda

Optional—these lighten up the flavor and add a nice touch:

2 tsp. honey

½ tsp. turmeric

Herb Bread.

Preheat oven to 300° F.

Grease a loaf pan with butter or coconut oil. We love using silicone bread pans because they're flexible and make it easier to get the bread out of the pan. If you use one, put the pan on a cookie sheet for greater ease in getting it into and out of the oven.

Put all ingredients in your mixing bowl or food processor with the S-blade and mix thoroughly. Pour the mixture into the greased pan and bake for 35–50 minutes, checking at the 35-minute mark.

Note: Grain-free breads don't rise much and tend to stay about the same level as the batter you pour into the pan. This bread will look a bit wet, even when it's done baking. It may look very moist and won't bounce as much as other breads when it's fully cooked. This is because it has very little actual "flour" and is rich in protein fats. When you touch the center to see if it's done, it will bounce a bit, so you'll feel a little firmness, but with plenty of moisture. You will know it's done because it will turn a light golden color on top and have that little bit of firmness when pressed.

Remove it from the oven when it's slightly golden brown, even if it still looks moist from the oils.

Allow the bread to cool completely on your countertop before taking it out of the pan; this will keep it from breaking. When it's completely cooled, run a butter knife around the edge, between the bread and pan, to loosen up the bread. Carefully remove it from the pan.

Store the bread in the refrigerator, where it will firm up because the oils will harden. Take it out of the refrigerator 20–30 minutes before serving to bring it to room temperature (or heat on lowest oven temperature to warm it up a bit before serving).

This bread freezes very well, so we recommend doubling the recipe and storing it in your freezer so you have a fast snack or bread for a dinner party. You can slice it before storing it, if you want to be able to remove and thaw a few slices at a time.

Serving suggestions:

Serve with the Pâté Plus, the Best Pâté Ever, or any of the salads or aspics in Chapter 10.

Spread with the Aioli, Lulu's French Rémoulade, butter, or coconut oil.

Dip in your favorite broth, soup, or stew.

MESSED-UP BUT SO DELICIOUS
PAN BREAD
(Grain Free)

This bread was a mistake. Not the flavor—the flavor is fantastic. It was a mistake because it was hard to work with. Overall, while we and our recipe testers loved the taste, we felt it was just too challenging because it could fall apart unless we were very careful getting it out of the fully cooled pan.

Then something happened. Not wanting to throw away good bread, we put the crumbles into a pan with some beef tallow and sautéed it up with some ground chicken for our Chicken Burger Salad. It was so delicious that we oohed and ahhed all the way through the meal.

We felt it would do you a disservice not to share this recipe, even though it's not the perfect "bread." If you're fortunate enough not to break the loaf, it's a great bread. If it does crumble, though, you will be just as happy with the meals you can achieve with it. It makes a wonderful hush puppy, stove-top stuffing, soup thickener, or complement to anything you want to sauté along with it.

> **Hands-on prep time:** 10 minutes
> **Total prep time:** 1 hour
> **Yield:** 1 loaf, with approximately 10 thick slices

1 cup bone broth (recommend chicken, but you can use any flavored or neutral broth)

1 egg

1 tsp. ground rosemary

1 tsp. basil

1 tsp. sea salt

1 tsp. black pepper

1 cup coconut butter

2 Tbsp. coconut oil

2 Tbsp. butter

¼ cup coconut flour

2 tsp. honey

½ tsp. turmeric

1 tsp. baking soda

Preheat oven to 300° F.

Grease a loaf pan with butter or coconut oil. We love using silicone bread pans because they're flexible and make it easier to get the bread out of the pan. If you use one, put the pan on a cookie sheet for greater ease in getting it into and out of the oven.

Put all ingredients in your mixing bowl or food processor with the S-blade and mix thoroughly. Pour the mixture into the greased pans and bake for 35–50 minutes, checking at the 35-minute mark.

Note: Grain-free breads don't rise much and tend to stay about the same level as the batter you pour into the pan. This bread will look a bit wet, even when it's done baking. It may look very moist and won't bounce as much as other breads when it's fully cooked. This is because it has very little actual "flour" and is rich in protein fats. When you touch the center to see if it's done, it will bounce a bit, so you'll feel a little firmness, but with plenty of moisture. You will know it's done because it will turn a light golden color on top and have that little bit of firmness when pressed.

Remove it from the oven when it's slightly golden brown, even if it still looks moist from the oils. Allow the bread to cool completely on your countertop before taking it out of the pan; this will keep it from breaking. However, this bread actually breaks very easily, so it may break anyway. Remember, you're using it for crumbles to sauté, as stuffing or soup thickener, or as a replacement for hush puppies.

When it's completely cooled, run a butter knife around the edge, between the bread and pan, to loosen up the bread. Carefully remove it from the pan.

Store in the refrigerator, where it will firm up because the oils will harden. Take it out of the refrigerator 20–30 minutes before serving to bring it to room temperature (or heat on lowest oven temperature to warm it up a bit before serving).

This bread freezes very well, so we recommend doubling the recipe and storing it in your freezer so that you have a fast snack or bread for a dinner party. You can slice it or take bits of the crumbled pieces and wrap them separately into the portions that you'll want to use later. This allows you to thaw only what you think you will need and save the rest in the freezer.

Serving suggestions:

Sauté in a skillet with butter, coconut oil, or animal fat; add spices if you like. It can be a stove-top stuffing or served like hush puppies with a salad, like the Chicken Burger Salad.

Sauté with bacon to absorb the bacon fat. Serve with eggs and bacon for a hearty breakfast.

Add to soups, stews, or broth to thicken them up.

HEALING
BUCKWHEAT <small>AND</small> VEGGIES

This recipe by medical intuitive **Rhonda Lenair** calls for the Healing Elixir Vegetable Stock. Unless you want an entirely vegan meal, you can also use any meat or poultry stock or broth that you have on hand.

This particular dish allows you to get a large dose of vegetables with a smaller amount of buckwheat grains, which can be wonderful for a gentle cleanse or detox. It's also perfect for dinner, especially when you're working on supporting your stomach, pancreas, and adrenals. A gluten-free grain dish with plenty of vegetables can help create a calm state of mind, aiding the body in winding down for more peaceful sleep.

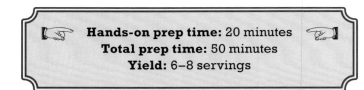

Hands-on prep time: 20 minutes
Total prep time: 50 minutes
Yield: 6–8 servings

3–4 cups Healing Elixir Vegetable Stock

10–12 cups shredded veggies (choose whatever you have on hand, like leeks, purple cabbage, onion, collards, kale with stems, cauliflower, carrots, and so on)

1 cup whole, fine, or medium granulation buckwheat

Optional: You do not have to add spices to this meal, but if you want, add sea salt and pepper, to taste; and perhaps add some fresh or dried thyme, rosemary, turmeric, basil, and coriander. Start with ½ tsp. of each, adding more if desired.

Optional: Sesame oil to drizzle over bowls upon serving

Add stock and all veggies to a large stockpot and bring to a boil.

Add buckwheat and boil for 5 minutes, then reduce the heat to low so that the water is just simmering. Add herbs, spices, and sea salt, if desired.

Cook for 20–30 minutes or until the water has been absorbed.

Serving suggestions:

Drizzle toasted sesame oil on top of each bowl you serve.

Serve with the Mashed Kabocha Squash.

Healing Buckwheat and Veggies.

QUINOA,
BROCCOLI,
and Leek Pilaf

This recipe is so flexible that you can use any bone broth, meat stock, or vegetable stock (just not fish stock); however, if you're practicing food combining, use vegetable stock.

When served warm, this dish is perfect for breakfast, lunch, or dinner. Many people are new to the idea of eating vegetables for breakfast; the most popular choices tend to be eggs and bacon, oatmeal, doughnuts, or cereal. This recipe makes a nice transition into vegetables for breakfast because it gently takes you there with grains as your ambassador.

We have made this as a tasty treat for traveling because it tastes just as good cold as it does warm. While cold meals for a full day of travel are not always pleasant, this one is really quite scrumptious and something to look forward to! For long trips or flights, you can add extra avocado for healthy fat and delicious flavor.

☞ **Hands-on prep time:** 15 minutes ☜
Total prep time: 35–45 minutes
(add 8–12 hours if you choose to soak the quinoa)
Yield: 6 servings

2 cups quinoa (red or white)

2 Tbsp. coconut oil or butter

2 tsp. curry powder (or turmeric)

2 tsp. black pepper

1 cup leeks, sliced thin

1–2 cups water

2 cups bone broth or stock

2 cups broccoli, cut into small florets

½ tsp. sea salt

Quinoa, Broccoli, and Leek Pilaf.

For optimal digestion, you can soak the quinoa according to the instructions at the beginning of this chapter, then drain the water and rinse. If you decide to skip soaking it, put the grains in a fine mesh strainer and rinse to remove the bitterness, which will make the quinoa taste better.

Put coconut oil, curry powder, pepper, and leeks into a large sauté pan and set the burner to low. Sauté for 5 minutes.

Now add the water (use 2 cups if you didn't soak the quinoa and only 1 cup if you're using soaked quinoa), broth or stock, and sea salt; turn the burner to high, bringing the liquid to a boil.

Once the liquid is boiling, turn the heat to medium low and add the quinoa. You'll want the liquid with quinoa to be simmering slowly and not boiling over, so adjust the heat accordingly. Allow to simmer for 10 minutes. This is a good time to cut up your broccoli, if you haven't already.

After 10 minutes of simmering, reduce the heat to low and add your broccoli. Put a lid on your pan; cook the quinoa and broccoli for 10 minutes or until the broccoli is soft and the quinoa is translucent. You'll see the little outer rings of the quinoa coming off of the grains, which will appear translucent, with no hard, white spots appearing. If you're using red quinoa, you'll see a similar effect with the red color going from a hard, dry look to a soft, wet, translucent look.

Continue to cook on low until all of the liquid is absorbed into the quinoa. If for some reason your quinoa isn't finished cooking and all the liquid has absorbed, no problem! Just add another ¼ cup water and let that simmer, adding more if you need to.

If you've soaked your quinoa on the longer side (12 hours or more), it may cook faster, but the liquid might not get fully absorbed. If this happens, you can get a fine mesh strainer and strain the liquid into a bowl (save for future use). This tends to happen if the burner is set too high. If you cook on low,

the liquid will tend to absorb slowly and uniformly. However you do it is okay!

Once the quinoa is cooked, remove from the heat and serve. You may want to have extra coconut oil, butter, ghee, or flaxseed oil on the table to drizzle over the dish, as some people like to customize the amount of healthy fats to their unique taste.

Add sea salt and black pepper to taste.

Serving suggestions:

Serve with your favorite broth or soup.

Add to the top of a bed of lettuce and drizzle with oil or dressing. The grains will warm up the lettuce for a nice comfort-food appeal.

Serve with the Best Brussels Sprouts or Simple Asparagus.

For travel:

Many people experience digestive upset during travel, so bringing along some healthy food that's easy on your system can calm your body, mind, and spirit.

Take this dish with you in a jar in a large plastic zip-top bag, with a disposable freezer pack. If you want to bump up the vegetables a bit, throw some romaine lettuce into the jar, too. Add some chunks of avocado and season with sea salt.

Alternatively, if you have a widemouthed thermos, you can keep your quinoa nice and warm for your trip. TSA standards typically allow for solid food to go through security—as long as your food is not full of liquid, the agents may want to look it over, but it's usually not a problem. This can be extra nice if you're in a hurry and don't want to scour the airport for the rare healthy-food vendor before sitting down at your gate and awaiting your flight.

Grains last up to 4 days in the refrigerator, so if you're going on a trip, you can ask the hotel you're staying in to provide a fridge in your room and take your quinoa for an on-the-road snack, breakfast, or alternative to restaurant meals.

BALANCED & BRIGHT
JASMINE RICE *with* SEASONAL VEGETABLES,
Golden Raisins, and Pistachios

This recipe by **Quinn Wilson,** owner of Balanced & Bright Bone Broth, calls for any bone broth or stock of your choice. You may want to aim for a neutral or lightly flavored broth or stock (or the Healing Elixir Vegetable Stock) to allow the flavors of this dish to shine through.

This recipe is great for breakfast, lunch, or dinner; it's a unique, savory, and sweet dish that adds new flavor and variety to your day. You get all the benefits of raw, seasonal vegetables that you'd enjoy in a salad, plus warm rice cooked in nourishing bone broth, and a veggie dressing to pull all of the tastes together.

☞ **Hands-on prep time:** 30 minutes ☜
Total prep time: 50 minutes if not
soaking the rice first (add 8–12 hours
if you're soaking the rice first)
Yield: 2–4 servings

Note on ingredients: This recipe has three parts that all come together for a great, one-bowl rice salad.

Rice ingredients:

1 cup uncooked jasmine rice

2 cups bone broth or stock of your choice

Dressing ingredients:

1 small shallot

1 clove garlic

2 Tbsp. flat-leaf parsley

2 Tbsp. red balsamic vinegar

2 tsp. fresh oregano

2 tsp. basil

⅓ cup extra-virgin olive oil

1 tsp. sea salt

1 tsp. black pepper

Salad ingredients:

2 cups bite-size pieces of assorted seasonal vegetables of your choice (such as cucumbers, tomatoes, beans, zucchini, peas, cabbage, beets, carrots, radishes, broccoli florets, and so on)

¾ cup hand-torn seasonal mixed leafy greens, sprouts, and herbs

⅓ cup chopped red, yellow, or white onion or green onions

¼ cup toasted pistachios, chopped (sunflower seeds and pine nuts are great alternatives)

¼ cup dried currants

Start the day before if you want to soak the rice (see instructions at beginning of this chapter).

Cook rice per the package directions using bone broth in place of water (1 cup of rice to 2 cups of bone broth will yield 2 cups cooked rice for this recipe).

Dressing instructions:

Place shallot, garlic, herbs, and vinegar in a blender or food processor, and blend until combined. Add sea salt and pepper.

With the blender or food processor running, slowly drizzle in oil. Process dressing until well combined.

Salad instructions:

Place salad ingredients in a large serving bowl.

Assembling the meal:

Drizzle the vegetables in your serving bowl with 3 Tbsp. dressing and toss to coat.

Serve over a bed of your cooked rice. Add additional dressing to individual bowls, to taste.

MAYA'S FINNISH
SOUROUGH
Rye Bread

This bread works well with any bone broth or stock.

Heather: Several years ago I traveled with Louise to Scotland for a Hay House event. We were excited because we were going see our dear friend Maya Labos. Maya is from Finland. She's beautiful, funny, and full of life. She's also a spitfire: She'll tell it like it is, and even if it's brutally honest, you'll love her for it. You can always count on Maya for a madcap story and a lot of laughs!

In Scotland, Maya bought five loaves of brown Irish soda bread to take on an upcoming cruise. Two weeks later, I got a call from her. "I could not believe it—I put the bread in paper, and when I got on the cruise five days later, it was all moldy," she said.

"Why did you think it wouldn't be moldy after five days in paper?" I asked her. That's when it hit me. She'd thought her soda bread was like the bread she grew up with.

I had just been doing some research in which I'd learned that people in other countries grew up eating sourdough that they hung on a pole for an entire month. Sourdough is actually alive—it's how our ancestors made bread full of probiotics that could last without refrigeration or freezing.

"Okay, I'm making you some authentic Finnish sourdough bread," I told Maya. After some more research, I found out how to get an authentic dry starter, and experimented with a recipe until it was perfected. This is the result of that recipe, which has now been modified to add bone broth—because we all deserve to have even better hair, skin, nails, and digestion while eating bread!

Maya has confirmed that this bread reminds her of her childhood. She loves to bake it until it's dry and slather it with butter. And she's not the only fan—everyone who tastes this bread loves it, and I've shared a bit of my activated starter with people all over the country. Once you have the activated starter, this no-knead bread is super easy to make. It's worth learning how to do because it makes the perfect travel food and snack. You're taking a grain with very little gluten and activating it with probiotics, so it becomes a living bread that delivers probiotics into your body. Add the bone broth, and you've got something really special.

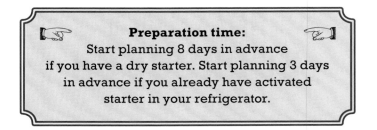

Preparation time:
Start planning 8 days in advance
if you have a dry starter. Start planning 3 days
in advance if you already have activated
starter in your refrigerator.

— *Dry starter*: It takes 7 days to activate a dry starter. Activating it basically means that you continue to make a flour and water mixture until it rises as it should, per the instructions that follow.

— *Activated starter*: Once you have an activated starter, making the bread is relatively quick. If you've just gotten your activated starter out of the refrigerator, you must revive it before making the bread. The steps for doing this (which follow) can take between 1–3 days, depending upon how recently you fed your activated starter. Reviving it consists of making sure the starter is rising properly, possibly feeding it with flour and water for a day or more, and then mixing the batter, letting it rise, and baking the bread.

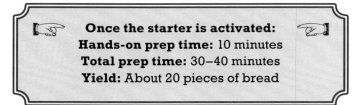

Once the starter is activated:
Hands-on prep time: 10 minutes
Total prep time: 30–40 minutes
Yield: About 20 pieces of bread

Preparation Notes—Before You Can Make Bread

Purchase a dry Finnish sourdough rye starter. We recommend Ed Wood's Sourdoughs International because they carry many authentic starters from around the world. You can order yours here: www .sourdo.com/cultures/finland/.

While you're waiting for your starter, watch some videos on how to make sourdough bread (YouTube has a bunch of options). You can look up how to make both sourdough and no-knead sourdough bread—this recipe is "no knead," which makes it extra easy. The hardest part is just understanding the steps. Once you get them, the whole thing is really simple; it's not as delicate a process as the videos lead you to believe. Sourdough rye is hardy and can take a lot of imperfect handling.

Once you receive your dry starter, follow the instructions to activate it. This requires about seven days of feeding the starter, which is essentially filling a jar with flour and water and watching it rise. It's easy, but it takes a 10-minutes-per-day commitment.

After you've activated your starter, store it in a quart-sized widemouthed jar, like a mason jar, with the lid loosened or just sitting on top so that air can get in

Maya's Finnish Sourdough Rye Bread

and out. You'll keep this starter in the refrigerator until you're ready to make bread.

Once a week, you'll "feed" the starter to keep it alive and well. To do so, open the jar and add 1 cup stone-ground organic rye flour and ¾ cup water. Mix this up well, making sure to get all of the flour mixed in. The starter is pretty hardy, so if you miss a week, you can still use it—see instructions for reviving your activated starter below.

When you're ready to bake bread, plan 2–4 days ahead (1–3 days of feedings and 1 day to let the bread rise). You might be able to cut corners and do 1–2 days ahead, but the recommendation is 3 days ahead (if your revived starter doubles in size when left overnight, you can make the bread the next day).

Here's how to revive your activated starter:

— Take it out of the refrigerator. If you haven't fed it in a while and it has some brown liquid on it (called hooch), you can either pour it off or stir it right back in. It's not "bad"; it's just been dormant.

— Feed the starter with 1 cup flour and ¾ cup water, and stir it all up well. Then leave it on your countertop, with the lid sitting so that air can flow through. (We like to feed our starter once per day. After being fed, it will grow, possibly doubling in size, and show some air bubbles in the mixture.) After letting the starter sit for 12–24 hours, assess whether it needs to be fed again. If your flour mixture has doubled in size in your jar, it's revived and ready to use in the bread recipe. If you haven't fed your starter in a long time and it's been sitting in your refrigerator, you may need to feed it a couple more times before it doubles in size and is ready to use in the recipe.

— After 12–24 hours, if your revived starter has not doubled in size, feed it again. You can take some of the starter out to make room for it to grow. Our recommendation is to take the starter out and begin a new jar so that you have a backup, and feed both of them. You could keep doing this and end up with a lot of jars! So unless your friends want some, use it for recipes or discard the extra when you go to feed it again. It will keep growing.

— If your revived starter has still not doubled in size after another 24 hours, feed it again for the 3rd time (3rd time's the charm!). Let it grow for 12–24 hours, and then you'll be ready to make your bread.

Whether it takes 1 or 3 feedings, after you've fed the sourdough starter and it's doubled in size, you'll be ready to use the bread recipe that follows. Allow 5–24 hours for the bread to rise.

Here are some tips:

— Watching a video does help! Here are some options: http://www.culturesforhealth.com/how-to-videos#sourdough_videos. The ones you'll want cover how to make sourdough bread and how to care for and feed your starter. Remember, you have a starter that has already been activated, so you'll need to feed it to get it ready to bake, but you don't have to begin from scratch with a dry starter.

— Rye has much less gluten than wheat breads or the like, so it won't rise as much (it also won't rise very much if you use stone-ground flour). It's a flatter bread, and as we've been told by Maya, flat bread is exactly what she was used to eating growing up in Finland.

— This dough is sticky, so rinse everything immediately after you make the bread to keep cleanup simple. We use a non-scratch scouring sponge to clean the dough off hands and utensils, and it works like a dream.

— When baking the bread, using the coconut oil or butter along with the sprinkled flour and caraway seeds makes all the difference in creating a perfect nonstick surface for the bread.

— Let your bread cool for at least 3 hours on a wire rack before cutting. Some say to let the bread "cure" or sit for 2 days before eating because the flavor really comes out. (We are rarely able to wait that long though!)

— Finnish people say to store the bread in a paper bag; Maya tells us it's because they like it dry and crispy. You might like it better stored in a plastic bag to keep it soft. Try both and see what you think.

— The bread should last longer than a week out of the fridge or freezer and still be delicious. In Finland, they leave it out for a month, which is possible to do without molding because it's a live bread. It does dry out over time, so we tend to leave ours out for a week and then slice up what we haven't used and put it in the freezer. You can pop a frozen piece or two in the toaster to warm up as needed.

2 cups organic sprouted rye flour (using sprouted flour makes the bread easier to digest, but optional)

2 Tbsp. blackstrap molasses

1½ Tbsp. caraway seeds

1 Tbsp. sea salt

1 cup bone broth (any flavored or neutral broth or stock)

¼ cup water

1¼ cups prepared rye flour starter

Mix up all ingredients well in a glass bowl. We usually stir it by hand using a wooden spoon; at least 50 strokes, or for 2–4 minutes. You will have a smooth, sticky dough. You do not need to knead it (hooray!).

Put a cover on the bowl and let it sit for 5 hours or overnight. The dough will almost double in size. (If the dough refuses to grow, you'll need to start over with activating your starter.)

Once it has doubled in size and you're ready to bake the bread, turn the dough onto a well-floured surface. This dough will be rather wet and sticky; have a lot of flour and water on hand so that you can use it to make everything easier to work with. Let the dough sit for 15–30 minutes to give it a "rest." While the dough is resting, preheat oven to 435° F.

Grease your bread pan with coconut oil or butter, sprinkle some flour over it, followed by some caraway seeds over the flour. This will make a nice non-stick surface.

You can use a regular loaf pan made of glass or silicone, but avoid metal. Since sourdough bread is fermented, it's acidic, and contact with metal (particularly any metal other than stainless steel) for the length of time it takes to bake the bread can cause a reaction resulting in discolored bread. Shorter contact, such as using stainless-steel mixing utensils, is not a problem. A lot of sourdough bread makers swear by using stone, like a LaCloche clay bread baker (which you can purchase online or at your local kitchen store). We've also made the bread in silicone and glass pans, which worked out really well.

Now put the bread dough into your pan—flouring your hands will help keep it from sticking to them. It may be very wet, but you can add more flour to the dough as you're working with it to get it into the pan (adding flour on top and on the sides to keep it from sticking).

Once you have the dough in the pan, take a sharp knife and put some slits (like a tic-tac-toe board) into the top. This will allow air to escape during cooking and give it a nice look once baked. If your knife sticks, wet the blade so that it slips through easily.

Bake for 30 minutes, and then check the bread, pressing the center to see if it's firm and bounces back. You'll likely need to bake for another 10–15 minutes. Turn the oven temperature down to 390° F for the last 10–15 minutes (and if you're using a LaCloche baker or other stoneware with a top, remove the top for the last 10–15 minutes of baking). Check with a meat thermometer—once the center of the bread reaches 220° F, it's done. The top should be brown a bit and get slightly drier.

Allow the bread to cool before removing from the pan. Make sure it's completely cool before slicing or it could become gummy.

PANCAKES or WAFFLES

(Grain Free)

On a weekend morning, when you just want to kick back and have some pancakes, this is the perfect recipe! After many experiments to come up with the perfect grain-free pancake recipe, we stumbled upon this lucky result one day. You can make several pancakes at once in the oven or one or two at a time on your stove top. You can also make waffles with this recipe.

Adorn with maple syrup, fruit, honey, butter, or whatever you feel drawn to. We've found that if you remove the honey from this recipe (or just use ½ tsp. honey at most), you can also make blinis for savory appetizers. These pancakes freeze well, too, so if you want to make extra, it's a great way to have a quick snack or meal on hand.

Indulge your inner child!

☞ **Hands-on prep time:** 10 minutes ☜
Total prep time: 20–30 minutes
Yield: 4–6 servings as a meal, and up to
10 servings if you make appetizer blinis

¼ cup coconut oil

½ cup coconut milk (you can make your own with ½ cup water and 1½ Tbsp. coconut butter, blended thoroughly in your blender)

¼ tsp. sea salt

2 cups almond flour

3 Tbsp. butter

1½ Tbsp. unflavored powdered beef gelatin

1½ Tbsp. honey

2 cups water

2 eggs

Note: Decide if you want to make the pancakes or waffles in the oven. You can purchase silicone waffle molds online and make several waffles at a time in your oven, if you like. If you decide to make them this way, preheat oven to 350° F.

Heat up 2 cups of water to just shy of boiling, and allow to cool for a few minutes. Add gelatin to the water and mix; then allow to sit for 5 minutes while the gelatin dissolves.

Add all ingredients, including the gelatin and water, to your mixing bowl or food processor with the S-blade and blend up completely. The batter will be thick; you can add more water if you want a thinner batter.

Oven method:

Grease silicone waffle molds—or, if you want pancakes, a baking sheet (a standard 9" x 13" or larger will work)—with butter or coconut oil. Pour the batter into the molds or on the baking sheets as desired. It will be easier if you put the waffle molds on a baking sheet, because the silicone pans are flexible and could use the structure of the baking sheet for ease of getting into and out of the oven. You can completely fill the waffle molds because the grain-free batter won't rise over the top.

Put the pancakes or waffles into the oven and bake at 350° F for about 10–15 minutes. Check at the 10-minute mark. The crust color will start to be like a drier white, without a bit of a golden color, and the edges will start to lift away from the pan or mold. When you press the crust, it will be slightly bouncy.

Once baked, remove the pancakes or waffles from the oven and allow the pans to cool for 10 minutes before doing anything with them. Once the pans have cooled, turn them over to gently remove the waffles, or use a spatula to gently lift the pancakes.

Stove-top method:

The popular way to make pancakes is in a skillet on the stove top. However, we find that this recipe is easier if you make it in the oven because the batter is a little tricky to work with when it comes time to flipping it in a skillet. If you make it in the oven, you don't have to turn the pancake and have a better chance for it to turn out perfectly. With careful attention, though, you can still make these pancakes on the stove top.

Put butter or coconut oil in a large skillet, and melt over medium low heat. Pour in a small round of batter; start small so that you learn how to handle pancakes as they cook. If you haven't made grain-free pancakes before, know that they will act differently than those made with grain, which have gluten and more flexibility, and hold together better.

As we mentioned, grain-free pancakes are best if you allow them to heat low and slow. When they start to get whiter in color and the edges appear to lift a bit, they're ready to flip onto the other side; carefully flip with a spatula. You can cook them as crispy as you like. Keep the pan well greaased as you make more.

Serving suggestions:

Serve with berries, sliced bananas, or warm apple slices and a dash of cinnamon.

Drizzle with honey, all-fruit jam, or maple syrup.

Enjoy on their own as an on-the-go snack.

Spread with a nut or seed butter and jelly, honey, or maple syrup; roll up as a snack.

Prepare the same recipe without honey (or just ½ tsp. of honey) and serve blini-style with the Best Liver Pâté Ever!, smoked salmon and avocado, the Tempting Tuna Salad, Aioli, or any of the aspics.

Sassy Green Smoothie.

CHAPTER 10

THE LIGHTER SIDE:
Salads, Pâtés, Aspics, and Smoothies

//

CHICKEN
BURGER
Salad

This 5-minute meal serves as a wonderful lunch or dinner. It even tastes good cold if you want to take it on the go.

What pushes this recipe over the top is if having some of the Messed-up but So Delicious Pan Bread (see recipe in Chapter 9) to go with it. It's not required, but is a wonderful addition. We'll give you some notes on how to incorporate it into the recipe if you have some on hand.

You will love this easy meal!

1 Tbsp. butter or coconut oil

1 tsp. dried thyme

½ tsp. turmeric

1 tsp. black pepper

¼ tsp. allspice (*optional*)

½ cup diced shallots

½ cup chicken bone broth (or any poultry broth or stock, vegetable stock, or neutral broth)

1½ lbs. ground chicken (any ground meat or poultry will work)

1 head of romaine lettuce, chopped; or 4 cups spring mix salad

Chicken Burger Salad.

Melt butter or coconut oil in a skillet on low heat.

Add spices and shallots, and heat on low until the shallots are translucent. If you have some of the Messed-up but So Delicious Pan Bread, put it in the skillet and get it nice and warm, so it soaks up the fat and spices. Then remove and set aside (it's okay if you remove the shallots when you're doing this).

Add bone broth and sea salt; turn the heat up to medium, simmering until broth has reduced by half. Add the ground meat to the skillet; set the burner to medium low. Break up the burger so that it's in small chunks. This will allow it to cook very fast—it will likely only take about 3–5 minutes.

While the meat is cooking, wash and chop the lettuce.

Prepare a bed of lettuce on each plate. Once the meat is done, take it off the burner and scoop some on top of the lettuce on each plate. (Add the warmed Messed-up but So Delicious Pan Bread, if you made it.)

Serving suggestions:

Enjoy on its own. If you want other vegetables with the salad, sliced radishes, cherry tomatoes, or thinly sliced cucumbers or carrots are nice, but not necessary for this great-tasting salad.

The Aioli, Lulu's French Rémoulade, and Do It Your Way Salad Dressing all go well with this dish, although the juices from the pan may be all you need for a salad dressing.

This dish goes wonderfully with the Cardamom Carrots and Best Brussels Sprouts.

EVERYONE'S
FAVORITE
Egg Salad

If you haven't made egg salad in a while, you're in for a treat. It's fantastic because it's full of good protein and healthy fat, and a great source of choline and vitamins A, D, E, and B complex. This salad calls for the Aioli recipe in Chapter 6, which calls for neutral broth or stock.

Whether you serve it as lunch, a snack, or an appetizer, you'll enjoy the rich, delicious taste of this egg salad. It's also a great option if you need a meal for a trip and don't mind carrying it in an insulated bag with an ice pack. We often slip insulated lunch bags into our carry-on bags if we want to bring our own food for long trips.

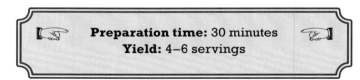

Preparation time: 30 minutes
Yield: 4–6 servings

3 tsp. sea salt

1 Tbsp. apple cider vinegar

6 eggs

½–1 cup Aioli

2 tsp. paprika

1 tsp. black pepper

Add 6 cups of water to a 3-quart saucepan and bring water to a boil. Add 2 tsp. sea salt and the apple cider vinegar.

Once the water is boiling, add the eggs, carefully putting them on the bottom of the pan with a large spoon. Boil uncovered for 1 minute.

Remove from heat and put the lid on the pan, leaving the eggs to sit in the hot water for 10–15 minutes.

While the eggs are sitting in warm water, make the Aioli.

Now back to your eggs: After 10–15 minutes, drain the warm water from the pan and put the eggs into a bowl, covering them with cold water. You can put the bowl of eggs and water in the refrigerator if you would like to chill it faster.

When the eggs are cold, crack each one lightly in one spot on a flat surface and roll it around—this will crack them in a way that makes them easier to peel. Peel the eggs and discard the shells or save them for a future bone broth.

Using your food processor with the S-blade or a potato masher, mix the eggs, paprika, pepper, and Aioli together until you have the consistency you like for egg salad. You'll likely want to use the pulse feature on your food processor so that you don't over-blend the eggs. Taste, and adjust salt and pepper.

Serving suggestions:

Serve in martini glasses or small bowls as an appetizer with Maya's Finnish Sourdough Rye Bread or the Herb Bread.

Serve with a plate of cut, raw vegetables.

Eat a scoop as a snack.

Roll in lettuce leaves, or serve on top of a green salad.

Serve with the Magic Zucchini and Carrots.

SIMPLY DELICIOUS
SALMON
Salad

Salmon is a superstar on the health scene for its nutritional profile and delicious taste. It's full of omega-3 fatty acids, B vitamins, and vitamins A, D, and E. Salmon is also protein-rich and has bioactive peptides, which provide antioxidants and protective properties for the heart, as well as inhibit cancer, type 2 diabetes, and inflammation.[1]

This salad calls for the Aioli recipe in Chapter 6, which is made with neutral broth or stock. If you're making a new batch for this recipe, you can use a neutral fish bone broth or stock if you like. Or if you have a healthy mayonnaise you'd like to use instead, that will work. You can also use Lulu's French Rémoulade recipe in Chapter 6, if you already have that ready-made.

If you choose canned salmon, you'll save time in making this recipe. Make sure to look for wild salmon and, for bonus points, a can that is free of the bisphenol A (BPA) toxin.

A *note about choosing sustainable fish*: As we write this book, wild sockeye salmon is a sustainable option, but it's important to check fishwatch.gov to see what's happening with salmon as time goes by.

Preparation time: 30 minutes
Yield: 4 servings

Simply Delicious Salmon Salad.

2 Tbsp. coconut oil

1½–2 lbs. fresh wild salmon (if using canned, use approximately 2½ cans)

½–1 cup Aioli

3 stalks celery, thinly diced (about ½ cup)

½ cup red onion, diced

½ tsp. sea salt

1 tsp. black pepper

Optional spices:

2 tsp. ground rosemary (or 1 Tbsp. fresh)

1 tsp. dried thyme

1 tsp. dried basil (or 1 Tbsp. fresh)

Rinse salmon steaks in cold water and pat dry.

Put coconut oil into a skillet and set burner to low, allowing the oil to melt. Add the celery, onions, black pepper, and any other spices you want to use. Heat for 2 minutes or until you smell their aroma—this allows the spices to release their medicinal benefits.

Put the salmon into the skillet and turn the heat to medium low. Sauté on one side for 5 minutes, then turn onto the other side for 3–4 minutes (or until it's done the way you like it). Reduce the heat to low if it's too hot.

When salmon is done, it should flake easily with a fork. You can always cut it in half and look at the inside: If you still see solid, wet-looking flesh in the middle, you may want to cook it longer, unless you like your fish to be more on the rare side. Be sure you don't overcook the fish or it will get dry and not taste as good.

Remove the salmon to a bowl, add the sea salt and Aioli, and mix thoroughly, mashing up the salmon with a large fork. Start with ½ cup Aioli and add more based on your desired texture. If you want to do this in your food processor, use the S-blade and pulse the fish, sea salt, and Aioli 5–10 times, until it reaches your desired consistency. Don't let the food processor go too long, or you will have more of a mushy pâté.

Serving suggestions:

Serve rolled in butter lettuce or romaine leaves, or add to the top of a salad.

Enjoy with a piece of the Herb Bread.

Have a scoop as a snack.

TEMPTING
TUNA
Salad

Tuna salad is a wonderful option for fast meals or lunches on the go.

This salad calls for the Aioli recipe in Chapter 6, which is made with neutral broth or stock. If you're making a new batch for this recipe, you can use a neutral fish bone broth or stock if you like. Or if you have a healthy mayonnaise you'd like to use instead, that will work. You can also make more of a salad Niçoise using our Do It Your Way Salad Dressing or Lulu's French Rémoulade.

For this recipe, you can use fresh or canned tuna. When choosing sustainable tuna, whether fresh or canned, it's important to look for pole-and-line or troll-caught wild tuna because it has the least impact on other marine life.[2] There are some canned options that state that the fish has been sustainably caught and wild, and the can is free of the bisphenol A (BPA) toxin. Greenpeace highlighted Wild Planet brand wild albacore canned tuna as one of the best in terms of sustainability.[3]

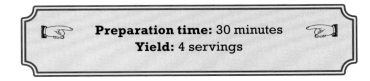

Preparation time: 30 minutes
Yield: 4 servings

2 Tbsp. coconut oil

1½–2 lbs. fresh tuna (if using canned, use approximately 2½ cans)

½–1 cup Aioli

3 stalks celery, thinly diced (about ½ cup)

4 green onions, thinly sliced

½ tsp. sea salt

½ tsp. black pepper

Optional spices:

1 tsp. dried basil (or 1 Tbsp. fresh)

1 tsp. dried thyme

¼ tsp. ground celery seed

Rinse tuna in cold water and pat dry.

Put coconut oil into a skillet and set burner to low, allowing the coconut oil to melt. Add the green onions, celery, black pepper, and any other spices you want to use. Heat the spices for 2 minutes or until you smell their aroma—this allows the spices to release their medicinal benefits.

Put the tuna into the skillet, and turn the heat to medium low. Sauté on one side for 5 minutes, then turn onto the other side for 3–4 minutes (or until it's done the way you like it). Reduce the heat to low if it's too hot.

When tuna is done, it should flake easily with a fork. You can always cut it in half and look at the inside: If you still see solid, wet-looking flesh in the middle, you may want to cook it longer, unless you like it more on the rare side. Be sure you don't overcook the fish or it will get dry and not taste as good.

Remove the tuna to a bowl, add the sea salt and Aioli, and mix thoroughly, mashing up the tuna with a large fork. Start with ½ cup Aioli and add more based on your desired texture. If you want to do this in your food processor, use the S-blade and pulse the fish, sea salt, and Aioli 5–10 times, until it reaches your desired consistency. Don't let the food processor go too long, or else you will have more of a mushy pâté.

Serving suggestions:

Serve rolled in butter lettuce or romaine leaves, or add to the top of a salad.

Enjoy with a piece of the Herb Bread.

Have a scoop as a snack.

LOBSTER
SALAD
Extravaganza

Lobster salad. It's what you have when you really want to treat yourself and the ones you love. It's a party for the mouth . . . truly an extravaganza! This recipe is worthy of a casual lunch or an upscale appetizer. (Note that it calls for the Aioli from Chapter 6, made with neutral bone broth. Lulu's French Rémoulade can also be used here, or you can use your favorite healthy mayo.)

Heather: During a week in Savannah, Georgia, Louise and I visited a restaurant called Maxwell's. We went there for three nights in a row because we fell in love with the food, the staff, and the owner, Catherine. We even met the chef. The funniest thing was that he refused to use butter, because the kitchen was too small! We laughed so hard when we heard this and brought our own butter for the next two nights.

Louise taught Catherine to do mirror work, and in her latest e-mail to us, she said she's still doing mirror work and benefitting from it very much!

One of the appetizers we had at Maxwell's was lobster salad. It was so delicious that we promptly went home and made our own version of this tasty treat. We're so excited to share it with you.

☞ Preparation time: 40–50 minutes **☜**
Yield: 6 servings

---

8 (7-oz.) lobster tails (3½ lbs. lobster total)

2 tomatoes

5 stalks celery, diced (about 1 cup)

¼ cup diced red onion

2 Tbsp. butter

2 tsp. thyme

1 tsp. turmeric

1 tsp. basil

1 tsp. black pepper

1 Tbsp. sea salt

¼–½ cup of Aioli

1 tsp. dried tarragon
(or 1 Tbsp. fresh)

2 Tbsp. finely chopped fresh
chives or green onions

Lobster Salad Extravaganza.

Cook the lobster tails (if you didn't purchase them already cooked):

If they're frozen, put them in your refrigerator overnight to thaw. They will be a brown-green color when uncooked.

When they're thawed and ready to cook, bring 6 cups of water with 1 Tbsp. sea salt to a boil. Add the lobster tails and boil for 8–10 minutes (uncovered) or until the tails turn bright red; the meat should feel tender when poked with a fork. Once they're cooked, remove from the water or drain in a colander. Allow the tails to cool to room temperature.

Cook the tomatoes and remove their skins:

Put 2 cups water into a saucepan and bring to a boil.

Put another 2 cups cold water into a large bowl.

Make an X cut in the bottom of each tomato (this makes it easier for the skin to come off). Put tomatoes into the boiling water and boil until the skin starts to come off (about 1 minute).

Once skin starts to come off, remove tomatoes from boiling water with a slotted spoon and put them into the cold water. After tomatoes are cool enough to handle, peel off the skins and then squeeze the tomatoes to remove the seeds.

Set the tomatoes aside to cool completely.

Sauté the celery, onions, and spices:

Add butter to a skillet and set the burner to low heat. Allow the butter to melt.

Add the celery, red onion, thyme, turmeric, basil, and pepper; heat on low for about 5 minutes or until the onions become translucent. Add the sea salt and heat for 1 more minute, mixing thoroughly, then set aside.

While everything is cooling, make the Aioli, unless you already have some on hand.

Assemble the lobster salad:

Chop your lobster tails into small pieces. If you feel they came out too rubbery, you can fix this by pulsing it in your food processor with the S-blade. Pulse 8–9 times.

Add the Aioli; celery, onion, and spice mixture; tarragon and chives; and tomatoes to the lobster in a large mixing bowl and mix thoroughly. It's now ready to serve or chill.

Serving suggestions:

Serve at room temperature, or chill in the refrigerator and serve up to two days later.

Serve as an appetizer in a martini glass or any other small serving dish.

Make a meal by adding on top of a green salad.

THE BEST
LIVER PÂTÉ
Ever!

Chicken livers do some pretty spectacular things for your body: They provide all the vitamin B$_{12}$ you need (and more) to help strengthen your brain health and nervous system. They help with low-iron anemia, and they more than provide the daily dose you need of vitamin A and folate. You also get copper and zinc—zinc is needed by every cell in the body, boosts immunity, and helps fight off pathogenic bacteria and viruses (those with small intestine bacterial overgrowth and candida, take note!).

Now here's the tricky part: chicken livers aren't too pretty, and they're an acquired taste. The people who love liver are big fans, but those who don't like it will avoid it like the plague. However, at a dinner party we had with our recipe testers, the Bone Broth Tribe, two self-admitted liver haters tried this dish and liked it.

This recipe uses meat bone broth or stock. (While neutral broth is preferred, you can use a flavored broth or the Healing Elixir Vegetable Stock.) What we love about it—and what the liver haters loved—is that it doesn't taste much like liver at all. The mix of spices makes a wonderful blend that tastes somewhat Moroccan, but with a bit of a twist. The spices give it exquisite flavor and boost the medicinal benefits. Check the "How to Work With Herbs and Spices" section in the Appendix for the healing benefits of the spices used in this recipe. Your body will love it!

☞ **Preparation time:** 15 minutes ☜
Yield: 4 servings as a meal,
and up to 10 servings as an appetizer

---

1 Tbsp. ghee or butter

½ cup thinly sliced onion (if you're going to pulse this in your food processor, don't worry about the size of the onion slices)

½ cup Madeira

½ cup bone broth (neutral broth, or any red meat broth or stock will work)

1 Tbsp. ground rosemary

2 tsp. lemongrass

2 tsp. allspice

2 tsp. paprika

1 tsp. black pepper

1 tsp. sea salt

7–8 organic chicken livers

Add the ghee and onion to a medium saucepan and set the burner to low heat. Warm the onion for a minute or two.

Add the bone broth and Madeira. Turn the heat up to medium; simmer for 5–10 minutes, stirring occasionally, until the liquid reduces by half. Add the spices and sea salt, and continue to simmer for 2 minutes.

Add the chicken livers and simmer on low until they turn from red to brown; this will take 5–7 minutes. You can cut a liver in half to see if it's still red inside. You can also use a meat thermometer and when the interior is 165° F, it's done.

Use an immersion blender to blend it up or put it in your blender or food processor with the S-blade and pulse a few times until it's the consistency you like.

Serving suggestions:

Serve goulash-style and warm over roasted zucchini slices, the Best Brussels Sprouts, cooked collards, or over a bed of shredded Romaine lettuce.

You can also serve this pâté-style with crudités.

This would be wonderful with the Herb Bread or Maya's Finnish Sourdough Rye Bread.

Serve with raw cultured vegetables, like sauerkraut or kimchi.

PÂTÉ
PLUS

This recipe by **Caroline Barringer,** NTP, CHFS, uses chicken bone broth. You can also use chicken stock or any neutral bone broth.

Heather: When I heard Caroline talk about this recipe, I knew we had to include it here! It brings the best parts of aspic, pâté, and bone broth together in a delicious, strengthening meal. Liver is incredibly good for mineral balancing, something I find that I'm supporting a lot of clients with today due to stress—which is often behind things like infertility, low thyroid, adrenal fatigue, weight gain, anemia, insomnia, addictions, and depression.

Liver is one of those healing foods our ancestors knew more about than we did. And I can tell you that once my clients start eating it, I get phone calls and e-mails full of joy and excitement because of the energy, calmness, and sleep they're getting.

Caroline really knows how to make a healing meal. You will love this!

☞ **Preparation time:** Start this recipe ☜
2 days before you plan to serve it.
While you can do it in 24 hours, you may
find it much easier to plan ahead and give it
plenty of time to firm up in the refrigerator.
Hands-on prep time: 50 minutes
Total prep time: 24–48 hours
Yield: 4–6 servings

4–6 strips pasture-fed bacon

2 cups chicken bone broth

3 Tbsp. unflavored powdered beef gelatin

½ tsp. sea salt

The Best Liver Pâté Ever! (see previous recipe)

¼ cup duck fat (or butter, ghee, or coconut oil)

1 Tbsp. fresh parsley, chopped

Instructions for Day 1— prepare the broth, bacon, and pâté:

Preheat oven to 400° F.

Bake the bacon strips in the oven until crispy. Crumble into small bits and place in a container in the refrigerator overnight.

Warm 2 cups of the chicken broth and whisk in the gelatin powder slowly to avoid lumps.

Evenly divide the broth with dissolved gelatin into 4 ramekins (small round bowls). If you don't have these, you can use small jars or any small bowl, or you can use a single rectangular glass container and serve from there. Place ramekins in the refrigerator and allow the broth to set firmly overnight.

Now prepare the Best Liver Pâté Ever! Be sure to put into your blender or food processor with the S-blade and pulse a few times until it's a smooth consistency. The blended contents will be more liquid at a warmer temperature, but will become solid when chilled. Put the pâté in a glass bowl; cover and chill overnight.

Instructions for Day 2—prepare the Pâté Plus:

Before doing anything, make sure of the following: your broth is completely gelled (thick and relatively solid). Your pâté is cold and somewhat congealed. The bacon is well chilled after being in the refrigerator overnight.

Next, warm the duck fat (or butter, ghee, or coconut oil) on a very low heat until it melts to a liquid. Immediately remove from heat.

Remove the ramekins, pâté, and bacon from the refrigerator. On top of the congealed layer of broth, spread on about a ½"-layer or more of the pâté. Be sure to leave some room for the final top layer.

Pour 1 Tbsp. of liquid duck fat over each ramekin, and sprinkle with bacon crumbles. Place the ramekins back into the refrigerator for 4–6 additional hours to chill and set. Just before serving, sprinkle with fresh chopped parsley.

This dish is recommended as an appetizer or a nutrient-dense snack. It will store in an airtight container for 5–7 days at a consistent refrigerator temperature of 38° F.

Serving suggestions:

Simply spoon out Pâté Plus directly from the ramekins and spread this delicious combination on lettuce leaves, the Herb Bread, or Maya's Finnish Sourdough Rye Bread.

Accompany with these condiments: raw cultured vegetables, beets, and or finely chopped organic red onion.

Enjoy with your favorite green salad, or serve with the Simple Asparagus.

OXTAIL PÂTÉ

Some people might not know what to do with the oxtail meat from making bone broth. This recipe is the perfect, easy, no-fuss way to use it to get a great meal or appetizer! It's great if you've just made an oxtail stock or bone broth, like Heather's Easy Oxtail Broth recipe, but it can use any meat broth or stock (neutral or flavored).

In many cultures, tougher cuts of meat (like shank meat, for example) are slow cooked in wine, broth, or water for 24 hours to get them perfectly tender and rich with flavor. Similarly, the meat in this recipe is tender and delicious.

Pâtés are meat with some fat added, which is perfect because oxtails already have a good amount of healthy fat (especially if organic and grass-fed). No additional fat is needed; just add seasoning and whiz it up in your food processor! It makes a nice, creamy, smooth pâté, and freezes well, too.

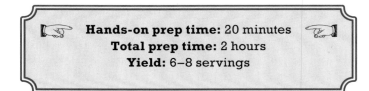

Hands-on prep time: 20 minutes
Total prep time: 2 hours
Yield: 6–8 servings

1 cup oxtail meat and fat

1–3 Tbsp. bone broth

Seasonings of your choice (you could just add sea salt and pepper to taste, but try the paprika and allspice, which is really delicious!):

- 1 tsp. black pepper
- ½ tsp. sea salt
- 2 tsp. paprika
- 1 tsp. allspice

Other options for seasonings per 1 cup of oxtail meat and fat:

If you decide you want to vary the taste of this pâté, you can get as creative as you like. Thyme, rosemary, and basil are wonderful options; you might like garlic or want to add some sautéed onions. Follow your intuition and have fun with it! Here's another spice combo we like:

- ¼ tsp. fennel
- ¼ tsp. five spice blend
- ¼ tsp. turmeric

Remove all oxtail meat and fat from the bones. Save the bones to either put back into the broth or to use for another round of meat stock or bone broth. (Many people use the bones multiple times—see Chapter 2 for more information.)

Make sure you get all bones out! Feel the meat between your fingers to make sure the little, thin "caps" of bones are removed as well.

Put your oxtail meat and fat, bone broth, and your choice of seasonings into your food processor with the S-blade or high-speed blender. Blend until you have the consistency you like. We like a smooth, creamy pâté with no chunks, so we leave the food processor going a bit longer. Taste and see if you want more sea salt; if so, add ¼ tsp. at a time.

That's it!

Serving suggestions:

Serve with cut vegetables, roll it up in lettuce leaves, or spoon it up on its own as an appetizer or snack.

Spread on the Herb Bread or Maya's Finnish Sourdough Rye Bread.

Serve with cultured vegetables, like sauerkraut or kimchi. These help aid digestion and add a wonderful, balancing sour taste.

Oxtail Pâté.

SO GOOD
LAMB SHANK
Pâté

This recipe uses the stock you'll get from cooking the lamb shanks, which keeps things simple. You'll get all the benefits of nutrient-rich meat and healthy fat in one delicious pâté that's easy to eat and digest!

This is a great snack or appetizer for a dinner party, and makes a basic, lovely pâté with a delicious mild flavor. We've included some flavor-enhancing ideas to spark your creativity and allow you to customize this recipe for your taste buds.

☞ **Hands-on prep time:** 20 minutes ☜
Total prep time: 4½–6½ hours
Yield: 4–8 servings if eaten as a snack,
or 10–12 servings as a party appetizer

Ingredients for lamb shanks:

2 lamb shanks

2 cups filtered water

1 Tbsp. ground rosemary

Ingredients for pâté:

Meat from 2 cooked lamb shanks

½ cup Aioli (or you can use ½ cup of the White Wine Mustard Sauce or Lulu's French Rémoulade; or use 2 Tbsp. butter and some of the optional spices we recommend)

1½ tsp. sea salt

1½ tsp. black pepper

1½ tsp. basil

2 tsp. thyme

1 Tbsp. thyme

1 Tbsp. basil

2 tsp. sea salt

1 tsp. black pepper

2 Tbsp. lamb stock from your slow cooker

Optional flavor additions—add one or a combination of the following if you want to experiment with new flavors:

¼ cup diced red onion

1 tsp. garlic powder or 1 clove fresh garlic (pressed or minced)

1 tsp. turmeric

1 tsp. cumin

Extra sea salt and ground pepper, to taste

Instructions for cooking lamb shanks:

Put all ingredients in a slow cooker. (If you don't have a slow cooker, you can make this dish in a braising pan or Dutch oven, on the lowest heat setting on your stove top.)

Decide when you want your lamb shanks ready to eat: If it's morning and you want them done by lunch, set your slow cooker to high, medium high, or the 4-hour setting. (Check the directions on your slow cooker for timing.) If it's nighttime and you want to have your lamb ready to take to work by the morning—or if it's morning and you want it ready for dinner—use the lowest setting, or the 8- or 10-hour setting.

Once your lamb shanks are done (they should fall off the bone and be very tender), remove them and allow them to cool.

You also have about 2 cups meat stock to use for other recipes now—bonus! You'll need 2 Tbsp. for this pâté and can save the rest for future use. There won't be any gelatin, but you can always add ½ Tbsp. unflavored powdered beef gelatin to get a gelled effect, if needed.

Time-saving suggestions: While the lamb shanks are cooking, you can make the Aioli, unless you have some on hand already. The White Wine Mustard Sauce and Lulu's French Rémoulade also work for this pâté, so if you have either of those on hand, use them to save time. Or you can use 2 Tbsp. butter and some of the spice suggestions we've made to enhance the flavor.

Instructions for pâté:

Put all ingredients into your food processor with S-blade or high-speed blender and mix up until fully blended.

Taste the pâté and decide if you want to add one or more of the optional flavor additions. If so, add them and blend up again, until blended thoroughly.

Serve cold.

This recipe freezes well, so you can freeze the extra and get it out for a quick meal, snack, or dinner party appetizer.

Serving suggestions:

Serve with Maya's Finnish Sourdough Rye bread, the Herb Bread, zucchini slices, or roll in a leaf of romaine lettuce.

Serve on a bed of lettuce as a salad or with your favorite cooked greens on the side.

ROCKET
STOCK
Blocks

This recipe by **Caroline Barringer,** NTP, CHFS, uses any bone broth of your choice.

Even though aspics surged in popularity in the 1960s, they fell out of favor—as most traditional foods did—during the TV-dinner generation. Nutritious aspics died a slow, jiggly death as Jell-O took center stage. (Think of Jell-O as an aspic with sugar.) However, we want to invite you to give aspics a try—they're budget-friendly, packed with nutrition, and tasty to boot. There's a good reason why they still grace the tables at the best French bistros today.

What's wonderful about this recipe is that it provides a way to turn bone broth into fast, portable food. There are two versions provided here: In the first option, you get gelatin-rich stock blocks for easy, on-the-go snacks and meals. In the second option, you get frozen flavor-rich stock blocks for use in sautés, soups, stews, and other meals you want to enhance with bone broth and spices.

When Caroline introduced these blocks to us, we could see all the benefits. First of all, they're a great source of easy-to-digest protein and collagen, as well as a wonderful blood sugar balancer. Since balancing blood sugar is responsible for many things, from brain health to weight to willpower and decision-making, it's great to have a quick snack that can keep it in check. Some people have also reported that eating the gelatin-rich stock blocks before bed helps them sleep better because of the calming minerals in the broth. And Caroline sometimes grabs a gelatin-rich block or even a frozen block and has it with avocado slices when she's on long conference calls for work.

Have fun with this recipe and use your own creativity as you make it with different spices and flavors. If you use a neutral broth, you can even sweeten your blocks for a little dessert treat, like gummies!

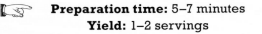
2 cups bone broth of your choice

Sea salt, to taste

1 Tbsp. butter or ghee

1 Tbsp. coconut oil

Variations (see instructions for more on this):

Option 1—high-protein, gelatin-rich:
   1 Tbsp. unflavored powdered beef gelatin

Combine broth (warmed if taken out of the fridge), sea salt, butter, and coconut oil in a blender and blend on high for 1–2 minutes. The mixture should be slightly frothy and emulsified.

Option 1—high-protein, gelatin-rich stock blocks:

Fully dissove gelatin in broth, and pour into silicone molds (often used for making gummy candies), silicone ice-cube trays, or a baking dish. With silicone, you may have to put it into a larger glass or Tupperware container for storage.

If you want to make more than 2 cups at a time, use this guideline: For every 2 cups of broth, add 1 heaping Tbsp. of gelatin.

Refrigerate for a minimum of 5 hours, until it gels. If you used a baking dish, simply cut the Rocket Stock into cubes. If you poured it into molds (kid-friendly) or ice-cube trays, just pop the shapes out. Rocket Stock Blocks (or shapes) will keep in the refrigerator for at least one full week.

Option 2—frozen, flavor-rich: **Add your favorite spices to make cooking with bone broth fast and easy. For example, you can use any or all of these spices:**

- 1 tsp. thyme
- 1 tsp. turmeric
- ½ tsp. ground rosemary
- ½ tsp. black pepper
- ½ tsp. allspice

Option 2—frozen, flavor-rich stock blocks:

Add your favorite herbs, spices, salt, and pepper to the emulsified broth; mix them in. (Note that you will not be adding in extra gelatin for this option.)

Allow stock to cool and pour into ice-cube trays. Place trays in the freezer until stock blocks are fully frozen. Once frozen, you can pop out the stock blocks and store in an airtight container in the freezer or just put the ice-cube tray right into the airtight container. Pop frozen stock blocks into stir-fry dishes, vegetable sautés, soups, and stews; or use them to infuse flavor and dense nutrition into any dish.

Serving suggestions:

Use the high-protein, gelatin-rich blocks for snacks at home or on the go, or to keep your blood sugar stable.

Serve for a fast-food lunch with pâté, eggs, a salad, or any leftovers you have in your refrigerator.

Use the frozen stock blocks to add flavor to any dish you want to make quickly, or if you've run out of bone broth and want the flavor and benefits in a meal you're preparing.

HAM HOCK,
RED LENTIL, AND
Yellow Squash Salad

This is a lovely, warm, comfort-food salad, punctuated with red chunks of ham. **Kaayla T. Daniel,** Ph.D., author of *Nourishing Broth: An Old-Fashioned Remedy for the Modern World,* first made a recipe like this back in the 1980s, during her vegetarian days—without the ham hock, of course. Now that she's an omnivore, she loves the rich flavor of the ham, as well as the added protein and health benefits of the gelatinous broth.

This recipe creates its own bone broth from the ham hock. Ham hocks are the knuckle of the pig, right near where it attaches to the foot. They have a small amount of meat and are full of collagen. You can also use smoked ham hock for added flavor.

Kaayla's family and friends all love this salad. Once you've got the hang of it, it's easy and fail-proof.

> **Hands-on prep time:** 30 minutes
> **Total prep time:** 16½ hours
> **Yield:** 4 servings

1 cup red lentils

1 tsp. apple cider vinegar

1 lb. ham hock

2 medium yellow onions, diced (about 2 cups)

2 sticks celery, diced

3 medium yellow squash, cut into bite-size chunks

¼ cup butter or ghee

Sea salt and black pepper, to taste

1 head romaine or red leaf lettuce (about 4–6 cups torn lettuce leaves)

Olive oil or salad dressing of your choice

In a glass bowl, add the lentils and just enough water to cover them. Mix in the apple cider vinegar, and cover with a lid or a plate. Leave the lentils to soak on your countertop for 4–5 hours, then drain the water, rinse the lentils, and leave them in your refrigerator until you cook them.

While the lentils are soaking, add 1½ quarts water, the ham hock, half the onions, and the celery into a stockpot or crockpot. Set the heat to high and bring the water to a boil, skimming off any foam that rises to the top. Allow to boil for 3 minutes, then reduce heat to low and simmer for 4–8 hours.

Strain the liquid into jars or a large glass bowl, and set aside to cool. Set aside the ham hock as well, but discard the vegetables. (After simmering, all of the nutrients from the vegetables have gone into the broth, and they may not taste very good. Some people like to keep them anyway and blend them up for fiber in other meals.)

Once the ham has cooled, cut or shred the meat into bite-size pieces, and save the bone for a future broth. Put the meat in a container, and store the meat and your cooled broth in your refrigerator overnight.

The next day, add your soaked lentils to a saucepan. Do not turn on the heat yet.

Remove your broth from your refrigerator and scrape off the fat cap from the top of the broth (see Chapter 2 for instructions on saving and using the fat). Add just enough broth to the saucepan to cover the lentils (around 1½ cups), set the heat to medium, and bring the liquid to a slow simmer. Simmer the lentils for about 10 minutes, or until the outsides are firm and the insides are soft. (Save the extra flavored broth for other recipes or for sipping.)

While the lentils are cooking, melt the butter or ghee in a skillet on low heat, and add the rest of the diced onion. Sauté 3–5 minutes, until onion becomes soft and translucent, then add the squash. Continue sautéing until the squash is as tender as you like it.

Add the cooked lentils and ham to the onion and squash mixture, then salt and pepper to taste. Continue to sauté until the liquid has completely reduced, mixing thoroughly.

Prepare a bed of lettuce on four plates, then evenly divide this mixture over each one. Drizzle with extra-virgin olive oil, our Aioli, the Do It Your Way Salad Dressing, or Louise's French Rémoulade.

Serving suggestions:

Serve with a slice of the Herb Bread.

FARM-TO-TABLE
ASPIC

This recipe results in a flavored bone broth that, once chilled, serves as the basis for a delicious aspic.

We love aspic, and while many people will insist the broth must be clear, we love to break the rules! With this recipe, we offer you a quick and easy dish that delivers all the nutrients and flavor you get in an aspic without the extra steps needed to clarify the broth. For those of you who love a really clear aspic, use the clarifying instructions in our other aspic recipes before dividing the broth into containers.

This no-fuss aspic reminds us of what we love most about simple, delicious farm-to-table eating.

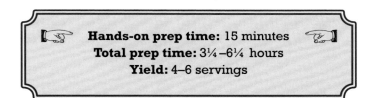

☞ **Hands-on prep time:** 15 minutes ☜
Total prep time: 3¼–6¼ hours
Yield: 4–6 servings

2 medium onions, diced (about 2 cups)

4 chicken feet or 1 Tbsp. powdered gelatin (either of these will help create a gelatin-rich aspic)

4 duck legs

2 tsp. sea salt

2 tsp. black pepper

2 tsp. ground rosemary

2 tsp. dried thyme

1 tsp. turmeric

If you are using the oven, preheat to 300° F.

Add 1 cup of water and the diced onion to a crock-pot, oven-safe lidded casserole dish, or Dutch oven.

Add chicken feet, rinsing first. Or, if using gelatin, mix the powder into the water and onions.

Rinse the duck legs, pat them dry and place them in the pot skin side up, on top of the onions. Mix the seasonings well and sprinkle them into the pot, over the duck legs.

Set your crockpot on low for 6 hours. If using the oven, place the lid on your casserole dish or Dutch oven and cook for 2–3 hours, or until the meat is fork tender.

Allow the broth to cool, then remove the duck legs and set aside on a plate or cutting board. Strain the broth through a fine-mesh strainer into a large glass or stainless steel bowl. Discard the onions. Taste the broth and season with more salt and pepper, as needed.

Remove the meat and skin from the bones, chopping it up into small, bite-size pieces. (You can save the skin for another recipe or use it in the aspic.)

Decide how you want to serve the aspic. If you want to provide individual portions, you may want to use small bowls or ramekins (6-oz. or 1-cup containers).

Ladle the broth into your bowls or ramekins, then add an equal amount of duck meat (and skin, if you're using it) into each serving container. Cover containers with lids, silicone tops, or plastic wrap, and place them in the refrigerator, ensuring that they are resting flat.

Refrigerate for a minimum of 24 hours, allowing the broth to completely gel. The aspic is ready to serve once it has gelled.

Serving suggestions:

Serve with your favorite green salad or cooked vegetables.

Serve with Herb Bread or Maya's Finnish Sourdough Rye Bread and Aioli.

TROTTING ON
EGGSHELLS

This recipe by **Brian Merkel,** head butcher at Belcampo Meat Co. in San Francisco, makes a neutral, clarified broth that can be used in dessert recipes or made into fantastic aspics, with great flavor options.

Pig's feet are also known as trotters or pettitoes and are used in cooking all over the world. They are becoming very popular these days, especially for bone broth enthusiasts. If you can't find them at your grocery store, though, check with your local butcher shop or the farmers' market.

This is a fun dish with the flexibility to be a neutral, sweet, or savory aspic. The broth is great chilled in 2-oz. shot glasses, so you can have a healthy "shot" on days when it's too hot for broth but you need your collagen and minerals. It's also wonderful for an on-the-go snack. Make sure to check out the aromatic flavor options, and have fun experimenting!

Hands-on prep time: 20 minutes
Total prep time: 38–55 hours
Yield: Approximately 3–4 quarts

Note: For the ingredients without measurements, feel free to play around with quantities up to 1 cup.

Pork skin (fat completely trimmed off)

Lean "tendony" pork trim (you can often get pork trimmings from your butcher shop)

4 whole pig's feet, split in half

Eggshells

Optional aromatic flavorings:

Slightly sweet: 1 Tbsp. lavender and ¼ cup honey

Savory: 2 cloves roasted garlic, ¼ tsp. ground juniper seed, 1 tsp. of some fresh herbs, and apple cider vinegar

Preheat oven to 400° F.

Place skin, trim, and pig's feet in thin layer on roasting tray(s). Roast in oven for 30–40 minutes, until lightly browned.

If you're getting your eggshells directly from the farmer, they may be a bit dirty because they're not washed in a chlorine bath. You can wash them in apple cider vinegar and water, or parboil them for 5 minutes in a saucepan of boiling water.

Place roasted items and eggshells in a slow cooker or large stockpot and just cover them with water. Set to a very gentle simmer—never boil! Skim occasionally. Simmer for at least 24 hours, or go as long as 48 hours.

Strain through a fine mesh strainer 1–3 times until you have a nice amber liquid, and there are no meaty bits floating around. Put broth back into the stockpot, and bring to a roaring simmer.

Beat 2–4 egg whites (depending on size of broth batch) and pour into broth. Turn off heat. The egg whites will float to the top and create a "raft," clarifying your broth. Remove "raft" and filter the broth through a fine mesh strainer again. Return broth to the stockpot.

At this point, you can add salt, aromatics, and flavors to your broth to taste.

Keep at a low simmer for an hour or so to infuse flavors. If you use lavender flowers, strain them out after 20 minutes. Discard any other solids, if you wish.

Store in your refrigerator for at least 6 hours (preferably overnight). The broth will chill into a more solid, yet jiggly aspic. Now it's ready to enjoy.

Serving suggestions:

Drink slightly sweet shots as a snack in the afternoon when you want an energy and blood sugar boost, but you don't want to spoil dinner.

Enjoy as a snack at work or on road trips.

Serve the savory or unflavored options with your favorite salad, pâté, or cooked vegetables.

Have as an appetizer along with a charcuterie board and sliced avocado.

OEUFS EN GELÉE
(EGGS IN ASPIC)

This is real French country-style aspic. This recipe calls for a chicken broth or any neutral broth (see ingredients for tips on using powdered unflavored gelatin, if needed). The broth is great chilled in small, clear glass bowls so that you can see how beautiful the aspic looks. You can also put it into tiny mason jars for that French-country touch.

Heather: I grew up in the days when aspic was no longer served at parties; instead, sugary Jell-O salads had taken its place. Talking about aspic brings these Jell-O salad molds to mind for many people. One of my friends said that her mother had 20 molds, and another said that she'd heard of a tomato aspic with Red Hots candies over a piece of iceberg lettuce. Um, no. This recipe is a twist on the one that Louise made when she was married and gave dinner parties with her husband. When she first told me about how she'd make oeufs en gelée years ago, I was so intrigued that all I could think was, *How would this chemistry magic happen?* Well, it's actually a lot easier than you think, once you get the knack of making a gelled broth (or bumping up the gel with powdered gelatin).

☞ **Hands-on prep time:** 20 minutes ☜
Total prep time: 6–9 hours
Yield: 4 servings

Ingredients:

1 Tbsp. butter or coconut oil

1 tsp. ground rosemary

1 tsp. thyme

½ tsp. black pepper

½ cup thinly sliced carrot rounds

½ cup diced onion

½ cup Madeira, divided

2 cups very gelled chicken or neutral bone broth (The broth should be fairly solid when chilled. If it's not, add 1½–2 Tbsp. unflavored powdered beef gelatin when you're heating up the broth.)

Ingredients to clarify the broth:

3 egg whites (save the yolks for another meal or soup)

Shells from the 3 eggs

2 tsp. fresh lemon juice

½ tsp. sea salt

1 cup thinly sliced zucchini half-moons

½ cup thinly sliced yellow squash half-moons

Oeufs en Gelée.

Put 1 Tbsp. butter or coconut oil into a braising pan and set the burner to low to melt the fat. Add the rosemary, thyme, and black pepper, allowing them to heat and release their aromas for 1 minute. Add carrots and diced onions; sauté for 4 minutes.

Add ¼ cup of the Madeira and continue to simmer on low, allowing it to reduce. Once the Madeira has reduced to about half, add about a cup of water along with the zucchini, yellow squash, and sea salt. Mix gently and put the lid on the pan to cook on low until the squash and zucchini are slightly soft (4–5 minutes).

While this is happening, you can put the bone broth into a saucepan and set the burner to medium high, bringing the broth to a vigorous simmer, just shy of boiling.

Clarify your broth: Beat 3 egg whites in a bowl with a whisk. Crush the eggshells and add those into the egg whites. Now add the remaining ¼ cup Madeira and 2 tsp. fresh lemon juice, and mix it all together. Pour this mixture into your broth; turn the heat down to the lowest temperature. The egg whites and shells will float to the top and create a "raft," clarifying your broth. Heat this way for about 5 minutes.

Use a fine mesh strainer with cheesecloth over it to filter out the raft and any solids from the broth.

Your broth should be clear. If it's not, you can heat it up again and make the raft one more time, then strain it again. That's only if it matters to you, though—you don't have to have a perfectly clear broth, it's only for looks!

Taste broth and adjust salt. Let the broth sit for 10 minutes; then pour into small jars, bowls, or ramekins with lids. Add ½ of a hard-boiled egg and some of the vegetables, arranged any way you like—you can just throw it in casually or do something artistic.

Put into your refrigerator for at least 2 hours, allowing the gelatin to set. Once it's completely gelled, it's ready to eat! You can either eat directly from the dishes or dip the bottom of each dish into hot water and gently turn over, allowing the aspic to slide out onto a chilled plate.

Refrigerate until you're ready to serve.

Serving suggestions:

Serve as a meal or snack on its own or with a side salad.

Enjoy with the Best Liver Pâté Ever!

Serve as an appetizer.

COLLAGEN-RICH
FRUIT
Smoothie

If you're new to smoothies, it may seem foreign to put a bunch of greens into a blender and drink it up, but the fruit will help introduce you to this practice. It makes a wonderful warm weather treat when fruits are abundant and in season.

This recipe uses collagen hydrolysate (collagen peptides). You can leave it out or use a neutral bone broth if you don't have any on hand. You can also customize this smoothie for your own tastes: Use any berries you love, switch out an avocado for the banana, change up the spices, or be creative to your heart's content!

☞ **Preparation time:** 5–10 minutes ☜
Yield: Approximately 3 cups

1 banana

1½ cups blueberries (fresh or frozen)

2 Tbsp. collagen hydrolysate (collagen peptides)

2–4 Tbsp. of nut or seed butter (like almond butter, tahini, sunflower butter, pumpkin seed butter, and so on)

Optional greens:

One of the following is nice to add some greens to your smoothie:

- 1–2 Tbsp. of your favorite green powder. NOW Foods organic Wheat Grass Juice powder (wheatgrass is not wheat gluten; it's a green grass), Premier Greens by Premier Research Labs, and Ormus Greens are a few popular organic options that you can get at Amazon.com and other online providers.

- ½ cup romaine lettuce leaves

Optional spices:

These spices are included because they help bring a balance to the sweet fruits in the smoothie, so you'll feel satisfied without triggering cravings, and they aid digestion. The cinnamon helps to warm the body, bringing balance to the cold smoothie. The sea salt is grounding and provides trace minerals:

- 1 tsp. cinnamon
- ¼ tsp. cardamom
- ¼ tsp. sea salt
- ⅛ tsp. fennel
- ⅛ tsp. nutmeg

If you want to do a spice-taste experiment, put all ingredients in your blender except for the spices and sea salt. Blend thoroughly, and then taste. What do you think? How do you feel? Do you like the taste? Do you feel balanced with the ingredients as is? If so, you can skip the spices and make sure to pay attention to how you feel for hours afterward. Write it down in your food journal—you're learning your own patterns and what keeps you grounded, calm, and centered.

If you feel that the recipe needs "something else," add the cinnamon, blend up, and taste again. Repeat the above process until you've got the taste combination that you really love.

Pour into glasses and enjoy! Store extra in your refrigerator for up to 3 days.

SASSY
GREEN
Smoothie

This is a light, slightly sweet smoothie that's easy on the digestive system. It's perfect for when you want some get-up-and-go without anything weighing you down. This recipe calls for collagen hydrolysate (collagen peptides) or neutral bone broth. The spices are good for balancing blood sugar, improving digestion, weight loss, eye health, fighting fungal and bacterial infection, heart health, regulating cholesterol, and reducing inflammation. If you need more grounding energy and strength, you could substitute a nut or seed butter for the coconut butter in this recipe.

This smoothie makes a great breakfast when your appetite is light and you don't want something heavy in your system. It also makes an ideal snack for late afternoon, when you're hungry and want something to tide you over till dinner, but don't want to ruin your appetite. In other words, it's a great blood sugar balancer that can satisfy your hunger, get some greens into your body, and keep you feeling light and energized. Drink this up and you'll still feel primed for the day's adventures!

☞ **Preparation time:** 5–10 minutes ☜
Yield: 2–3 servings

2 cups lettuce (such as romaine or red leaf)

¼–½ cup flat parsley

1 Granny Smith apple

¼ cup coconut butter (You could use almond butter or tahini, although the coconut butter tends to be lighter on the digestive system. If you're really hungry and need a strengthening option, try a nut butter.)

2 Tbsp. unflavored beef collagen hydrolysate powder (you can also use 2 Tbsp. neutral beef bone broth or stock)

2 heaping Tbsp. goji berries (Skip this if you don't have them. You can use extra apple, 1 Tbsp. tart cherry juice concentrate, or 1 Tbsp. camu camu powder or pomegranate powder as alternatives, if you like.)

1 Tbsp. cinnamon

1 tsp. fennel

1 tsp. enugreek

½ tsp. sea salt

Optional:

¼ tsp. cloves for added digestive support

Optional sweeteners:

2 tsp.–1 Tbsp. honey

1 Tbsp. molasses (if you want more potassium)

1–4 drops stevia in each glass when served (start with one drop, mix it in, and taste; add more drops, one at a time, until you achieve the taste you like)

Put all ingredients, except the optional sweeteners, into your blender and blend well. Taste the smoothie and decide if you want to add one of the sweeteners. Mix thoroughly and serve.

Store extra in your refrigerator and consume over the next day or two.

Serving suggestions:

Serve as is—no embellishments needed!

If you like, squeeze a few drops of fresh lemon juice or a couple drops of Urban Moonshine citrus bitters into your glass for flavor and added digestive support.

LULU'S SALAD
IN A GLASS
Smoothie

This recipe uses collagen hydrolysate (collagen peptides). If you don't have any collagen hydrolysate on hand, you can use a neutral bone broth instead.

Louise: I call my morning smoothie a shake because it's so good! It's really like a salad in a glass. I use whatever I have in my refrigerator, and it's a little different every time. I'm going to give you some great ideas for how to make your own salad in a glass. Your body will love it!

Preparation time: 5–10 minutes
Yield: Approximately 3–4 cups

---

2 cups of liquid—we vary this and sometimes use a combination of the following:

- Young coconut water
- Green juice
- Tart cherry juice concentrate
- Pomegranate juice
- Pineapple juice
- Almond milk
- Coconut milk

Vegetables—we look in the refrigerator for about a cup of raw vegetables, especially green vegetables, which could include a combination of the following:

- 1 Tbsp. cultured vegetables, like sauerkraut
- Asparagus
- Celery
- Collards
- Green beans
- Kale
- Lettuce
- Swiss chard
- Zucchini

A protein powder source of your choice:

- 2 Tbsp. collagen hydrolysate (collagen peptides)
- 1 Tbsp. colostrum (this is the "first mother's milk" after a calf is born and has many immune-boosting and digestion-enhancing properties)

- 1–2 Tbsp. of your favorite protein powder
- 1 Tbsp. chia seed powder
- 1 Tbsp. hemp seed powder
- 1 Tbsp. flax meal

Green powder for added vitamins and minerals:

- 1–2 Tbsp. of your favorite green powder

A protein fat for grounding energy:

- 2 Tbsp. of nut or seed butter, such as almond butter, tahini (sesame seed butter), sunflower seed butter, or pumpkin seed butter
- Coconut butter
- 1 raw egg yolk

Optional additions for flavor and medicinal value:

- 1 Tbsp. salad dressing, like Lulu's French Rémoulade or the Do It Your Way Salad Dressing (Chapter 6)
- 1 Tbsp. camu camu for whole-food vitamin C

Spices are full of antioxidants and health benefits, and help add flavor and balance of tastes. Here are some we like:

- 2 tsp. cinnamon
- ¼ tsp. cardamom
- ¼ tsp. Himalayan salt or dulse (a sea vegetable full of minerals)
- ¼ tsp. fennel
- ¼ tsp. fenugreek

If you want to do a spice-taste experiment, put all ingredients in your blender except for the spices and sea salt. Blend thoroughly, and then taste. What do you think? How do you feel? Do you like the taste? Do you feel balanced with the ingredients as is? If so, you can skip the spices and make sure to pay attention to how you feel for hours afterward. Write it down in your food journal—you're learning your own patterns and what keeps you grounded, calm, and centered.

If you feel that the recipe needs "something else," add the cinnamon, blend up, and taste again. Repeat the above process until you've got the taste combination that you really love.

Pour into glasses and enjoy! Store extra in your refrigerator for up to 3 days.

CHAPTER 11

THE CELEBRATION: Decadent Desserts

CHOCOLATE DROP COOKIES, AND THE GREAT CHOCOLATE Experiment

This recipe calls for neutral beef bone broth, unflavored powdered beef gelatin, and bone marrow (we have substitutions in case you don't have bone marrow on hand).

Heather: Louise and I love chocolate drop cookies, so we decided to make a healthy version. While we were creating this recipe, we started to have fun with the chocolate drop part of the recipe. We ended up making 4 layers of taste, starting with a very simple recipe and then layering in spices.

This will give you an idea about how I like to use spices—the whole goal is to create balance. When I make a recipe, I'm looking for a taste that keeps my energy in the center of my body, the hara or power center. This area is in the abdomen and often represents the third chakra, your self-esteem and self-empowerment. I find that when something is too sweet or off balance, my energy feels like it goes up into my head and buzzes around. This can create a feeling of brain fog or difficulty concentrating. It's not unlike what happens to kids and adults when they eat too much sugar.

A recipe that is balanced across six tastes in Ayurvedic medicine (or five tastes in Chinese medicine) tends to create a feeling of balance in the body and mind. It keeps your energy grounded so that you can go about your day at your best. It also keeps your body free of cravings, which usually happen when your energy has left the center of your body and is buzzing somewhere up in your head, creating ungrounded dissatisfaction and confusion. (To learn more about this, see the "How to Work with Herbs and Spices" section in the Appendix.)

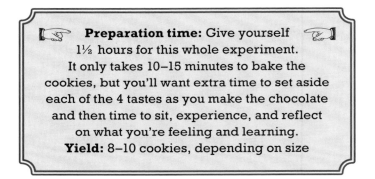

Preparation time: Give yourself 1½ hours for this whole experiment. It only takes 10–15 minutes to bake the cookies, but you'll want extra time to set aside each of the 4 tastes as you make the chocolate and then time to sit, experience, and reflect on what you're feeling and learning.
Yield: 8–10 cookies, depending on size

How to Do the Great Chocolate Experiment

To take this journey with us, all you have to do is make the whole recipe completely, but take a large scoop out at each point (taste #1, taste #2, taste #3, and taste #4). Then sit down when you have plenty of time and taste each one. *Tip:* Conduct your chocolate-tasting experiment after your cookies are made so that the baking does not get in the way of your focus.

Tune into each taste with all your senses: Smell it. Take your time chewing and savoring each bite, and see how it feels in your mouth. Then as you swallow, see how it feels in your body. Notice what you feel drawn to or what resonates most with you at a deep level—much deeper than just your taste buds. Notice which taste makes you feel the most satisfied in your body, mind, and spirit. Once you

identify that, you'll have an idea of how to layer spices for your own needs!

This is a great way to tune into all of your senses. You're basically doing a very deep level of mindful eating—not just paying attention to your meal, but paying attention to every sense and then to how your body feels afterward.

If you want, you can write down what you learned. Write down the spices you used, as many times you can use these same spices in other desserts and cooking. If you're new to food preparation, you can lean on these for a while until you're ready to branch out, learning to use this tasting process as you're cooking all of your food, so you can customize it with the kind of ingredients that bring balance to your mind, body, and spirit.

Taste #1—Base Recipe, No Spices:

1 cup Medjool dates, pitted

½ cup cooked bone marrow left over
   from your broth making (Bone marrow
   makes a wonderful chocolate, so do
   use it if you can. Note that even if your
   bone marrow has a slight beef taste,
   it will still be hidden in the recipe.)
   If you don't have bone marrow, use
   butter or ghee.

½ cup raw cacao powder

½ cup coconut butter

½ cup coconut oil

½ tsp. sea salt

Put dates in hot water and allow them to soften up (5–15 minutes); drain the water, and mash the dates. You can skip this step if you're using a food processor or high-speed blender.

Put all ingredients into your mixing bowl, food processor, or high-speed blender. Blend until all ingredients are thoroughly mixed and smooth.

Set 2 Tbsp. of this mixture aside in a bowl. Leave the rest in the mixing bowl, blender, or food processor.

Now add the ingredient for taste #2.

//

Taste #2—Add Bone Broth, No Spices:

½ cup neutral beef bone broth
   (Heather's Oxtail Bone Broth or any
   neutral beef broth works well)

Add the bone broth to your mixing bowl, blender, or food processor; blend up completely.

Take 2 Tbsp. out and set aside in a separate bowl.

Now add the ingredients for taste #3.

//

Taste #3: Add Balance with Spices:

These spices will add a deeper and more
 mysteriously layered flavor. They start
 to bring the taste "down" in a way
 that keeps your energy in your hara or
 power center:

- 2 tsp. cinnamon
- ½ tsp. allspice
- ½ tsp. cardamom
- ¼ tsp. cloves

Add all spices to your mixing bowl, blender, or food processor, and blend completely.

Take 2 Tbsp. out and set aside in a separate bowl.

Now add the ingredients for taste #4.

///

Taste #4—Rich Vanilla and Balancing Spices:

This adds a sense of richness and elegance
 to the recipe. Vanilla extract brings out
 the flavor and makes it more chocolatey:

- 2 tsp. vanilla extract
- ½ tsp. sea salt
- ½ tsp. black pepper

Add vanilla, sea salt, and pepper to your mixing bowl, blender, or food processor, and blend completely.

Take 2 Tbsp. out and set aside in a separate bowl.

You are now finished making the chocolate drops, and it's time to make the shortbread cookies.

///

Recipe for shortbread cookies:

1 Tbsp. gelatin	1½ Tbsp. honey
2 cups almond flour	½ tsp. vanilla extract
¼ tsp. sea salt	½ tsp. fennel
3 Tbsp. butter, coconut oil, or ghee	½ tsp. fenugreek
1 egg	¼ tsp. nutmeg

Making Chocolate Drop Cookies.

Preheat oven to 350° F.

Grease a cookie sheet with butter, ghee, or coconut oil.

Heat up ¼ cup water so that it's hot, but not boiling. Remove from heat and put into a bowl, mixing in the gelatin and allowing it to dissolve for 5 minutes.

In a separate mixing bowl, food processor with the S-blade, or high-speed blender, add all ingredients. Add in the water and gelatin mixture. Blend everything thoroughly.

Now put the cookies onto your greased cookie sheet. You can form them with any amount of batter you choose, based on the size of cookies you want. If you like, you can use 1–2 Tbsp. of batter and flatten them into round shapes on the cookie sheet. It helps if you create a little dip in the middle of each cookie by pressing the center of the raw dough with your thumb. This gives you a nice space to fill with chocolate once the cookies are baked and cooled.

Bake the cookies for 10–15 minutes, checking at the 10-minute mark. They're done when they look drier and slightly golden in color.

Take the cookies out of the oven and allow them to cool completely. (Note that they freeze well.)

With a 1 tsp. measuring spoon, scoop out the chocolate-drop mixture and put it on top of each cooled cookie. You could use a cake frosting piping kit to make a pretty frosting drop, if you like.

Store cookies in the refrigerator. Take them out a few mintues before serving, allowing them to come to room temperature.

Now you are ready to conduct your Great Chocolate Experiment. Take your time and have fun with this sensory experience!

APPLE
TARTE
Tatin

This recipe, which calls for neutral bone broth, is a French version of apple pie. The crust is baked on top and then, just for added flair, turned upside down so that the once-on-top crust is on the bottom for serving. This is pretty brilliant because it leaves the top free and ready for a dollop of ice cream!

Heather: The first time I ever had apple tarte tatin was on a recent trip to Bruges with Louise and several friends. One of our friends and I chose to split the dessert. I'm not big on restaurant desserts, so I figured I'd have a couple bites and pass it on. However, the tarte was so good that I literally had to hold myself back from finishing the whole thing. (I was a good friend and shared half—I think it was half anyway!—but everyone could tell I wanted to sequester the tarte all for myself.) So here is a healthy, grain-free, and refined sugar–free recipe, so you can experience this delicious version of apple pie.

Because our recipe uses a grain-free crust, the cooking instructions are different from what you may be familiar with when making a tarte tatin pastry crust. If you decide to use your favorite unbaked pastry crust instead, you may want to modify the cooking instructions so that there is more time in the oven and less time on top of the stove.

Hands-on prep time: 35 minutes
Total prep time: 1½ hours
Time-saving tip: The crust freezes well,
so if you can find a flat space in your freezer
(or space to rest a tray with the wrapped crust on it),
you can plan way ahead and save time on
the day you want to serve this dessert!
Yield: 1 large pie or 2 small pies,
approximately 10–12 servings

Ingredients for the apple filling:

8 Granny Smith apples

1 cup Medjool dates, pitted

½ cup bone broth, neutral flavor (if you don't have neutral broth on hand, put ½ cup warm water in a bowl and dissolve 1 tsp. unflavored powdered beef gelatin in the water for about 5 minutes)

2 Tbsp. butter or ghee

1 Tbsp. cinnamon

Ingredients for the grain-free crust:

1½ Tbsp. unflavored powdered beef gelatin

1 cup water

¼ cup unrefined coconut oil

½ can coconut milk, approximately 7 oz. (or make your own with ½ cup water and 1½ Tbsp. coconut butter, blended thoroughly in your blender)

⅛ tsp. sea salt

2 cups almond flour

3 Tbsp. butter

½ Tbsp. honey

1 egg

Instructions for the apple filling:

Peel the apples, then cut them into quarters and remove the core. You don't have to be perfectly precise with this, just do your best. (To help yourself out later on, cut a small bit off the top of the apple so that there is a flat top.) Set apple quarters aside to air dry. You can do this up to 2 days in advance of making the tarte tatin, storing the apple pieces in the refrigerator. It doesn't matter if they start to turn brown.

Put the bone broth (or gelatin in water) and pitted dates into a pan on low and heat for 5 minutes. Press the dates down flat into the liquid while warming; remove from the heat and allow them to sit in the liquid and soften. When they're soft enough to mash (about 15 minutes), mash the dates into a paste with a fork, or blend them in your blender or food processor.

Put the butter into a braising pan (3½–5 quart with a lid) and set the burner to low, melting the butter. Add the cinnamon and allow the aromas and medicinal properties to be released (about 2 minutes). Add the date paste and mix in with the butter and cinnamon; heat for 1 additional minute.

Now remove from the heat and add the apple quarters. You'll start by taking one quarter and putting it cut-side down (the side where you removed the core will go down flat-ish on the pan) in the center of the pan. You're now going to rest all of the other apple slices on each other around this middle piece—this is why you cut the small piece of apple off the top, so you have a flat edge to rest the apples on. Take each apple quarter and rest it on its flat top edge, so it's leaning on the middle apple. Once you've surrounded that middle apple, start building the rest of the quarters around the little circle you made. The apples will be placed a bit like standing dominoes, each one sitting on its small flat side and resting on the apple quarter in front of it. This actually works pretty well, but if they fall a bit, it's okay! Just keep building the circle until you've used all of your apple quarters.

If you don't have enough apple quarters to fill the whole pan, that's perfectly fine. If you have too many, save them for a snack. Your goal is to have a nice, reasonably tightly packed circle of apples leaning on one another.

Set your burner on the lowest temperature and heat the apples for about 30 minutes with the lid on. Check after 15 and then 20 minutes to see how soft the apples are. When they're soft and very easily pierced by a fork, remove pan from the heat and set aside. While all of this is slow cooking, you can start making your crust. (If you use a softer apple than a Granny Smith, such as a Golden Delicious, the apples will cook much faster.)

Apple Tarte Tartin with Moroccan Vanilla Spice Ice Cream and Heavenly Marshmallow Cream Whipped Topping.

Instructions for the grain-free crust:

Preheat oven to 350° F.

Heat up 1 cup of water to just shy of boiling and allow to cool for a few minutes. Add gelatin to the water and mix, then allow to sit for 5 minutes while the gelatin dissolves.

Add all ingredients, including the gelatin and water, to your mixing bowl or food processor with the S-blade; blend up completely. The mixture should be the consistency of thick pancake batter.

Line a large baking sheet (a standard 9" x 13" or larger will work) with either parchment paper or a silicone baking mat (it's okay if the mat is smaller than the area of your baking sheet). Grease the parchment paper or silicone mat with butter or coconut oil, including the edges of the pan around the parchment or mat. You're using this liner to make it easy to flip the crust onto the tarte tatin.

Pour the crust batter onto the lined baking sheet. It's okay if the batter goes over the edges of the paper or silicone mat a bit (as long as it's still on the baking sheet!). Flatten into a circle or oval that is roughly the size of your braising pan with the apples in it—it doesn't have to be perfect. Flatten the circle or oval with a rubber spatula or the back of your mixing spoon.

Put the crust into the oven and bake at 350° F for about 10–15 minutes, checking at the 10-minute mark. The crust color will start to look like a drier white, without much golden color, and the edges will start to lift from the mat or parchment paper. When you press the crust, it will be slightly bouncy. You're still going to bake the crust again on the apples, so it doesn't have to be completely cooked through, just cooked enough that it will easily lift from the baking sheet.

Remove the crust from the oven and allow to cool before doing anything with it. Leave your oven set at 350° F.

When your apples are soft and you've removed them from the heat, you'll almost be ready to assemble the tarte. Just make sure the crust has had enough time to cool down.

Once completely cooled, lift the parchment paper or mat from the baking sheet and gently flip the crust on top of the apples in your braising pan. Tuck the edges of the crust down into the pan. If any breakage happens, that's okay; it won't show once you're done!

Take the crust-covered apples in their braising pan and put it in the oven, baking for another 10–20 minutes (closer to 10 minutes if the apples are already really soft). This is just to let everything settle in and warm up together. This is also a good time for the apples to soften up, if they hadn't already. You want them soft enough to cut with a butter knife for serving.

After 10–20 minutes, and when your apples are very soft, remove the braising pan from the oven. Set the pan on your stove top and allow it to cool a bit while you grease a deep-dish pie plate or large serving platter. You want to choose something with depth so that you can turn the braising pan upside down into it, so the crust will be on the bottom.

After the braising pan has cooled a bit and your serving piece is greased, take the braising pan with your oven mitts on and gently turn it upside down over your dish. (It's helpful to have some good oven mitts that allow you some dexterity with your hands.) Everything will come right out into the dish, but sometimes there's a shift and the apples move around. Just adjust anything that needs to be adjusted, shifting the crust a bit or fixing the arrangement of apples—it's all part of the process! You can even hide a bit of crust breakage with the apples.

Serving suggestions:

Serve warm with a scoop of the Moroccan Vanilla Spice Ice Cream. The 5-Minute Banana Cinnamon Ice Cream is a good second best if you want to save some time.

BEST
PUMPKIN PIE
Ever

This has to be the best pumpkin pie, ever! Full of healthy ingredients, you could even eat it for breakfast. The almond-meal crust is so delicious and easy to make, yet does not taste at all like almond; it marries well with the pumpkin pie filling. However, you can make this dessert without a crust if you so desire.

This recipe calls for neutral bone broth; there's also a powerhouse of spices in it, making it delicious and healthy. (Learn more about their healing benefits in the "How to Work with Herbs and Spices" section in the Appendix.) The surprise spice making an appearance is turmeric, a healing hero of a spice. Don't be scared off by its addition—all of our taste testers agreed that it made the recipe sing and enhanced the overall flavor of the pie.

This whole recipe is from scratch, from crust to pie filling (we'll give you some shortcuts in case you're on a time constraint). Making the pie entirely from scratch is fairly simple and makes a big difference in the taste, so if you do have the time, go for it!

If you do want to make everything from scratch, it's best to start 2 days ahead, especially if you're serving the pie for a party or holiday gathering.

— *Two days before serving*: Soak the almond flour. (This is optional, but so easy!).

— *One day before serving*: To keep preparation really easy, bake the pumpkin and make the pie the day before, so that you can chill it in your refrigerator overnight (since it needs to chill for at least 6 hours).

☞ **Hands-on prep time:** 40 minutes ☜
Total prep time: 8 hours and 40 minutes
Yield: 1 pie, approximately 8–10 servings
with generous slices

Ingredients for the pie crust:

2 cups almond flour ¼ tsp. sea salt

2 Tbsp. coconut oil

1 egg yolk

2 Tbsp. gelled neutral bone broth (add 1 tsp. powdered unflavored beef gelatin to ¼ cup bone broth if the broth you have on hand didn't gel well)

1 tsp. ground fenugreek

Ingredients for the pumpkin pie filling:

1 (2-lb.) sugar pumpkin or butternut squash (you can bake it yourself with the instructions that follow, or feel free to substitute with canned organic pumpkin)

1 cup Medjool dates, pitted

1 (16-oz.) can coconut milk (or make your own with 1 cup water and 2½ Tbsp. coconut butter, blended thoroughly in your blender)

½ cup neutral bone broth

¼ cup honey

½ cup flax meal

¼ cup coconut oil

1 Tbsp. blackstrap molasses

2 Tbsp. apple cider vinegar

2 eggs, plus 1 egg yolk

2 tsp. cinnamon

1 tsp. ginger

½ tsp. cardamom

½ tsp. turmeric

⅛ tsp. cloves

½ tsp. sea salt

½ tsp. lemon zest

1 tsp. fresh lemon juice

Instructions for the pie crust:

If you want to make your own almond flour or soak your packaged almond flour (both of which are optional), follow the instructions in Chapter 9. If you have the time and interest, you might try an experiment, making one pie crust with soaked flour and one without. See how you feel afterward (notice any and all symptoms—mood and digestion), and you'll know if it's worth it for you!

Preheat oven to 350° F.

Add the almond flour and all the other ingredients into a mixing bowl. You can do this in your food processor with the S-blade, if you have one. Mix until the batter forms a ball

Press dough into a greased 9" pie dish. You can make this crust very thin—it's actually better this way. Make sure that the edges around the outside bottom edge of the pie are thin as well (as the crust is pressed into the crease of the pie plate at the bottom). It should be about ¼" thick or so. This crust keeps its shape well and holds the pie filling beautifully.

Once your pie filling is done, pour it into the crust.

Instructions for the pumpkin pie filling:

Keep oven at 350° F. (If you're using a glass pie plate, lower the oven temperature to 300° F.)

If you're baking your own pumpkin, the easiest way to do this is to poke about 10 holes in your sugar pumpkin (or butternut squash), put it in a baking dish with about 2" water, and bake until you can easily insert a knife into the pumpkin (or squash). Remove from the oven, allow to cool, then cut down the middle and scoop out the seeds (you can set them aside if you want to clean them and make pumpkin or squash seeds, which are delicious!). You'll get approximately 2 cups (give or take) of pumpkin from a 2-lb. sugar pumpkin.

If you're making your own coconut milk, do so while the pumpkin is baking, then chill for 1–2 hours so that it gets really thick.

Scoop out 2 cups of pumpkin and save any excess for another pie or a side dish for another meal. Put the pumpkin in your food processor with the S blade (you can also use a high-speed blender or mixer). Add dates and puree.

Now add the coconut milk and the rest of the ingredients and puree until fully blended; taste and see if you like it. At this point, the adventurous cook can add more dates or honey for sweetness, or more of any spice you want to emphasize, according to your taste.

Assembling and baking the pie:

Preheat oven to 425° F (reduce the heat to 375° F if you're using a glass pie plate).

Add the pumpkin pie filling into the crust you've already prepared, and fill right to a tad beneath the rim of the pie plate. (If you're not using a crust, just pour the pie filling into the pan.)

Put the pie in the oven and bake for 15 minutes, then reduce the heat to 350° F (300° F for a glass pie plate). Bake for 40–50 minutes.

Remove from the oven and cool for 2 hours. Cover with a lid or plastic wrap (if we use plastic wrap, we make sure it's tight and doesn't touch the pie, only the plate), and refrigerate for at least 6 hours before serving.

Serving suggestions:

Serve on its own or, for a real treat, add a scoop of the Moroccan Vanilla Spice Ice Cream on the side.

Best Pumpkin Pie Ever with Heavenly Marshmallow Cream Whipped Topping.

CHOCOLATE MOUSSE
WITH A TWIST

Most chocolate desserts are so sweet that they induce cravings for more. This one is different because it takes you on a journey through layers of tastes—the spices in this mousse are designed to boost your metabolism, balance your blood sugar, and reduce or eliminate cravings. Note that it must use neutral bone broth. If you don't have any on hand, you can use 1 tsp. unflavored powdered beef gelatin and warm it up with the dates in the first step.

When you eat this dessert mindfully, you may feel that your energy stays grounded, so you feel satisfied without stirring up fuzzy brain or difficulty concentrating. Most sweets on the market today create an attention deficit by causing blood sugar to surge and zinging your energy all over the place. This makes concentration, creativity, and true satisfaction challenging.

With this mousse, you'll be creating a flavor sensation that is unusually satisfying and takes you on a journey that supports digestive health, a deeply grounded feeling, and the energy to enjoy life to the fullest. Get ready for a real treat!

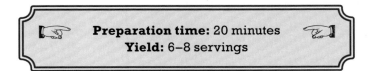

Preparation time: 20 minutes
Yield: 6–8 servings

20 Medjool dates, pitted

1 cup water

1 cup bone broth (A nice gelled neutral broth is best. If you don't have any on hand, use 1 tsp. unflavored powdered beef gelatin.)

2 cups coconut butter

6 egg yolks

1 cup raw cacao powder

2 Tbsp. molasses

2 Tbsp. honey

2 Tbsp. cinnamon

1½ Tbsp. cardamom

2 tsp. ginger

1½ tsp. sea salt

1 tsp. black pepper

½ tsp. nutmeg

¼ tsp. cloves

10 drops Urban Moonshine Organic Citrus Bitters (alternatives: 8 drops of juice from a fresh orange, 3 drops of orange extract, or 4 drops juice of a fresh lemon)

Heat up water and put in a bowl; add dates to soften up. During this step, if you don't have neutral bone broth on hand, add 1 tsp. unflavored powdered beef gelatin to the hot water and mix in. Allow everything to sit and dissolve (about 10 minutes).

Add the softened dates to your electric mixer, food processor with the S-blade, or high-speed blender; blend thoroughly. (If you don't have a food processor or high-speed blender, wait until the dates get so mushy that you can easily blend them up with a fork. This might take 20–30 minutes.)

Add the rest of the ingredients and continue to blend up until everything is thoroughly mixed.

Put this mixture into a glass bowl with a lid, and store in your refrigerator for up to 4 days. After this, store any leftovers in your freezer for up to 4 months. This recipe freezes very well and is wonderful to take out as a fast dessert, even for a dinner party.

Serving suggestions:

Enjoy as is.

Add raspberries, thin orange slices, strawberries, or goji berries.

DECADENT TWO-LAYER
CHOCOLATE CAKE
(Grain Free)

We first served this cake as a special treat when our dear friend and Hay House author Nancy Levin was visiting San Diego. It got rave reviews and has since continued to top the charts for healthy, decadent desserts. This cake is moist and has a rich chocolate taste from raw cacao. Even your friends who don't consider themselves healthy eaters will enjoy this—not realizing that it's good for them, too!

This recipe calls for neutral bone broth; beef bone broth would be best, but you can use any neutral bone broth or meat stock. You'll also see that, like several other recipes we've included in this book, it has quite a few spices. If you've already done the Great Chocolate Experiment (included as part of the Chocolate Drop Cookies recipe earlier in the chapter), you'll begin to understand that we've designed this recipe for balance and so that it won't trigger cravings. If you feel like you have a good sense of your own tastes concerning spices, feel free to modify the ones in this recipe according to your own preferences. Have fun with it!

☞ **Hands-on prep time:** 40 minutes ☜
Total prep time: Approximately 45 minutes
Yield: Two ½" layers for a
two-layer cake; 10–12 servings

Tips for making this cake:

You can make the cake batter ahead of time, refrigerate it, and bake it a day or two later, if you want. You can also make the frosting a couple of days, or even weeks, ahead and store it in the freezer for later use.

If you make your own almond flour (see instructions at the beginning of Chapter 9), you'll want to plan ahead an extra day, or maybe just make a large batch to freeze and have on hand for other recipes as needed).

Cake ingredients:

10 Medjool dates, pitted (you can substitute with ¼ cup honey)

½ cup bone broth

½ cup blackstrap molasses

½ cup coconut oil, melted

½ cup coconut butter

1 cup water

6 eggs, room temperature

3 cups almond flour (store-bought or make your own)

¼ cup coconut flour

2 cups raw cacao powder

3 Tbsp. vanilla powder (or vanilla extract)

1 Tbsp. cinnamon

2 tsp. baking soda

1½ tsp. sea salt

2 tsp. cardamom

1 tsp. ginger

¼ tsp. fennel

¼ tsp. cloves

¼ tsp. black pepper

Frosting ingredients:

1 ripe avocado

½ cup coconut butter

½ cup raw cacao

¼ cup honey

¼ tsp. allspice

1 Tbsp. vanilla extract

½ tsp. sea salt

1 tsp. cinnamon

½ tsp. cardamom

Cake instructions:

Preheat oven to 350° F.

Grease two 8"–9" round cake pans (or 9" x 9" square pans) with coconut oil. We like using silicone cake pans, but you can use rectangular loaf pans if that's all you have. If using glass pans, reduce heat to 300° F, since glass bakeware gets hotter than silicone or metal.

Begin with the dates (or honey) as follows:

— If using a blender or food processor with the S-blade: Put the dates and liquid ingredients in first and blend well. Then add the dry ingredients, and mix everything thoroughly.

— If using a mixer or mixing by hand: Soak dates in ½ cup hot water for an hour, or until they become a very mushy paste and can be mixed up with a fork. (Alternatively, substitute ¼ cup honey for the dates.)

Mix up all wet ingredients until fully blended, then add dry ingredients and blend well.

Once the batter is fully blended, taste to see if you like the flavor or want to add a bit of honey, sea salt, or spices (we sometimes add more cinnamon, vanilla, or sea salt). The batter will taste a lot like the final baked cake, so trust your judgment here.

Pour the batter into the cake pans and bake for between 30–45 minutes. Baking times vary based on how much batter you poured into your pan, the type of cake pan used, and other factors. You'll know the cake is done when you touch the center and it bounces back a bit, or if you put a toothpick into the center and it comes out clean.

While the cake is baking, make the frosting (see instructions that follow). When the cake is done, remove from oven and allow to cool on your countertop. Make sure you don't try to remove the cake

Decadent Two-Layer Chocolate Cake.

from the pans until they have cooled, and you can actually touch it safely with your bare hands.

After cooling, insert a butter knife between the pan and cake, and run the butter knife gently around the edge of the cake, to loosen it from the pan. We like to get a large plate and turn the pan upside down over the plate, allowing the cake to come out right onto the plate (using a plate for each layer of cake).

Frosting instructions:

Put all ingredients into your mixing bowl, blender, or food processor with the S-blade; mix thoroughly.

If you make this frosting ahead of time and you've stored it in the freezer or refrigerator, allow it to come to room temperature before frosting the cake so that it goes on smoothly and easily.

Serving suggestions:

Garnish with strawberries, raspberries, goji berries, walnuts, shredded coconut, or edible flowers.

Serve as is, or with the Moroccan Vanilla Spice Ice Cream.

5-MINUTE
BANANA CINNAMON
ICE CREAM
(Non-Dairy)

When you need ice cream in a rush and don't have an ice-cream maker, this is the perfect recipe! It's simple, delicious, and can be enjoyed on its own or as a side dish for the Apple Tarte Tatin or Cinnamon New Year Cake.

☞ **Preparation time:** 5 minutes ☜
Yield: 4 servings

---

3 bananas (frozen)

1 Tbsp. powdered unflavored beef gelatin (dissolved in 2 Tbsp. hot water)

2 tsp. ground cinnamon

2 Medjool dates, pitted ¼ tsp. sea salt

Tip: When freezing bananas, it's easiest if you peel them first and wrap them in wax paper or parchment paper. You can also cut them into smaller pieces that fit into your food processor or blender. If you want, you can freeze bananas in their skins, but they may be a little more difficult to peel once you remove them (you can let them thaw just a little to make them easier to peel).

Put all ingredients in your blender or food processor with the S-blade, and blend until mushy and fully mixed.

If you make a big batch, you can store it in your freezer in a glass jar. Make sure you don't fill the jar completely (leave ⅓ cup of room between the ice cream and the top of the jar). We like to put the glass jar in a freezer bag to protect it from breakage. You may want to label the bag, so you'll know what dish it is and the date that you made it.

Serving suggestions:

Serve immediately on its own, or with pie, cake, or fresh berries.

If you're serving the ice cream after dinner, you may want to take it out of your freezer and put it into your refrigerator when the meal begins, so that it will be soft enough to scoop when it's time to serve dessert.

CINNAMON
NEW YEAR CAKE
(Grain Free)

Some believe that on the Chinese New Year, if you eat a piece of this special cake, you'll have good luck for the whole year to come. We like the sound of that! This is a new twist on a traditional Chinese New Year cake—we've created a grain-free option with some added spices for flavor and balance, and using neutral bone broth. You may enjoy it on its own, or with the Cinnamon Orange Coconut Frosting we're including here, which can really dress up the cake and make it very special.

Note that grain-free breads don't rise much because it's the grains (especially gluten!) that stretch and trap air bubbles from leavening, so things get all light and airy in the oven. You'll still have a nice, moist cake, but it will only rise a tiny bit.

This is really fun to serve if you have a Chinese Hot Pot meal (see the dinner-party menus in Chapter 3). But you can eat a piece any time of year and affirm your good luck!

☞ **Hands-on prep time:** 10 minutes ☜
Total prep time: Approximately 40 minutes
Yield: 2 flat, rectangular layers for a 2-layer cake;
10–12 servings

Cake ingredients:

6 eggs

2 cups coconut flour

1 cup almond flour

4 cups coconut milk (or ½ cup coconut butter and 4 cups water)

1 cup honey

½ cup bone broth (neutral bone broth or 1 tsp. unflavored powdered beef gelatin dissolved in ½ cup hot water)

¼ cup butter

1 Tbsp. cinnamon

½ tsp. sea salt

¾ tsp. baking soda

¼–½ cup shredded coconut (*optional*)

Optional, but fun spices for balance and flavor:

1 tsp. fennel

½ tsp. paprika

½ tsp. lemongrass

Optional Cinnamon Orange Coconut Frosting ingredients:

½ cup coconut oil

¼ cup honey (or dates; the honey will be a lighter color, and the dates will make it darker)

2 Tbsp. vanilla extract

2 Tbsp. juice from a fresh orange (*optional—you could substitute 3 drops orange extract or leave this out*)

1 Tbsp. cinnamon

½ tsp. sea salt

Cinnamon New Year Cake, unfrosted.

Cake instructions:

Preheat oven to 350° F

Put all ingredients in a large mixing bowl; or to make it really easy, put them in your stand mixer, food processor with the S-blade, or high-speed blender. Mix thoroughly. If mixing by hand, gentlly heat the coconut butter and honey to make it easier to stir.

Grease 2 loaf pans with butter or coconut oil. Pour the mixture into the greased pans.

Note: Some Chinese New Year cakes just have a light sprinkling of shredded coconut on top. If you want to do this, sprinkle about ¼–½ cup shredded coconut on top of the cakes before baking.

Put the pans into the oven and bake for 30–40 minutes, checking at the 30-minute mark. You'll know it's done when the cake has risen a tiny amount and the bread is firm and bouncy to the touch. It will also be slightly browned on top and possibly get a small crack or two on the surface. Open the oven, touch the center of the cake with your finger, and if it feels firm and bouncy, it's done. Remove from oven and allow to cool on your countertop. If you want to use the Cinnamon Orange Coconut Frosting, make that now.

Frosting instructions:

Put all ingredients into a food processor with the S-blade and mix until completely blended.

Serving suggestions:

Drizzle the Cinnamon Orange Coconut Frosting over the top of the cake and enjoy! Garnish with orange slices and mint leaves.

You can use your favorite frosting, a layer of crushed berries, or sliced bananas between the layers and on top of the cake, or use a layer of Moroccan Vanilla Spice Ice Cream between layers when preparing the cake to serve.

Serve with Moroccan Vanilla Spice Ice cream

Serve with sliced bananas and the Heavenly Marshmallow Cream Whipped Topping—this got rave reviews from our recipe testers, the Bone Broth Tribe.

Slice cake and eat pieces as a snack, without frosting. This cake is almost like French toast, so it would be wonderful with some butter or coconut oil as a breakfast treat, especially if you're moving away from a standard American breakfast, like doughnuts!

Cinnamon New Year Cake with Cinnamon Orange Coconut Frosting.

HEAVENLY
MARSHMALLOW CREAM
Whipped Topping, and Marshmallows

These recipes use neutral bone broth and unflavored powdered beef gelatin. If you don't have a really gelled neutral bone broth, add 2 Tbsp. unflavored beef gelatin to 1 quart of neutral stock or broth to get it to gel very firmly.

Okay, seriously, who doesn't like marshmallows? Is there anything else that brings out the inner child in every one of us? Memories of toasted marshmallows by the campfire or eating s'mores in the summertime often come up anytime we mention this treat. We have a few stories of our own involving marshmallows:

Louise: When I was a little girl, I won a very unusual contest, which involved seeing how fast you could get a marshmallow attached to a string into your mouth. This meant you had to have a very strong tongue. Well, I did, because I won the contest every time! When Heather heard this story, she decided we needed to make some healthy marshmallows and try this contest ourselves!

Heather: When I decided to make my first batch of marshmallows a couple of years ago, I didn't have a stand mixer. I figured I could use my immersion blender with whisk attachment instead, which required me to hold the "on" button the whole time in order to make it work. I had placed a tea towel around the bowl to keep the marshmallow from splattering.

This makeshift solution was going as well as it could until my cat, Willie, came in from the enclosed patio. He was chasing a bee, and I began to worry that he'd get stung. I called out for my husband, Joel, who was likely ignoring me thinking I was going to ask him to do some chore. As I looked over at Willie, I inadvertently lifted the whisk out of the bowl, but was still pushing the on button . . . which resulted in the tea towel winding around the running whisk and marshmallow covering every surface of the floor, stove, and cabinets. (Joel came down once it was all cleaned up.) These days, I have a stand mixer with a splatter-proof bowl. It's amazing how effortless making marshmallows is now!

Our recipe testers, the Bone Broth Tribe, said this recipe was so good that they wanted to take a bath in the marshmallow cream. It makes a wonderful whipped topping. We're also including suggestions for making more traditional marshmallows, which are moister, healthier, and tastier than the store-bought version. We hope you enjoy both versions of this recipe, and perhaps you will have your own marshmallow stories to tell for years to come.

HEAVENLY MARSHMALLOW CREAM WHIPPED TOPPING

This may appear to form in a pan but will not be firm at room temperature, and will be easy to scoop and use as a whipped topping or frosting substitute for cake. You can refrigerate or freeze it and still have a nice, whipped-cream-type consistency.

> **Preparation time:** 10–20 minutes
> **Yield:** 10–12 servings

¼ cup neutral bone broth (you can substitute
  2 tsp. unflavored powdered gelatin)

½ cup water

1 cup raw honey

1 tsp. sea salt

2 tsp. vanilla extract

Optional spices. These are what pushed the marshmallow cream over the top to "heavenly" and "otherworldly" for our recipe testers. The spices ground the marshmallow cream so that it's not too sweet and does not trigger cravings:

- ¼ tsp. cinnamon
- ¼ tsp. cardamom
- ¼ tsp. fenugreek
- 6–10 drops citrus bitters

Add honey, water, vanilla, and sea salt into a saucepan; heat on medium high until the honey gets to 220° F when measured with a candy thermometer (you can also use a meat thermometer that goes up to 220° F). Typically, when it gets to this stage, you're seeing big bubbles as the mixture boils, and you may notice that the smell changes just a bit or you become aware of the aroma. (We have made this without a thermometer and just used our visual and olfactory senses, and done pretty well.) In the beginning, you may want the reassurance of a candy or meat thermometer, just to confirm that it's where you want it to be. The mixture will look golden colored, like the honey, but will change to white when you mix it!

Pour the mixture into a mixing bowl; add bone broth. If you need to use powdered gelatin instead of neutral bone broth, add it in with the warmed mixture and let it dissolve and cool down for 10–15 minutes.

Once cooled a bit, turn on your mixer. A stand mixer is the easiest because you just turn it on and let it go; you can also use a hand mixer. It helps if you have a splatter protector over your bowl, although you could use a tea towel if you're careful and pay attention while mixing (so you don't have a mishap like Heather did!).

You'll know that the cream is done when it gets thick and white, almost like it stands up by itself when you make a peak with it. This may take about 7–10 minutes.

Now taste—see if you like it as is or if that feels too sweet for you. We like to see if there's energy going right up to the head after tasting. If that feeling happens, it's likely too sweet, and this is a good sign to add some spices. You could start first by adding the cinnamon; mix it in and taste. If you're feeling adventurous, add the rest of the spices. Note that the bitters aid digestion and add a nice, balancing flavor; alternatively, you could add 2 drops of lemon or orange juice, or 1 drop of either orange or lemon extract.

Mix all spices thoroughly and you're ready to transfer everything to your pan. Pour the mixture into a large glass dish and cover with a lid, if you have one. A rubber spatula can help get out all the goodness, unless you want to leave a little there for licking the mixer and bowl.

Store in your refrigerator for up to 4 days, or in your freezer for up to a month. Even if you freeze this marshmallow cream, it will still be soft and ready to serve within a few minutes of removing it from the freezer.

Serving suggestions:

Use as a topping for ice cream.

Serve over berries or sliced bananas

Serve with the Apple Tarte Tatin recipe as an alternative to ice cream.

This topping also works beautifully as an alternative to frosting. Try it on the Cinnamon New Year Cake with sliced bananas. Yum!

MARSHMALLOWS

These will be firm at room temperature and closer to store-bought marshmallows, except that they'll be moister in texture.

☞ **Hands-on prep time:** 10–20 minutes ☜
Total prep time: 4 hours and 20 minutes
Yield: 12 servings

6 Tbsp. neutral bone broth (Make sure it is very gelled. It should have little movement when you shake the chilled bone broth that has been in the refrigerator for at least 24 hours. If it's not that gelled, add 1 Tbsp. of powdered gelatin. If it's completely liquid, add 2½ Tbsp. powdered gelatin.)

1 cup honey

2 tsp. vanilla extract

1 tsp. sea salt

2 Tbsp. powdered beef gelatin

Optional spices. These spices ground the marshmallows so that they're not too sweet and do not trigger cravings:

- ¼ tsp. cinnamon
- ¼ tsp. cardamom

- ¼ tsp. fenugreek
- 3 drops of Urban Moonshine Citrus Bitters

Optional coloring and toppings:

- You can use natural food dyes, such as elderberry tincture and tart cherry juice concentrate, to color these if you're making Easter Peeps for kids or want to add pizzazz for a party.

- Be creative and have fun with your own inventions! After the marshmallows are put into the pan, some people sprinkle theirs with camu camu powder (a natural source of vitamin C and pink in color), raw cacao, cinnamon, cloves, fennel, ground pumpkin seeds, shredded coconut, or whatever catches their fancy!

Follow all of the instructions for the Heavenly Marshmallow Cream Whipped Topping, except you won't be using water for this recipe. Once you add the bone broth, honey, vanilla, and sea salt to your mixing bowl, add the 2 Tbsp. powdered gelatin, mix it in just a bit, and allow the mixture to sit (about 10 minutes). Then proceed with mixing it up as described in the marshmallow cream recipe (about 10 minutes in the mixer), until it stands in peaks.

Once the mixing is finished and you have added the spices you want to include, leave everything in the bowl and decide whether you want to use any optional coloring ingredients. If you want to use the elderberry tincture and/or tart cherry juice concentrate, add those into the mixing bowl and mix thoroughly before transferring to a pan. If you want to make Peep-style treats, you can get a pastry bag and tips (used in cake decorating) and pipe Peep-shaped treats.

If you want to add any other ingredients to top your marshmallows (such as camu camu powder, raw cacao, or shredded coconut), these can be added after you transfer the marshmallows to the pan.

Once your marshmallows are in the pan (or piped into shapes) and sprinkled with optional ingredients, leave them on your countertop (or put in the refrigerator) to completely set, which will take about 5 hours. At this point, you can slice them, remove them from the pan, and serve.

Store in your refrigerator for up to 7 days, and in your freezer for longer periods.

Serving suggestions:

Eat as is.

Eat with a scoop of sunflower butter or tahini sprinkled with sea salt for a nice treat.

Serve with sliced strawberries or bananas.

Tie one to a string and do Louise's contest-winning trick, trying to get the marshmallow up into your mouth! There are many websites and books with kids' games involving marshmallow races like this. Have fun!

Heavenly Marshmallow Cream Whipped Topping.

Moroccan Vanilla Spice Ice Cream.

MOROCCAN
VANILLA SPICE
ICE CREAM
(Non-Dairy)

This recipe must use neutral bone broth. If you don't have any on hand, you can use 2 Tbsp. unflavored powdered beef gelatin and warm it up with the dates in the first step of the instructions.

Oh my, ice cream! This delicious recipe got rave reviews from our recipe testers, the Bone Broth Tribe. What makes this an extra-nice treat is that it can be easily scooped straight out of the freezer. (Many non-dairy ice creams need about 20 minutes or so to soften a bit in the refrigerator or on the countertop before serving.) You can also make it with or without an ice-cream maker.

Because of the spices used, this vanilla ice cream almost has a hint of coffee flavor. If you love coffee ice cream and want to kick this up a notch, you can add a little organic coffee extract or finely ground organic coffee beans (about 1 tsp. of either should work and decaf is fine). You can get organic coffee extract online or in the spice section of some health-food stores, near the vanilla extract. Note that coffee haters love this recipe, too, because it's not enough of a coffee flavor to turn them off. It's pretty much the best of both worlds!

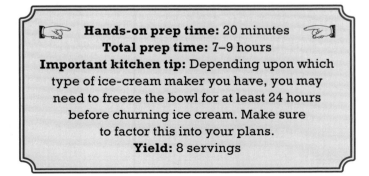

Hands-on prep time: 20 minutes
Total prep time: 7–9 hours
Important kitchen tip: Depending upon which type of ice-cream maker you have, you may need to freeze the bowl for at least 24 hours before churning ice cream. Make sure to factor this into your plans.
Yield: 8 servings

10 Medjool dates (approximately 1 cup), pitted

5–6 cups water

½ cup beef bone broth (A nice gelled neutral broth is best. If you don't have any on hand, use 2 Tbsp. unflavored powdered beef gelatin.)

1 cup sunflower butter

2 cups coconut oil

½ cup maple syrup

3 egg yolks

½ tsp. turmeric

1 tsp. fenugreek

2 tsp. ginger

2 Tbsp. vanilla powder (or extract)

1 Tbsp. cinnamon

1 tsp. sea salt

¼ tsp. cloves

¼ tsp. allspice

You can use an electric mixer, food processor with the S-blade, or high-speed blender for this recipe. Heat up 1 cup of the water and put in a bowl; add the dates to soften up. During this step, if you don't have neutral bone broth on hand, add 2 Tbsp. unflavored powdered beef gelatin to the hot water and mix in, allowing everything to sit and dissolve.

Wait 10 minutes for the dates to soften. (If you don't have a food processor or high-speed blender, wait until the dates get so mushy that you can easily blend them up with a fork. This might take 20–30 minutes.)

Once the dates are soft, put them in your blender, food processor, or mixing bowl and blend thoroughly. Add in the rest of the ingredients, and continue to blend up until everything is thoroughly mixed.

When you taste the mixture, it's important to know that it will taste similar once it's been made into ice cream, but it will lose a little flavor after freezing, so don't be alarmed if it's a little more intense than you expected.

Put this mixture into a glass bowl with a lid, and chill in your refrigerator before making ice cream.

If you have an ice-cream maker:

After 6 hours or more of chilling in your refrigerator, put the mixture into your ice-cream maker and churn until the mixture is frozen and holds together well. You should be able to take some out on a wooden spoon and turn it upside down with none of the ice cream dripping off.

Store in a lidded glass container n your freezer. Place a piece of wax paper or parchment paper over the ice cream before putting on the lid, to keep it from developing freezer burn. It will keep for several months.

If you don't have an ice-cream maker:

Take a large stainless steel bowl and fill it halfway with ice. Add some rock salt (or any coarse salt, such as kosher) and mix it up. The salt won't be touching the ice cream—it's there to lower the temperature of the ice so that it gets cold enough to freeze the mixture effectively.

Put a smaller stainless steel or ceramic bowl into the big bowl of ice and salt. Make sure it's set well into the ice, so that ice is going up the sides of the smaller bowl, but not into the bowl itself. Then fill the smaller bowl halfway up with ice cream mixture.

Now take a handheld mixer or immersion blender with whisk attachment and blend the ice-cream mixture for 10 minutes.

Take both bowls and put them in the freezer for 1–2 hours. Then take the bowls out and use your hand mixer again for another 10 minutes.

Cover with some natural parchment paper (sitting directly on the mixture), then put a top on the smaller bowl and allow the ice cream to set in your freezer.

Serving suggestions:

Eat alone or serve with the Cinnamon New Year Cake, Apple Tarte Tatin, Vanilla Cake with Berry White Chocolate Frosting, or your favorite baked apples or berries.

cee

VANILLA CAKE
with BERRY WHITE CHOCOLATE FROSTING
(Grain Free)

This recipe must use neutral bone broth. If you don't have any on hand, you can use 2 tsp. unflavored powdered beef gelatin and warm it up with the dates in the first step of the instructions.

This cake was deemed so moist by our recipe testers that it needs no adornments! As they sampled the cake, all we could hear from the Bone Broth Tribe was "ooohhh" and "ahhhh," so we knew we were on to something good!

You can use your favorite berries for the frosting, or leave them out altogether for a simple, white chocolate frosting.

Preparation time: You can make the frosting up to 3 days before the cake to save time. The frosting also freezes well.
Hands-on prep time: 45 minutes
Total prep time: Approximately 1½ hours
Yield: Approximately 10 servings

Cake ingredients:

2 cups coconut butter

½ cup ghee

½ cup almond flour

½ cup honey

5 eggs

1 cup bone broth (A nice gelled neutral broth is best. If you don't have any on hand, use 2 tsp. unflavored powdered beef gelatin.)

3 Tbsp. vanilla extract

½ tsp. sea salt

Optional spices—these are wonderful to bring balance to the tastes in this recipe to reduce cravings, create a sense of satisfaction, and to aid digestion:

- 1 tsp. fennel
- 1 tsp. cardamom

Frosting ingredients:

1 cup strawberries (you could also use raspberries, blackberries, or even cherries)

½ cup raw cacao butter

¼–½ cup honey (amount will depend on which fruit you use and how sweet you like it)

½ cup ghee

½ cup almond flour

1½ Tbsp. vanilla extract

¼ tsp. sea salt

Pinch cloves

Cake instructions:

Preheat oven to 300° F.

Grease two 8"–9" round cake pans (or 9" x 9" square pans) with coconut oil or butter. We like using silicone cake pans, but you can use rectangular loaf pans if that's all you have. Glass works, too, just be sure to reduce heat to 250° F, since glass bakeware gets hotter than silicone or metal pans.

Add all ingredients into your food processor, high-speed blender, or mixing bowl (you can use a motorized mixer or mix by hand); blend up thoroughly.

Taste and decide if you want the optional spices. Add them if desired and blend thoroughly.

Pour the batter into your greased pans and bake for 30 minutes. Note that baking times vary based on how much batter you poured into your pan, the type of cake pan used, and other factors.

While the cake is baking, make the frosting.

Important tip: This cake bakes sort of "wet" in that it will still look very moist and not bounce when it's fully cooked. In other words, when you touch the middle, it won't bounce back, but you'll feel a little give. Take the cake out when it's browned on top, and allow it to cool completely before removing it from the pan.

After cooling, insert a butter knife between the pan and cake, and run the butter knife gently around the edge of the cake, to loosen it from the pan. This should allow you to remove the cake. We like to get a large plate and turn the pan upside down over the plate, allowing the cake to come out right onto the plate (using a plate for each layer of cake).

This cake will be very moist and resemble pineapple upside-down cake on the bottom, once you've taken it out of the pan. This is why so many people love it!

Frosting instructions:

Make sure the cake is completely cool before frosting it. If you break some, that's okay. This is what frosting is for—to disguise the little breaks in the cake!

If you're not using a food processor or high-speed blender, mash up the berries you are using with a fork to get them soft, and set them aside. (If you're using cherries, be sure to cut them in half and remove the pits, and then mash them up.)

Melt the raw cacao butter in a small saucepan on the lowest burner setting. If you measure out a heaping ½ cup, you should have approximately that amount once it's melted. Make sure the raw cacao butter doesn't get too hot or else it will burn; watch it melt so that you remove it from the burner as soon as it's fully melted.

Add the raw cacao and all ingredients (starting with just ¼ cup honey at first) into your mixer, high-speed blender, or food processor with the S-blade. You can also mix this by hand to build a little muscle!

You may find that the resulting mixture has more of a liquid texture than you'd expect for frosting. That's okay because it will firm up in the refrigerator. Taste the frosting to see if you want it a bit sweeter;

if so, add some honey and taste again. We like to add 1 Tbsp. at a time and taste, just to get the right amount of sweetness.

Put it in a covered container in your refrigerator for at least 30 minutes.

If your frosting has been in the refrigerator for more than a couple of hours, take it out about 20 minutes before frosting your cake. This will allow it to soften up so that it's easily spreadable on your cake. Since the cake has to finish baking and then cool, you have plenty of time for your frosting to firm up before you'll need it.

When the frosting is thick and ready to spread, take a butter knife or rubber spatula and frost one cake; put the top layer on, and then frost the top layer and sides.

You're now ready to decorate as desired and serve! We like to keep things simple and decorate with fresh berries, goji berries, banana slices, or edible flowers.

Serving suggestions:

This cake is wonderful on its own. You can also serve with berries or the Moroccan Vanilla Spice Ice Cream.

Louise, holding a Sidecar; and Heather, holding a Negroni Cocktail; toast over a pot of bone broth.

⋅⋅ CHAPTER 12 ⋅⋅

THE SASSY:
Cocktails with Benefits

In his book *Blue Zones: Lessons for Living Longer from the People Who've Lived the Longest*, Dan Buettner found that having a drink or two of wine, beer, or spirits factored into the habits of many of the longest-living people on the planet. His research suggested that drinking in moderation (a drink or two, max) had some health benefits. This is a highly personal decision, though, and for those of you who do choose to drink alcohol, we wanted to share some cocktails that would augment the health benefits.

Bone broth cocktails and hot toddies are gracing the menus of restaurants and bars in many cities across the country. While this may seem new, such drinks have actually been around for as long as bone broth itself. We were inspired to put a twist on this tradition by creating cocktails that taste just as they were intended, but without any added refined sugar. Our simple syrup uses neutral bone broth and honey, for instance, and the rest play on the intended taste of the original cocktail recipe.

Heather: When my husband, Joel, and I went to Scotland, we visited the oldest Scotch seller in Edinburgh. The expert at the establishment explained to us that the liquor sold as Scotch today, even from the most expensive brands, has gone through processing that removes all of the good stuff (like essential fatty acids) and adds back sugar and caramel color. He proceeded to do a tasting with us of their Scotch, which had all the good stuff still in it but none of the artificial additives. The taste was dramatically different and better.

As someone with one foot in the health world and another in the culinary world, I recognize that many people want to live a life that offers choice—one of moderation rather than denial. Alcohol is often a part of the equation for foodies because they love to experience the flavors and crafts of a particular region or culture. Craft beers, spirits, and wine have moved from the trendy to mainstream, and we are fortunate that more artisans are making organic and sulfite-free options.

Cocktails, beer, and wine in moderation can be a fun part of a really good meal with friends. Some innovative bars have healthy cocktails that provide higher-quality ingredients. The ones that Louise and I include in this chapter go the extra mile by adding amino acids and minerals in bone broth for fortification and grounding, bitters to aid digestion, and lemon for a touch of cleansing. We think you'll love them!

The Sidecar.

THE
SIDECAR

Rumor has it this 1920s cocktail was created by an American soldier in Paris. Many people who know their cocktails will tell you that it's their favorite, and with good reason. This drink is easy to make and has a delicious, light flavor with a tiny touch of natural sweetness. While most sidecar recipes do not contain bone broth or bitters, we really love how these two additions round out the drink with health benefits, but without taking anything away from the fabulous taste.

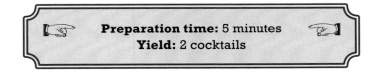

Preparation time: 5 minutes
Yield: 2 cocktails

¼ cup (2 oz.) neutral bone broth or stock

⅓ cup (approximately 2½ oz.) Cointreau

⅓ cup lemon juice

⅔ cup (approximately 5¼ oz.) cognac

10–12 drops Urban Moonshine Citrus Bitters
(or your favorite citrus bitters)

Take your broth out of the refrigerator and allow to sit on the countertop to become more liquid. If it's really gelled, heat on the lowest temperature in a saucepan, then cool to room temperature.

Put all ingredients in a large glass, and then pour into a cocktail shaker full of cracked ice. Shake well, then strain into 2 chilled cocktail glasses. These are extra fun poured into martini glasses.

MANHATTAN

This cocktail is believed to have been created in New York City in the late 1800s and was quite popular with bourbon lovers during Prohibition. These days the tasty Manhattan is enjoying a resurgence (and with good reason!), often with a bartender's own interpretation of this timeless classic.

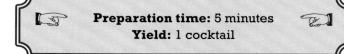

Preparation time: 5 minutes
Yield: 1 cocktail

1 oz. (2 Tbsp.) bone broth

¼ cup (2 oz.) rye or bourbon—we used Redemption high-rye bourbon, which worked well for this cocktail

1½ oz. (3 Tbsp.) sweet vermouth

10 drops Urban Moonshine Citrus Bitters (or your favorite citrus bitters)

3–5 drops Dynamic Health tart cherry juice concentrate,

3 drops Scrappy's Cardamom Bitters

Lemon twist or cherry, for garnish

Take your broth out of the refrigerator and allow to sit on the countertop to become more liquid. If it's really gelled, heat on the lowest temperature in a saucepan, then cool to room temperature.

Put all ingredients in a large glass, and then pour into a cocktail shaker full of cracked ice. Shake well, then strain into a chilled cocktail glass (some people love this in a martini glass, while others prefer a lowball glass).

Garnish with a lemon or cherry twist.

A Manhattan.

Negroni Cocktail.

NEGRONI
COCKTAIL

This oh-so-sophisticated 1920s cocktail is experiencing a renaissance today. Drinking it may bring you right back to Florence, Italy, when Count Negroni decided to add gin to his cocktail instead of soda water. This easy-to-make, easy-to-drink cocktail has since become a beloved classic, much like the Manhattan. Our version offers a healthy twist with bone broth, bitters, and lemon to aid your digestion, along with a touch of honey instead of refined sugar.

Note that the simple syrup concentrate requires neutral bone broth or stock, and when you make it you'll have extra left over for a couple more cocktails.

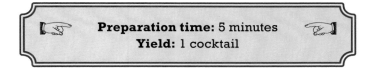

Preparation time: 5 minutes
Yield: 1 cocktail

Ingredients for the simple syrup concentrate:

½ Tbsp. honey

½ cup neutral bone broth or stock

Ingredients for the cocktail:

1½ oz. simple syrup concentrate (3 Tbsp.)

1½ oz. red vermouth (3 Tbsp.)

1½ oz. Campari (3 Tbsp.)

1½ oz. (3 Tbsp.) dry gin (Barr Hill Gin is a nice option)

7 drops Urban Moonshine Citrus Bitters (or your favorite citrus bitters)

1 tsp. lemon juice

Optional: 1–2 oz. sparkling mineral water or Prosecco—this is really good if you want a lighter taste

Orange twist, for garnish

Heat broth with honey on the lowest temperature in a saucepan, then cool to room temperature.

Put all ingredients (except sparkling water and orange twist) into a large glass, and then pour it into a cocktail shaker full of cracked ice. Shake well, then strain into a chilled cocktail glass. Top with sparkling water or Prosecco, if using.

Garnish with an orange twist.

Bone Broth Scotch.

BONE
BROTH
Scotch

Called a "corrected Scotch" in Scotland, where it's served soup-style in a bowl with lamb broth, celery, carrots, and onions,[1] we have changed it up a little by using Scotch and sea salt as a type of "finisher" for this easy cocktail. We suggest using a neutral bone broth or stock, although some people like a slightly flavored lamb broth with this recipe. The broth and sea salt really adds a nourishing, grounding feel to this drink.

Preparation time: 5 minutes
Yield: 1 cocktail

½ cup neutral broth or stock

¼ cup (2 oz.) Scotch

Dash of sea salt for balance
and extra minerals

Take your broth out of the refrigerator and allow to sit on the countertop to become more liquid. If it's really gelled, heat on the lowest temperature in a saucepan, then cool to room temperature. If you want to make this a hot toddy, heat it up and then remove from heat to cool down a bit.

Pour the bone broth and Scotch into a glass, and mix together with a dash of sea salt. Serve warm, at room temperature, or on ice.

CHAPTER 13

THE DIY:

Beautiful Skin and Hair Masks

///

SKIN-SO-SMOOTH
HONEY GELATIN
Face Mask

This face mask is food for all skin types, including sensitive skin, and neutral bone broth is preferred for this recipe.

As with all skin masks, make sure you test some of this on your inner forearm before using it on your face. Every person's body is different and while reactions are rare, they could happen.

1 tsp. bone broth that has a nice, thick gel consistency. Neutral bone broth works best because it won't have any additives to create a "soup-like" scent or other additives that could irritate skin. Alternatively, you can use ½ tsp. unflavored beef gelatin powder.

1 tsp. raw honey

— If *you're using bone broth*: Mix chilled broth and honey thoroughly with a fork or whisk. You'll have enough for 2 masks. Store extra in the refrigerator.

— If *you're using gelatin powder*: Add the gelatin powder to 2 tsp. warm water and allow to sit for 5 minutes. Heat the honey in a saucepan gently on low. Once it's warm and melted, take off heat and add the water and gelatin. Mix well and wait 15 minutes until it's cooled down and has a paste-like gelatin consistency that you can still spread on your face. You can put this in the refrigerator if you need to firm things up a bit.

Lightly coat your face with the mask, using your fingers, a clean makeup brush, or a soft, unused paintbrush. Avoid eye area and lips. Do your neck if you like as well.

Let sit on your face for 10–20 minutes or until dry.

Wash off thoroughly with warm water, and then use some toner (optional) and your favorite serum or moisturizer. Some people may use coconut oil or beef tallow on their skin as a natural moisturizer.

DIY
NOSEY PERFECT
Pore Cleanser

Here's an all-natural way to clean out the pores on your nose, using a fun home remedy that you can make in minutes!

We've used pore strips and found them to be not only overly drying, but also full of chemicals that we'd rather not put on our skin. Remember, what you put on your skin gets absorbed into your body. This is why it's just as important to choose quality ingredients for your skin as for your food.

This recipe uses unflavored powdered beef gelatin. If you happen to have kefir on hand, it's a great way to get the beneficial properties of probiotics into your skin as well!

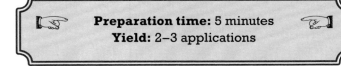

Preparation time: 5 minutes
Yield: 2–3 applications

2 tsp. unflavored powdered beef gelatin

2 tsp. milk, kefir, goat's milk, or coconut milk
(Any percentage milk fat should work, but
use coconut milk if you're allergic to dairy.)

Add gelatin and milk to a very small saucepan. Mix thoroughly until you have a thick, chunky texture.

Set burner to low and heat the mixture, mixing regularly until it's a thick liquid. If you're using coconut milk and the mixture gets too clumpy, add a little water to help dissolve the clumps (start with 1 Tbsp. water). Remove from burner and allow to cool to room temperature.

Test the cooled mixture on the inside of your arm before applying to your face. This is to make sure you're not sensitive to it. If you have any unpleasant reactions, *do not* use this cleanser on your face.

With a clean makeup brush; a small, soft, unused paintbrush; or your fingers, brush the mixture over your nose, including the sides and bottom.

Keep the mixture on until it's dry to the touch; this will take approximately 10 minutes. Once it's dry, carefully pull it off of your nose with your fingers. If you remove it carefully, it will come off in strips that are mostly intact, almost like a pore strip.

You may notice the oil and dirt from clogged pores that has been removed from the skin on your nose. If you have small pores already, you may notice some sebum on the strip and some still on your nose. Using your fingernails or a soft warm washcloth, you can gently scrape off the sebum still on your nose.

Follow up with your favorite toner and serum or lotion.

Store extra pore cleanser in a jar in your refrigerator and heat up on low when you're ready for your next use.

SO SHINY
BEAUTIFUL
Hair Mask

Whether you plan a full day of beauty or just take 20–30 minutes to pamper yourself, you will love this gelatin hair treatment for soft, shiny, manageable hair! It greatly nourishes your hair with its protein-rich and moisturizing ingredients.

While your hair mask is working its magic, play some soft music, take a bath, do mirror work, or meditate. Of course, you might just want to put on your favorite music and dance around your bathroom—it's a perfect time for a dance break!

Do this treatment once or twice per month.

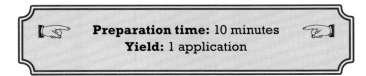

Preparation time: 10 minutes
Yield: 1 application

½ cup water

1 Tbsp. unflavored powdered beef gelatin

1 egg yolk

Optional: coconut oil for the ends of your hair

Heat the water until hot; add the gelatin and mix thoroughly. Allow to cool. When the mixture has reached room temperature, add the egg yolk and mix thoroughly.

Apply mask to your hair without rubbing into your scalp. Leave your ends free of the mask and put coconut oil on them, if you desire, as it is very moisturizing. If you like, you can put a shower cap over your hair to let everything set.

Leave the mask on your hair for 20–30 minutes. Rinse your hair with warm water, and then shampoo as usual.

Alternative for removing hair-product buildup:

If you want to remove product buildup in your hair, replace the egg yolk with 1 tsp. apple cider vinegar, and mix everything together thoroughly.

✧ CHAPTER 14 ✧

TO YOUR HEALTH, HAPPINESS, AND LONGEVITY

At 89 years old, Louise has some excellent insights on what it takes to live a long, healthy, happy life. She shares them here with us:

> On my 80th birthday, Hay House threw a big party for me. That day, I announced to all of my employees, friends, and loved ones: "My 80s are going to be the best decade of my life so far!" And I used this affirmation all through my 80s.
>
> Now, at 89, I look back over the past 9 years and realize I was right. I am healthy, strong, and happier than ever. I have wonderful friendships. I have decided that from now on, I am going by the name "Louise Play" because this is the energy I'm bringing into my life. If there is anything I can leave you with in this book, it's that your health is the greatest blessing. For me, health is as simple as getting my thoughts right with positive affirmations, and getting my food right by eating whole foods and bone broth. These are the things that nourish my mind and body. They give me the energy to experience the joy that is all around me. They allow me to play with friends of all ages, to dance, and to giggle.
>
> Remember, Life loves you! You can step into your kitchen and take your health into your own hands. Maybe grab some friends or family members who will help make the whole thing even more fun. Let's all affirm: I *deserve the best, and I accept it now!*

In a world that has been enticed by magic pills and fast food, bone broth may be dismissed as "just soup." People might try it for a week and be on to the next big trend. And yet with all of our modern science and time-saving prepared foods, we're witnessing a decline in energy, an increase in stress, and a widely held negative affirmation that *the body falls apart at* 40. We invite you to change this belief and create new affirmations for your health, such as: I *am healthy, whole, and complete in every stage of my life*.

Bone broth and whole foods are not a one-time magic pill. They are a daily practice, like meditation and affirmations. Each day, consuming bone broth reminds your body that it's supported and deserves gentle, easy-to-digest nutrients. When consumed regularly, you deliver to your body key components that help keep it going.

While other foods contain amino acids, vitamins, and minerals, bone broth has a unique way of delivering denatured collagen as well. You might think of your stockpot as a collagen-delivery device; a way to nourish the connective tissues that make up and support your body from head to toe, from bones to skin. When you love your body this way, it's no wonder it will begin to heal and thrive.

NATURE HEALS

For more than a thousand years, we have moved farther away from the land. And yet we still know and feel its healing powers when we walk in the woods, climb a mountain, or stroll barefoot on sandy beaches. Somewhere deep inside, we know that nature helps us heal. It calms, soothes, and balances us.

Natural, whole foods are one way that we can reconnect with nature every single day. We can live exciting, modern lives and still allow nature to ground us every time we sit down to a meal. We strengthen this connection because making food requires us to slow down and focus on nourishment; we strengthen it even more when we share a meal with loved ones. In consuming food from the earth, we take all of that healing energy into our bodies,

and the alchemical process of digestion transforms that energy into healing nutrients for our bodies. This is why so many wise thought leaders like the Dalai Lama say, "Food is life." Food from nature has the ability to transform us, in body and soul.

We live in a world of hard evidence, which can sometimes make light of nature in favor of science. Yet if we look closely enough, there is often science to back up what we know deep inside. It may take longer for it to show up, but it eventually does. Today, science knows that we are all an experiment—each one of us has a body that is different from the other. When we learn to go inside and listen, we find that there is a truth, a knowing, deep within us, which recognizes what we need to feel nourished, loved, and healed.

In our kitchens, we can prepare healing foods from our ancestors who were closer to the land and more instinctively knew its healing properties. The time we take in our kitchens is an investment in our own nourishment. It is a declaration to ourselves that we matter, and another way we can love ourselves. We can learn to tailor tastes and textures that delight us, finding creative ways to express our art through food. As we prepare and consume this food, we can be mindful of the love that went into it. This love that is entering our bodies, soothing our soul, and calming stress.

There is nothing that can do this like broth. In fact, broth is one of the easiest foods to prepare and digest. It warms us to the bone, reminding us of our beloved grandmothers. It gives us the vitality to go out there into the world and live a fabulous, beautiful, vibrant life. One where we put on feathered flapper headbands and bold lipstick, take baths with our hats on, and celebrate life with the heart, soul, and energy of teenagers.

We invite you to take your own journey into healing broth. Whether you're on this journey to heal, celebrate wellness, or embrace your own inner child, we hope you enjoy the culinary adventures that broth provides.

HEALING AFFIRMATION AND MEDITATION

Here is a healing affirmation and meditation that you can do anytime you want to remind yourself that you are worth the time it takes to nourish yourself. Put one hand on your heart and one hand on your belly; take three deep, slow breaths; and say these words:

I am unfolding in fulfilling ways. Only good can come to me. I now express health, happiness, prosperity, and peace of mind. I am worth the time it takes to nourish myself, from planning to shopping to preparing and enjoying food. I am willing to release old, negative beliefs that kept me from taking time for myself. They are only thoughts that stand in my way. My new thoughts are positive and fulfilling. I now find ways to love nourishing and caring for myself. I am learning to feel comfortable with my culinary skills. I am in charge. I am safe, and I am free.

My kitchen is a place of joy, adventure, and creativity. In my kitchen, I see all the ways that I can nourish myself. As I step into my kitchen, I create peacefulness in my mind, and my body reflects this peacefulness as perfect health. I am open to experimenting with new foods and new approaches, listening to my inner wisdom for what works for me. My food preparation is my presence practice and my mindfulness meditation. Every moment presents a wonderful new opportunity to become more of who I am.

My body is always working toward optimal health. My body wants to be whole and healthy. I cooperate and become healthy, whole, and complete. I am love, and I nourish myself with love. I allow the love from my own heart to wash through me, cleansing and healing every part of my body. I know I am worth healing. I share this love with all who enter my home and sit at my table. I greet the new with open arms. I trust life to be wonderful! And so it is.

⤜APPENDIX⤛

Bone Broth Healing Stories

EYTON SHALOM'S STORY:
HEALING BACK PAIN AND WARMING THE BODY

Eyton Shalom is a licensed acupuncturist and expert in Chinese medicine and Ayurvedic medicine. He's also a talented cook with expertise in working with healing herbs and spices.

I discovered bone broth in 1991, when I was in my second year at acupuncture school and was working full-time as well. With all the stress, I got bronchitis, which developed into walking pneumonia. I had a constant dry cough that would not go away. I felt weak and my lungs were chronically irritated. I was treated by a student in the clinic at my acupuncture school, and he taught me to make chicken bone marrow soup (bone broth), made into a porridge with rice. After 3 days of consuming this, my strength returned, and I felt much better. (See Eyton's Healing Chicken Soup in Chapter 5.)

My second experience with bone broth was in 1992, during my third year of acupuncture school. A back injury I had sustained at age 17 was exacerbated that year due to overwork and sitting so long on hard seats at school. I learned to make a beef bone broth with Chinese medicinal herbs, and that helped my body heal and strengthen up even more.

Prior to discovering bone broth, I was a vegetarian for 12 years and always felt cold, especially in my hands and feet. After incorporating bone broth and soups with a bone broth base into my diet, my body temperature warmed right up—I no longer have cold hands and feet. I'm fascinated by the healing properties of food and especially broths. In the world of food, the way we can promote life is by respecting the laws of digestion. For our bodies, digestion is a warm process of transforming food into energy. When we make bone broth, we're doing the same thing. We are warming the bones and other ingredients and transforming them into energy that promotes life.

QUINN WILSON'S STORY: BEAUTIFUL SKIN AND NAILS, HEALING TEETH AND STOMACH

Quinn Wilson is founder and owner of Balanced & Bright Bone Broth, a small company making and selling bone broth in the San Diego area.

I began to take an interest in traditional foods several years ago. I had heard of the benefits of bone broth, and it made sense as I looked at my great-grandmother's pre–Civil War cast iron cauldron, imagining that it must have produced bone broth for many generations before it was passed down to me. I had no expectations about what broth would do when I started drinking it in place of coffee. I was experimenting rather than trying to fix food intolerance or heal an illness.

After two weeks of sipping bone broth, I noticed that the skin on my hands started to look shiny and supple, my complexion became radiant and clear, and my nails were healthy and strong. The real magic happened within the next month and a half, though. Twenty years earlier, a ski accident had left me without front teeth, and I endured dental implants and many surgeries over the years as a result. A more recent surgery had created chronic pain, yet after sipping bone broth for a couple months, the pain just stopped. I could tell that the broth, which was rich in amino acids and minerals, had given my body what it needed to heal my mouth. Another month after that, my erratic stomach issues began to resolve—it's been several years now, and I have no stomach issues to speak of.

As I looked around, I could see that the desire for convenience—one I'd participated in myself—had been shortchanging our health. Advances in modern science and kitchen convenience seem to have prompted a decline in our overall health as a nation. Along with my own health issues, I noticed how many people around me had gluten intolerance, food allergies, IBS, Crohn's disease, fatigue, diabetes, and allergies. And I became aware of the niche markets that had popped up in the food and medical industries, all coming to cash in on our nationwide dilemma.

I became so passionate about bone broth that I started to make and sell it myself. What I found is that there is a large and growing group of consumers who want broth made with organic, pasture-fed animals and organic vegetables. They're choosing to use food as medicine and skip the hefty prices on supplements with magnesium, phosphate, silicon, chondroitin, and glucosamine, and get these nutrients in their daily bone broth instead.

CATHY'S STORY: HEALING CHRONIC FATIGUE, DIGESTIVE PROBLEMS, AND DEPRESSION

Cathy, a marketing executive and mom of three, is one of Heather's clients.

When I began working with Heather Dane on my health, I had chronic fatigue, digestive problems, and depression. Heather guided me to get my minerals and genetics tested. What she found is that my minerals were very low, which was contributing to all of my symptoms. Looking at my 23andMe genetic profile, Heather was able to tailor a nutrition, supplement, and life-style program that was targeted to my unique needs.

Because of some of the depression and mood challenges I was having, Heather suggested I start with meat stocks and plenty of soups. She also had me take a sea-mineral supplement, whole-food vitamin C, and some active vitamin B supplements like methyl B$_{12}$ (active vitamin B$_{12}$) and L-methylfolate (active folate).

I also began to make the lifestyle changes she recommended, most of which were designed to decrease stress. Heather explained that stress burns through minerals, and it was contributing to my low energy and the rest of my symptoms. I have to admit, it was a real overhaul in changing my food and my lifestyle, but it was so worth it!

The supplements gave me energy within the first 2 weeks, and that helped me get into the kitchen and learn how to make new foods. The meat stock was so much easier than I expected —I make it every week now, and I won't do without it.

Within a month, my digestion had improved so much that I was no longer bloated and uncomfortable after every meal. I actually felt light again. I noticed that my body looked leaner and I had less cellulite. I had no idea that could

happen! Within 6 months, I was feeling fully alive again. I felt happier and more motivated, and I started to enjoy my work again. My libido improved, which Heather told me is another sign of my adrenals healing. Within 8 months, I was having daily bowel movements, which hadn't happened for years.

After 10 months, I was feeling solid in my moods and switched to bone broth. My digestion continued to improve. I love making soups and other meals with the broth, and it's a big part of my life now. I would never have believed I could feel this good from changing my diet. While I know I did several things to recover, I feel that the meat stock was the real foundation for my healing. Lately, my friends keep asking what I'm doing to look and feel so good, so I've started going into their kitchens to teach them to make stock and broth, too.

ANNIE'S STORY: HEALING DEBILITATING PAIN AND TOOTH DECAY

Annie Dru Allshouse turned to bone broth because she began suffering debilitating pain. After finding Sally Fallon Morell's book *Nourishing Traditions*, Annie decided to regain her health in the kitchen. She began making bone broth—and from the first sip, she could feel her cells awaken. Within 9 months, her pain was gone, and her mobility and moods improved. She found it mind-blowing that something as simple as bone broth could be so healing. And yet even if we don't hear much about it, the science behind the gut-brain connection is there: *anything with restorative impact on the digestive tract translates into mood-enhancing chemicals to the brain.*

Annie's teenage son became hooked on bone broth when his dentist wanted to do a root canal on a diseased tooth. After seeing how well Annie had done with broth, he asked her to help him save his tooth. He focused on bone broth as part of his healing diet, and within a year, his dentist gave him a clean bill of health.

KIM SCHUETTE: HELPING CLIENTS REGAIN ENERGY, RESOLVE A GENETIC SEIZURE DISORDER, AND HEAL BROKEN BONES

Kim Schuette, a certified nutritionist and certified Gut and Psychology Syndrome (GAPS) practitioner, has been helping her clients heal with bone broth and nutritional balancing for more than a decade at her healing center in Southern California, Biodynamic Wellness.

Kim shares some stories of her personal experience with broth:

When my friend broke 6 bones in her foot, her doctor said it would take 6 weeks to heal. She drank 32 ounces of bone broth daily, and took some other nutritional supplements like cod-liver oil, and recovered within 3 weeks.

Also, one of my clients had a newborn named Conner, who had a genetic seizure disorder that caused him to experience seizures anywhere from 40 to 120 times per day. His mom came to me after consulting multiple medical professionals, and I handed her a recipe for a meat stock formula designed specifically for Conner's needs. The mom looked at me and said, "I don't even know how to boil an egg." I went to her house and taught her how to cook. About a month later, she came back to me looking more energized and feeling empowered because she could take care of her own and her family's health. And Conner continued to improve over time, until he was no longer having seizures. He's now on a gut-healing GAPS program and doing well. His parents are thrilled.

I've noticed that once my clients see the benefits of bone broth, they begin to feel satisfied that this healing came from their own kitchen. One of the benefits of healing with food is giving the body and mind a chance to slow down to prepare food. This is a foreign concept in modern culture. Most people say they don't have time to prepare food for themselves. What we're really saying when we say that is, "I don't have time to take care of myself." As Louise would remind us, that's an affirmation! From the beginning of humankind, we had to hunt, gather, and prepare food. These days, our schedules can get so full that we resist this primal part of our humanity.

Most of my clients actually like to cook once they start feeling better. When the gut heals, their brain chemicals start stabilizing, and their moods and energy come back into balance. This is when they become more motivated to nourish themselves well.

ARIANE RESNICK: HEALING FROM LYME DISEASE, HASHIMOTO'S DISEASE, AND FERTILITY ISSUES

Ariane Resnick is author of *The Bone Broth Miracle: How an Ancient Remedy Can Improve Health, Fight Aging and Boost Beauty*. She was a vegetarian for nearly 30 years. When she became a certified nutritionist and personal chef, she found herself creating meals for people on special diets (such as gluten-free, dairy-free, soy-free, and so on) and found that by the time all of the sensitive foods were removed, meat was more important to the diet.

As she worked with her clients, she found that bone broth was not only full of healing benefits, but it completely shifted her opinion about meat as well. Ariane recovered from chronic/neurological late stage Lyme disease, and bone broth was one of the key foods she used in her recovery. At her sickest, she had severe fibromyalgia and could not walk more than a few steps. She saw tremendous benefits from broth in her own health and the health of her clients.

For example, she had a client who had leaky gut and Hashimoto's disease (an autoimmune condition where the immune system attacks the thyroid), and she wanted to recover her health so that she could get pregnant. For the past couple of years, she'd been unsuccessful with in vitro fertilization and came to Ariane for a nutritional healing protocol. Its mainstays were turmeric tea and gallons of bone broth to keep inflammation down, heal the gut, and strengthen the body.

After some time on this protocol, her client went for another round of in vitro fertilization, and her doctor was amazed by the strength of her eggs. Ariane's client is now halfway to term with twins and tells everyone that they're her bone broth miracle babies.

Ariane believes that food is the most sacred part of our lives because we are quite literally what we eat. She's passionate about bone broth because she believes this simple food made from leftovers is chock-full of bioavailable, easily digested nutrients.

YOUR HEALING STORY

You are healthy, whole, and complete. How do you feel when you read those words? Sometimes when we have symptoms or a diagnosis, we become fearful or forget to trust our bodies to heal. We might even feel angry and upset that our body is in the state it's in. Remember, the thoughts you think and the words you speak matter. What if you believed that symptoms were messages from your body, asking you to take loving steps toward healing?

We invite you to listen to your body and let it guide you. Here is an affirmation you can use anytime you want to build trust in the signals your body is giving you and to affirm your best health.

In the infinity of life where I am, all is perfect, whole, and complete. Each one of us, myself included, has been encoded with the innate ability to heal. I now look at the past with love, choosing to learn from my old experiences and experiment with new discoveries. I am open to loving myself so much that I take small, gentle actions each day to nurture myself. I trust my body to guide me in each moment. If I experience a symptom, I take the time to ask the symptom what it wants me to know. Then I wrap it in love and thank it for awakening me to how I can support myself. My body is brilliant, and I listen for the foods that nourish me best.

The past is over and done. There is only the experience of this moment. I love myself for bringing myself through the past and into this present moment. I listen for what I need, and I speak my truth. I know I am worth nourishing myself. I know I am worth healing. All is well in my world. And so it is.

❧ HOW TO WORK ❧
with Herbs and Spices

The Flavor and Healing Heroes

Here is a list of common herbs and spices, many of which are flavor and healing stars in our finishers, elixirs, and recipes.

1. The Basics

Sea salt and black pepper or white pepper work with any herbs and spices. They tend to show up in just about every recipe, and for good reason!

— **Sea salt or pink Himalayan salt.** These types of salt add flavor and enhance the flavors of the ingredients in a recipe (a little goes a long way). These natural salts add important trace minerals. If you study minerals, you'll find that they're the body's spark plugs, giving us energy. Yet they also keep us anchored and rooted, helping us stay grounded and calm. This is helpful when making food with the sweet taste because it keeps the body in balance. These natural salts can be used interchangeably, and it's nice to change it up a bit because they each offer a slightly different mineral profile.

— **Black pepper.** This was considered the "king of spices" in the Middle Ages, and that's an appropriate title: Indian black pepper in particular is rich in nutrients that aid your digestion.

All black pepper in fact aids digestion, helps prevent or treat constipation, has heart- and blood pressure–regulating properties, and aids memory and thyroid health.[1] You can substitute white pepper in recipes if desired, though, for similar flavor and health benefits. And while desserts don't tend to have pepper, you will see it in our recipes. We like to add pepper to desserts that need a touch of the "hot" flavor to balance the tastes.

2. Herbs

You can pretty much combine any of these herbs and you'll get a great taste. Remember, if you're just starting out using herbs and spices, start with a small amount (like ⅛ tsp.) and sample your dish after each addition.

Here are some common herbs and their health benefits:

— **Basil** has been shown to have beneficial properties for type 2 diabetes, cholesterol, pain, stress, ulcers, and high triglycerides.

— **Bay leaf** is great for joint pain, indigestion, ulcers, and arthritis; treating cancer; regulating cholesterol and triglycerides, as well as blood sugar; and can even repel mosquitoes for up to two hours.

— **Dill** provides great flavor for fish, vegetable dishes, and dressings. It can support healthy digestion, aid in bone density, and create a calm energy.

— **Lemongrass** offers a hint of sour flavor to balance out a dish; we use it in pâtés, desserts, and other recipes. Lemongrass is an antianxiety remedy and has been shown to have beneficial effects for type 2 diabetes, epilepsy, insomnia, cancer, cholesterol, thrush (oral candida infection), high triglycerides, and vaginal yeast infection.

— **Mint** is wonderful for digestion, anxiety, fatigue, nasal congestion, menopause, menstrual cramps, and allergies.

— **Rosemary** has been shown to reduce anxiety, alleviate pain in arthritis, and help lower blood sugar. It also helps improve your memory and protect your skin from the sun's UV radiation.

— **Sage** has been shown to support memory, the heart, and the skin. It also benefits herpes, cancer, ulcers, psoriasis, and eczema.

— **Tarragon** is a good source of antioxidants, minerals, and vitamins A, B complex, and C. It can help with heart and eye health, and reducing blood sugar levels.

— **Thyme** is a very flexible herb that we use almost daily in our kitchens. It's been shown to be antiaging and good for the heart, colds, colitis, bacterial infections, and ulcers.[2]

3. Chinese Herbs

These herbs have wonderful healing benefits and are used in the healing elixir recipes contributed by Eyton Shalom, M.S., L.Ac. (We offer suggestions on where to find them in the Resources section.)

— **Astragalus (Huang qi).** This adaptogenic herb (which means that it helps the body deal with stress) is an immune booster used in Chinese medicine to regain strength and vitality.

— **Codonopsis (Dang shen).** Sometimes referred to as "poor man's ginseng," codonopsis is an adaptogenic herb with some of the same strengthening and energizing effects as ginseng. It's been used to clear mucus in the lungs and for symptoms like headaches, diarrhea, anemia, hemorrhoids, and high blood pressure.

— **Dioscorea (Shan yao).** Also referred to as Chinese yam, dioscorea is used in Chinese medicine to restore energy, nourish the blood, and clear heat-related illness.

— **Dong quai (Angelica sinensis).** Known as Chinese Angelica, this herb is known to be beneficial for menopause or premenstrual syndrome (PMS), but it's great for hormone balance in women *and* men. Avoid using this herb if you are pregnant, or have diarrhea or abdominal pain.

— **Goji berry.** Also called Chinese wolfberry, goji berries moved into the category of superfood during the raw-food movement in the United States for their ability to promote longevity. These antioxidant-, vitamin-, and mineral-rich berries are used in Chinese medicine to support the kidneys, lungs, and liver.

— **Lily bulb (Bai he).** This herb helps with chronic cough, clearing the lungs, calming the mind for restful sleep, and calming the spirit. Avoid using if you have diarrhea.

— **Ophiopogon (Mai men dong)** is used in Chinese medicine to reduce inflammation, protect the body from bacterial infections, relieve constipation, and strengthen the stomach.

— **Schizandra (Wu wei zi).** This herb is used in Chinese medicine to create a calm energy, clear the skin, strengthen the liver, and balance the nervous system.

4. Spices

Just like herbs, most spices go together. You almost can't go wrong, and it's the perfect way to use your intuition and your senses as you create your own recipes.

— **Allspice** is wonderful in just about any recipe, as it's a flavorful and high-antioxidant spice. It's helpful for menopause and high blood pressure and contains more than 24 healing compounds.

— **Caraway seeds** are great for digestion, constipation, acid reflux, and regulating cholesterol.

— **Cardamom** helps with asthma, constipation, bad breath, and indigestion, and has been shown to lower blood pressure and histamine.

— **Cinnamon** is anti-inflammatory, helps promote healthy bacteria in your gut (those good guys that help you digest and assimilate your food), and keeps your blood sugar stable (which helps give you willpower!). It can also help with heart health and can prevent diabetes.

— **Clove** is great for your teeth and gums, helps fight bad bacteria like H. pylori (responsible for ulcers), and can inhibit viruses like herpes and hepatitis C.

— **Coriander** helps regulate digestion, bloating, cholesterol levels, blood pressure, skin issues (such as rosacea or eczema), and vaginal yeast infections.

— **Cumin** has beneficial properties for cancer, epilepsy, type 2 diabetes, and bone health.

— **Fennel** can help with arthritis, calms cramps (including menstrual cramps) and colic, and is a powerful digestive aid and anti-inflammatory.

— **Fenugreek** has been found to help with weight loss, improved moods, blood sugar balance, cataracts, kidney stones, and gallstones. It can also help prevent or reverse non-alcoholic fatty liver disease.

— **Ginger** is an anti-inflammatory spice that can help with arthritis, nausea, morning sickness, and migraines. It is also amazing for your digestion.

— **Nutmeg** can protect your skin from wrinkles due to the breakdown of elastin in the skin and skin-damaging ultraviolet (UV) rays, provides anti-anxiety and anti-depression benefits, and inhibits the viral cause of diarrhea. And some studies have found that nutmeg has aphrodisiac activity and increases libido.

— **Paprika** helps with indigestion, cardiovascular health, and circulation; is antibacterial and anti-inflammatory; and contains vitamins A, E, K, and C.

— **Saffron** has been shown to help with mood issues (such as depression or anxiety), insomnia, blood pressure, menstrual cramps, multiple sclerosis, Parkinson's disease, memory issues, and erectile dysfunction.

— **Turmeric** is wonderful as an anti-inflammatory if you're experiencing arthritis, swelling, or inflammation around your menstrual period, or any other autoimmune-type symptoms. Incidentally, it's wonderful for your skin and a natural anti-wrinkle remedy. It can also protect against radiation from the sun or x-rays.

— **A special note about vanilla.** We like to think of vanilla as the bringer of richness. Adding vanilla to almost any dessert gives it a much richer flavor: It can bring a more pastry-like flavor to breads and biscuits. It adds richness to chocolate, deepening the flavor. It almost seems like it's adding a sweeter taste, and that's because it is! Not because it has any kind of sugar, but because its characteristic taste is more on the naturally sweet side, from an Ayurvedic-medicine perspective. Full of antioxidants, vanilla can also be used to add a rich flavor to some butter and cream sauces for savory dishes. As you become more familiar with using vanilla, you can decide whether you like to use the beans (a little more effort, but a wonderful flavor result), powder, or extract.[3]

The Six Tastes and Herbs and Spices[4]

In our recipes, we use herbs and spices for their flavor and medicinal properties. We also use them to create balance.

Today's food manufacturers create foods that manipulate sweet, salty, and fat tastes in order to boost cravings; this leaves the body wanting more. Instead, if you think about balancing the six tastes, your body feels more satisfied and grounded. And when you're satisfied and grounded, you feel calmer and more able to concentrate. In desserts, this means that you tend to feel more satisfied with one or two cookies, for example, instead of craving the whole plate.

All of our recipes are designed to do this, so there's no guesswork for you! For those of you who love to experiment, we offer this overview of the six tastes, and the types of herbs and spices that you can use to get the balance you are seeking (see next page).

These are some of the spices we love to use most. From left to right, and top to bottom: cinnamon sticks, whole cloves, fresh parsley, fenugreek, allspice, paprika, turmeric, thyme, ginger, basil, fennel seeds, fresh thyme, and fresh sage.

TASTE *and* MEDICINAL PROPERTIES	HERB, SPICE, *or* FLAVORING

Sweet
 	
Has strengthening, cleansing,
    and cooling properties
Slowing, relaxing
Builds and strengthens tissues
    and energy
	Allspice
	Cardamom
	Cinnamon
	Coriander
	Dill
	Fennel
	Mint
	Nutmeg
	Tarragon
	Vanilla

Salty Cooling effect Moistens dryness Softens hardened lumps and stiffness Aids digestion and detoxification	Sea salt Pink Himalayan salt Fish sauce Umeboshi plum Bonito flakes Tamari Seaweed

Sour
 	
Cooling effect
Helpful for dripping or loose
    conditions like perspiration,
    diarrhea, hemorrhoids, prolapse
	Caraway
	Juniper berry
	Lemongrass
	Pomegranate

Astringent Cool, dry, and heavy Can stop bleeding and aid in healing ulcers Has blood-purifying qualities	Basil Cinnamon Dill Fennel Pomegranate Saffron Tarragon
Bitter Cooling effect Can help dry excess fluids or calm excessive personalities Reduces inflammation, constipation	Bay leaf Cumin Fenugreek Saffron Tarragon Turmeric
Pungent Warming effect Stimulates circulation of energy, digestion Can help improve liver function	Allspice Bay leaf Caraway Celery seed Clove Cumin Fenugreek Garlic Ginger Hing (asafoetida) Oregano Paprika Rosemary Sage Thyme

Here's how to become an herb and spice expert in five easy steps:

1. Treat yourself to some well-loved staple herbs and spices (see the previous lists of herbs and spices and their health benefits).

2. Use the herbs and spices in our recipes and notice how they taste. The best cooks taste as they're preparing their food. In many of our recipes, we give you optional spices that you can add or not—taste what it's like before adding them, and then if you do add them, taste again. Notice the difference. You will be learning which flavors work best for you and how they make your body feel.

Make sure to set aside a little time to do the Great Chocolate Experiment in our Chocolate Drop Cookies recipe (Chapter 11). We offer you four levels of flavor by adding various spices. This is a great way to see how you can layer flavor and also to determine what level your body resonates with most!

3. Use the rest of your senses:

- Smell the herbs and spices, and then smell the food you're making. A lot of times, the scent will let you know if the spices and food goes together. Do they smell similar, like they might go together? If so, then try it and see—you'll likely be right!

- Notice the sensations in your body as you taste the food. Does it make you feel satisfied? This goes beyond taste; rather, after you taste, notice how you feel. Your taste buds were designed to know what you need. The more you use them, the more they will guide you better than any chef. Ask your body if you feel like something else is needed for balance.

- Use your intuition. When you open your spice cabinet, allow your intuition to guide you to the herbs and spices you feel most drawn to. Sometimes, without even knowing why, you'll pick spices with exactly the medicinal qualities your body needs. Have fun with this—it's a great way to develop your intuition!

4. Start small. If you only put in a little of an herb or spice, like ⅛ tsp., you almost can't go wrong. If you're not sure, take ⅛ tsp. and put it in the food, mix it up, and taste. If you like it, add another ⅛ tsp. and go from there. Another option is to take a separate cup of what you're making and try mixing a pinch of the herb or spice in there and give it a taste. This way, you won't mess anything up.

5. Just go for it! Try things out; experiment. We often find that things we think are big mistakes turn out to be the best-tasting recipes ever. If you're afraid to make mistakes, you'll miss out on all the fun you could have. This is exactly where you'll want to have a "what the hell" attitude.

Chilled bone broth with a fat cap on top.

⌁RECIPE⌁
Contributors

In all of our years in the traditional-foods movement, we have met some talented chefs, butchers, farmers, nutritionists, health professionals, and educators in the sustainable, nose-to-tail food movement. We thought it would be fun to share a small number of recipes from these professionals to give you a look at how they prepare broths and broth-based meals (see Part II of this book for more).

This section will introduce you to our contributors, so that you can get to know a little bit about them and their areas of expertise.

CAROLINE BARRINGER

Caroline Barringer is the founder and CEO of Immunitrition, senior lead instructor for the Nutritional Therapy Association (NTA), former NTA vice president and board of directors member, Master Certified Healing Foods Specialist (CHFS), Certified GAPS Practitioner (CGP), Certified Birth Renaissance Practitioner (BRP), published health author, and lecturer.

Caroline's mission is to change the way the world eats through nutrition education, performance, and publication, and to help empower individuals to make responsible and healthful food choices for restoring and maintaining a higher quality of life. Putting her entrepreneurial skills to work, she founded Immunitrition, LLC, in 2005; since then, the company has been manufacturing cultured foods for national distribution. Her newest project is "Freeway Foodies," a nationwide road tour/Internet TV show that will share holistic resources, showcase people and practitioners, and visit new and exciting places of great influence in today's rapidly growing healing-arts industry.

Caroline began her career as a professional singer and voice actor, but her fascination with food took center stage when she was first introduced to the age-old concept of lacto-fermentation in her early 20s. With a rigorous and demanding performance schedule, Caroline noticed that her health was taking a hit, so she began researching the many ways to ferment or "culture" a wide variety of foods, including meats, vegetables, fruits, fish, dairy, juices, teas, nuts, seeds, grains, and legumes. Witnessing restorative health benefits, Caroline decided to make cultured foods and nutrition education a core element in her life and career.

Caroline found a new lease on life with bone broth, but she only started drinking it reluctantly. Having been a vegetarian for 15 years, she did everything she could to recover with vegetarian practices. After repeated illnesses, however, she found herself walking past a pizzeria in New York City one day when the smell of pepperoni made her want to jump over the counter and eat it all off the top of the pizza. First, she thought, E*eew*. Then she thought, I *think this is life trying to tell me something*. She began to look into bone broth but didn't want to participate in animal suffering. Soon she found out that she could source humanely raised animals, but she still wasn't ready to eat meat. Bone broth seemed like a good compromise.

Caroline was astounded by the difference bone broth made in her health. Her energy came back; her digestion improved; and today, at 41 years old, she has hardly any wrinkles. She attributes her health to bone broth, and it's become a way of life for her.

Read more about Caroline at: immunitrition.com and freewayfoodies.com.

NICK BRUNE

Nick Brune was born and raised in the heart of "flavor country," Baton Rouge, Louisiana—where he began cooking and experimenting with food at a very young age. Becoming infatuated with the flavor and design of food, he then moved to Los Angeles and worked as head chef of some of the top catering companies in the city, coordinating some of the biggest events in L.A. Nick co-founded Eco Caters in 2007 alongside Adam Hiner to bring fresh, seasonal, organic food to the tables of events throughout Southern California. In 2011, Nick and Adam opened a new restaurant in San Diego called Local Habit. Today, Nick has dedicated his talents to creating artful, seasonal, organic dining experiences that are full of flavor and zest.

Nick grew up with a love of the land. His grandfather was a farmer in East Texas; however, 60 years ago, the government came and told him he was going to have to change his farming practices. The new government rules included practices that did not honor the land, the animals, or humans. Nick's grandfather made the tough, emotional decision to leave farming behind. His grandfather's commitment —coupled with Nick's own observation of the push for mass farming, along with pollution in the rivers of his hometown—created his fervor for changing the food system.

Underneath it all, Nick has a passion for nourishing people. That passion comes from the melting pot of tastes from his childhood in Louisiana, where Creole—the mix of rich and poor European, African, and Native American people, and all of their cultures, music, and cooking styles—came together. He has a love of the jazz that came from a European and African population that became united when they heard each other's music and knew it would sound better together.

And that is Nick's message: We are better together. We are better when we blend a love of the land, animals, and people from all cultures, races, and backgrounds. We are better together when we eat foods that nourish our bodies so we can be strong and healthy. And we are better together when we share our music.

Read more about Nick at: ecocaters.com.

KAAYLA T. DANIEL, PH.D., CCN

Kaayla Daniel earned her Ph.D. in Nutritional Sciences and Anti-Aging Therapies from the Union Institute and University in Cincinnati, and is certified as a clinical nutritionist (CCN) by the Clinical Nutrition Certification Board of the International and American Association of Clinical Nutritionists in Dallas. Dr. Daniel is Vice President of the Weston A. Price Foundation, a member of the board of directors of the Farm-to-Consumer Legal Defense Fund, and received the Weston A. Price Foundation's Integrity in Science Award in 2005.

She is also co-author (with Sally Fallon Morell) of the best-selling Nourishing Broth: An Old-Fashioned Remedy for a Modern World and author of The Whole Soy Story: The Dark Side of America's Favorite Health Food. Her books have been endorsed by leading health experts including Larry Dossey, Joseph Mercola, Doris Rapp, JJ Virgin, Jonathan Wright, and many others.

Kaayla remembers her days in college— getting caught up in Fig Newtons, Coca-Cola, and ice cream—during which her health tanked. She began to take interest in what she was eating; luckily, just after graduation, Julia Child's sense of humor and joie de vivre inspired Kaalya to get back into the kitchen. In the 1990s Kaayla began researching cartilage with Dr. John F. Prudden, known as "the father of cartilage therapy," so she's had this information for years, which fit beautifully into her book with Sally Fallon Morell. These days, Kaayla is known as "the Naughty Nutritionist" because of her ability to outrageously and humorously debunk nutritional myths.

Read more about Kaayla at: drkaayladaniel .com.

DAVE HEAFNER AND LESLIE PESIC

Dave Heafner and Leslie Pesic own Da-Le Ranch, a small, sustainable family farm, located just outside San Diego. All of the animals are grass- or pasture-fed and treated humanely with love, from beginning to end. Dave had the vision to start the farm, and Leslie is the "animal whisperer"—according to Dave, she has a way with all the animals. They have their own signature way of making bone broth, and we can tell you that it's absolutely delicious!

We met Dave at a local farmers' market while doing research for this book and wanted to share his story with you. Before he became a farmer, Dave was a very successful professional in the financial-services industry who had a near-death experience that resulted in a series of events that included losing his entire savings. He did some soul searching and realized he'd been so caught up in making money that he'd lost himself.

As Dave began to think about what really mattered, he felt called to live off the land and become a farmer. While he loved farming, he hadn't fully committed to having a "farm business" until one of his customers convinced him to start selling at farmers' markets. His customers began coming to him with tears in their eyes, thanking him for the food that reminded them of home, or of their grandmother's cooking. People were coming for healing food and expressing their gratitude, which moved Dave so much that he and Leslie made a full commitment to serving the area with humanely raised, healthy meats, poultry, game, and a variety of eggs (even large, wonderful goose eggs!). They also sell bones for broth and make custom-requested batches of broth for regular customers. And they're constantly looking for better, healthier ways to feed their animals, like using fermented grasses, which the animals love.

Many challenges had to be overcome in their farming journey, including months where they didn't know if they'd make the mortgage, but they remain committed to their dream, putting their savings into giving people jobs as opposed to buying toys. Somehow, things always turned out okay.

Talking with Dave reminded us that it's worth believing in a dream and staying the course. And that no matter what details show up to get in our way—no matter what ripples and turbulence life brings—there is one thing that matters: how we support, nourish, and connect with one another. Many of us may dream of living off the land; in the absence of that, the people who reconnect us to this ideal are farmers like Dave and Leslie. We take our hats off to them at every meal.

Read more about Dave and Leslie at: da-le-ranch.com.

RHONDA LENAIR

Rhonda Lenair is a prophet and medical intuitive; she is also known as the healer of addictions by tens of thousands of clients worldwide. As a medical intuitive, she has been compared over and over to the "Sleeping Prophet," Edgar Cayce.

Rhonda founded a non-medical paradigm called the Self(s) Healing Experience (SHE) that provides immediate access to the state of enlightenment and the sanctity of inner peace. SHE is legendary for producing a phenomenon—a "predictable miracle"—whereby all desires and cravings, along with the need to self-destruct with addictions and other out-of-control issues, effortlessly cease without pain, withdrawals, treatments, or therapy.

Heather shares a story about working with Rhonda:

> I remember when I first heard about Rhonda Lenair. I was reading a local magazine about natural health, and there was an article about her. I had never been to a medical intuitive before and didn't know what to think. I decided

to take a chance and see if she could help me recover my digestive health.

Rhonda is not like other medical intuitives. She doesn't want you to tell her anything. She just looks into your body and being and then, like water, reflects back what she sees. What she sees is your entire "system" in all its possibility. When she speaks, it's clear that she's speaking as the part of you that you can't hear—letting you know what your best all-dimensional self wants you to know. Rhonda helped me hear what my body and life were crying out for, and inspired me to take loving care of myself. Part of loving and caring for myself involved preparing home-cooked foods that would nourish my body back to health.

Read more about Rhonda at: lenair.com.

BRIAN MERKEL

Brian Merkel came to butchery by way of art, design, and charcuterie in 2008. After earning an art degree, he moved to Detroit in 2009 and started Porktown Sausages & Charcuterie, using the finest local meats and working in small batches to create his savory delights. Brian is now head butcher at Belcampo Butcher Shop & Restaurant in one of San Francisco's most beloved neighborhoods, Russian Hill. Belcampo's mission is to ensure humane treatment of their animals, traditional methods, and farm-to-fork traceability.

Brian says, "We started making bone broth at Belcampo to meet consumer demand, mostly for health and healing. Since I'm around it all the time, I've been drinking it regularly and have noticed that my complexion is better and that my fingernails are much stronger. Today, we can barely keep it on the shelves because so many people are coming in to order it. We sell it in takeaway coffee cups and by the quart. As a full-service butchery and restaurant, we have been pleasantly surprised at the huge demand for bone broth. It's become a big part of our business. Our bone broth is gelatin-rich and neutral in flavor, making it perfect for any recipe you might want to make. We offer some 'finishers' for our broths so that people can add flavor on the go."

NICK POLIZZI

Nick Polizzi has been making documentary films for the past ten years. The titles he has been a part of include *The Sacred Science*; *Simply Raw: Reversing Diabetes in 30 Days*; and *The Tapping Solution*.

While filming his most recent project, *The Sacred Science*, Nick was intrigued by the exotic ingredients, cooking styles, and recipes that he was exposed to as he worked in the Amazon rain forest of Peru. His fascination with the role that indigenous plants played in the culture of the tribes that he observed up close led him to expand his scope and explore the traditional recipes of remote cultures all around the world.

Taking note along the way of certain dishes, in a variety of cultures, that have passed the test of time, he realized a common theme: People passed family food traditions from generation to generation, not only because they tasted good, but because they nurtured health and wellness. His latest book, *The Sacred Cookbook*, is a collection of those recipes.

Heather remembers meeting Nick for the first time:

> Louise and I met Nick Polizzi at a dinner party with a group of dear friends and Hay House authors. Louise and I showed up in our flapper feathers, making a scene in a good way, and right away we liked Nick; his wife, Michelle; and their baby, River. That night, we all sat at a long table, family style, overlooking the ocean. We enjoyed delicious, healthy food, and the sound we heard most at the table was laughter.
>
> Not wanting our good time to end, we all proceeded across the street to the hotel where everyone was staying. We found a circle of comfortable chairs and couches, and everyone tried on Louise's and my flapper headbands— even the men! That prompted a scarf exchange, which somehow resulted in Nick wearing a scarf-hat on his head that Louise had made. The pictures from the great scarf-and-headband exchange still make me laugh to this day. I love how sharing a meal not only brings in-the-moment enjoyment, but memories and ripple effects that can last a lifetime.
>
> Nick, whose mom owned a restaurant, has been cooking since he was 12 and has a passion for food as medicine. Louise and I loved working with his cookbook.

Read more about Nick at: thesacredscience .com.

PRICE-POTTENGER NUTRITION FOUNDATION

The Price-Pottenger Nutrition Foundation (PPNF) feels like family to us. Their vision is "a world where optimal nutrition is the standard, the environment fosters the health of all living things, and people are thriving." How awesome is that?

A leading resource for the work of Weston A. Price, D.D.S.; Francis M. Pottenger, Jr., M.D.; and others who have discovered the underlying causes of disease and degeneration and how to prevent or reverse these conditions, PPNF has a mission to educate people about food, lifestyle habits, and healing modalities that promote vibrant health.

As we chose the PPNF recipes to feature in our book, we met with Joan Grinzi, R.N. (executive director), Edward Bennett (president and journal editor), and Annie Dru Allshouse (advisory board member and ancestral cuisine educator). Joan, Ed, and Annie all include bone broth in their daily routines, but came to it for different reasons. Ed developed a love of food from growing up with a garden. Joan's mother introduced her to the work of Edgar Cayce, and her interest continued to blossom from there. Annie turned to bone broth to heal debilitating pain. Yet all three of them seemed to echo one important principle: *When you taste broth, you just know you feel good. And sometimes, that's all that matters.*

Read more about PPNF at: ppnf.org.

ARIANE RESNICK

Ariane Resnick is a private chef and certified nutritionist who specializes in organic farm-to-table cuisine and creates indulgent, seemingly "normal" food out of impeccably clean, whole-food ingredients. She has cooked for celebrities including Gwyneth Paltrow, Chris Martin, Matt Groening, Lisa Edelstein, and Jeff Franklin; and has been featured in Yahoo! Health, *Well + Good* NYC, *In Style*, *Star*, Goop.com, Food.com, the Huffington Post, Refinery29.com, *Muscle & Fitness*, and *Men's Fitness*, and on Food Network's *Chopped*. She is also a survivor of late stage Lyme disease and chemical poisoning, and recovered holistically from both. When not crafting beautifully presented tasty dishes that accommodate any combination of dietary restriction, Ariane consults with individuals and chefs on wellness and nutrition, and provides hands-on instruction for simple ways to cook more healthfully. She lives in West Hollywood, California.

Read more about Ariane at: arianecooks.com.

AARON ROCCHINO

Aaron Rocchino and his wife, Monica, own the Local Butcher Shop in Berkeley, California, which they opened in 2011. Prior to opening their business, Aaron (a chef) and Monica (a catering executive) noticed that there was a shortage of local, humanely raised, sustainable meat available for consumers. Today, the Local Butcher Shop offers grass- and pasture-fed meats and poultry. They focus on nose-to-tail meats and develop close relationships with their source farms, so they can ensure the purity of their meats. Consumers are invited to visit the farms they work with and learn more about their practices as well.

Aaron and Monica started offering bone broth at the Local Butcher Shop because so many customers were requesting it; today, they offer a variety of broth and stock. Their bone broth is healing, incredibly gelatin-rich, and perfect for use in any recipe (including desserts) because it's neutral in flavor.

Aaron's little-known tip when it comes to making bone broth? More cooking is not always better. At some point, after the 36-hour mark, "There is a point where you can cook it too long," he told us. He learned after experimenting with timing that there's a point where the broth can start to taste more bitter. This is usually when the bones disintegrate, get brittle, and fall apart.

Read more about Aaron at: thelocalbutcher shop.com.

ROBERT RUIZ

Robert Ruiz put himself through college in Hawaii by diligently tackling all jobs, including mopping floors and cleaning fryers as a short-order cook. When Ian Whittemore of the famed Kona Inn Restaurant noticed his potential, Robert leaped at this mentorship opportunity. The next three years were spent focusing on French-cooking techniques, basic butchering, and sautéing. This extensive training and preparation enabled him to join Alan Wong at the five-diamond Hualalai resort. Here, Robert developed his keen sense of Hawaiian regional cuisine by working at all three restaurants on the property, re-creating Wong's signature dishes and embracing the master chef's philosophies. Under the continued tutelage of Hualalai's executive chef, Etsuji Umezu, Robert's distinct love of being a sushi chef was born. Umezu fostered his confidence as a sushi chef, even giving him the honor of serving the princess of Japan.

After extensive training and privileged apprenticeship under Hawaii's finest chefs, Robert has become one of San Diego's best non-traditional sushi chefs. His mentors taught him to know the source of every ingredient in each dish, and to make sure those ingredients were fresh. After witnessing fraudulent fish practices—such as restaurants misidentifying fish or passing off inferior-quality fish—he decided to find a way to provide truthful information to customers about fish species and sustainability. Working with NOAA (National Oceanic and Atmospheric Administration) fishery scientists, he developed the concept of an edible QR (quick reference) code for sushi with NOAA FishWatch information so that customers could make informed choices about their food.

Today, as owner and chef of the Land & Water Company in Carlsbad, California, Robert's boundless creativity and delicious food creates word-of-mouth ripples throughout the community. His commitment to saving and preserving our oceans through his sustainability efforts is changing how fish and sushi will be served worldwide. Robert taught us that fish are seasonal, just like fruits and

vegetables. We've eaten many times at his restaurant, where everything is sustainable, organic, and made with great passion for the land and sea. One of our Bone Broth Tribe members describes Robert's food as a "psychedelic trip for the tongue." It's that good.

Read more about Robert at: landandwaterco.com.

KIM SCHUETTE

Kim Schuette, CN, Certified GAPS Practitioner, has been in private practice in the field of nutrition since 1999. In 2002, she established Biodynamic Wellness, now located in Solana Beach, California. Her love for organic gardening, gourmet cooking, and healing through foods and real food-based nutritional therapies led her into a practice where she offers private consultations specializing in nutritional and biotherapeutic drainage therapy to address gut/bowel and digestive disorders, male and female hormonal imbalances, cancer support, ADD/ADHD challenges, and a myriad of other health concerns.

Kim introduced the GAPS Diet to clients in 2006, and in 2011 became a Certified GAPS Practitioner under the guidance of Dr. Natasha Campbell-McBride. Kim teaches numerous workshops centered on the work of Drs. Weston Price, Francis Pottenger, and Melvin Page; she received the Activist Award from the Weston A. Price Foundation in 2012 for her work in children's nutrition and preconception nutrition. Additionally, she was named "Best Alternative Health Practitioner of 2013" by *Ranch & Coast Magazine* in their annual "Best of

San Diego" edition. She serves on the board of directors of the Weston A. Price Foundation, as well being the co-leader of as the San Diego chapter.

Read more about Kim at: biodynamic wellness.com.

EYTON SHALOM

Eyton J. Shalom, M.S., L.Ac., has dedicated his life to helping others heal from the inside out. In his private practice in San Diego, he uses acupuncture, herbology, Ayurveda, and nutritional/dietary therapies to get long-lasting relief from disease and pain, while at the same time treating the underlying root causes. For over 20 years, Eyton has been empowering his patients to take control of their health with diet, therapeutic exercise, stress management, breathing, and meditation practice.

Eyton has been an herbal medicine consultant and subject matter expert for the California Acupuncture Licensing Exam, and has been an instructor and clinical supervisor at Pacific College of Oriental Medicine for the past five years, teaching herbal medicine, acupuncture, medical history, and nutrition. He has also taught at San Diego's Mesa College, and at the California College of Holistic Studies. Eyton was the author of the popular columns "Tao of Health" on jadedragon.com and "Living with the Seasons" in the *Mission Hills News*, and has been published in the *Oriental Medicine Journal*.

Read more about Eyton at: bodymind wellnesscenter.com.

QUINN WILSON

A San Diego native, Quinn Wilson spent eight years in the interior-design industry, only to discover that her true life's passion had always been in food. A few years ago, she became interested in traditional foods as a lifestyle and began making bone broth regularly at home. Quinn realized the direct benefits to her health and wellness within the first two weeks of drinking it on a regular basis.

In 2012, Quinn decided that she'd bring bone broth to the mainstream marketplace, making an arduous and time-consuming process accessible to everyone. She designed her bone broth recipe to be an easy-to-drink tea, versatile in all ways: it can be consumed hot, cold, sweet, salty, or plain. It also slips easily into any recipe that calls for stock or broth. Currently she works full-time growing Balanced & Bright Bone Broth out of Carnitas Snack Shack in Del Mar, California. Quinn also works on occasion as a freelance food stylist and food writer with an emphasis on traditional foods. Most recently she worked on an international cookbook that was published in spring 2015.

Heather recalls first meeting Quinn:

Louse and I met Quinn in the most auspicious of ways. On a lark, we decided to go to a party that *Edible San Diego* magazine was holding at a local restaurant. When we walked in, the lovely woman at the door pointed out the magazine's managing editor, Britta Turner. As we told Britta about our book, she told us about her friend Quinn Wilson, who was so passionate about the healing benefits from bone broth that she'd started her own business. We found that Quinn makes high-quality broth with bones from organic, grass-fed animals, and spent years perfecting her broth for flavor and color so that it can be used in a wide variety of ways. Incidentally, that same night, Britta also pointed out Nick Brune, executive chef of Local Habit and owner of Eco Caters, whose recipes are also included in this book.

Read more about Quinn at: balancedand bright.wordpress.com.

Metric Conversion Chart

The recipes in this book use the standard United States method for measuring liquid and dry or solid ingredients (teaspoons, tablespoons, and cups). The following charts are provided to help cooks outside the U.S. successfully use these recipes. All equivalents are approximate.

Standard Cup	Fine Powder (e.g., flour)	Grain (e.g., rice)	Granular (e.g., sugar)	Liquid Solids (e.g., butter)	Liquid (e.g., milk)
1	140 g	150 g	190 g	200 g	240 ml
¾	105 g	113 g	143 g	150 g	180 ml
⅔	93 g	100 g	125 g	133 g	160 ml
½	70 g	75 g	95 g	100 g	120 ml
⅓	47 g	50 g	63 g	67 g	80 ml
¼	35 g	38 g	48 g	50 g	60 ml
⅛	18 g	19 g	24 g	25 g	30 ml

Useful Equivalents for Liquid Ingredients by Volume				
¼ tsp			1 ml	
½ tsp			2 ml	
1 tsp			5 ml	
3 tsp	1 tbsp		½ fl oz	15 ml	
	2 tbsp	⅛ cup	1 fl oz	30 ml	
	4 tbsp	¼ cup	2 fl oz	60 ml	
	5⅓ tbsp	⅓ cup	3 fl oz	80 ml	
	8 tbsp	½ cup	4 fl oz	120 ml	
	10⅔ tbsp	⅔ cup	5 fl oz	160 ml	
	12 tbsp	¾ cup	6 fl oz	180 ml	
	16 tbsp	1 cup	8 fl oz	240 ml	
	1 pt	2 cups	16 fl oz	480 ml	
	1 qt	4 cups	32 fl oz	960 ml	
			33 fl oz	1000 ml	1 l

Useful Equivalents for Dry Ingredients by Weight

(To convert ounces to grams, multiply the number of ounces by 30.)

1 oz	¹⁄₁₆ lb	30 g
4 oz	¼ lb	120 g
8 oz	½ lb	240 g
12 oz	¾ lb	360 g
16 oz	1 lb	480 g

Useful Equivalents for Cooking/Oven Temperatures

Process	Fahrenheit	Celsius	Gas Mark
Freeze Water	32° F	0° C	
Room Temperature	68° F	20° C	
Boil Water	212° F	100° C	
Bake	325° F	160° C	3
	350° F	180° C	4
	375° F	190° C	5
	400° F	200° C	6
	425° F	220° C	7
	450° F	230° C	8
Broil			Grill

Useful Equivalents for Length

(To convert inches to centimeters, multiply the number of inches by 2.5.)

1 in			2.5 cm	
6 in	½ ft		15 cm	
12 in	1 ft		30 cm	
36 in	3 ft	1 yd	90 cm	
40 in			100 cm	1 m

⋯RESOURCES⋯

Here are some wonderful resources to get you started on your bone broth and nose-to-tail, farm-to-table, sustainable food journey!

Grass- or Pasture-Fed Meats and Poultry, Wild-Caught Fish

- US Wellness Meats: grasslandbeef.com

- Belcampo Meat Co. has local options around California and an online store for delivery: belcampomeatco.com/shop

- The Local Butcher Shop takes local orders from the store only in Berkeley, CA: thelocalbutchershop.com

- Vital Choice: vitalchoice.com/shop/pc/home.asp

Bone Broth Purveyors to Check Out

We recommend doing a search for bone broth in your area or asking your local farmer, chef, or butcher for recommendations. There are also many restaurants, including ethnic restaurants and farm-to-table restaurants, that offer bone broths or soups. Some farmers do custom orders. Here are some ideas to get you started (note that many of these will deliver):

- Au Bon Broth offers organic chicken and grass-fed beef bone broth (neutral and flavored): aubonbrothbonebroth.com

- Balanced & Bright Bone Broth. Quinn Wilson sells high-quality bone broth locally in the greater San Diego area, and will soon be offering online ordering for national delivery: balancedandbright.wordpress.com

- Bare Bones offers broth from animals that are pasture-raised, hormone- and antibiotic-free, and fed grain-free diets (also available for pickup in Southern Oregon and some Northern California locations): barebonesbroth.com

- Belcampo Meat Co. is a great source of meat, bones, and neutral bone broth in six locations in California: belcampomeatco.com

- Brodo, the New York City bone broth to-go window that helped set the trend, offers organic chicken and grass-fed beef broth: brodonyc.com

- The Brothery offers organic chicken and grass-fed beef bone broth: thebrothery.com

- Da-Le Ranch owners Dave and Leslie offer grass- and pasture-fed chicken and beef broth as custom orders for their customers: da-le-ranch.com

- The Flavor Chef, Lance Roll, sells his organic chicken and grass-fed beef broth in health-food stores and butcher shops in the greater San Diego area: theflavorchef.com

- The Local Butcher Shop is a great source of meat, bones, and neutral bone broth and stock in Berkeley, CA: thelocalbutchershop.com

- Proposition Chicken sells tasty chicken bone broth by the coffee cup to go in San Francisco, using Mary's Free Range chickens, which have been pasture-fed with non-GMO feed, and no hormones or antibiotics: propositionchicken.com

- Salt, Fire & Time offers organic pasture-fed bone broth for pickup or delivery in the Portland, OR, area: saltfireandtime.com

- Wise Choice market: wisechoicemarket.com/bone-broth

Education, Information, and Resources on Traditional Diets and Healing with Whole Food

- Price-Pottenger Nutrition Foundation: ppnf.org

- Weston A. Price Foundation: westonaprice.org

- The Environmental Working Group provides information to help consumers make healthy choices. Find the latest information on pesticides in fruit and vegetables, including the annual "dirty dozen" list: ewg.org.

Where to Find Real Food, Bone Broth Makers, and Sustainable and Humane Farms and Suppliers

- Eat Wild. You can search their database of international pasture-based farms and ranches: eatwild.com

- Weston A. Price Foundation. Check to see if you have a local chapter in your area, as local chapters can point you to suppliers and resources: westonaprice.org/get-involved/find-local-chapter/

- Local Certified Gut and Psychology Syndrome Practitioner (GAPS). Do an Internet search to find a GAPS chapter or practitioner in your area.

- E*dible* magazine. Browse (in print or online) information about local, seasonal foods and providers: ediblecommunities.com

- Local Amish farms and farmers' markets: localamishfarms.com

- Find real food, farmers' markets, and farmers in your area: localharvest.org

- Online organic produce: Melissas.com

- Specialty food products (such as nut flours, raw cacao, green powders, coconut butter, collagen hydrolysate, and so on):
  - Amazon.com
  - shop.goldminenaturalfoods.com
  - iHerb.com
  - PureFormulas.com
  - ThriveMarket.com
  - Vitacost.com

Herbs, Spices, and Chinese Herbs

- Mountain Rose Herbs (organic and wild-crafted herbs and spices): MountainRoseHerbs.com

- Spring Wind Dispensary (carries all of the herbs in our elixir recipes and has quality standards for pure herbs):
  - Phone: (415)921-9990
  - e-mail: Orders@SpringWindDispensary.com
  - List of herbs sold: www.springwinddispensary.com/products_list.php

- Fat Turtle Herb Company: fatturtleherbs.com

- Asian markets (may carry fresh or dried Chinese herbs)

- Health food stores (may carry some of the more common Chinese herbs, such as astragalus, codonopsis, schizandra, and goji berries).

Slow Cookers

There are many great options on the market at a variety of price ranges that you can buy, but be sure to avoid models with aluminum or nonstick interiors.

If you're concerned about lead, here are some options that use materials other than the glazed ceramic:

—VitaClay Smart Organic Multicooker. This slow cooker is also a rice cooker and yogurt maker, and the clay pot insert is unglazed and lead-free. Clay pot cooking is popular because of its ability to produce very tender meats, which may make it a superior option for slow cooking grass- and pasture-fed meats. This model is programmable, so you can boil and then simmer, and program other cooking options and times. The timer can be set in 10-minute increments up to 5 hours, so you'll have to reset it for longer cooking times. It also has a keep-warm setting and a delayed timer, so you can set it to start at a later time. One caveat is to avoid their discontinued model, the VF7900-3, which may be sold on the secondary market (such as on eBay or in thrift shops) or that are sometimes left over at Amazon.com. This model has a Teflon nonstick coating on the heating element (not in contact with food). Due to customer concerns about breathing in Teflon fumes, the company discontinued the model and has a green ceramic-coated heating unit now (again, not in contact with food).

When we polled our bone broth enthusiasts, the VitaClay Smart Organic Multicooker was deemed to be the best as a slow cooker for those who want both lead-free peace of mind and more programmable heating and timing options in a slow cooker.

— VitaClay Stoneware Yogurt Maker and Slowcooker. This is approximately $50 and has a low, medium, high, and yogurt-maker temperature setting. Like the Organic Multicooker by VitaClay, this model has an unglazed, lead-free clay pot insert. This is a great option for those who want a more budget-friendly slow cooker.

— Instant Pot IP Duo or IP Lux. This is a pressure cooker, slow cooker, rice cooker, and yogurt maker, which also browns and sautés. The Instant Pot has an 18/8 stainless steel cooking pot with a 3-ply bottom. This model has a lot of options for programming: The slow-cooker timer goes from 30 minutes to 20 hours, and has a keep-warm feature up to 10 hours, which is nice for making long-cooked bone broths. Some of the GAPS experts and health enthusiasts have tried this and liked it better as a pressure cooker than a slow cooker. The consensus was that when used more like a slow cooker, you could not adjust the temperature to low, medium, or high, which can lead to overcooking some foods. However, when used as a pressure cooker, we've heard that the broth is among the best.

Nutritional Consulting by Phone and Skype

Gut-brain health and nutrigenomics (how food and supplements impact gene expressions):

Heather Dane: HeatherDane.com

Donna Johnson, R.N.: MTHFRAlliance.com

Kim Schuette: BiodynamicWellness.com

Mineral testing and mineral balancing nutrition consulting:

Morley Robbins: GotMag.org

⸙ENDNOTES⸕

Chapter 1

1. Laura Stampler, "Organic Food Sales on the Rise," *Time,* May 13, 2014, http://time.com/97949/organic-food-sales-on-the-rise/.

2. Ibid.

3. Janet Clarkson, *A Global History* (London: Reaktion Books, 2010).

4. Encyclopaedia Britannica Online, s. v. "restaurant," accessed April 15, 2015, http://www.britannica.com/topic/restaurant.

5. Jean-Louis Flandrin and Massimo Montanari. *Food: A Culinary History from Antiquity to the Present.* (New York: Columbia University Press, 1999).

6. "Global Collagen Market to Reach $4.4 Billion By The Year 2020," Meticulous Research, March 14, 2015, http://www.meticulousresearch.com/press/global-collagen-market-to-reach-4-4-billion-by-the-year-2020/.

7. Harvey Lodish, et al., *Molecular Cell Biology, 4th edition* (New York: W. H. Freeman, 2000).

8. Ibid.

9. Angelica Carrillo Leal, "Why Does Your Skin Age?" *Dartmouth Undergraduate Journal of Science* (January 28, 2013), http://dujs.dartmouth.edu/news/why-does-your-skin-age#.VceIkXjkS8F.

10. Sara Sibilla et al., "An Overview of the Beneficial Effects of Hydrolysed Collagen as a Nutraceutical on Skin Properties: Scientific Background and Clinical Studies," *The Open Nutraceuticals Journal* 8 (2015): 29–42, doi:10.2174/1876396001508010029; V. Kahan et al., "Stress, Immunity, and Skin Collagen Integrity: Evidence from Animal Models and Clinical Conditions," *Brain Behavior and Immunity* (November 2009): 1089-95, doi:10.1016/j.bbi.2009.06.002.

11. A. L. Boskey and R. Coleman, "Aging and Bone," *Journal of Dental Research* 89.12 (December 2010): 1333–1348, doi:10.1177/0022034510377791; Usha Kini and B.N. Nandeesh, "Physiology of Bone Formation, Remodeling, and Metabolism," *Radionuclide and Hybrid Bone Imaging* (2012) 29–57, doi:10.1007/978-3-642-02400-9_2; Sibilla "Overview."

12. Nicholas E. Diamant, "Pathophysiology of Gastroesophageal Reflux Disease," *GI Motility Online* (2006), doi:10.1038/gimo21.

13. Silke K. Schagen, et al., "Discovering the Link between Nutrition and Skin Aging." *Dermatoendocrinology* 4.3 (2012): 298–307, doi: 10.4161/derm.22876; N. Takasao, et al., "Cinnamon Extract Promotes Type I Collagen Biosynthesis via Activation of IGF-I Signaling in Human Dermal Fibroblasts," *Journal of Agricultural and Food Chemistry* 60.5 (February 2012):1193–200, doi: 10.1021/jf2043357; R. Jugdaohsingh, "Silicon and Bone Health." *The Journal of Nutrition, Health & Aging* 11.2 (2007): 99–110; D. Jean-Gilles, et al., "Anti-inflammatory Effects of Polyphenolic-enriched Red Raspberry Extract in an Antigen-induced Arthritis Rat Model," *Journal of Agricultural and Food Chemistry* 60.23 (June 2012): 5755–62 doi:10.1021/jf203456w; Ivana Binic, et al., "Skin Ageing: Natural Weapons and Strategies." *Evidence-Based Complementary and Alternative Medicine* (2013): doi:10.1155/2013/827248.

14. Nathan Ralph Gotthoffer, *Gelatin in Nutrition and Medicine* (Grayslake Gelatin Company, 1945).

15. Ibid.

16. Kim Schuette, "Stock vs. Broth: Are You Confused?" BioDynamicWellness.com, accessed March 24, 2015.

17. Ibid.

18. L. C. Junqueira and G. S. Montes. "Biology of Collagen-proteoglycan Interaction," *Archivum Histologicum Japonicum* 46.5 (December 1983): 589–629, http://www.ncbi.nlm.nih.gov/pubmed/6370189.

19. A. P. Simopoulos, "The Importance of the ratio of omega-6/omega-3 essential fatty acids" *Biomedicine & Pharmacotherapy* 56.8 (October 2002) 365–79, National Institutes of Health. Oct 2002, http://www.ncbi.nlm.nih.gov/pubmed/12442909.

20. S. R. Schwartz and J. Park, "Ingestion of BioCell Collagen(®), a novel hydrolyzed chicken sternal cartilage extract; enhanced blood microcirculation and reduced facial aging signs," *Journal of Clinical Interventions in Aging, 7* (267–73), 2012, doi: 10.2147/CIA.S32836.

21. Kaayla T. Daniel, "Is There a Natural Remedy for Cellulite? Think Bone Broth," NourishingBroth.com, April 8, 2015, http://nourishingbroth.com/hot-news/is-there-an-all-natural-remedy-for-cellulite-think-bone-broth/.

22. Ray Peat, "Gelatin, Stress, Longevity," RayPeat.com, accessed April 12, 2015, http://raypeat.com/articles/articles/gelatin.shtml.

23. Tyson, "The Effect of Gelatin."

24. Peat, "Gelatin, Stress, Longevity."

25. P. Li, et al. "Amino acids and immune function," *British Journal of Nutrition* 98.2 (August 2007): 237–52, doi: 10.1017/S000711450769936X.

26. Barbara O. Rennard, et al., "Chicken Soup Inhibits Neutrophil Chemotaxis In Vitro." *Chest* 118.4 (October 2000): 1150–7, PubMed (PMID: 11035691).

27. Marian Burros, "So Listen to Mother Already: For Flu, Take Chicken Soup," *Eating Well* (blog), *The New York Times,* February 3, 1999, http://www.nytimes.com/1999/02/03/dining/eating-well-so-listen-to-mother-already-for-flu-take-chicken-soup.

28. S. Hasegawa, et al., "Cysteine, histidine and glycine exhibit anti-inflammatory effects in human coronary arterial endothelial cells," *Clinical and Experimental Immunology,* 167.2 (February 2012): 269–74, doi:10.1111/j.1365-2249.2011.04519.x; A. Z. de Souza, et al., "Oral Supplementation with L-Glutamine Alters Gut Microbiota of Obese and Overweight Human Adults: A Pilot Study," *Nutrition* 31.6 (January 2015): 884–9, doi:10.1016/j.nut.2015.01.004.

29. Rennard, "Chicken Soup Inhibits."

30. C. Palacios, "The role of nutrients in bone health, from A to Z," *Critical Reviews in Food Science and Nutrition,* 46.8 (2006), Pub Med (PMID: 17092827).

31. P. J. Turnbaugh, et al., "An obesity-associated gut microbiome with increased capacity for energy harvest," *Nature* 444 (December 2006): 1027–31, doi:10.1038/nature05414.

32. de Souza, "Oral Supplementation."

33. Julie E. Flood and Barbara J. Rolls, "Soup preloads in a variety of forms reduce meal energy intake," *Appetite* 49.3 (November 2007) 626–34, PubMed (PMCID: PMC2128765).

34. M. L. Ray, et al., "Effect of sodium in a rehydration beverage when consumed as a fluid or meal," *Journal of Applied Physiology* 85.4 (October 1998) 1329–36, PubMed (PMID: 9760324).

35. R. J. Maughan, et al., "Factors influencing the restoration of fluid and electrolyte balance after exercise in the heat." *British Journal of Sports Medicine* 31.3 (September 1997): 175–82, PubMed Central (PMC1332513).

36. E. L. Dillon, et al., "Amino acid metabolism and inflammatory burden in ovarian cancer patients undergoing intense oncological therapy," *Clinical Nutrition* 26.6 (December 2007): 736–43, doi:10.1016/j.clnu.2007.07.004.

37. Dan Hurley, "Your Backup Brain," *Psychology Today,* November 1, 2011, accessed May 10, 2015, https://www.psychologytoday.com/articles/201110/your-backup-brain.

38. Leo Galland, "Do You Have Leaky Gut Syndrome?" The Huffington Post, September 10, 2010, http://www.huffingtonpost.com/leo-galland-md/do-you-have-leaky-gut-syn_b_688951.html.

39. Federation of American Societies for Experimental Biology, "Why inflammation leads to a leaky blood-brain barrier: MicroRNA-155," ScienceDaily, June 2, 2014, http://www.sciencedaily.com/releases/2014/06/140602104749.htm.

40. Ana-Maria Enciu et al, "Triggers and Effectors of Oxidative Stress at Blood-Brain Barrier Level: Relevance for Brain Ageing and Neurodegeneration," Oxidative Medicine and Cellular Longevity (2013), doi:10.1155/2013/297512; Tanya K. Murphy, Roger Kurlan, and James Leckman, "The Immunobiology of Tourette's Disorder, Pediatric Autoimmune Neuropsychiatric Disorders Associated with *Streptococcus,* and Related Disorders: A Way Forward," *Journal of Child and Adolescent Psychopharmacology* 20.4 (August 2010): 317–331, doi: 10.1089/cap.2010.0043; George Szmukler et al., "Anorexia Nervosa and Bulimic Disorders: Current Perspectives: Proceedings of the Conference on Anorexia Nervosa and Related Disorders, Held at University College, Swansea, Wales on 3-7 September 1984.

41. Amy Nett, "Beyond MSG: Could Hidden Sources of Glutamate Be Harming Your Health?" ChrisKresser.com, September 16, 2014, https://chriskresser.com/beyond-msg-could-hidden-sources-of-glutamate-be-harming-your-health/.

42. "Review of: Excitotoxins: The Taste that Kills," *Nutrition Digest* 37.3, http://americannutritionassociation.org/newsletter/review-excitotoxins-taste-kills.

43. Sally Fallon Morell, "Broth Is Beautiful," The Weston A. Price Foundation, January 1, 2000, http://www.westonaprice.org/health-topics/broth-is-beautiful/.

Chapter 2

1. Mary V. Gold, "Organic Production/Organic Food: Information Access Tools," Alternative Farming Systems Information Center, June 2007, last updated May 2015, http://www.nal.usda.gov/afsic/pubs/ofp/ofp.shtml.

2. Stanley A. Fishman, *Tender Grassfed Meat: Traditional Ways to Cook Healthy Meat* (Alamo, CA: Alanstar Games, 2009).

3. Ibid.

4. "The Judicious Use of Medically Important Antimicrobial Drugs in Food-Producing Animals," Guidance for Industry #209, April 13, 2012, http://www.fda.gov/downloads/AnimalVeterinary/GuidanceComplianceEnforcement/GuidanceforIndustry/UCM216936.pdf.

5. "GMO Facts," The Non-GMO Project.

6. "Evaluation of five organophosphate insecticides and herbicides," *IARC Monographs* Volume 112, International Agency for Research on Cancer, World Health Organization, March 20, 2015, http://www.iarc.fr/en/media-centre/iarcnews/pdf/MonographVolume112.pdf.

7. Sheryl Ryan, "Which Are the Healthiest and Most Responsible Fish to Eat?" Greenopedia, accessed April 23, 2015.

8. "Iodine: Fact Sheet for Consumers," National Institutes of Health, last reviewed June 24, 2011, https://ods.od.nih.gov/factsheets/Iodine-Consumer/.

9. Michael Conathan, "Fukushima Fallout Not Affecting U.S.-Caught Fish," *Voices: Ocean Views* (blog), *National Geographic,* September 11, 2013, http://voices.nationalgeographic.com/2013/09/11/fukushima-fallout-not-affecting-u-s-caught-fish/.

10. R. A. McCance, W. Sheldon, and E. M. Widdowson, "Bone and Vegetable Broth," *Archives of Disease in Childhood* 9.52 (August 1934): 251–8.

11. Ibid.

12. Harvey Lodish, et al., *Molecular Cell Biology,* 4th edition.

13. Sally Fallon Morell and Kaayla T. Daniel, *Nourishing Broth: An Old-Fashioned Remedy for the Modern World* (Grand Central Life & Style, 2014).

Chapter 3

1. Karen Marley, Karen, "The Fantastic 5: Antioxidant Spice Heroes or How to Keep That Pesky 'Eat Healthy' Resolution!" Spice Sherpa, January 26, 2011, http://www.spicesherpa.com/the-fantastic-5-antioxidant-spice-heroes-or-how-to-keep-that-pesky-eat-healthy-resolution/.

Chapter 4

1. "Lamb Broth," *Health and Healing Wisdom* 21.4 (Winter 1997), Price-Pottenger Nutrition Foundation.

Chapter 5

1. Bharat B. Aggarwal with Debora Yost, *Healing Spices: How to Use 50 Everyday and Exotic Spices to Boost Health and Beat Disease* (Sterling, January 2011).

2. Ibid.

3. Ariane Resnick, *The Bone Broth Miracle: How An Ancient Remedy Can Improve Health, Fight Aging, and Boost Beauty* (New York: Skyhorse Publishing, 2015).

Chapter 6

1. K. El-Mostafa, et al., "Nopal cactus (Opuntia ficus-indica) as a source of bioactive compounds for nutrition, health and disease," *Molecules* 19.9 (September 17, 2014): 14879–901, doi:10.3390/molecules190914879.

2. Nick Polizzi, *The Sacred Cookbook: Forgotten Healing Recipes of the Ancients* (Three Seed Productions, 2013).

3. Ibid.

4. Pat Connolly, "Chard Soup," *Health and Healing Wisdom* 30.4 (Winter 2006), Price-Pottenger Nutrition Foundation.

Chapter 7

1. "Baked Lemon Turkey Breast," *Health and Healing Wisdom* 16.4 (1992), Price-Pottenger Nutrition Foundation.

2. "Breakfast Lamb Stew," *Health and Healing Wisdom* 21.4 (Winter 1997), Price-Pottenger Nutrition Foundation.

Chapter 10

1. Miriam Meister, "Salmon contain health-promoting bioactive peptides," National Food Institute, the Technical University of Denmark, September 4, 2014, http://www.food.dtu.dk/english/News/2014/09/Salmon-contain-health-promoting-bioactive-peptides.

2. "Tuna Shopping Guide: How Does Your Can Stack Up?" Greenpeace, http://www.greenpeace.org/usa/oceans/tuna-guide/.

3. Ibid.

Chapter 12

1. Warren Bobrow, *Apothecary Cocktails: Restorative Drinks of Yesterday and Today* (Fair Winds Press, 2013).

Appendix

1. Aggarwal, *Healing Spices.*

2. Ibid.

3. Ibid.

4. "Ayurveda & Diet: Food Chart: Spices," allAyurveda.com, accessed April 14, 2015, http://www.allayurveda.com/dietp_spices.asp; Aggarwal, *Healing Spices*; Paul Pitchford, *Healing with Whole Foods: Asian Traditions and Modern Nutrition, 3rd edition* (Berkeley, CA: North Atlantic Books, 2002).

⸙GENERAL INDEX⸙

A

Acid reflux, finisher recipes for easing, 108
Affirmations
    about: benefits of, xi, 11; guidelines for, 11;
        Louise and, 4
    for boosting immunity, 12
    for challenges with health issues, 4
    for common cold/bronchitis, 12
    for digestion, 19
    for fatigue or exercise capacity, 14
    for fighting inflammation, 12
    for healing (with meditation), 319
    for hydration issues, 13
    for listening to your body, 326
    for mood issues, 14
    for muscle care, 14
    for starting bone broth journey, 19
    for strengthening bones/teeth, 13
    for weight challenges, 13
Allergies, finisher recipe for, 108
Allshouse, Annie Dru, 324, 340
Amino acids, in bone broth, 8–9
Anxiety, finisher recipes for easing, 108–109
Ayurveda, 40, 46, 107, 270, 330, 343

B

Back pain, healing story, 321–322
Beauty treatments. *See* Index of Recipes

Benefits of bone broth. *See* Bone broth
Beverage, bone broth as, 45
Blenders, 25
Bloating, finisher recipes to alleviate, *111*
Blood sugar balance, 11, 109, 132, 251, 252,
    264, 281, 328, 330
Bone broth
    about: overview of authors' perspectives, 4
    basic nature of, xii
    bioavailable collagen in, 6–8. *See also*
        collagen
    bioavailable nutrients in, 6, 8–9
    bones and ingredients for, 26–27
    healing benefits of. *See* Healing, health
        and; Healing stories
    healing flavor enhancement of, 6, 10
    history of, 5–6
    magic pills and, 317–318
    making. *See* Index of Recipes
    meat stock and. *See* Meat stock
    panacea question clarified, 15–16
    ready-made, buying, 42
    real food, grandma's soups and, 4–5
    reasons to consume, 6–10, 317–318
    resources, 347–351
    slowing down to cook with, 324–325
    TV dinners, media, and return to, 5
    using. *See* Bone broth, action plan for

enjoying; Bone broth, guidelines for using

waste minimization of, 6, 9–10

what it is, 5–6

Bone broth, action plan for enjoying, 67–71. *See also* Index of Recipes

about: overview of, 67

assessing kitchen and storage tools, 68–69

deciding how to start, 67

listening to your body, 71

making broth, 70

making plan, 68–69

repeating the process, 71

shopping for ingredients, 69

slow, gentle approach, 70

storing broth and fat, 70

using broth and fat, 70–71

Bone broth, guidelines for using

action plan. *See* Bone broth, action plan for enjoying

adapting to work for you, 16–19

affirmations for, 11–14, 19. *See also* Affirmations

daily consumption, 30, 45, 46

discomfort remedies, 17

discomfort remedies/affirmations, 18–19

drinking in cup, 45

genetic intolerances and, 19

gentler place to start, 17, 18

getting gut-health practitioner input, 18–19

ideas for incorporating into routine, 45–46

journaling experiences, 17–18

making fast soup, 45–46

meat stock as gentler option, 16, 17, 18

menu ideas. *See* Index of Recipes

MSG, glutamates and, 16–17. *See also* Glutamates

as quickie meal, 46

removing fat from broth, 17

starting journey, 19

starting other recipes, 46

supporting digestion, 17

tracking (journaling) experiences, 17–18

traveling and, 46

use tips, 45–46

at work, 46

Bones (animal). *See* Index of Recipes

Bones (human), healing broken, 324

Bones (human), strengthening, 12–13

Book overview, using this book, xiv–xv

Boron, 12

Boulanger, A., 5–6

Browning bones, 28

B vitamins, 12, 96, 234

B12, 96, 242, 323

B6, 96

B complex, 7, 232, 328

C

Calcium, 9, 12

Campbell-McBride, Dr. Natasha, 18, 29, 40, 42, 343

Cancer

dashi broth and, 104

Louise dealing with, 47, 134

preventative herbs/foods, 112, 134, 234, 328, 330

therapy, bone broth and, 14

Cathy's story, 323

Chinese herbs, 118, 321, 328–329, 349

Chinese medicine, 115, 116, 270, 321

Chinese New Year, 288

Chondroitin, 9, 322

Chronic fatigue, healing story, 323

Cleansing, finisher recipes for, 109

Cobalt, 9

Colanders or strainers, 23

Cold and bronchitis

affirmation for relieving, 12

alleviating, 12

Collagen. *See also* Gelatin

animal protein as source of, 7

bioavailable, in bone broth, 7

bone broth benefits and, 10–11

bone selection and, 26–27

denatured, 10–11

digestion-boosting roles, 8

Ehlers-Danlos syndrome and, xiv
factors causing decline in, 7
foods that support (but don't contain), 8
glucosaminoglycans and, 9, 10, 15
healing effects of, 10–11
hydrolyzed. *See* Collagen hydrolysate
   (peptides)
importance of, 7
increasing nutritional values, 8
levels, affecting broth consistency, 32–33
loss of, effects, 7
making bone broth unique, 6
only food source of, 7
plant foods and, 8
protecting, sealing intestine, 8
rebuilding, 16
skin health and, 10
supplements, skin and, 10
as "the great supporter," 7
types of, 7
vegetable stock and, 18
what it is, what it does, 7
Collagen hydrolysate (peptides)
benefits of, 8
brands to buy, 55
gelatin, MSG and, 41–42
gelatin vs., 41
protein drink, 267
recipes with, 154–155, 262–263, 264–265,
   266–268
using in recipes, 33
what it is, 8, 10
where to buy, 349
Containers
Ball/mason jars, 24
filling with bone broth, 31
minimizing breakage, 31
for on-the-go use, 24–25
putting in plastic bags, 24, 31
Copper, 7, 9, 12, 242

D

Dane, Heather, xii, xiii–xv, 323, 351, 379
Depression, healing story, 323
Detoxification, finisher recipes for, 109
Diabetes, 11, 15, 234, 322, 328, 330, 339

Digestion
affirmations for, 19
collagen boosting, 8
finisher recipes for, 109
healing stories, 322, 323

E

Education resources, 348
Electric mixers, 25
Energy, finisher recipes for, 108
Energy, regaining, healing story, 324
Essential fatty acids, 8, 10
Exercise capacity, restoring, 13–14

F

Fat caps, 31
Fatigue, affirmation for, 14
Fatigue, chronic, healing story, 323
Fat(s)
digestive challenges with, 17
healthy, 9, 55
removing from broth, 17, 29
rendering, 31–32
saving and using, 31–32
shopping list, to buy, 55
skimming or not (making broth), 29
storing, 70. *See also* Storing bone broth
using, action plan, 67–71
Fertility, healing story, 325
Finished broths/finishers, 26, 105–111. *See also*
   Index of Recipes (Medical finishers and
   healing elixirs)
Fluoride, 9
Food journal, keeping, 17–18
Funnel, stainless-steel, 24

G

GAPS. See Gut and Psychology Syndrome
   (GAPS) diet
Gas, finisher recipes to alleviate, 111
Gelatin
buying, 55
collagen hydrolysate vs., 41
as denatured collagen, 7, 10–11
healing benefits of, 10–14

rich, key ingredients for, 26–27
unflavored powder form. *See* Collagen hydrolysate (peptides)
Genetically modified organisms (GMOs), 37
Genetic seizure disorder, healing story, 324
Glucosamine, 9, 322
Glucosaminoglycans (GAGs), 9, 10, 15
Glutamates, 16–17, 18, 42, 56
Glutamic acid, 8, 16–17
Glycine, 8, 11, 12
GMOs, 37
Guiding principles. *See* Principles, guiding
Gut and Psychology Syndrome (Campbell-McBride), 18
Gut and Psychology Syndrome (GAPS) diet, 15, 18, 26, 324, 342
Gut health
    leaky gut and leaky brain, 15, 16, 17, 51
    mood and, 14, 15
    talking with practitioner about, 18–19

H

Hair masks. *See* Index of Recipes (Beauty treatments)
Hashimoto's disease, healing story, 325
Hay, Louise
    affirmations of. *See* Affirmations
    background and outlook, 47
    breakfast options, 48
    Chinese new year hot pot party, 66
    daily meal routine, 47–49
    dessert and snack preferences, 49
    on health, happiness, and love, 317
    as Louise Play, 4, 317
    lunch and dinner options, 48–49
    pre-breakfast routine, 48
    preparing for parties "Louise Play" style, 63
Healing, health and. *See also* specific health issues
    bone broth and, xii, 10–14, 317–319
    conditions impacted by bone broth, 11–14
    guiding principle applicable to, 50–53
    healing affirmation and meditation, 319
    healing flavor enhancement of bone broth, 6, 10

loving yourself and, xi
making healing elixirs, 46
natural healing, 318–319
principles of, xi–xii
recipes for. *See* Index of Recipes, (Medical finishers and healing elixirs)
right food and, xii
right thoughts and, xi
whole food resources, 348
Healing stories, 321–326
    about: Annie's story, 324; Ariane Resnick and clients' stories, 325; Cathy's story, 323; Eyton Shalom's story, 321–322; Kim Schuette and clients' stories, 324–325; Quinn Wilson's story, 322
    back pain, 321
    beautiful skin and nails, 322
    broken bones, 324
    chronic fatigue, 323
    depression, 323
    digestion and stomach issues, 322, 323
    fertility, 325
    Hashimoto's disease, 325
    Lyme disease, 325
    regaining energy, 324
    resolving genetic seizure disorder, 324
    tooth pain and decay, 322, 324
    warming the body, 321–322
    yours (with affirmation), 325–326
Heart health, 90, 108–109, 330
Histamines, finisher recipe to lower, 108
Hydration
    affirmation for, 13
    bone broth for, 13
    restoring exercise capacity with, 14
Hydroxyproline, 8, 11

I

Ice-cube trays, silicone, 24
Immersion blenders, 25
Immunity, boosting, 12
Inflammation, fighting
    affirmation for, 12
    bone broth for, 12, 14, 325
    finisher recipes for, 109
    herbs/spices for, 51, 329, 330
    recipes for, 234–235, 264–265

Ingredients. *See* Index of Recipes
Intuition ("inner ding")
    choosing restaurant meals and, 22
    making bone broth and, 30, 43
    spice use and, 329, 333
    trusting, 30, 40, 43, 47
Iron, 9, 12, 96
Irritable bowel syndrome (IBS), finisher recipes
    to alleviate, 111

J

Jars. *See* Containers
Journal, keeping, 17–18

K

Kitchen equipment. *See also* specific equipment
    about: overview of, 21, 22
    assessing tools, 68
    for Chinese hot pot dinner party, 66
    essential items, 22–24
    optional items, 24–25
Kitchen, guiding principle about, 50

L

Labeling jars of bone broth, 24
Ladles, 24
Leaky gut, 15, 16, 17, 51
Leftovers, using, 34–35
L-glutamine/-glutamic acid, 12, 13, 16
Louise. *See* Hay, Louise
Love, Louise on health, happiness and, 317
Love, of self, xi
Lyme disease, healing story, 325

M

Magnesium, 9, 12, 17, 322
Making bone broth. *See* Index of Recipes (Bone
    broth, making)
Manganese, 9, 12
Masks, facial/hair. *See* Index of Recipes (Beauty
    treatments)
Meat stock
    bones and ingredients for, 26–27

compared to bone broth, 18
    as gentler option than broth, 17, 18
    guidelines for using, 18
    making, 17, 18. *See also* Index of Recipes
    starting with, 18
Meditation, healing affirmation and, 319
Memory, finisher recipes to boost, 111
Mesh strainers, 23
Minerals. *See* specific minerals; Vitamins and
    minerals
Mixers, 25
Mood
    affirmation for, 14
    bone broth for, 14
    dancing improving, 50
    disorders, what to do for, 17–18
    gut health/bacteria and, 14, 15
    meat stock for, 18
    nutrients for, 9
Mood, finisher recipes to boost, 111
MSG, glutamates vs., 16–17. *See also* Gluta-
    mates
Muscle, building, 9, 14

N

Nails, beautiful, bone broth user story, 322
Nutrients, in bone broth, 8–9. *See also* specific
    nutrients
Nutritional consulting resources, 351

O

Omega-3 fatty acids, 38, 234

P

Parboiling bones, 28
Phosphate, 322
Phosphorus, 9, 12
Planet, less waste with bone broth, 6, 9–10
Potassium, 9, 12
Preparing bones, 27–28
Principles, guiding, 50–53
    kitchen is where we play, 50
    learning to work with herbs/spices, 52

turning mistakes into delicious mistakes, 52–53

you are worth healing, 50–52

Proline, 8, 11

R

Recipes and recipe contributors. *See* Index of Recipes

Rendering fat, 31–32

Resources, 347–351

Restaurant food, 21–22

Routine, incorporating bone broth into, 45–46

S

Selenium, 9

Self-love, xi

Silicon, 7, 322

Silicone ice-cube trays, 24

Simmering ingredients, 28–29

Skimmers, 24

Skin, beautiful, bone broth user story, 322

Skin care. *See* Index of Recipes (Beauty treatments)

Slow cookers
  brands and models, 350
  making bone broth with. *See* Index of Recipes (Bone broth, making)
  safety precautions, 28
  selecting, features and types, 23, 350

Spoons and ladles, 23–24

Stand mixers, 25

Stomach issues, healing story, 322. *See also* Digestion

Stories, healing. *See* Healing stories

Storing bone broth
  action plan, 70
  assessing if broth good or not, 30, 71
  assessing tools for, 68
  Ball/mason jars for, 24
  consumption rate and, 30
  guidelines, 30–31
  labeling and, 24
  minimizing jar breakage, 31
  on-the-go containers for, 24–25

putting jars in plastic bags, 24, 31
  shelf life, 30

Strainers or colanders, 23

Stress, finisher recipes for easing, 108–109

Sulfur, 7, 9

Sweeteners, whole-food, 55

T

Teeth, healing stories, 322, 324

Teeth, strengthening, 13

Testimonials. *See* Healing Stories

V

Vegetarians, bone broth and, 321–322, 325, 336

Vitamin A, 7, 9, 12, 232, 234, 328, 330

Vitamin B. *See* B vitamins

Vitamin C, 7, 12, 59, 323, 328, 330

Vitamin D, 7, 9, 12, 232, 234

Vitamin E, 7, 9, 232, 234, 330

Vitamin K, 9, 12, 330

Vitamins and minerals. *See also* specific vitamins and minerals
  in bone broth, 9, 12, 16
  in plant foods, 7, 18, 39

W

Warming the body, healing story, 321–322

Waste, minimization of, 6, 9–10

Weight loss, affirmation for, 13

Weight loss, bone broth promoting, 13

Weight loss, finisher recipes to promote, 109

Z

Zinc, 9, 12, 96, 242

⌐INDEX OF RECIPES⌐

Note: Page numbers in *italics* indicate recipes. Page numbers in **bold** indicate biographical sketches of recipe contributors.

A

Aioli: Garlic Mayonnaise with a Healthier Twist, *148–149*
Aioli, Louise's French rémoulade with, *150–151*
Alcohol. *See* Cocktails with benefits
Allspice, properties of, 329, 332
Almonds. *See* Nuts and seeds
Apple cider vinegar
    adding to bone broth, 27, 39–40
    amount to use, 27
    choosing, 39
    functions of, 40
    shopping list, 57
Apple Tarte Tatin, *274–277*
Artichoke Tahini Sauce, *152–153*
Asparagus
    Louise's Healing Asparagus Soup, *134–135*
    Simple Asparagus, *199–200*
Aspics. *See* Salads, pâtés, and aspics
Astragalus (Huang qi), properties of, 329

B

Baked Lemon Turkey Breast, *170–171*
Balanced & Bright Beef Bone Broth (Neutral), *86–87*
Balanced & Bright Jasmine Rice with Seasonal Vegetables, Golden Raisins, and Pistachios, *219–220*
Balanced & Bright Quick Pho and Lunches to Go, *146–147*
Balanced & Bright Seared Veggie Sauté, *201–202*
Balsamic Vinaigrette, *155*
Bananas
    Collagen-Rich Fruit Smoothie, *262–263*
    5-Minute Banana Cinnamon Ice Cream (Non-Dairy), *286–287*
Barringer, Caroline, 29, 60, **114**, *123–125*, *244–245*, *251–252*, **335–336**
Basil, properties of, 328, 332
Bay leaf, properties of, 328, 332
Beans, shopping list, 56
Beauty treatments, 311–316
    about: using bone broth for, 46

DIY Nosey Perfect Pore Cleanser, *313–314*
Skin-So-Smooth Honey Gelatin Face Mask, *311–312*
So Shiny Beautiful Hair Mask, *315–316*
Beef
    about: broth for healing elixirs, 115; conventional vs. factory farmed, 35–37; gold standard, 35; grass- or pasture-fed, 35–36, 347; hormone and antibiotic free, 36; organic, 35; shopping list, 54–55; sustainable, humanely raised, 38; ways to enjoy oxtail meat, 81
    Balanced & Bright Beef Bone Broth (Neutral), *86–87*
    Beef or Lamb Stock or Broth (Lightly Flavored), *98–99*
    Crispy Short Ribs with Lime, Cilantro, and Mint, *162–163*
    Easy Eye of Round Roast, *164–167*
    Farm-to-Table Aspic, *255–256*
    Farmer Leslie's Bone Broth Recipe (Neutral or Flavored), *88–89*
    Hearty Hamburger Soup, *132–133*
    Heather's Easy Oxtail Meat Stock and Bone Broth (Neutral), *79–81*
    Kitchen Sink Bone Broth (Neutral), *84–85*
    Local Butcher Shop Bone Broth (Neutral), *82–83*
    Louise's Favorite Bone Broth or Vegetable Broth (Neutral or Flavored), *76–77*
    Oxtail Pâté, *246–247*
    Savory Beef Broth with Aromatic Spices (Flavored), *90–91*
Berries
    Berry White Chocolate Frosting (Grain Free), *299–301*
    Collagen-Rich Fruit Smoothie, *262–263*
Best Brussels Sprouts, *187–188*
Best Liver Pâté Ever!, *242–243*
Best Pumpkin Pie Ever, *278–280*
Beverages. *See also* Cocktails with benefits; Smoothies
    Bone Broth Hot Chocolate, *108–109*

Chai Drink, *109*
Energizing Chai Hot Chocolate or Latte, *108*
Saffron Tea, *108, 109*
Bison Meatloaf Cupcakes with Mashed Celery Root Topping, *159–161*
Bitters, about, 57
Bitters, drinks with. *See* Cocktails with benefits
Blocks, Rocket Stock, *251–252*
Blueberries. *See* Berries
Bone broth, action plan for enjoying, 67–71
    about: overview of, 67–68
    assessing kitchen and storage tools, 68
    deciding how to start, 67
    listening to your body, 71
    making broth, 70. *See also* Bone broth, making
    making plan, 68–69
    repeating the process, 71
    shopping for ingredients, 69
    slow, gentle approach, 70
    storing broth and fat, 70–71
    using broth and fat, 71
Bone Broth Hot Chocolate, *108–109*
Bone broth, making, 25–33. *See also* Bones (animal); Ingredients, bone broth
    aim of, 32
    attitude toward, 42–43
    basic broth recipes. *See* Broths and stocks, basic
    browning bones, 27–28
    buying ready-made instead of, 42
    clear-broth cooking tip, 29
    consistency target, 32
    consumption rate and, 30
    egg-white "raft" to soak up cloudiness, 29
    fat caps and, 31–32
    filling stockpot/slow cooker with ingredients, 28
    finished broths, 26, 75
    flavored broths, 26, 75
    gelling or not, 32–33
    getting ready to use/using broth, 31–33

guiding principles for, 50–53
intuition and, 30
neutral/flavorless broths, 26, 75
parboiling bones, 28
powdered gelatin for, 33. *See also* General Index (Collagen hydrolysate)
preparing bones, 27–28
ready-made instead of, 42
reusing bones, 33
simmering ingredients, 28–29
simmering more (remouillage), 33
skimming fat (or not), 29
storing after, 30–31. *See also* General Index (Storing Bone Broth)
straining broth, 29, 30
using broth made. *See* Bone broth, action plan for enjoying
what-the-hell approach to, 42–43
Bone broth, ready-made, 42
Bone Broth Scotch, *310*
Bones (animal)
browning, 27–28
meaty, 27
mixing types (or not), 27
parboiling, 28
preparing, 27–28
reusing, 33
for rich gelatin, 26
selecting, 26–27
shopping list, 54–55
Bones (human), strengthening, 12–13
Bonito flakes, about, 57
Bragg Liquid Aminos, about, 57–58
Breads. *See* Grains, breads, and pancakes
Breakfast
about: Louise's pre-breakfast and, 48; menu ideas, 60–61
Breakfast Lamb Stew, *175–177*
Broccoli
Balanced & Bright Seared Veggie Sauté, *201–202*
Quinoa, Broccoli, and Leek Pilaf, *216–218*
Broths and stocks, basic, 75–104

about: finished broths, 75; flavored broths, 75; gathering ingredients for, 77; neutral/flavorless broths, 75; overview of, 75; recipe sources, 75
Balanced & Bright Beef Bone Broth (Neutral), *86–87*
Beef or Lamb Stock or Broth (Lightly Flavored), *98–99*
Chicken and Pork Bone Broth (Flavored), *92–93*
Chicken, Pheasant, or Turkey Stock or Broth (Flavored), *100–101*
Dashi Fish Stock (Flavored), *104*
Farmer Leslie's Bone Broth Recipe (Neutral or Flavored), *88–89*
Fish Stock or Broth (Flavored), *102–103*
Healing Elixir Vegetable Stock (Vegan; Lightly Flavored), *94–95*
Heather's Easy Oxtail Meat Stock and Bone Broth (Neutral), *79–81*
Kitchen Sink Bone Broth (Neutral), *84–85*
Lamb Broth (Lightly Flavored), *96–97*
Local Butcher Shop Bone Broth (Neutral), *82–83*
Louise's Favorite Bone Broth or Vegetable Broth (Neutral or Flavored), *76–77*
Savory Beef Broth with Aromatic Spices (Flavored), *90–91*
Brune, Nick, *90–91*, *92–93*, *162–163*, **336–337**, 344
Brussels sprouts, best, *187–188*
Buckwheat and veggies, *214–215*

C

Cacao. *See* Chocolate
Cacao butter, about, 59
Cactus and Seafood Soup, *123–125*
Cakes
Cinnamon New Year Cake (Grain Free), *288–290*
Decadent Two-Layer Chocolate Cake (Grain Free), *283–285*

Vanilla Cake with Berry White Chocolate Frosting (Grain Free), *299–301*
Camu camu powder, about, 59
Caramelized Onions, *191–192*
Caraway seeds, properties of, 329, 332
Cardamom Carrots, *189–190*
Cardamom, properties of, 329, 332
Carrots
    Balanced & Bright Seared Veggie Sauté, *201–202*
    Cardamom Carrots, *189–190*
    Magic Zucchini and Carrots, *193–194*
Celery root
    Bison Meatloaf Cupcakes with Mashed Celery Root Topping, *159–161*
    Mashed Celery Root, *195–196*
Chai Drink, *109*
Chai, energizing hot chocolate or latte, 108
Chard Soup, *140–141*
Chia seed powder, about, 59
Chicken. *See* Poultry
Chinese hot pot party menu, 64–66
Chocolate
    about: cacao for, 59
    Bone Broth Hot Chocolate, *108–109*
    Chocolate Drop Cookies, and The Great Chocolate Experiment, *269–273*
    Chocolate Mousse with a Twist, *281–282*
    Decadent Two-Layer Chocolate Cake (Grain Free), *283–285*
    Energizing Chai Hot Chocolate or Latte, *108*
    Vanilla Cake with Berry White Chocolate Frosting (Grain Free), *299–301*
Cholesterol regulation, finisher recipes for, *108–109*
Cilantro soup, cleansing, *126–127*
Cinnamon
    about: properties of, 329, 332
    Cinnamon New Year Cake (Grain Free), *288–290*
    Cinnamon Orange Coconut Frosting, *289–290*
    5-Minute Banana Cinnamon Ice Cream (Non-Dairy), *286–287*
Citrus
    Cinnamon Orange Coconut Frosting, *289–290*
    Lemon Vinaigrette, *155*
Cleanser recipes, vegetable. *See* Vegetable dishes
Cleansing Cilantro Soup, *126–127*
Clove, properties of, 330, 332
Cocktails with benefits, 303–310
    about: bitters in, 57; overview of bone broth cocktails, 303–304; popularity of, 303–304; simple syrup concentrate, *309*
    Bone Broth Scotch, *310*
    Manhattan, *306*
    Negroni Cocktail, *309*
    The Sidecar, *305*
Coconut aminos, about, 58
Coconut butter, about, 58
Coconut water, for smoothies, 60
Codonopsis (Dang shen), properties of, 329
Collagen-Rich Fruit Smoothie, *262–263*
Colostrum, about, 59
Cookies, chocolate drop, and the great chocolate experiment, *269–273*
Coriander, properties of, 330, 332
Cornish game hens
    about: dinner party menu, 63–64
    Cornish Game Hen with White Wine Mustard Sauce, *181–183*
Crispy Short Ribs with Lime, Cilantro, and Mint, *162–163*
Cumin, properties of, 330, 332

D

Daniel, Kaayla T. Ph.D., CCN, 10, 40, 42, *253–254*, **337**
Dashi Fish Stock (Flavored), *104*
Decadent Two-Layer Chocolate Cake (Grain Free), *283–285*
Desserts, 269–301
    about: Louise's preferences, 49; menu ideas, 63, 64, 65–66; pie crust recipe, *279*

Apple Tarte Tatin, *274–277*
Best Pumpkin Pie Ever, *278–280*
Chocolate Drop Cookies, and The Great
    Chocolate Experiment, *269–273*
Chocolate Mousse with a Twist, *281–282*
Cinnamon Orange Coconut Frosting,
    289–290
5-Minute Banana Cinnamon Ice Cream
    (Non-Dairy), *286–287*
Cinnamon New Year Cake (Grain Free),
    288–290
Decadent Two-Layer Chocolate Cake
    (Grain Free), *283–285*
Heavenly Marshmallow Cream Whipped
    Topping, and Marshmallows, *291–295*
Moroccan Vanilla Spice Ice Cream (Non-
    Dairy), *297–298*
Shortbread Cookies, *272–273*
Vanilla Cake with Berry White Chocolate
    Frosting (Grain Free), *299–301*
Digestion, remedy for, *120–121*
Dill, properties of, 328, 332
Dinner party menus. *See* Menus, dinner party
Dioscorea (Shan yao), properties of, 329
Dips. *See* Sauces, dips, and dressings
DIY Nosey Perfect Pore Cleanser, *313–314*
Do It Your Way Salad Dressing, *154–155*
Dong quai (Angelica sinensis)
    about: medicinal properties/precautions,
        329
    Dong Quai Chicken Soup, *118–119*
Dressings. *See* Sauces, dips, and dressings
Drinks. *See* Beverages; Cocktails with benefits

E

Easy Eye of Round Roast, *164–167*
Easy Homemade Tomato Sauce, *128–129*
Easy Turkey Meatloaf Cupcakes with Kabocha
    Squash Topping, *172–174*
Eggs and eggshells
    about: buying, 37; egg drop soup, 131;
        eggshells, 37; poaching eggs, 131
    Eggs Your Way Soup, *130–131*

Everyone's Favorite Egg Salad, *232–233*
Oeufs en Gelée (Eggs in Aspic), *259–261*
Trotting on Eggshells, *257–258*
Energizing Chai Hot Chocolate or Latte, *108*
Everyone's Favorite Egg Salad, *232–233*

F

Face mask, honey gelatin, *311–312*
Farm-to-Table Aspic, *255–256*
Farmer Leslie's Bone Broth Recipe (Neutral or
    Flavored), *88–89*
Fat(s). *See* General Index
Fennel, properties of, 330, 332
Fenugreek, properties of, 330, 332
Fermented Turmeric Finisher, *112–113*
Finishers. *See* Medicinal finishers and healing
    elixirs
Finnish sourdough rye bread, Maya's, *221–225*
Fish and seafood
    about: choosing wild vs. farmed, 38; iodine
        content, 38; Louise making fish broth
        first time, 102; mercury concerns, 38;
        radiation concerns, 38; sustainable,
        humanely raised, 38
    Cactus and Seafood Soup, *123–125*
    Dashi Fish Stock (Flavored), *104*
    Fish Stock or Broth (Flavored), *102–103*
    Lobster Salad Extravaganza, *239–241*
    Pan-Seared Snapper or Halibut, *184–185*
    Simply Delicious Salmon Salad, *234–235*
    Tempting Tuna Salad, *237–238*
    Tom Yum Soup, *138–139*
Flaxseeds/flax meal, buying, 58
Flours (specialty), 57
Fruits
    about: collagen-supporting, 7; shopping
        list, 54
    Collagen-Rich Fruit Smoothie, *262–263*

G

Game, wild
    about: Cornish game hen dinner party
        menu, 63–64; overview and selection, 37

Bison Meatloaf Cupcakes with Mashed Celery Root Topping, *159–161*

Chicken, Pheasant, or Turkey Stock or Broth (Flavored), *100–101*

Cornish Game Hen with White Wine Mustard Sauce, *181–183*

Rabbit in White Wine Mustard Sauce, *178–179*

Garlic

    Aioli: Garlic Mayonnaise with a Healthier Twist, *148–149*

    Louise's French Rémoulade with Aioli, *150–151*

Genetically modified organisms (GMOs), 37

Ginger, pickled, *203–204*

Ginger, properties of, 330, 332

GMOs, 37

Goat

    about: broth for healing elixirs, 115

    Goat and Vegetable Stew, *144–145*

Goji berry, properties of, 329

Grains, breads, and pancakes, 205–227

    about: activating/reviving sourdough starter, 222–224; gluten-free shopping list, 56; how to soak nut, seeds, and grains, 205–206

    Balanced & Bright Jasmine Rice with Seasonal Vegetables, Golden Raisins, and Pistachios, *219–220*

    Herb Bread (Grain Free), *209–211*

    Healing Buckwheat and Veggies, *214–215*

    How to Make Your Own Almond Flour, *207–208*

    Maya's Finnish Sourdough Rye Bread, *221–225*

    Messed-up but So Delicious Pan Bread (Grain Free), *212–213*

    Pancakes or Waffles (Grain Free), *226–227*

    Quinoa, Broccoli, and Leek Pilaf, *216–218*

Grass- or pasture-fed animals, 35–36, 347

Green bean soup, pureed, *142–143*

Green powders, about, 59

Greens

Chard Soup, *140–141*

Sassy Green Smoothie, *264–265*

Grocery shopping. *See* Shopping list, master

H

Hair mask, *315–316*

Hamburger soup, *132–133*

Ham Hock, Red Lentil, and Yellow Squash Salad, *253–254*

Heafner, Dave, 88–89, **337–338**

Healing Buckwheat and Veggies, *214–215*

Healing Chicken Soup, *116–117*

Healing elixirs. *See* Medicinal finishers and healing elixirs

Hearty Hamburger Soup, *132–133*

Heather's Easy Oxtail Meat Stock and Bone Broth (Neutral), *79–81*

Heavenly Marshmallow Cream Whipped Topping, and Marshmallows, *291–295*

Hemp-seed powder, about, 60

Herb Bread (Grain Free), *209–211*

Herbs and spices, 27, 327–333. *See also* specific herbs and spices

    about: overview of benefits, 40–41

    astringent, 332

    basics (salt and pepper), 327–328

    benefits of, 40

    bitter, 332

    guidelines for using, 333

    guiding principle regarding, 52

    herbs (including Chinese), 328–329, 332

    itemized, with benefits, 327–330

    learning to work with, 52, 333

    medicinal properties, 332

    pepper, 327–328

    pungent, 332

    resources for, 349

    salt, 327

    salty taste, 332

    shopping list, 56

    six tastes, 40, 331–332

    sour, 332

    spices, 329–330, 332

sweet, 332
Herby Vinaigrette, *155*
Honey Dijon, *155*
Honey gelatin face mask, *311–312*
Honey Mustard Chicken, *168–169*

I

Ice cream
    5-Minute Banana Cinnamon Ice Cream
      (Non-Dairy), *286–287*
    Moroccan Vanilla Spice Ice Cream (Non-
      Dairy), *297–298*
Indigestion and Joint Health Remedy, *120–121*
Ingredients, bone broth. *See also* Bones (ani-
    mal); Fish and seafood; Meat; Poultry
    about: ethical farming and, 34, 38
    apple cider vinegar, 27, 57
    buying. *See* Shopping list, master
    gathering at your pace, 76–77
    guiding principle for, 50–52
    herbs and spices, 27
    high quality of, 50–52
    leftover use, 34–35
    optional items, 27, 38–41
    resources for, 347–348
    selecting, 26–27, 38–41
    vegetables (organic), 27, 39
    water, 27
Ingredients, other. *See* Shopping list, master;
    specific main ingredients

J

Joint health remedy, *120–121*

K

Katsuobushi, buying, 58
Kitchen Sink Bone Broth (Neutral), *84–85*
Kombu seaweed, buying, 58

L

Lamb
    about: broth for healing elixirs, 115; buy-
      ing, 96; nutritional benefits, 96

Beef or Lamb Stock or Broth (Lightly Fla-
    vored), *98–99*
Breakfast Lamb Stew, *175–177*
Farmer Leslie's Bone Broth Recipe (Neutral
    or Flavored), *88–89*
Lamb Broth (Lightly Flavored), *96–97*
Louise's Favorite Bone Broth or Vegetable
    Broth (Neutral or Flavored), *76–77*
So Good Lamb Shank Pâté, *248–250*
Leeks, in Quinoa, Broccoli, and Leek Pilaf,
    216–218
Lemon. *See* Citrus
Lemongrass, properties of, 328, 332
Lemons. *See* Citrus
Lenair, Rhonda, *94–95, 214–215,* **338–339**
Lily bulb (Bai he), properties of, 329
Liver pâtés. *See* Salads, pâtés, and aspics
Lobster Salad Extravaganza, *239–241*
Local Butcher Shop Bone Broth (Neutral),
    82–83
Louise's Favorite Bone Broth or Vegetable
    Broth (Neutral or Flavored), *76–77*
Louise's French Rémoulade with Aioli, *150–*
    151
Louise's Healing Asparagus Soup, *134–135*
Lulu's Salad in a Glass Smoothie, *266–268*
Lunch and dinner
    Louise's daily meal routine, 48–49
    menu ideas, 61

M

Magic Zucchini and Carrots, *193–194*
Manhattan cocktail, *306*
Maori Puha Boil Up, *136–137*
Marshmallows, Heavenly Marshmallow Cream
    Whipped Topping and, *291–295*
Mashed Celery Root, *195–196*
Mashed Kabocha Squash, *197–198*
Masks. *See* Beauty treatments
Maya's Finnish Sourdough Rye Bread, *221–225*
Mayonnaise. *See* Sauces, dips, and dressings
Measurement conversion charts, *345–346*
Meat. *See also* Fish and seafood; Poultry; specif-
    ic meats

about: overview of what to buy, 35
conventional vs. factory farmed, 36–37
gold standard, 35
grass- or pasture-fed, 35–36; grass-fed
    and grain-finished, 36; grass-fed and
    grass-finished, 36; resources for, 347
hormone and antibiotic free, 36
organic, 35
shopping list, 54–55
sustainable, humanely raised, 38
wild game, 37
Meatloaf cupcakes
    about: casual dinner party with, 62
    Bison Meatloaf Cupcakes with Mashed
        Celery Root Topping, *159–161*
    Easy Turkey Meatloaf Cupcakes with Kabo-
        cha Squash Topping, *172–174*
Meat stock
    as gentler option to bone broth, 17, 18
    making, 17, 18
    recipes. *See* Broths and stocks, basic
Medicinal finishers and healing elixirs,
    105–122
    about: beef, pork, lamb, goat broths for
        healing elixirs, 115; chicken broth for
        healing elixirs, 115; choosing broths,
        115; customizing elixirs, 115; finishers
        (add-ins), 105–106; healing elixirs,
        115; *jing* energy and, 115; overview of,
        105–106; tips for, 106
    Dong Quai Chicken Soup, *118–119*
    Fermented Turmeric Finisher, *112–113*
    Finisher Recipes (targeted), *107–111*; about:
        invent your own, 111; for all-day
        energy, *108*; to alleviate gas, bloating,
        IBS, *111*; for anti-stress, anti-anxiety,
        cholesterol regulation, heart health,
        108–109; to boost mood and memory,
        111; for cleansing, anti-inflammatory,
        detoxifying, *109*; to combat allergies
        or high histamine, *108*; to ease acid
        reflux, *108*; to enhance digestion,
        balance blood sugar, promote weight

loss, *109*
    Healing Chicken Soup, *116–117*
    Healing Elixir Vegetable Stock (Vegan;
        Lightly Flavored), *94–95*
    Indigestion and Joint Health Remedy,
        120–121
    Probiotic Tonic Recipe, *122*
    Rocket Stock, *114*
Menus
    breakfast, 60–61
    dessert, 62
    dinner party. *See* Menus, dinner party
    Louise's daily meal routine and, 47–49
    lunch and dinner, 61
    snack, 61–62
Menus, dinner party, 62–67
    about: Louise's Chinese new year hot pot
        party, 66; preparing for parties "Louise
        Play" style, 63
    Chinese hot pot party, 64–67; broth, 64–
        65; dessert, 65–66; dipping sauces, 65;
        meat, poultry, and fish, 65; noodles,
        65; tools for, 66–67; vegetables, 65
    Cornish game hen easy-yet-elegant party,
        63–64; appetizers, 63–64; dessert, 64;
        main meal, 64
    meatloaf cupcakes casual dinner party, 62;
        appetizers, 62; dessert, 63; main meal,
        62
Merkel, Brian, *84–85*, 111, *112–113*, *257–258*,
    339
Messed-up but So Delicious Pan Bread (Grain
    Free), *212–213*
Metric conversion charts, 345–346
Mint, properties of, 328, 332
Moroccan Vanilla Spice Ice Cream (Non-
    Dairy), *297–298*
Mousse, chocolate with a twist, *281–282*
Mustard
    about: buying, 58
    Honey Dijon, *155*
    Honey Mustard Chicken, *168–169*
    White Wine Mustard Sauce, *156–157*

N

Negroni Cocktail, *309*
Nutmeg, properties of, 330, 332
Nuts and seeds
    about: collagen-supporting, 8; drying,
        206; how to soak, 205–206
    How to Make Your Own Almond Flour,
        207–208

O

Oeufs en Gelée (Eggs in Aspic), *259–261*
Oils, healthy, shopping list, 55
Onions, caramelized, *191–192*
Ophiopogon (Mai men dong), properties of,
    329
Organics
    GMOs and, 37
    meat, 35
    shopping for, 53
Oxtail. *See* Beef

P

Pan bread (grain free), *212–213*
Pancakes or Waffles (Grain Free), *226–227*
Pan-Seared Snapper or Halibut, *184–185*
Paprika, properties of, 330, 332
Party menus. *See* Menus, dinner party
Pasture-fed meat. *See* Grass- or pasture-fed
    animals
Pâtés. *See* Salads, pâtés, and aspics
Pepper, about, 327–328
Pesic, Leslie, *88–89*, **337–338**
Pho, quick, and lunches to go, *146–147*
Pickled Ginger, *203–204*
Polizzi, Nick, *136–137*, *138–139*, **339–340**
Pomegranate juice, for smoothies, 60
Pomegranate molasses, about, 59
Pore cleanser, *313–314*
Pork
    about: broth for healing elixirs, 115; con-
        ventional vs. factory farmed, 36–37;
        gold standard, 35; grass- or pasture-fed,

35–36, 347; hormone and antibiotic
    free, 36; organic, 35; shopping list, 54;
    sustainable, humanely raised, 38; wild
    game, 37
Chicken and Pork Bone Broth (Flavored),
    92–93
Farmer Leslie's Bone Broth Recipe (Neutral
    or Flavored), *88–89*
Ham Hock, Red Lentil, and Yellow Squash
    Salad, *253–254*
Kitchen Sink Bone Broth (Neutral), *84–85*
Local Butcher Shop Bone Broth (Neutral),
    82–83
Louise's Favorite Bone Broth or Vegetable
    Broth (Neutral or Flavored), *76–77*
Trotting on Eggshells, *257–258*
Poultry
    about. *See also* Cornish game hens
        chicken broth for healing elixirs, 115;
        conventional vs. factory farmed, 36–37;
        eggshells, 37; gold standard, 35; grass-
        or pasture-fed, 35–36; hormone and
        antibiotic free, 36; organic, 35; over-
        view of what to buy, 35; sustainable,
        humanely raised, 38; wild game, 37
Baked Lemon Turkey Breast, *170–171*
Best Liver Pâté Ever!, *242–243*
Chicken and Pork Bone Broth (Flavored),
    92–93
Chicken Burger Salad, *229–231*
Chicken, Pheasant, or Turkey Stock or
    Broth (Flavored), *100–101*
Dong Quai Chicken Soup, *118–119*
Easy Turkey Meatloaf Cupcakes with Kabo-
    cha Squash Topping, *172–174*
Farmer Leslie's Bone Broth Recipe (Neutral
    or Flavored), *88–89*
Healing Chicken Soup, *116–117*
Honey Mustard Chicken, *168–169*
Indigestion and Joint Health Remedy,
    120–121
Kitchen Sink Bone Broth (Neutral), *84–85*
Louise's Favorite Bone Broth or Vegetable

Broth (Neutral or Flavored), *76–77*
Maori Puha Boil Up, *136–137*
Pâté Plus, *244–245*
Price-Pottenger Nutrition Foundation, *96–97*,
    140–141, *170–171*, *175–177*, **340**, 348
Principles, guiding, for recipes, 50–53
    kitchen is where we play, 50
    learning to work with herbs/spices, 52
    turning mistakes into delicious mistakes,
       52–53
    you are worth healing, 50–52
Probiotic Tonic Recipe, *122*
Puha, in Maori Puha Boil Up, *136–137*
Pumpkin pie, best ever, *278–280*
Pureed Green Bean Soup, *142–143*

Q

Quinoa
    about: flakes, 48; soaking and cooking,
       218; for travel, 218
    Quinoa, Broccoli, and Leek Pilaf, *216–218*

R

Rabbit in White Wine Mustard Sauce, *178–179*
Raspberries. *See* Berries
Recipe contributors, 335–344
    Barringer, Caroline, 29, 60, *114*, *123–125*,
       244–245, *251–252*, **335–336**
    Brune, Nick, *90–91*, *92–93*, *162–163*,
       336–337, 344
    Daniel, Kaayla T. Ph.D., CCN, 10, 40, 42,
       253–254, **337**
    Heafner, Dave, *88–89*, **337–338**
    Lenair, Rhonda, *94–95*, *214–215*, **338–339**
    Merkel, Brian, *84–85*, 111, *112–113*,
       257–258, **339**
    Pesic, Leslie, *88–89*, **337–338**
    Polizzi, Nick, *136–137*, *138–139*, **339–340**
    Price-Pottenger Nutrition Foundation,
       96–97, *140–141*, *170–171*, *175–177*,
       340, 348
    Resnick, Ariane, *122*, 325, **341**
    Rocchino Aaron, 33, *82–83*, **341**

Ruiz, Robert, 38, *104*, **341–342**
Schuette, Kim, *98–99*, *100–101*, *102–103*,
    324, **342–343**, 351
Shalom, Eyton, 107, 115, *116–117*, *118–*
    119, *144–145*, 321–322, 328, **343**
Wilson, Quinn, *86–87*, *146–147*, *201–202*,
    219–220, 322, **343–344**
Recipes. *See also* specific main ingredients
    cleanser. *See* Vegetable dishes
    comfort. *See* Sauces, dips, and dressings;
       Soups and stews
    foundation. *See* Broths and stocks, basic
    guiding principles for, 50–53
    healing. *See* Medicinal finishers and heal-
       ing elixirs
    healing worthiness and, 50–52
    herbs, spices and. *See* Herbs and spices
    kitchen as play area and, 50
    starting with bone broth, 46
    strengthening. *See* Strengtheners
    turning mistakes into delicious mistakes,
       52–53
Rendering fat, 31–32
Resnick, Ariane, *122*, 325, **341**
Resources, 347–351
Rice
    about: to buy, 56
    Balanced & Bright Jasmine Rice with Sea-
       sonal Vegetables, Golden Raisins, and
       Pistachios, *219–220*
Rocchino Aaron, 33, *82–83*, **341**
Rocket Stock, *114*
Rocket Stock Blocks, *251–252*
Rooster. *See* Poultry
Rosemary, properties of, 328, 332
Ruiz, Robert, 38, *104*, **341–342**
Rye bread, Finnish sourdough, *221–225*

S

Saffron, properties of, 330, 332
Saffron Tea, *108*, *109*
Sage, properties of, 328, 332
Salad dressings. *See* Sauces, dips, and dressings

Salads, pâtés, and aspics, 229–261
    Best Liver Pâté Ever!, *242–243*
    Chicken Burger Salad, *229–231*
    Everyone's Favorite Egg Salad, *232–233*
    Farm-to-Table Aspic, *255–256*
    Ham Hock, Red Lentil, and Yellow Squash
        Salad, *253–254*
    Lobster Salad Extravaganza, *239–241*
    Lulu's Salad in a Glass Smoothie, *266–268*
    Oeufs en Gelée (Eggs in Aspic), *259–261*
    Oxtail Pâté, *246–247*
    Pâté Plus, *244–245*
    Rocket Stock Blocks, *251–252*
    Simply Delicious Salmon Salad, *234–235*
    So Good Lamb Shank Pâté, *248–250*
    Tempting Tuna Salad, *237–238*
    Trotting on Eggshells, *257–258*
Salmon salad, *234–235*
Salt
    to buy, 56
    salty taste and, 332
    types and properties, 327
Sassy Green Smoothie, *264–265*
Sauces, dips, and dressings
    about: dipping sauce menu ideas, 65
    Aioli: Garlic Mayonnaise with a Healthier
        Twist, *148–149*
    Artichoke Tahini Sauce, *152–153*
    Balsamic Vinaigrette, *155*
    Do It Your Way Salad Dressing, *154–155*
    Easy Homemade Tomato Sauce, *128–129*
    Herby Vinaigrette, *155*
    Honey Dijon, *155*
    Lemon Vinaigrette, *155*
    Louise's French Rémoulade with Aioli,
        150–151
    White Wine Mustard Sauce, *156–157*
Savory Beef Broth with Aromatic Spices (Fla-
    vored), *90–91*
Schizandra (Wu wei zi), properties of, 329
Schuette, Kim, *98–99*, *100–101*, *102–103*, 324,
    342–343, 351
Scotch, bone broth, *310*

Shalom, Eyton, 107, 115, *116–117*, *118–119*,
    144–145, 321–322, 328, **343**
Shopping list, master, 53–60
    about: overview of, 53
    animal protein, bones, gelatin, 54–55
    fats and oils, 55
    flours (specialty), 57
    fruits, 54
    grains and beans, 56
    herbs and spices, 56
    miscellaneous specialty ingredients, 57–60
    shopping for items on, 69
    sweeteners, 55
    vegetables, 54
    whole/organic foods, 53
    wine, vinegar, sauces, lemons, 56–57
Shortbread Cookies, *272–273*
Sidecar, the, *305*
Simple Asparagus, *199–200*
Simple syrup concentrate, *309*
Simply Delicious Salmon Salad, *234–235*
Skin care. *See* Beauty treatments
Skin-So-Smooth Honey Gelatin Face Mask,
    311–312
Smoothies, 262–268
    about: ingredients for, 59–60; liquids for,
        267; powders (protein/green) for, 267;
        spices for, 267; vegetables for, 267
    Collagen-Rich Fruit Smoothie, *262–263*
    Lulu's Salad in a Glass Smoothie, *266–268*
    Sassy Green Smoothie, *264–265*
Snacks
    Louise's preferences, 49
    menu ideas, 61–62
Soaking grains, 206
Soaking nuts and seeds, 205
So Good Lamb Shank Pâté, *248–250*
So Shiny Beautiful Hair Mask, 315–316
Soups and stews
    about: making fast bone broth soup,
        45–46; thermos broth for work/travel,
        133

Balanced & Bright Quick Pho and Lunches to Go, *146–147*
Breakfast Lamb Stew, *175–177*
Cactus and Seafood Soup, *123–125*
Chard Soup, *140–141*
Cleansing Cilantro Soup, *126–127*
Eggs Your Way Soup, *130–131*
Goat and Vegetable Stew, *144–145*
Healing Chicken Soup, *116–117*
Hearty Hamburger Soup, *132–133*
Louise's Healing Asparagus Soup, *134–135*
Maori Puha Boil Up, *136–137*
Pureed Green Bean Soup, *142–143*
Tom Yum Soup, *138–139*
Sourdough rye bread, Finnish, *221–225*
Squash
    Best Pumpkin Pie Ever, *278–280*
    Easy Turkey Meatloaf Cupcakes with Kabocha Squash Topping, *172–174*
    Ham Hock, Red Lentil, and Yellow Squash Salad, 253–254
    Magic Zucchini and Carrots, *193–194*
    Mashed Kabocha Squash, *197–198*
Strawberries. *See* Berries
Strengtheners, 159–185
    Baked Lemon Turkey Breast, *170–171*
    Bison Meatloaf Cupcakes with Mashed Celery Root Topping, *159–161*
    Breakfast Lamb Stew, *175–177*
    Cornish Game Hen with White Wine Mustard Sauce, *181–183*
    Crispy Short Ribs with Lime, Cilantro, and Mint, *162–163*
    Easy Eye of Round Roast, *164–167*
    Easy Turkey Meatloaf Cupcakes with Kabocha Squash Topping, *172–174*
    Honey Mustard Chicken, *168–169*
    Pan-Seared Snapper or Halibut, *184–185*
    Rabbit in White Wine Mustard Sauce, *178–179*
Sweeteners, whole-food, 55

T
Tahini sauce, artichoke, *152–153*
Tamari, buying, 60
Tamarind paste, about, 60
Tarragon, properties of, 328, 332
Tempting Tuna Salad, *237–238*
Thyme, properties of, 328, 332
Tomato sauce, easy homemade, *128–129*
Tom Yum Soup, *138–139*
Travel, food for, 46, 196, 216, 218, 221
Trotting on Eggshells, *257–258*
Tuna salad, *237–238*
Turmeric, in Fermented Turmeric Finisher, *112–113*
Turmeric, medicinal properties, 330, 332

V
Vanilla
    about: properties of, 330, 332; using, 330
    Moroccan Vanilla Spice Ice Cream (Non-Dairy), *297–298*
    Vanilla Cake with Berry White Chocolate Frosting (Grain Free), *299–301*
Vegetable dishes, 187–204
    Balanced & Bright Seared Veggie Sauté, *201–202*
    Best Brussels Sprouts, *187–188*
    Caramelized Onions, *191–192*
    Cardamom Carrots, *189–190*
    Magic Zucchini and Carrots, *193–194*
    Mashed Celery Root, *195–196*
    Mashed Kabocha Squash, *197–198*
    Pickled Ginger, *203–204*
    Simple Asparagus, *199–200*
Vegetables. *See also* specific vegetables
    about: in bone broth, 27, 39; collagen-supporting, 7–8; organic, 39; rainbow of colors, 54; selecting, 39; shopping list, 54
    Balanced & Bright Jasmine Rice with Seasonal Vegetables, Golden Raisins, and Pistachios, *219–220*

Balanced & Bright Quick Pho and Lunches
    to Go, *146–147*
Goat and Vegetable Stew, *144–145*
Healing Buckwheat and Veggies, *214–215*
Louise's Favorite Bone Broth or Vegetable
    Broth (Neutral or Flavored), *76–77*
Vegetable stock
    about: building to bone broth with, 18
Vinaigrette. *See* Sauces, dips, and dressings
Vinegar. *See* Apple cider vinegar

W

Waffles (grain free), *226–227*
Water, for bone broth, 27
White Wine Mustard Sauce, *156–157*
Wild game. *See* Game, wild
Wilson, Quinn, *86–87, 146–147, 201–202,
    219–220*, 322, **343–344**

Z

Zucchini. *See* Squash

ABOUT THE AUTHORS

Louise Hay, the author of the international bestseller *You Can Heal Your Life*, is a metaphysical lecturer and teacher with more than 50 million books sold worldwide. For more than 30 years, Louise has helped people throughout the world discover and implement the full potential of their own creative powers for personal growth and self-healing. Louise is the founder and chairman of Hay House, Inc., which disseminates books, audios, DVDs, and other products that contribute to the healing of the planet. Visit www.LouiseHay.com

Heather Dane, the "21st-century medicine woman," is a certified health coach specializing in applying functional medicine and nutrigenomics protocols to resolve chronic health conditions, addictions, and out-of-balance lifestyles. After recovering naturally from several so-called incurable illnesses, Heather discovered that symptoms are signposts for the road back to health. She has worked with many of the great minds in medicine, natural health, nutrition, and energy healing, and designs delicious recipes to nourish body and soul. Visit www.HeatherDane.com

Hay House Titles of Related Interest

CRAZY SEXY JUICE: 100+ Simple Juice, Smoothie & Nut Milk Recipes to Supercharge Your Health, by Kris Carr

CULTURED FOOD FOR HEALTH: A Guide to Healing Yourself with Probiotic Foods, by Donna Schwenk

KALE AND COFFEE: A Renegade's Guide to Health, Happiness, and Longevity, by Kevin Gianni

MAKE YOUR OWN RULES COOKBOOK: More Than 100 Simple, Healthy Recipes Inspired by Friends and Family Around the World, by Tara Stiles

NUTRITION FOR INTUITION, by Doreen Virtue and Robert Reeves, N.D.

ONE SPIRIT MEDICINE: Ancient Ways to Ultimate Wellness, by Alberto Villoldo, Ph.D.

THE TAPPING SOLUTION FOR PAIN RELEF: A Step-by-Step Guide to Reducing and Eliminating Chronic Pain, by Nick Ortner

All of the above are available at your local bookstore, or may be ordered by contacting Hay House (see next page).

❧

We hope you enjoyed this Hay House book. If you'd like to receive our online catalog featuring additional information on Hay House books and products, or if you'd like to find out more about the Hay Foundation, please contact:

Hay House, Inc., P.O. Box 5100, Carlsbad, CA 92018-5100
(760) 431-7695 or (800) 654-5126
(760) 431-6948 (fax) or (800) 650-5115 (fax)
www.hayhouse.com® • www.hayfoundation.org

ℭℯ

Published and distributed in Australia by: Hay House Australia Pty. Ltd., 18/36 Ralph St., Alexandria NSW 2015 • *Phone:* 612-9669-4299 • *Fax:* 612-9669-4144 • www.hayhouse.com.au

Published and distributed in the United Kingdom by: Hay House UK, Ltd., Astley House, 33 Notting Hill Gate, London W11 3JQ • *Phone:* 44-20-3675-2450 • *Fax:* 44-20-3675-2451 • www.hayhouse.co.uk

Published and distributed in the Republic of South Africa by: Hay House SA (Pty), Ltd., P.O. Box 990, Witkoppen 2068 • info@hayhouse.co.za • www.hayhouse.co.za

Published in India by: Hay House Publishers India, Muskaan Complex, Plot No. 3, B-2, Vasant Kunj, New Delhi 110 070 • *Phone:* 91-11-4176-1620 • *Fax:* 91-11-4176-1630 • www.hayhouse.co.in

Distributed in Canada by: Raincoast Books, 2440 Viking Way, Richmond, B.C. V6V 1N2
Phone: 1-800-663-5714 • *Fax:* 1-800-565-3770 • www.raincoast.com

ℭℯ

Take Your Soul on a Vacation

Visit www.HealYourLife.com® to regroup, recharge, and reconnect with your own magnificence.
Featuring blogs, mind-body-spirit news, and life-changing wisdom from Louise Hay and friends.

Visit www.HealYourLife.com today!